Discipline and History

Discipline and History

Political Science in the
United States

Edited by
James Farr and Raymond Seidelman

Ann Arbor
THE UNIVERSITY OF MICHIGAN PRESS

Copyright © by the University of Michigan 1993
All rights reserved
Published in the United States of America by
The University of Michigan Press
Manufactured in the United States of America

1996   1995   1994   1993   4   3   2   1

*A CIP Catalogue record for this book is available from
the British Library.*

Library of Congress Cataloging-in-Publication Data

Discipline and history : political science in the United States /
  edited by James Farr and Raymond Seidelman.
       p.   cm.
    Includes bibliographical references and index.
    ISBN 0-472-09512-9 (alk. paper).—ISBN 0-472-06512-2 (pbk. :
alk. paper)
    1. Political science—United States—History.   I. Farr, James,
1950–   .   II. Seidelman, Raymond.
  JA84.U5D57   1993   92-39346
  320′.0973—dc20   CIP

Preface

This anthology brings together historical essays about the discipline of political science in the United States. The contributors include prominent political scientists from the past, current leaders of the discipline, and contemporary disciplinary historians. Written at different times and for different purposes, the essays collectively present a panorama of views about the discipline from the late nineteenth century to the present. Taken together, they reveal the methodological, theoretical, and political diversity that has amply characterized political science over the course of its history. The essays also suggest that the identity of the discipline has been and continues to be constituted not by agreements over fundamental principles but by long-standing debates over the meaning of politics, the methods of science, the theories of behavioralism or the state, and the responsibilities of public professionals and civic educators. Political science is, as it were, the history of its debates, and the state of the discipline at any one time is the state of its debates, in light of their history.

Several edited volumes on "the state of the discipline" have been published in recent years, providing more or less detailed accounts of the theories and methods that presently dominate the various subfields of political science. These have been of considerable interest and assistance to political scientists both for the purpose of teaching and reflection. This anthology shares some common concerns with these other volumes. However, it takes a decidedly more historical perspective on the discipline as a whole, with somewhat special emphasis on the subfields of American politics and political theory. There are twenty-three essays from or about four different periods in the development of the discipline. Thus the present anthology not only includes earlier and contemporary essays, but each is in part about the history of political science. Whatever their format and ostensible end—a public lecture inaugurating a chair of political science, a presidential address to the American Political Science Association, a critical review of methodological tendencies, a plea for a new research agenda, or an interpretative recovery of previously held theories—these essays reveal the necessity and inevitability of historical interpretation and reinterpretation. This is obvious not only when political scientists try to remember their discipline's past but also when they try to understand its present and chart its future.

We are indebted to several colleagues and friends for guidance and criticism in helping us to complete this volume. John Gunnell, David Easton, Terence Ball, and Theodore Lowi were particularly generous in their various efforts on our behalf. Conversations with Mary Dietz, John Dryzek, Edwin Fogelman, and Stephen Leonard contributed to the volume's present shape, whether they were fully aware of it or not. Colin Day, director of The University of Michigan Press, was helpful and encouraging at every turn. We would also like to thank Julia Smedley for helpful historical research and keen editorial sleuthing. The American Political Science Association, through the kind offices of Jean Walen, was very expeditious in contacting the authors of essays originally published in the *American Political Science Review,* as well as extremely generous in waiving its permission fees. Similar generosity was extended to us by the Johns Hopkins University Press, the University of Texas Press, and Sage Publications. We thank them and all individual authors for reducing the fiscal burdens of this project.

Three essays were written expressly for inclusion in this volume, and thanks (by one or both editors) are due to their authors—Terence Ball, Raymond Seidelman, and Helene Silverberg. Essays by Francis Lieber, John W. Burgess, Woodrow Wilson, W. W. Willoughby, and Charles A. Beard are now part of the public domain. We are grateful to the presses—and the authors where applicable—for permission to reprint the remaining essays in a slightly edited form. Essays were edited, where necessary, with an eye on the volume's overall length. Acknowledgments are provided at the foot of each essay's opening page.

Finally, each of the editors would like to thank the other for the friendly collaboration.

Contents

General Introduction   1

Part 1: Beginnings/1857–1903

Introduction   15

History and Political Science, Necessary Studies
in Free Countries
Francis Lieber   21

The Study of Administration
Woodrow Wilson   33

The Idea and Forms of the State
John W. Burgess   49

The American Political Science Association
W. W. Willoughby   59

Political Science and the State
James Farr   63

The Development of the Social Sciences
Dorothy Ross   81

Part 2: Developments/1903–1945

Introduction   107

Politics
Charles A. Beard   113

Recent Advances in Political Methods
Charles E. Merriam   129

The Bias of American Political Science
Benjamin E. Lippincott   147

Specialists on Intelligence
Harold D. Lasswell   159

Contradictions of a Political Discipline
David M. Ricci   165

American Political Science, Liberalism,
and the Invention of Political Theory
John G. Gunnell   179

Part 3: Debates/1945–1970

Introduction   201

American Political Science in Its Postwar Political
Context
Terence Ball   207

Political Science, Mid-Century
Leonard D. White   223

The Idea of a Political System and the Orientation of
Political Research
David Easton   229

The Behavioral Approach in Political Science: Epitaph
for a Monument to a Successful Protest
Robert A. Dahl   249

Political Science and Political Education
Norman Jacobson   267

Part 4: Departures/1970–1992

Introduction   285

Political Science in the United States: Past and Present
David Easton   291

Political Scientists, Disenchanted Realists, and
Disappearing Democrats
Raymond Seidelman   311

Another State of Mind
Charles E. Lindblom   327

The Two-Party System and Duverger's Law: An Essay
on the History of Political Science
William H. Riker   345

Gender Studies and Political Science: The History of
the "Behavioralist Compromise"
Helene Silverberg   363

The State in Political Science: How We Become What
We Study
Theodore J. Lowi   383

Contributors   397

Bibliography   403

Index   417

General Introduction

In educating students and edifying colleagues, political scientists repeatedly pose questions that bear upon the identity of political science itself. What is the discipline's purpose or mission? What theories, methods, standards, or disciplinary boundaries does the profession seek to establish? What civic roles, public policies, or educational programs should the discipline encourage? What, in short, should political science be, what should it do, and where should it go?

These and many other questions are often subsumed under a single broad one: What is the state of the discipline? This question has been asked by and of political scientists in the United States during periods of disciplinary self-reflection.[1] This question figures most prominently, perhaps, in the annual presidential addresses to the American Political Science Association and to the various regional associations. Programmatic essays that lay claim to new territory or that prescribe new directions to take often begin with this question. So, too, do numerous texts that canvas the scope and methods of the discipline or that advocate a new or renewed public role for political science. In attempting to answer this question, political scientists sometimes hail the progress and the promise of the discipline, usually as regards one tradition, program, or group within it. At other times, they applaud the discipline for its pluralism and openness, either within the liberal arts or in the service of a wider public. At still other times, they diagnose the crises of the discipline as instances of intellectual purposelessness, methodological fragmentation, professional overspecialization, or political irrelevance.

The history of the discipline is implicated in two general ways in connec-

---

1. To judge by recent volumes, we are currently in a period of considerable disciplinary self-reflection. Among the more general and prominent volumes, we would include Ada W. Finifter, ed., *Political Science: The State of the Discipline* (Washington, DC: American Political Science Association, 1983); Herbert Weisberg, ed., *Political Science: The Science of Politics* (New York: Agathon, 1986); and William J. Crotty, ed., *Political Science: Looking to the Future* (Evanston, IL: Northwestern University Press, 1991), 4 volumes. Somewhat more specialized collections include Naomi B. Lynn and Aaron Wildavsky, eds., *Public Administration: The State of the Discipline* (Chatham, NJ: Chatham House, 1990); and Heinz Eulau, ed., *Crossroads of Social Science: The ICPSR 25th Anniversary Volume* (New York: Agathon, 1989).

tion with the practice of analyzing its present state. First, as a matter of logic, a political scientist must provide at least a sketch of the history of the discipline in order to explain or to judge the present progressiveness (or decline) of the discipline. Such a sketch might attend to the founding of the discipline in order to state how it is now foundering, or it might address today's successes by allusion to yesterday's failures. Although such a sketch may or may not go very far back into the past or dig very deeply into the historical record, it must surely draw upon the past if only in rough outline in order to portray the route or routes of the present.

Second, as a matter of fact, the practice of analyzing the state of the discipline goes back to the formative association of the profession in the United States in the opening years of this century. Indeed, the practice is even more time-honored than that, for it goes back to the nineteenth century when the discourse of a "science of politics" was finding an academic site in departments and curricula around the country. For a century and more, then, political scientists have, in fact, been analyzing the state of the discipline and, in doing so, have necessarily called up what they took to be their past.

Yet, the systematic probing of political science's past and the detailed narration of its history has varied considerably over this period of time. And it has varied not only from one political scientist to another but from one era to another. Indeed, it would appear that American political science has only recently emerged from an era—extending roughly from the mid-1950s to the mid-1980s—in which sustained investigations or reflections about the history of political science, at least as measured by books and monographs, were relatively rare. In one notable exception to this rule—*The Development of American Political Science: From Burgess to Behavioralism* (1967)—Albert Somit and Joseph Tanenhaus noted that "most American political scientists are largely unfamiliar with the origins and early evolution of the discipline. . . . An adequate history of the field has yet to be written, and the available literature . . . affords at best a fragmentary and partial account."[2]

By contrast, political scientists before the mid-twentieth century were

---

2. Albert Somit and Joseph Tanenhaus, *The Development of American Political Science: From Burgess to Behavioralism* (Boston: Allyn and Bacon, 1967), p. 2. Other important exceptions during this period include Herbert J. Storing, ed., *Essays on the Scientific Study of Politics* (New York: Holt, Rinehart, and Winston, 1962); and Dwight Waldo, "Political Science: Tradition, Discipline, Profession, Science, Enterprise," in Fred I. Greenstein and Nelson W. Polsby, eds., *Handbook of Political Science* (Reading, MA: Addison-Wesley, 1975), vol. 1: 1–130. Also see the more specialized studies of disciplinary founders as found in Paul F. Kress, *Social Science and the Idea of Process: The Ambiguous Legacy of Arthur F. Bentley* (Urbana: University of Illinois Press, 1973); and Barry O. Karl, *Charles E. Merriam and the Study of Politics* (Chicago: University of Chicago Press, 1974).

rather (though in many cases not exceptionally) more knowledgeable about the past when analyzing the state of the discipline. For those writing around the turn of the century, this was perhaps a consequence of their taking a more historical view of the scope and methods of political science. This was certainly the view of Francis Lieber in the 1850s, when he became the first officially named professor of political science in the United States, as well as of such scholars as John W. Burgess, Woodrow Wilson, and W. W. Willoughby, who followed Lieber in developing analytical or comparative-historical methods for political science. This was also Frederick Pollock's message in his *Introduction to the History of the Science of Politics* (1890) as well as J. R. Seeley's general motto: "History without Political Science has no fruit; Political Science without History has no root." Charles Merriam, whose work became somewhat less historical in the years after his 1903 classic, *History of American Political Theories,* nonetheless proposed in 1925 the adoption of several "new aspects of political science" against the backdrop afforded by "the recent history of political thinking." In the same year, but with a more distant past in mind, Robert H. Murray prefaced his *History of Political Science from Plato to the Present* with the observation that there was not "a single controversy of our day without a pedigree stretching into the distant ages." And in the 1930s, Anna Haddow provided pedagogical reflections of a systematically historical kind in her *Political Science in American Colleges and Universities, 1636–1900.*[3]

Even the opening salvos of the (second) "behavioral revolution" during the decade after World War II were fired in part by competing narratives of the history of political science. Most notably in *The Political System,* David Easton made his powerful brief in 1953 for behavioral systems theory (modeled on the assumptions of the natural sciences) by, among other things, diagnosing the malaise of political science "since the Civil War" and by sketching out "the decline of modern political theory." Three years later, Bernard Crick wrote a dissertation on the history of American political science—later published as *The American Science of Politics: Its Origins and Conditions* (1959)—criticizing these and similar views. Crick's principal theme was that behavioralist aspirations to "science" were neither new nor politically innocent nor much worth holding. "By scorning history and phi-

3. Frederick Pollock, *An Introduction to the History of the Science of Politics* (London: 1890); John R. Seeley, *Introduction to Political Science* (London: 1896), p. 3; Charles Merriam, *New Aspects of Politics* (Chicago: University of Chicago Press, 1925), ch. 3; Robert H. Murray, *The History of Political Science from Plato to the Present* (New York: Appleton, 1925), preface; Anna Haddow, *Political Science in American Colleges and Universities, 1636–1900* (New York: Appleton, 1939).

losophy," Crick concluded, "the idea of a science of politics" showed itself to be but "a caricature of American liberal democracy."[4] Alongside contemporaries such as Easton and forbears such as Merriam, Crick dramatically underscored the point—already amply evident in presidential addresses and scope-and-methods texts—that in organizing "the facts" of the discipline's past, a great variety of interpretations was possible and perhaps even inevitable.

The history of political science has lately recaptured the attention of scholars, in and outside the discipline. Exactly why this should be so is not entirely clear. But among the possible reasons might be the need of both newer and older generations of political scientists to come to grips with, and possibly to resolve, the crises that continue to beset the discipline, the recent revolution in historiography at last breaking upon political science, and the increasing historical self-awareness of the other social sciences. As a sign of the latter, consider the emergence or continuing viability of journals such as the *History of Sociology,* the *History of Anthropology,* the *History of Political Economy,* the *History of the Human Sciences,* and the *Journal of the History of the Behavioral Sciences* (the catholicity of whose title fails to conceal the hegemony of psychology within). While political science does not yet have a similar journal, its history has nonetheless motivated the labors of a number of disciplinary historians. The variety of interpretations, so evident in the past, can once again be seen in David Ricci's *The Tragedy of Political Science* (1984), Raymond Seidelman and Edward Harpham's *Disenchanted Realists* (1985), Andrew Janos's *Politics and Paradigms* (1986), and Dorothy Ross's *The Origins of American Social Science* (1991). Ricci chronicles the moral contradictions of a science of democracy; Seidelman and Harpham, the repeated disenchantments of a tradition of liberal reformers; Janos, the diversified progress of theories of change; and Ross, the persistence of American exceptionalism in the very categories of political science. Along with the publication of a series of interviews with leading political scientists of the past and present in *Political Science in America: Oral Histories of a Discipline,* these works clearly suggest that we are in an era of heightened historical consciousness about the discipline.[5]

---

4. David Easton, *The Political System: An Inquiry into the State of Political Science* (New York: Knopf, 1953), p. 38 and chap. 10; Bernard Crick, *The American Science of Politics: Its Origins and Conditions* (Berkeley: University of California Press, 1959), p. 227. Also during this period, see Dwight Waldo, *Political Science in the United States: A Trend Report* (Paris: UNESCO, 1956).

5. David Ricci, *The Tragedy of Political Science: Politics, Scholarship, and Democracy* (New Haven: Yale University Press, 1984); Raymond Seidelman with the assistance of Edward J. Harpham, *Disenchanted Realists: Political Science and the American Crisis, 1884–1984* (Albany: State University of New York Press, 1985); Andrew C. Janos, *Politics and Paradigms: Changing Theories of Change in the Social Sciences* (Stanford: Stanford University Press, 1986);

Reflections upon these and other works have also served to deepen this historical consciousness by directing our attention to the methods or historiographical principles implicit in them. According to one set of reflections, Janos presents an example of "Whig" historiography because he tells a teleological story of progress in theories of change that led to the present state of the discipline. Ricci and Seidelman, on the other hand, proved to be "skeptics" because their histories are critical of the scientific or liberal democratic aspirations of political scientists in the discipline's past and present.[6] Another set of reflections seizes upon and criticizes the artificially constructed notion of "tradition" in Seidelman, the overly dramaturgical allusion to "tragedy" in Ricci, and the borrowed philosophical idea of "paradigm" in Janos.[7] The ground for these different methodological reflections—particularly the reference to "paradigms"—was laid in earlier debates in the history and philosophy of science, especially over the work of Thomas Kuhn and its applicability to political science.[8] The ground for these reflections—particularly the reference to "traditions"—had also been laid in more recent debates over the interpretation of the history of political thought, especially over the contextualist work of Quentin Skinner and J. G. A. Pocock.[9] The historiography of

---

Dorothy Ross, *The Origins of American Social Science* (Cambridge: Cambridge University Press, 1991); Michael A. Baer, Malcolm E. Jewell, and Lee Seligman, eds., *Political Science in America: Oral Histories of a Discipline* (Lexington: University Press of Kentucky, 1991). Further signs of a heightened historical consciousness about political and social science may be found, for example, in Stefan Collini, Donald Winch, and John Burrow, *That Noble Science of Politics: A Study in Nineteenth Century Intellectual History* (Cambridge: Cambridge University Press, 1983); JoAnne Brown and David van Keuren, eds., *The Estate of Social Knowledge* (Baltimore: Johns Hopkins University Press, 1991); Gabriel Almond, *A Discipline Divided* (Beverly Hills: Sage, 1990); and David Easton, John G. Gunnell, and Luigi Graziano, eds., *The Development of Political Science: A Comparative Survey* (New York: Routledge, 1991).

6. John S. Dryzek and Stephen T. Leonard, "History and Discipline in Political Science," *American Political Science Review* 82 (1988): 1245–60. See also the subsequent controversy, James Farr et al., "Can Political Science History Be Neutral?" *American Political Science Review* 84 (1990): 587–607. The reference to "Whig" historiography originates with Herbert Butterfield, *The Whig Interpretation of History* (New York: Penguin, 1931).

7. James Farr, "The History of Political Science," *American Journal of Political Science* 32 (1988): 1175–95.

8. Thomas Kuhn, *The Structure of Scientific Revolutions* (Chicago: University of Chicago Press, 1962). On Kuhn and related applications of the philosophy of science, see Richard J. Bernstein, *The Restructuring of Social and Political Theory* (Philadelphia: University of Pennsylvania Press, 1978); Gary Gutting, ed., *Paradigms and Revolutions: Applications and Appraisals of Thomas Kuhn's Philosophy of Science* (Notre Dame: University of Notre Dame Press, 1980); and Terence Ball, ed., *Idioms of Inquiry: Critique and Renewal in Political Science* (Albany: SUNY Press, 1987).

9. Essays by and about Skinner are collected in James Tully, ed., *Meaning and Context: Quentin Skinner and His Critics* (Princeton: Princeton University Press, 1988). Also see, among other places, J. G. A. Pocock, *Politics, Language, and Time* (London: Methuen, 1972); and

Pocock is singled out by Ross as inspiring or best describing her historiographical approach in *The Origins of American Social Science*. Yet her explanation of the persistence of American exceptionalism turns upon larger social forces, such as modernization and secularization, as well as upon the causal role of professionalization and the rise of the research university.[10] This is already reanimating a debate—heard earlier and elsewhere—about whether the history of political science, or of any science, should consist essentially in a narrative about "external" forces or in one about the "internal" development of scientific ideas and theories themselves.[11]

One very general and humbling consequence follows from the variety of arguments and perspectives contained in the various works of history and historiography mentioned above. As John G. Gunnell has observed: "Although the study of the history of political science may not be as fully developed as that of some of the other social sciences, this area of research in the United States has now reached a point where it is difficult any longer to contemplate a single general treatment."[12] Yet, while no "single general treatment" may be possible, any treatment at all of the history of American political science must proceed in terms of certain general themes that inform the narration of the past or an analysis of the present. These themes may be understood in part as templates that overlay and help organize the disparate facts of the discipline's past. However, these themes have also fueled the

---

Richard Rorty, J. B. Schneewind, and Quentin Skinner, eds., *Philosophy in History* (Cambridge: Cambridge University Press, 1984). On "tradition," see John G. Gunnell, *Political Theory: Tradition and Interpretation* (Cambridge, MA: Winthrop, 1986). A vast related literature has also developed in the history of anthropology and sociology. For beginnings, see, for example, George W. Stocking, "On the Limits of 'Presentism' and 'Historicism' in the Historiography of the Behavioral Sciences," *Journal of the History of the Behavioral Sciences* 1 (1965): 211–18; and Steven Seidman, Robert Alun Jones, R. Stephen Warner, and Stephen Turner, "The Historicist Controversy: Understanding the Sociological Past," *Sociological Theory* 3 (1985): 13–28.

10. Ross, *The Origins,* xvii. On the professionalization of American social science more generally, see Robert H. Wiebe, *The Search for Order, 1877–1920* (New York: Hill and Wang, 1967); Mary O. Furner, *Advocacy and Objectivity: A Crisis in the Professionalization of American Social Science, 1865–1905* (Lexington: University of Kentucky Press, 1975); and Thomas L. Haskell, *The Emergence of Professional Social Science: The American Social Science Association and the Nineteenth Century Crisis of Authority* (Urbana: University of Illinois Press, 1977).

11. John G. Gunnell, *The Descent of Political Theory* (Chicago: University of Chicago Press, forthcoming). The competing claims of "genealogy" and "archaeology" will also fuel this debate, particularly as the works of Michel Foucault continue to be felt among political scientists and disciplinary historians. For a clear overview that is especially attentive to Foucault's substantive history of the human sciences in *The Order of Things,* see Gary Gutting, *Michel Foucault's Archaeology of Scientific Reason* (Cambridge: Cambridge University Press, 1990).

12. John G. Gunnell, "In Search of the State: Political Science as an Emerging Discipline in the U.S.," in Peter Wagner, Bjorn Wittrock, and Richard Whitley, eds., *Discourses on Society: The Shaping of the Social Science Disciplines* (Boston and Dordrecht: Kluwer Academic Publishers, 1991), p. 123.

persistent debates that past political scientists themselves have been engaged in for over a century or so. Indeed, it is these long-standing debates, not some agreement on fundamental principles, that give the discipline the identity it now has.

By our reckoning, there are at least nine general themes (several of which could be collapsed into fewer heads or others added to them):

1. The *diversity of theories and methods* that have been developed and that have vied for the intellectual allegiance of the discipline
2. The central role that the concept of *the state* has played in focusing the debates that attend this diversity, even when the concept is ostensibly rejected
3. The equally central role that *behavioralism* has played in focusing these debates, even when it too is rejected
4. The claims about the character of a *science* of politics, and the *contested meanings* of science that have informed these claims
5. The intellectual *confluences with other disciplines*, especially history and the social sciences
6. The *professionalization* of the discipline and the *institutional associations* it has forged internally and with other professions, especially history and the social sciences
7. The *public roles* that political scientists have played or should play, and particularly their responsibilities as *civic educators* of one kind or another
8. The roles that *women and minorities* have played or been denied in the discipline, as well as the silence about or fitful incorporation of *gender and race* into the theories and methods of the discipline
9. The broader *ideological debates* of American politics that have engaged political scientists in their role as public intellectuals, especially debates about liberalism and American exceptionalism, socialism and social classes, even when political science promises an end of ideology

The present volume brings together several essays that individually and collectively highlight and historicize these general themes. Commentary on the significance and connections of the individual essays is left to the section introductions below, as is a sense of the relevant contexts, events, or forces that helped to shape and define the four formative periods of the discipline. Here we provide a few general observations about the essays and the volume as a whole.

The volume includes several documentary essays on "the state of the discipline," written at different times by different political scientists, as well as a few interpretative narratives written in the past few years by various disciplinary historians. The authors are divisible into three general groupings. First, there are prominent figures in the discipline's less recent past, including Francis Lieber, John W. Burgess, Woodrow Wilson, W. W. Willoughby, Charles A. Beard, Charles E. Merriam, Harold D. Lasswell, Benjamin E. Lippincott, and Leonard D. White. Second, there are current or recent leaders of the discipline, including David Easton, Robert A. Dahl, William H. Riker, Norman Jacobson, Charles E. Lindblom, and Theodore J. Lowi. Third, there are contemporary historians of the discipline, including Dorothy Ross, John G. Gunnell, David M. Ricci, Terence Ball, Helene Silverberg, the editors, and again David Easton. Overall, the volume brings together essays *from* or *about* the history of the discipline, organized into four general periods from the latter half of the nineteenth century to the present.

The essays cover considerable intellectual and historical ground. Several invoke or criticize many of the more important theories and theoretical traditions of political science (such as the study of administration, political economy, systems theory, institutionalism, and especially the state). Several recall or denounce some of the discipline's more striking methodological approaches (such as comparative history, rational choice, political psychology, gender analysis, and especially behavioralism). Several champion or castigate a number of the public roles that political scientists have served (as civic educators, liberal reformers, specialized experts, or exporters of the American way of life). Other essays critically recount key episodes in the professionalization of the discipline or discuss some of its signal debates during the late nineteenth century, the Progressive era, the New Deal, the aftermath of World War II, the 1960s, and the 1980s.

Most of the essays analyze the state of the discipline by providing general proclamations about the discipline that were (or are) influential or provocative in their time. All are also self-consciously historical in that they recall their past, in greater or lesser scholarly detail. We thereby witness not only different states of the discipline at different times but also systematically changing perspectives on the discipline's past over time. Indeed, it would only be a slight exaggeration to refer to them as the discipline's different pasts, given the range of remembrances and the variety of historical interpretations that attend analyses of the state of the discipline.

This sense of historical plurality is strongly reinforced and complemented by the other essays written by disciplinary historians. These writers exhibit a range of critical and sympathetic judgments about political science as well as about what disciplinary history should principally focus upon, whether it be theories or personalities or institutional developments. When surveyed as a whole, the essays in the volume also present a variety of different methodological principles and historiographical perspectives. Whigs and skeptics, textualists and contextualists, internalists and externalists are all given voice here. One can hear different axes grinding and witness the partisan and less-partisan uses of history. This was intentional. No methodological uniformity, historiographical hegemony, or political rectitude was sought or imposed in bringing these essays together. We hope that the volume thereby underscores the necessity and inevitability of historical interpretation when reflecting on the discipline, even as it acknowledges and encourages the great range of styles, principles, and contents that pass muster as histories of political science.

The *American Political Science Review* is amply (though not, we hope, overly) represented in the pages below. Such prominence is perhaps understandable given that the *Review* is the journal of the national association and that it frequently features just the sorts of diagnoses and remembrances of the discipline that appear in this volume. The annual presidential addresses are standardly of this sort. However, this volume includes only two such addresses, even though several authors—Willoughby, Wilson, Beard, Merriam, Lasswell, White, Dahl, Easton, Lindblom, Riker, and Lowi—were at one time or another presidents of the American Political Science Association. A study of the presidential addresses in the *Review,* perhaps alongside the presidential addresses in the journals of the regional associations, would make an interesting study. It would certainly be one kind of contribution to disciplinary history; however, this volume is not such a study, as much as several of its essays may sound presidential in tone or judgment.

The essays' general themes apply to the historical sweep of American political science as a whole. Taken together, therefore, the essays at least touch upon all of the various subfields of political science in the United States, including comparative politics, international relations, and political methodology, as well as American politics and political theory. But, admittedly, the essays address the subfield of American politics in a much more direct and sustained fashion; and, to a lesser extent, they also address the subfield of political theory insofar as its history is tied to the history of the study of American politics. Thus, for example, the general themes about behavioralism and about the state are evidently relevant to all of the discipline's subfields, although these themes are addressed below in essays drawn mainly from American politics and political theory. Or, to take a different example, one could suggest (as some of our authors do below) that one or another of the themes of American exceptionalism—that American politics was an exception to Old World politics or that Americans faced historically special trials in the New World or that Americans were uniquely positioned to make novel contributions to human thinking, including a science of politics—may be found in the categories and theories of all of the various subfields of political science. But the themes of American exceptionalism are surely most persuasive when political scientists and political theorists are studying America itself or reflecting upon the place of political science in American public life. In any case, for better or worse, the discipline has had at its core the study of American politics, and the students and theoretical critics of American politics have been particularly prone to assess the state of the discipline and to reflect upon its past.

The dates governing the periodization used in the volume pick out important events and developments in the history of the discipline in the context of American political life—such as the creation of America's first professorship of political science (1857), the founding of the American Political Science Association (1903), the end of World War II (1945), and the challenge to (and from) behavioralism (around 1970). We acknowledge that our periodization is a conventional construction designed to forward our pluralistic purposes. The dates and events variously reflect and make concrete some of the general themes about the history of political science mentioned above, especially the discipline's increasing professionalization, its various public roles in American politics, and its internal methodological debates. Like all periodizations, ours is, of course, open to dispute or to reconstruction for different purposes. Indeed, at least two of the essays below—the one by Merriam, and the second of the two by Easton—provide rather different four-stage periodizations of the discipline's history.

The periods of the discipline's history are described in the section introductions that follow. But, at a glance, we begin with the creation of the first chair of political science, a signal instance of the institutionalization of the profession in the United States. The first period (Beginnings) that it helps to demarcate embraces the theoretical articulations of "the state" and their practical applications to administration, as well as the formation of a comparative-historical method. The creation of the American Political Science Association accelerates the institutionalization of the discipline, and this we use to inaugurate a second period (Developments). This period witnesses a terminological shift away from "the state" along with an increasingly realistic assessment of American politics coupled with the hopes for Progressive reform led in part by political scientists. The invocation of psychology and sociology also helps to inaugurate the first behavioral revolution and to distance empirical political scientists from émigré political theorists.

World War II had an enormous effect on American political scientists, as it did on people the world over. Not only did it quash certain kinds of reformism, but it mobilized political scientists in the war effort. We use its conclusion to begin our third period (Debates), a period in which the research university expands and political scientists seek out a much-expanded fiscal basis in league with the other social and now "behavioral" sciences. The second behavioral revolution helps to define this period, as do the challenges to behavioralism that come in part as a consequence of facing urban riots and the Vietnam War. The postbehavioral era, as it is sometimes called, may be seen to begin around 1970; it constitutes our most recent period (Departures). A pervasive sense of crisis, a call for an expanded dialogue at the discipline's center, and a profusion of new modes of inquiry, most notably rational choice theory and theories of gender, have characterized our most recent round of debates. Perhaps this volume, too, and historical studies like it, should be understood as a product of our discipline's present departures, even though the appeal and argument are decidedly historical.

In conclusion, this volume has been designed to capture some sense of and appreciation for the diverse theoretical, methodological, and political aspects of the discipline of American political science over the course of a century and more. It goes without saying that much else in the history of the discipline had to be passed over in silence and what is not passed over is open to different interpretations. Certainly, many readers will wish that we had included other essays or covered other episodes in the history of the discipline. In a collection of this or any size, this is probably unavoidable. But if readers who have this reaction do so nonetheless by remembering the past as a gauge to understanding the present, the volume will even then have served its purpose. Our aim in editing this collection of essays will be realized only to the extent that readers seriously return to the historical record in order to reflect on the state of the discipline and on the politics that we profess to study.

Part 1
Beginnings/1857–1903

Introduction

Political science emerged as an academic discipline in the United States in the latter half of the nineteenth century. The year 1880 figures as an important symbolic date, for in that year, the School of Political Science was formed at Columbia University under the directorship of John W. Burgess. This same year also lies at the exact midpoint between two other dates of institutional significance: 1857, the year in which Francis Lieber was named America's first professor of history and political science at Columbia, and 1903, the year in which the American Political Science Association (APSA) was founded. During this half-century, political science became an independent course of study, increasingly distanced not only from moral philosophy from which it evolved at colleges and universities around the country, but also from the other newly individuated social sciences, such as economics, psychology, and sociology. The professionalization of the various social sciences was also marked by the creation of independent associations that emerged (as somewhat belatedly did the APSA) out of the reformist American Social Science Association (ASSA).[1]

Before the latter half of the nineteenth century, "political science" was a term used in the United States by publicists and statesmen of the American Enlightenment. Aware of the novelty of their task and the modernity of their context, these publicists and statesmen drew upon classical and modern sources to interpret and promulgate the republican experimentation and citizen education under way in the New World. Figures such as John Adams, Alexander Hamilton, and James Madison alleged to draw upon, among others, Cicero, Grotius, Montesquieu, and Hume as inspirations for what Adams called "the divine science of politics" directly at work in republican America. In their writings and in those that followed them, "political science" provided a terminological framework to understand, debate, and reform national ideals,

---

1. See works on professionalization and on the social science associations cited in the General Introduction and in Dorothy Ross's essay below.

institutions, and processes. In the course of America's first half-century, they succeeded in bringing about "a new political science for a world itself quite new," which de Tocqueville had called for in 1835.[2]

This sense of America's novelty and uniqueness was carried over into the later nineteenth-century context, as "political science" increasingly became the name for a subject of higher education and a new academic discipline.[3] The forces of modernization—especially secularization, nationalization, and democratization—at work on the American republic were also at work on political science itself. Another force of modernization—the centralization of the state—came to give political science its late-century identity as "the science of the state." "The national popular state alone," Burgess proclaimed, "furnishes the objective reality upon which political science can rest in the construction of a truly scientific political system." These sentiments of *Political Science and Comparative Constitutional Law* (1891) were prefigured in Lieber's *Manual of Political Ethics* (1838) and Theodore Dwight Woolsey's *Political Science: Or, the State Theoretically and Practically Considered* (1877), and they were seconded in W. W. Willoughby's *The Nature of the State* (1896) and the future president Woodrow Wilson's *The State: Elements of Historical and Practical Politics* (1889).

These works on the state displayed considerable differences, but they collectively provided a theoretical expression of nationalism in the period after the Civil War. They were concerned to explore the normative foundations of the modern nation-state, finding it in some combination of popular sovereignty, the organic community, the rule of law, and the natural liberties of citizens. But contrary to later misconceptions, they were even more concerned with explaining the state's governmental apparatus, legal structure, formal evolution, and practical manifestation in parties and public opinion. There was considerable methodological reflection attendant to this formal and empirical task as well. Some of this reflection praised natural science as a model for political science; some of it hailed the advances in the collection of statistics; and some of it insisted upon the inextricable connections between inquiries in history and in political science. In more concrete terms, it was what Wilson called the "historical, comparative method" that provided the main intellectual resources for understanding the American state in comparison to other states, past and present.

The administration of the state—or, as some thought, its veritable

---

2. John Adams, *Thoughts on Government*, in Charles S. Hyneman and Donald S. Lutz, eds., *American Political Writing during the Founding Era* (Indianapolis: Liberty Press, 1983), vol. 1, p. 402; Alexis de Tocqueville, *Democracy in America* (Garden City, NY: Anchor Books, 1969), p. 12.

3. For this development, see Anna Haddow, *Political Science in American Colleges and Universities: 1636–1900* (New York: Appleton, 1939).

absence—also came to focus the practical and political vision of political scientists. The point was not only to understand the state but to change it—if only to develop and modernize its administrative structure. The reformist agenda of the ASSA was taken up by the various new disciplinary associations, including the APSA. "Civil service reform" was particularly important for political scientists who hoped that administration might prove "businesslike." Such reform was viewed by many political scientists like Wilson, whose words these are, as a requirement of "this industrial and trading age." It could thereby be "removed from the hurry and strife of politics," especially of a narrowly partisan or populist kind, and certainly from a socialist agenda advocated by certain sociologists such as Albion Small and certain economists such as Richard T. Ely. Following their republican forbears, political scientists generally avowed their moderation and what Lieber had called the "calming effect" of their science on students and civil servants. Despite considerable disagreements about what, if anything, should be reformed about national policy or race and gender relations, political scientists mainly ranged across the classical liberal spectrum, from Burgess's modern conservatism to Wilson's democratic idealism. In these various ways, political science in the latter half of the nineteenth century proved to be a science *of* politics and a science *for* politics in the changing new world that America most dramatically exemplified.

The essays that follow highlight some of the more important features of this brief sketch of the beginnings of a discipline. Lieber's inaugural address (here much shortened) was delivered at Columbia College in early 1858 when he formally assumed the chair of history and political science that had been created for him the previous year. Warning his audience of "the threatened cleaving of this broad land," Lieber begins his late antebellum address with a cry of nationalism and a call for a national university on the German model. Critical of "idolatrous patriotism," communism, and much else, Lieber praises America's unique liberties and republican institutions in a neo-Kantian way that underscores the mutuality of citizens' rights and duties. Itself an exercise in civic education, the address goes on to identify political science as the science that treats of "man as a jural being—as citizen," especially in "the highest institution—the state." It also delineates the subfields of political science, including political economy, and demarcates its boundaries with history, "the very science for nascent citizens of a republic."

The essays by John W. Burgess and Woodrow Wilson exemplify the focus as well as the range of thinking of Gilded Age scientists of the state. The differences are as important as the similarities. Burgess raises more abstract questions about the state, whereas Wilson surveys more practical ones about its administration. While Burgess simply nods in the direction of "a better organization of the state outside of the government," Wilson explicitly advocates reform of the civil service, as would Frank Goodnow, the APSA's first president. Wilson's advocacy of "the historical, comparative method" finds its complement in Burgess's boast (in the preface to *Political Science and Comparative Constitutional Law;* not printed here) that the novelty of his "comparative study" lies in its "attempt to apply the method, which has been so productive in Natural Science to Political Science and Jurisprudence." In practice, however, Burgess's method generally proved to be much more legalistic and formalistic, something that Wilson himself criticizes as dogmatic. Expressing the sense of New World uniqueness that many thinkers have since called American exceptionalism, Burgess emphasizes "the distinctive lessons of our institutions" when compared to those of European states; and Wilson insists that "we Americanize" the study of administration and allow civil servants to "inhale much free American air." Both political scientists also freely exhale the language of democracy, in rather marked contrast to earlier nineteenth-century writers. But we cannot look back without remembering the avowed features of such talk. Burgess's "democratic state" needed a "national harmony" based upon a consensus over "rights and wrongs" and upon what he hoped would become Teutonic racial homogeneity; Wilson's "democratic state" needed an expert bureaucracy far "removed from the common political life of the people, its chiefs as well as its rank and file." In short, in these essays we get a glimpse of the ambivalences about the meaning and extent of popular democracy that characterized late nineteenth-century political science in America.

Burgess and Wilson were professional political scientists, whatever else they were. Wilson's essay appeared in 1887 in the second volume of *Political Science Quarterly* (*PSQ*), the new professional journal brought out by Burgess's School of Political Science at Columbia. Other journals and schools followed, as did other marks of a profession, especially the creation of a national association in 1903. W. W. Willoughby, another theorist of the state from Johns Hopkins's own school of political science, records this event in a brief note for the 1904 *PSQ*. Besides remembering the names of its founders and first officers—including Wilson, Goodnow, and Willoughby himself—the note calls attention to the collective judgments within the association about the three principal subfields of political science, the need for their methodical study, and their intellectual distance from "the other so-called social sciences." Disavowing any specifically "partisan position," the APSA nonetheless intended to include nonacademic members and to speak broadly to questions of practical politics.

In the two closing essays, disciplinary historians James Farr and Dorothy Ross place these various developments—and indeed the whole of late nineteenth-century political science—within different, broader frameworks. Farr looks closely at the mutual evolution of the concepts of "political science" and "the state" not only in the writings of later nineteenth-century figures such as Burgess, Wilson, and Willoughby but in those of earlier Federalists and especially Francis Lieber. This broader intellectual context forces a considerable qualification on claims that Americans thought of themselves as "stateless" before the Gilded Age or were merely mimicking German theorists at the close of the century. It also allows us to see a conceptual unity amidst considerable theoretical diversity that characterized the intellectual formation of the discipline.

Noting many intellectual differences among the social sciences and providing considerable detail about the various individuals who brought them about, Ross nonetheless emphasizes the similar processes of their professionalization, as explained by university reform and—during Wilson's "industrial and trading age"—the requirements for expert knowledge prompted by industrialization itself. Ross also reveals how a new generation of reform-minded experts turned to new conceptions and methods of science in order to break with traditionalists—only to have this metamorphose into scientism in the opening decades of the twentieth century.[4] Charles E. Merriam stands out in this development; and the mention of his name takes us into the next period of political science.

---

4. Ross has recently explored this phenomenon more systematically and connected it expressly to American exceptionalism in *The Origins of American Social Science* (Cambridge: Cambridge University Press, 1991).

History and Political Science, Necessary Studies in Free Countries

Francis Lieber

Before I proceed to perform the honorable duty of this evening, I ask your leave to express on this, the first opportunity which has offered itself, my acknowledgment for the suffrages which have placed me in the chair I now occupy. You have established a professorship of political science in the most populous and most active city of our whole, wide commonwealth—a commonwealth of an intensely political character; and this chair you have unanimously given to me. I thank you for your confidence.

Sincere, however, as these acknowledgments are, warmer thanks are due to you, and not only my own, but I believe I am not trespassing when I venture to offer them in the name of this assemblage, for the enlargement of our studies. You have engrafted a higher and a wider course of studies on your ancient institution which in due time may expand into a real, a national university, a university of large foundation and of highest scope, as your means may increase and the public may support your endeavors. So be it.

We stand in need of a national university, the highest apparatus of the highest modern civilization. We stand in need of it, not only that we may appear clad with equal dignity among the sister nations of our race, but on many grounds peculiar to ourselves. A national university in our land seems to have become one of those topics on which the public mind comes almost instinctively to a conclusion, and whose reality is not unfrequently preceded by prophetic rumor. They are whispered about; their want is felt by all; it is openly pronounced by many until wisdom and firmness gather the means and resolutely provide for the general necessity. There is at present in many countries of Europe an active movement in reference to university reforms; others have institutions of such completeness as was never known before, and we, one of the four leading nations, ought not to be without our own, a

"An Inaugural Address Delivered on the 17th of February, 1858, on Assuming the Chair of History and Political Science, in Columbia College, New York." Reprinted in a much shortened version from *Miscellaneous Writings* (Philadelphia: J. B. Lippincott, 1881), vol. 1, pp. 329–68.

21

university, not national, because established by our national government; that could not well be, and if it were, surely would not be well; but I mean national in its spirit, in its work and effect, in its liberal appointments and its comprehensive basis. I speak fervently; I hope I speak knowingly; I speak as a scholar, as an American citizen; as a man of the nineteenth century in which the stream of knowledge and of education courses deep and wide.

The *patria* of us moderns ought to consist in a wide land covered by a nation, and not in a city or a little colony. Mankind have outgrown the ancient city-state. *Countries* are the orchards and the broad acres where modern civilization gathers her grain and nutritious fruits. The narrow garden-beds of antiquity suffice for our widened humanity no more than the short existence of ancient states. Moderns stand in need of nations and of national longevity, for their literatures and law, their industry, liberty, and patriotism; we want countries to work and speak, write and glow for, to live and to die for. The sphere of humanity has steadily widened, and nations alone can nowadays acquire the membership of that great commonwealth of our race which extends over Europe and America. Has it ever been sufficiently impressed on our minds how slender the threads are that unite us in a mere political system of states, if we are not tied together by the far stronger cords of those feelings which arise from the consciousness of having a country to cling to and to pray for, and unimpeded land and water roads to move on?

Should we, then, not avail ourselves of so well proved a cultural means of fostering and promoting a generous nationality, as a comprehensive university is known to be? Shall we never have this noble pledge of our nationality? All Athens, the choicest city-state of antiquity, may well be said to have been one great university, where masters daily met with masters, and shall we not have even one for our whole empire, which does not extend from bay to bay like little Attica, but from sea to sea, and is destined one day to link ancient Europe to still older Asia, and thus to help completing the zone of civilization around the globe? All that has been said of countries, and nations, and a national university would retain its full force even if the threatened cleaving of this broad land should come upon us. But let me not enter on that topic of lowering political reality, however near to every citizen's heart, when I am bidden by you to discourse on political philosophy, and it is meet for me not to leave the sphere of inaugural generalities.

Those branches which I teach are important, it seems, in all these respects and for every one, whatever his pursuits in practical life may be. To me have been assigned the sciences which treat of man in his social relations, of humanity in all its phases in society. Society, as I use the term here, does not only mean a certain number of living individuals bound together by the bonds of common laws, interests, sympathies, and organization, but it means these and the successive generations with which they are interlinked, which have belonged to the same portion of mankind, and whose traditions the living have received. Society is a continuity. Society is not arbitrarily made up by men, but man is born into society; and that science which treats of men in their social relations in the past, and of that which has successively affected their society, for weal or woe, is history. Schloezer, one of the first who gave currency to the word *statistik,* of which we have formed statistics, with a somewhat narrower meaning, has well said, History is continuous Statistik; Statistik, History arrested at a given period.

The variety of interests and facts and deeds which history deals with, and the dignity which surrounds this science, for it is the dignity of humanity itself in all its aspirations and its sufferings, give to this branch of knowledge a peculiarly cultivating and enlarging character for the mind of the young.

If the nourishing character inherent in the study of history is true; if history favors the growth of strong men and is cherished in turn by them, and grows upon their affection as extended experience and slowly advancing years make many objects of interest drop like leaves, one by one; if history shows us the great connection of things, that there is nothing stable but the progressive, and that there is Alfred and Socrates, Marathon and Tours, or, if it be not quaint to express it thus, that there is the microcosm of the whole past in each of us; and if history familiarizes the mind with the idea that it is a jury whose verdict is not rendered according to the special pleadings of party dogmas, and a logic wrenched from truth and right—then it is obvious that in a moral, practical, and intellectual point of view it is the very science for nascent citizens of a republic. There are not a few among us who are dazzled by the despotism of a Caesar, appearing brilliant at least at a distance—did not even Plato once set his hopes on Dionysius?—or are misled by the plausible simplicity of democratic absolutism, that despotism which believes liberty simply to consist in the irresponsible power of a larger number over a smaller, for no other reason, it seems, than that ten is more than nine. All absolutism, whether monarchical or democratic, is in principle the same, and the latter always leads by short transitions to the other. We may go farther; in all absolutism there is a strong element of communism. The theory of property which Louis the Fourteenth put forth was essentially communistic. There is no other civil liberty than institutional liberty, all else is but passing semblance and simulation. It is one of our highest duties, therefore, to foster in the young an institutional spirit, and an earnest study of history shows the inestimable value of institutions. We need not fear in our eager age and country that we may be led to an idolatry of the past—history carries sufficient preventives within itself—or to a worship of institutions simply because they are institutions. Institutions, like the sons of men themselves, may be wicked or good; but it is true that ideas and feelings, however great or pure, retain a passing and meteoric character so long as they are not embodied in vital institutions, and that rights and privileges are but slender reeds so long as they are not protected and kept alive by sound and tenacious institutions; and it is equally true that an institutional spirit is fostered and invigorated by a manly study of society in the days that are gone.

A wise study of the past teaches us social analysis, and the separation of the permanent and essential from the accidental and superficial, so that it becomes one of the keys by which we learn to understand better the present. History, indeed, is an admirable training in the great duty of attention and the art of observation, as in turn an earnest observation of the present is an indispensable aid to the historian. A practical life is a key with which we unlock the vaults containing the riches of the past. Many of the greatest historians in antiquity and modern times have been statesmen; and Niebuhr said that with his learning alone, and it was prodigious, he could not have understood Roman history, had he not been for many years a practical officer in the financial and other departments of the administration, while we all remember Gibbon's statement of himself, that the captain of the Hampshire militia was of service to the historian of Rome. This is the reason why free nations produce practical, penetrating, and unravelling historians, for in them every observing citizen partakes, in a manner, of statesmanship. Free countries furnish us with daily lessons in the anatomy of states and society; they make us comprehend the reality of history. But we have dwelled sufficiently long on this branch.

The branch which treats of the necessity, nature, and effects, the promotion and the hindrances of production, whether it be based almost exclusively on appropriation, as the fishery; or on coercing nature to furnish us with better and more abundant fruit than she is willing spontaneously to yield, as agriculture; or on fashioning, separating, and combining substances which other branches of industry obtain and collect, as manufacture; or on carrying the products from the spot of production to the place of consumption; and the character which all these products acquire by exchange, as values, with the labor and services for which again products are given in exchange, this division of knowledge is called political economy—an unfit name; but it is the name, and we use it. Political economy, like all the other new sciences, was obliged to fight its way to a fair acknowledgment against all manners of prejudices. The introductory lecture which Archbishop Whately delivered some thirty years ago, when he commenced his course on political economy in the University of Oxford, consists almost wholly of a defence of his science and an encounter with the objections then made to it on religious, moral, and almost on every conceivable ground, or suggested by the misconception of its aims. Political economy fared, in this respect, like vaccination, like the taking of a nation's census, like the discontinuance of witch-trials.

The economist stands now on clearer ground. Opponents have acknowledged their errors, and the economists themselves fall no longer into the faults of the utilitarian. The economist indeed sees that the material interests of men are of the greatest importance, and that modern civilization, in all its aspects, requires an immense amount of wealth, and consequently increasing exertion and production, but he acknowledges that "what men can do the least without is not their highest need." He knows that we are bid to pray for our daily bread, but not for bread alone, and I am glad that those who bade me teach Political Economy, assigned to me also Political Philosophy and History. They teach that the periods of national dignity and of the highest endeavors have sometimes been periods of want and poverty. They teach abundantly that riches and enfeebling comforts, that the flow of wine and costly tapestry, do not lead to the development of humanity, nor are its tokens; that no barbarism is coarser than the substitution of gross expensiveness for what is beautiful and graceful; that it is manly character, and womanly soulfulness, not gilded upholstery or fretful fashion—that it is the love of truth and justice, directness and tenacity of purpose, a love of right, of fairness and freedom, a self-sacrificing public spirit and religious sincerity, that lead nations to noble places in history; not surfeiting feasts or conventional refinement. The Babylonians tried that road before us.

But political economy, far from teaching the hoarding of riches, shows the laws of accumulation and distribution of wealth; it shows the important truth that mankind at large can become and have become wealthier, and must steadily increase their wealth with expanding culture.

It is, nevertheless, true that here, in the most active market of our whole hemisphere, I have met, more frequently than in any other place, with an objection to political economy, on the part of those who claim for themselves the name of men of business. They often say that they alone can know anything about it, and as often ask: What is Political Economy good for? The soldier, though he may have fought in the thickest of the fight, is not on that account the best judge of the disposition, the aim, the movements, the faults, or the great conceptions of a battle, nor can we call the infliction of a deep wound a profound lesson in anatomy.

What is Political Economy good for? It is like every other branch truthfully pursued, good for leading gradually nearer and nearer to the truth; for making men, in its own sphere, that is the vast sphere of exchange, what Cicero calls *mansucti,* and for clearing more and more away what may be termed the impeding and sometimes savage superstitions of trade and intercourse; it is, like every other pursuit of political science of which it is but a branch, good for sending some light, by means of those that cultivate it as their own science, to the most distant corners, and to those who have perhaps not even heard of its name.

If it is now generally acknowledged that Political Economy ought not to be omitted in a course of superior education, all the reasons apply with greater force to that branch which treats of the relations of man as a jural being—as citizen, and most especially so in our own country, where individual political liberty is enjoyed in a degree in which it has never been enjoyed before. Nowhere is political action carried to a greater intensity, and nowhere is the calming effect of an earnest and scientific treatment of politics more necessary. In few countries is man more exposed to the danger of being carried away to the worship of false political gods and to the idolatry of party than in our land, and nowhere is it more necessary to show to the young the landmarks of political truth, and the essential character of civil liberty—the grave and binding duties that man imposes upon himself when he proudly assumes self-government. Nowhere seem to be so many persons acting on the supposition that we differ from all other men, and that the same deviations will not produce the same calamities, and nowhere does it seem to be more necessary to teach what might well be called political physiology and political pathology. In no sphere of action does it seem to me more necessary than in politics, to teach and impress the truth that "logic without reason is a fearful thing." Aristotle said: The fellest of things is armed injustice; History knows a feller thing—impassioned reasoning without a pure heart in him that has power in a free country—the poisoning of the well of political truth itself. Every youth ought to enter the practical life of the citizen, and every citizen ought to remain through life deeply impressed with the conviction that, as Vauvenargue very nobly said, "great thoughts come from the heart," so great politics come from sincere patriotism, and that without candid and intelligent public spirit, parties, without which no liberty can exist, will raise themselves into ends and objects instead of remaining mere means. And when the words party, party consistency, and party honor are substituted for the word Country, and, as Thucydides has it, when parties use each its own language, and men cease to understand one another, a country soon falls into that state in which a court of justice would find itself where wrangling pleaders should do their work without the tempering, guiding judge—that state of dissolution which is the next step to entire disintegration. Providence has no special laws for special countries, and it is not only true as Talleyrand said: *Tout arrive;* but everything happens over again. There is no truth, short of the multiplication table, that, at some time or other, is not drawn into doubt again, and must be re-asserted and re-proved.

One of the means to insure liberty—that difficult problem in history, far more difficult than the insurance of despotism, because liberty is of an infinitely more delicate organization—is the earnest bringing up of the young in the path of political truth and justice, the necessity of which is increased by the reflection that in our period of large cities man has to solve, for the first time in history, the problem of making a high degree of general and individual liberty compatible with populous cities. It is one of the highest problems of our race, which cannot yet be said to have been solved.

Political philosophy is a branch of knowledge that ought to be taught not only in colleges; its fundamental truths ought to be ingrained in the minds of every one that helps to crowd your public schools.

A complete course of political philosophy, to which every course, whether in a college or a university, ought to approximate, as time and circumstances permit, should wind its way through the large field of political science somewhat in the following manner.

We must start from the pregnant fact that each man is made an individual and a social being, and that his whole humanity with all its attributes, moral, religious, emotional, mental, cultural, and industrial, is decreed forever to revolve between the two poles of individualism and socialism, taking the latter term in its strictly philosophical adaptation. Man's moral individualism and the sovereign necessity of his living in society, or the fact that humanity and society are two ideas that cannot even be conceived of, the one without the other, lead to the twin ideas of Right and Duty. Political science dwells upon this most important elementary truth, that the idea of right cannot be philosophically stated without the idea of obligation, nor that of duty without that of right, and it must show how calamitous every attempt has proved to separate them; how debasing a thing obligation becomes without corresponding rights, and how withering rights and privileges become to the hand that wields the power and to the fellow being over whom it sways, if separated from corresponding duty and obligation.

Right and duty are twin brothers; they are like the two electric flames appearing at the yard-arms in the Mediterranean, and called by the ancient mariners Castor and Pollux. When both are visible, a fair and pleasant course is expected; but one alone portends stormy mischief. An instinctive acknowledgment of this truth makes us repeat with pleasure to this day the old French maxim, *Noblesse oblige,* whatever annotations history may have to tell of its disregard.

That philosopher, whom Dante calls *il maestro di color che sanno,* and whom our science gratefully acknowledges as its own founder, says that man is by nature a political animal. He saw that man cannot divest himself of the state. Society, no matter in how rudimental a condition, always exists, and society considered with reference to rights and duties, to rules to be obeyed, and to privileges to be protected, to those that ordain, and those that comply, is the political state. Government was never voted into existence, and the state originates every day anew in the family. God coerces man into society, and necessitates the growth of government by that divinely simple law, which has been alluded to before, and consists in making the young of man depend upon the parents for years after the period of lactation has ceased. As men and society advance, the greatest of institutions—the state—increases in intensity of action, and when humanity falters back, the state, like the function of a diseased organ, becomes sluggish or acts with ruinous feverishness. In this twinship of right and duty lies the embryonic genesis of liberty, and at the same time the distinction between sincere and seasoned civil liberty, and the wild and one-sided privilege of one man or a class; or the fantastic equality of all in point of rights without the steadying pendulum of mutual obligation.

This leads us to that division which I have called elsewhere Political Ethics, in which the teacher will not fail to use his best efforts, when he discourses on patriotism—that ennobling virtue which at times has been derided, at other times declared incompatible with true philosophy or with pure religion. He will not teach that idolatrous patriotism which inscribes on its banner, Our country, right or wrong, but that heightened public spirit, which loves and honors father and mother, and neighbors, and country; which makes us deeply feel for our country's glory and its faults; makes us willing to die, and, what is often far more difficult, to live for it; that patriotism which is consistent with St. Paul's command: Honor all men, and which can say with Montesquieu, "If I knew anything useful to my country but prejudicial to Europe or mankind, I should consider it as a crime;" that sentiment which made the Athenians reject the secret of Themistocles, because Aristides declared it very useful to Athens, but very injurious to Sparta and to the other Greeks. The Christian citizen can say with Tertullian, *Civitas nostra totus mundus,* and abhors that patriotism which is at best bloated provincialism, but he knows, too, that that society is doomed to certain abasement in which the indifference of the *blasé* is permitted to debilitate and demoralize public sentiment. The patriotism of which we stand as much in need as the ancients is neither an amiable weakness, nor the Hellenic pride. It is a positive virtue demanded of every moral man. It is the fervent love of our own country, but not hatred of others, nor blindness to our faults and to the rights or superiorities of our neighbors.

We now approach that branch of our science which adds, to the knowledge of the "end and reasons of political societies," the discussion of the means by which man endeavors to obtain the end or ought to obtain it; in one word, to the science of government, and a knowledge of governments which exist and have existed. The "end and reasons of political societies" involve the main discussion of the object of the state, as it is more clearly discerned with advancing civilization, the relation of the state to the family, its duties to the individual, and the necessary limits of its power. Protection, in the highest sense of the word,[1] both of society, as a whole, and of the component individ-

---

1. That I do not mean by this material protection only, but the protection of all interests, the highest no less so than the common ones, of society as a unit, as well as of the individual human

uals, as such, without interference, and free from intermeddling, is the great object of the civilized state, or the state of freemen. To this portion of our science belong the great topics of the rights as well as the dependence of the individual citizen, of the woman and the child; of primordial rights and the admissibility or violence of slavery, which, throughout the whole course of history wherever it has been introduced, has been a deciduous institution. The reflection on the duties of the state comprehends the important subjects of the necessity of public education (the common school for those who are deprived of means, or destitute of the desire to be educated; and the university, which lies beyond the capacity of private means); of the support of those who cannot support themselves (the pauper, and the poor orphans, and sick); of intercommunication and intercommunion (the road and the mail); of the promotion of taste and the fine arts, and the public support of religion, or the abstaining from it; and the duty of settling conflicting claims, and of punishing those that infringe the common rules of action, with the science and art of rightful and sensible punition, or, as I have ventured to call this branch, of penology.

The comprehensive apparatus by which all these objects, more or less dimly seen, according to the existing stage of civil progress, are intended to be obtained, and by which a political society evolves its laws, is called government. I generally give at this stage a classification of all governments, in the present time or in the past, according to the main principles on which they rest. This naturally leads to three topics, the corresponding ones of which, in some other sciences, form but important illustrations or constitute a certain amount of interesting knowledge, but which in our science constitute part and parcel of the branch itself. I mean a historical survey of all governments and systems of law, Asiatic or European; a survey of all political literature as represented by its prominent authors, from Aristotle and Plato, or from the Hindoo Menu, down to St. Simon or Calhoun—a portion of the science which necessarily includes many historians and theologians on the one hand, such as Mariana, De Soto, and Machiavelli, and on the other hand statesmen that have poured forth wisdom or criminal theories in public speech, Demosthenes or Webster, Chatham, Burke, Mirabeau or Robespierre and St. Just. And lastly, I mean that division of our science which indeed is, properly, a subdivision of the latter, but sufficiently important and instructive to be treated separately—a survey of those model states which political philosophers have from time to time imagined, and which we now call Utopias, from Plato's Atlantis to Thomas More's Utopia, Campanella's Civitas Solis or Harrington's Oceana to our socialists, or Shelley's and Coleridge's imaginings

being, will be well known to the reader of my Political Ethics. I do by no means restrict the meaning of protection to personal security, nor do I mean by this term something that amounts to the protection of an interest in one person to the injury of others.

and the hallucinations of Comte. They are growing rarer and, probably, will in time wholly cease. Superior minds, at any rate, could feel stimulated to conceive of so-called philosophical republics, in ages only when everything existing in a definite form—languages, mythologies, agriculture, and governments—was ascribed to a correspondingly definite invention, or, at times, to an equally definite inspiration, and when society was not clearly conceived to be a continuity; when far less attention was paid to the idea of progress, which is a succession of advancing steps, and to the historic genesis of institutions; and when the truth was not broadly acknowledged that civilization, whether political or not, cannot divest itself of its accumulative and progressive character.

This Utopology, if you permit me the name, will include those attempts at introducing, by sudden and volcanic action, entirely new governments resulting from some fanatical theory, such as the commonwealth of the anabaptists in Germany, or the attempts at carrying out Rousseau's equalitarian hatred of representative government, by Marat and Collot d'Herbois. They have all been brief and bloody.

When an account is given of the imaginary governments, which the greater or lesser philosophers have constructed as ideal politics, attention must be directed to the striking fact that all Utopists, from Plato to our times, have been more or less communists.

The radical error of the communist consists in his exclusive acknowledgment of the principle of socialism, and his endeavors to apply it even to that which has its very origin and being in individualism—to property. Man cannot exist without producing; production always presupposes appropriation; both are essentially individual, and where appropriation consists in occupation by a society as a unit, this is no less exclusive or individual property, with reference to all other societies, than the property held by a single man. The communist does not seem to see the absurdity of demanding common property for all men in France, upon what he considers philosophic grounds, yet excluding the rest of mankind from that property. The radical error of the individualist, on the other hand, is, that he wholly disavows the principle of socialism, and, generally, reasons on the unstable and shaking ground of expediency alone. He forgets that both, individualism and socialism, are true and ever-active principles, and that the very idea of the state implies both; for, the state is a society, and a society consists of individuals who never lose their individual character, but are united by common bonds, interests, organizations, and a common continuity.

Act on individualism alone, and you would reduce society to a mere crowd of egotistical units, far below the busy but peaceful inmates of the anthill; act on socialism alone, and you reduce society to loathsome despotism, in which individuals would be distinguished by a mere number, as the inmates of Sing Sing. Despotism, of whatever name, is the most equalitarian government. The communist forgets that communism in property, as far as it can exist in reality, is a characteristic feature of low barbarism. Herodotus tells us what we find with existing savages. Mine and Thine in property and marriage is but dimly known by them. The communist wants to "organize," as he calls it, but in fact to disindividualize everything, even effort and labor, and a garden of the times of Louis XV., in which the ruthless shears have cramped and crippled every tree into a slavish uniformity, seems to delight his eye more than a high forest, with its organic life and freedom. Hobbes, who, two centuries ago, passed through the whole theory of all-absorbing power conveyed to one man by popular compact, which we now meet with once more in French Caesarism, defined religion as that superstition which is established by government, and we recollect how closely allied all despotism is to communism. The highest liberty—that civil freedom which protects individual humanity in the highest degree, and at the same time provides society with the safest and healthiest organism through which it obtains its social ends of protection and historic position—may not inaptly be said to consist in a due separation and conjunction of individualism and socialism.

One more remark. It is a striking fact that the old adage, all extremes meet, has been illustrated by none more forcibly than by the socialists; for the most enthusiastic socialists of France, America, and Germany have actually come to the conclusion that there need be and ought to be no government at all among men truly free, except, indeed, as one of our own most visionary socialists naïvely adds, for roads and some such things. For them Aristotle discovered in vain that: Man is by nature a political animal.

The political philosopher will now take in hand, as a separate topic, our own polity and political existence; and this will lead to our great theme, to a manly discussion of Civil Liberty and Self-Government. We are here in the peristyle of a vast temple, and I dare not enter it with you at present, for fear that all the altars and statues and votive tablets of humanity, with all the marbled records of high martyrdom and sanguinary errors, would detain us far beyond the midnight hour. It is our American theme, and we, of all men, are called upon to know it well, with all the aspirations, all the duties and precious privileges, all the struggles, achievements, dangers and errors, all the pride and humiliation, the checks and impulses, the law and untrammelled action, the blessings and the blood, the great realities, the mimicry and licentiousness, the generous sacrifices and the self-seeking, with all these memories and actualities—all wound up in that one word Liberty.

And now the student will be prepared to enter upon that branch which is the glory of our race in modern history, and possibly the greatest achievement of combined judgment and justice, acting under the genial light of culture and religion—on International Law, that law which, without the sword of justice, encompasses even the ocean. The ancients knew it not in their best time; and life and property, once having left the shore, were out of the pale of law and justice. Even down to our Columbus, the mariner stood by the helm with his sword, and watched the compass in armor.

Political science treats of man in his most important earthly phase; the state is the institution which has to protect or to check all his endeavors, and, in turn, reflects them. It is natural, therefore, that a thorough course of this branch should become, in a great measure, a delineation of the history of civilization, with all the undulations of humanity, from that loose condition of men in which Barth found many of our fellow beings in Central Africa, to our own accumulated civilization, which is like a rich tapestry, the main threads of which are Grecian intellectuality, Christian morality and trans-mundane thought, Roman law and institutionality, and Teutonic individual independence, especially developed in Anglican liberty and self-government.

Need I add that the student, having passed through these fields and having viewed these regions, will be the better prepared for the grave purposes for which this country destines him, and as a partner in the great commonwealth of self-government? If not, then strike these sciences from your catalogue. It is true, indeed, that the scholar is no consecrated priest of knowledge, if he does not love it for the sake of knowledge. And this is even important in a practical point of view; for all knowledge, to be usefully applied, must be far in advance of its application. It is like the sun, which, we are told, causes the plant to grow when he has already sunk below the horizon; yet I acknowledge without reserve, for all public instruction and all education, the token which I am in the habit of taking into every lecture-room of mine, to impress it ever anew on my mind and on that of my hearers, that, following Seneca, we teach and learn:

NON SCHOLAE SED VITAE, VITAE UTRIQUE.

The Study of Administration

Woodrow Wilson

I suppose that no practical science is ever studied where there is no need to know it. The very fact, therefore, that the eminently practical science of administration is finding its way into college courses in this country would prove that this country needs to know more about administration, were such proof of the fact required to make out a case. It need not be said, however, that we do not look into college programmes for proof of this fact. It is a thing almost taken for granted among us, that the present movement called civil service reform must, after the accomplishment of its first purpose, expand into efforts to improve, not the *personnel* only, but also the organization and methods of our government offices: because it is plain that their organization and methods need improvement only less than their *personnel*. It is the object of administrative study to discover, first, what government can properly and successfully do, and, secondly, how it can do these proper things with the utmost possible efficiency and at the least possible cost either of money or of energy. On both these points there is obviously much need of light among us; and only careful study can supply that light.

Before entering on that study, however, it is needful:

I. To take some account of what others have done in the same line; that is to say, of the history of the study.
II. To ascertain just what is its subject matter.
III. To determine just what are the best methods by which to develop it, and the most clarifying political conceptions to carry with us into it.

Unless we know and settle these things, we shall set out without chart or compass.

Reprinted in a somewhat shortened version from *Political Science Quarterly* 2 (1887): 197–222.

I.

The science of administration is the latest fruit of that study of the science of politics which was begun some twenty-two hundred years ago. It is a birth of our own century, almost of our own generation.

Why was it so late in coming? Why did it wait till this too busy century of ours to demand attention for itself? Administration is the most obvious part of government; it is government in action; it is the executive, the operative, the most visible side of government, and is of course as old as government itself. It is government in action, and one might very naturally expect to find that government in action had arrested the attention and provoked the scrutiny of writers of politics very early in the history of systematic thought.

But such was not the case. No one wrote systematically of administration as a branch of the science of government until the present century had passed its first youth and had begun to put forth its characteristic flower of systematic knowledge. Up to our own day all the political writers whom we now read had thought, argued, dogmatized only about the *constitution* of government; about the nature of the state, the essence and seat of sovereignty, popular power and kingly prerogative; about the greatest meanings lying at the heart of government, and the high ends set before the purpose of government by man's nature and man's aims. The central field of controversy was that great field of theory in which monarchy rode tilt against democracy, in which oligarchy would have built for itself strongholds of privilege, and in which tyranny sought opportunity to make good its claim to receive submission from all competitors. Amidst this high warfare of principles, administration could command no pause for its own consideration. The question was always: Who shall make law, and what shall that law be? The other question, how law should be administered with enlightenment, with equity, with speed, and without friction, was put aside as "practical detail" which clerks could arrange after doctors had agreed upon principles.

That political philosophy took this direction was of course no accident, no chance preference or perverse whim of political philosophers. The philosophy of any time is, as Hegel says, "nothing but the spirit of that time expressed in abstract thought"; and political philosophy, like philosophy of every other kind, has only held up the mirror to contemporary affairs. The trouble in early times was almost altogether about the constitution of government; and consequently that was what engrossed men's thoughts. There was little or no trouble about administration—at least little that was heeded by administrators. The functions of government were simple, because life itself was simple. Government went about imperatively and compelled men, without thought of consulting their wishes. There was no complex system of public revenues and public debts to puzzle financiers; there were, consequently, no financiers to be puzzled. No one who possessed power was long at a loss how to use it. The great and only question was: Who shall possess it? Populations were of manageable numbers; property was of simple sorts. There were plenty of farms, but no stocks and bonds: more cattle than vested interests.

I have said that all this was true of "early times"; but it was substantially true also of comparatively late times. One does not have to look back of the last century for the beginnings of the present complexities of trade and perplexities of commercial speculation, nor for the portentous birth of national debts. Good Queen Bess, doubtless, thought that the monopolies of the sixteenth century were hard enough to handle without burning her hands; but they are not remembered in the presence of the giant monopolies of the nineteenth century. When Blackstone lamented that corporations had no bodies to be kicked and no souls to be damned, he was anticipating the proper time for such regrets by full a century. The perennial discords between master and workmen which now so often disturb industrial society began before the Black Death and the Statute of Laborers; but never before our own day did they assume such ominous proportions as they wear now. In brief, if difficulties of governmental action are to be seen gathering in other centuries, they are to be seen culminating in our own.

This is the reason why administrative tasks have nowadays to be so studiously and systematically adjusted to carefully tested standards of policy, the reason why we are having now what we never had before, a science of administration. The weightier debates of constitutional principle are even yet by no means concluded; but they are no longer of more immediate practical moment than questions of administration. It is getting to be harder to *run* a constitution than to frame one.

There is scarcely a single duty of government which was once simple which is not now complex; government once had but a few masters; it now has scores of masters. Majorities formerly only underwent government; they now conduct government. Where government once might follow the whims of a court, it must now follow the views of a nation.

And those views are steadily widening to new conceptions of state duty; so that, at the same time that the functions of government are every day becoming more complex and difficult, they are also vastly multiplying in number. Administration is everywhere putting its hands to new undertakings. The utility, cheapness, and success of the government's postal service, for instance, point towards the early establishment of governmental control of the telegraph system. Or, even if our government is not to follow the lead of the governments of Europe in buying or building both telegraph and railroad lines, no one can doubt that in some way it must make itself master of masterful corporations. The creation of national commissioners of railroads, in addition to the older state commissions, involves a very important and delicate extension of administrative functions. Whatever hold of authority state or federal governments are to take upon corporations, there must follow cares and responsibilities which will require not a little wisdom, knowledge, and experience. Such things must be studied in order to be well done. And these, as I have said, are only a few of the doors which are being opened to offices of government. The idea of the state and the consequent ideal of its duty are undergoing noteworthy change; and "the idea of the state is the conscience of administration." Seeing every day new things which the state ought to do, the next thing is to see clearly how it ought to do them.

This is why there should be a science of administration which shall seek to straighten the paths of government, to make its business less un-businesslike, to strengthen and purify its organization, and to crown its duties with dutifulness. This is one reason why there is such a science.

But where has this science grown up? Surely not on this side of the sea. Not much impartial scientific method is to be discerned in our administrative practices. The poisonous atmosphere of city government, the crooked secrets of state administration, the confusion, sinecurism, and corruption ever and again discovered in the bureaux at Washington forbid us to believe that any clear conceptions of what constitutes good administration are as yet very widely current in the United States. No; American writers have hitherto taken no very important part in the advancement of this science. It has found its doctors in Europe. It is not of our making; it is a foreign science, speaking very little of the language of English or American principle. It employs only foreign tongues; it utters none but what are to our minds alien ideas. Its aims, its examples, its conditions, are almost exclusively grounded in the histories of foreign races, in the precedents of foreign systems, in the lessons of foreign revolutions. It has been developed by French and German professors, and is consequently in all parts adapted to the needs of a compact state, and made to fit highly centralized forms of government; whereas, to answer our purposes, it must be adapted, not to a simple and compact, but to a complex and multiform state, and made to fit highly decentralized forms of government. If we would employ it, we must Americanize it, and that not formally, in language merely, but radically, in thought, principle, and aim as well. It must learn our constitutions by heart; must get the bureaucratic fever out of its veins; must inhale much free American air.

If an explanation be sought why a science manifestly so susceptible of being made useful to all governments alike should have received attention first in Europe, where government has long been a monopoly, rather than in England or the United States, where government has long been a common franchise, the reason will doubtless be found to be twofold: first, that in Europe, just because government was independent of popular assent, there was more governing to be done; and, second, that the desire to keep government a monopoly made the monopolists interested in discovering the least irritating means of governing. They were, besides, few enough to adopt means promptly.

The countries of the continent for a long time desperately struggled against all change, and would have diverted revolution by softening the asperities of absolute government. They did at last give the people constitutions and the franchise; but even after that they obtained leave to continue despotic by becoming paternal. They made themselves too efficient to be dispensed with, too smoothly operative to be noticed, too enlightened to be inconsiderately questioned, too benevolent to be suspected, too powerful to be coped with. All this has required study; and they have closely studied it.

On this side of the sea we, the while, had known no great difficulties of government. With a new country, in which there was room and remunerative employment for everybody, with liberal principles of government and unlimited skill in practical politics, we were long exempted from the need of being anxiously careful about plans and methods of administration. We have naturally been slow to see the use or significance of those many volumes of learned research and painstaking examination into the ways and means of conducting government which the presses of Europe have been sending to our libraries. Like a lusty child, government with us has expanded in nature and grown great in stature, but has also become awkward in movement. The vigor and increase of its life has been altogether out of proportion to its skill in living. It has gained strength, but it has not acquired deportment. Great, therefore, as has been our advantage over the countries of Europe in point of ease and health of constitutional development, now that the time for more careful administrative adjustments and larger administrative knowledge has come to us, we are at a signal disadvantage as compared with the transatlantic nations; and this for reasons which I shall try to make clear.

Judging by the constitutional histories of the chief nations of the modern world, there may be said to be three periods of growth through which government has passed in all the most highly developed of existing systems, and through which it promises to pass in all the rest. The first of these periods is that of absolute rulers, and of an administrative system adapted to absolute rule; the second is that in which constitutions are framed to do away with absolute rulers and substitute popular control, and in which administration is neglected for these higher concerns; and the third is that in which the sovereign people undertake to develop administration under this new constitution which has brought them into power.

Those governments are now in the lead in administrative practice which had rulers still absolute but also enlightened when those modern days of political illumination came in which it was made evident to all but the blind that governors are properly only the servants of the governed. In such governments administration has been organized to subserve the general weal with the simplicity and effectiveness vouchsafed only to the undertakings of a single will.

Such was the case in Prussia, for instance, where administration has been most studied and most nearly perfected. Of similar origin was the practice, if not the plan, of modern French administration with its symmetrical divisions of territory and its orderly gradations of office. The recasting of French administration by Napoleon is, therefore, my second example of the perfecting of civil machinery by the single will of an absolute ruler before the dawn of a constitutional era.

Among those nations, on the other hand, which entered upon a season of constitution-making and popular reform before administration had received the impress of liberal principle, administrative improvement has been tardy and half-done. Once a nation has embarked in the business of manufacturing constitutions, it finds it exceedingly difficult to close out that business and open for the public a bureau of skilled, economical administration. There seems to be no end to the tinkering of constitutions. Your ordinary constitution will last you hardly ten years without repairs or additions; and the time for administrative detail comes late.

Here, of course, our examples are England and our own country. The English race has long and successfully studied the art of curbing executive power to the constant neglect of the art of perfecting executive methods. It has exercised itself much more in controlling than in energizing government. It has been more concerned to render government just and moderate than to make it facile, well-ordered, and effective. English and American political history has been a history, not of administrative development, but of legislative oversight—not of progress in governmental organization, but of advance in law-making and political criticism. Consequently, we have reached a time when administrative study and creation are imperatively necessary to the well-being of our governments saddled with the habits of a long period of constitution-making. That period has practically closed, so far as the establishment of essential principles is concerned, but we cannot shake off its atmosphere. We go on criticizing when we ought to be creating. We have reached the third of the periods I have mentioned—the period, namely, when the people have to develop administration in accordance with the constitutions they won for themselves in a previous period of struggle with absolute power; but we are not prepared for the tasks of the new period.

Such an explanation seems to afford the only escape from blank astonishment at the fact that, in spite of our vast advantages in point of political liberty, and above all in point of practical political skill and sagacity, so many nations are ahead of us in administrative organization and administrative skill. Why, for instance, have we but just begun purifying a civil service which was rotten full fifty years ago? To say that slavery diverted us is but to repeat what I have said—that flaws in our constitution delayed us.

Of course all reasonable preference would declare for this English and American course of politics rather than for that of any European country. We should not like to have had Prussia's history for the sake of having Prussia's administrative skill; and Prussia's particular system of administration would quite suffocate us. It is better to be untrained and free than to be servile and systematic. Still there is no denying that it would be better yet to be both free in spirit and proficient in practice. It is this even more reasonable preference which impels us to discover what there may be to hinder or delay us in naturalizing this much-to-be-desired science of administration.

What, then, is there to prevent?

Well, principally, popular sovereignty. It is harder for democracy to organize administration than for monarchy. The very completeness of our most cherished political successes in the past embarrasses us. We have enthroned public opinion; and it is forbidden us to hope during its reign for any quick schooling of the sovereign in executive expertness or in the conditions of perfect functional balance in government. The very fact that we have realized popular rule in its fulness has made the task of *organizing* that rule just so much the more difficult. In order to make any advance at all we must instruct and persuade a multitudinous monarch called public opinion—a much less feasible undertaking than to influence a single monarch called a king.

Wherever regard for public opinion is a first principle of government, practical reform must be slow and all reform must be full of compromises. For wherever public opinion exists it must rule. This is now an axiom half the world over, and will presently come to be believed even in Russia. Whoever would effect a change in a modern constitutional government must first educate his fellow citizens to want *some* change. That done, he must persuade them to want the particular change he wants. He must first make public opinion willing to listen and then see to it that it listen to the right things. He must stir it up to search for an opinion, and then manage to put the right opinion in its way.

To know the public mind of this country, one must know the mind, not of Americans of the older stocks only, but also of Irishmen, of Germans, of negroes. In order to get a footing for new doctrine, one must influence minds cast in every mould of race, minds inheriting every bias of environment, warped by the histories of a score of different nations, warmed or chilled, closed or expanded by almost every climate of the globe.

So much, then, for the history of the study of administration, and the peculiarly difficult conditions under which, entering upon it when we do, we must undertake it. What, now, is the subject matter of this study, and what are its characteristic objects?

II.

The field of administration is a field of business. It is removed from the hurry and strife of politics; it at most points stands apart even from the debatable ground of constitutional study. It is a part of political life only as the methods of the counting-house are a part of the life of society; only as machinery is part of the manufactured product. But it is, at the same time, raised very far above the dull level of mere technical detail by the fact that through its greater principles it is directly connected with the lasting maxims of political wisdom, the permanent truths of political progress.

The object of administrative study is to rescue executive methods from the confusion and costliness of empirical experiment and set them upon foundations laid deep in stable principle.

It is for this reason that we must regard civil-service reform in its present stages as but a prelude to a fuller administrative reform. We are now rectifying methods of appointment; we must go on to adjust executive functions more fitly and to prescribe better methods of executive organization and action. Civil-service reform is thus but a moral preparation for what is to follow. It is clearing the moral atmosphere of official life by establishing the sanctity of public office as a public trust, and, by making the service unpartisan, it is opening the way for making it businesslike. By sweetening its motives it is rendering it capable of improving its methods of work.

Let me expand a little what I have said of the province of administration. Most important to be observed is the truth already so much and so fortunately insisted upon by our civil-service reformers; namely, that administration lies outside the proper sphere of *politics*. Administrative questions are not political questions. Although politics sets the tasks for administration, it should not be suffered to manipulate its offices.

This is distinction of high authority; eminent German writers insist upon it as of course. Bluntschli, for instance, bids us separate administration alike from politics and from law. Politics, he says, is state activity "in things great and universal," while "administration, on the other hand," is "the activity of the state in individual and small things. Politics is thus the special province of the statesman, administration of the technical official." "Policy does nothing without the aid of administration"; but administration is not therefore politics. But we do not require German authority for this position; this discrimination between administration and politics is now, happily, too obvious to need further discussion.

There is another distinction which must be worked into all our conclusions, which, though but another side of that between administration and politics, is not quite so easy to keep sight of: I mean the distinction between *constitutional* and administrative questions, between those governmental adjustments which are essential to constitutional principle and those which are merely instrumental to the possibly changing purposes of a wisely adapting convenience.

A clear view of the difference between the province of constitutional law and the province of administrative function ought to leave no room for misconception; and it is possible to name some roughly definite criteria upon which such a view can be built. Public administration is detailed and systematic execution of public law. Every particular application of general law is an act of administration. The assessment and raising of taxes, for instance, the hanging of a criminal, the transportation and delivery of the mails, the equipment and recruiting of the army and navy, etc., are all obvious acts of administration; but the general laws which direct these things to be done are as obviously outside of and above administration. The broad plans of governmental action are not administrative; the detailed execution of such plans is administrative. Constitutions, therefore, properly concern themselves only with those instrumentalities of government which are to control general law. Our federal constitution observes this principle in saying nothing of even the greatest of the purely executive offices, and speaking only of that of the President of the Union who was to share the legislative and policy-making functions of government, only of those judges of highest jurisdiction who were to interpret and guard its principles, and not of those who were merely to give utterance to them.

This is not quite the distinction between Will and answering Deed, because the administrator should have and does have a will of his own in the choice of means for accomplishing his work. He is not and ought not to be a mere passive instrument. The distinction is between general plans and special means.

There is, indeed, one point at which administrative studies trench on constitutional ground—or at least upon what seems constitutional ground. The study of administration, philosophically viewed, is closely connected with the study of the proper distribution of constitutional authority. To be efficient it must discover the simplest arrangements by which responsibility can be unmistakably fixed upon officials; the best way of dividing authority without hampering it, and responsibility without obscuring it. And this question of the distribution of authority, when taken into the sphere of the higher, the originating functions of government, is obviously a central constitutional question. If administrative study can discover the best principles upon which to base such distribution, it will have done constitutional study an invaluable service. Montesquieu did not, I am convinced, say the last word on this head.

To discover the best principle for the distribution of authority is of greater importance, possibly, under a democratic system, where officials serve many masters, than under others where they serve but a few. All sovereigns are suspicious of their servants, and the sovereign people is no exception to the rule; but how is its suspicion to be allayed by *knowledge?* If that suspicion could but be clarified into wise vigilance, it would be altogether salutary; if that vigilance could be aided by the unmistakable placing of responsibility, it would be altogether beneficent. Suspicion in itself is never healthful either in the private or in the public mind. *Trust is strength* in all relations of life; and, as it is the office of the constitutional reformer to create conditions of trustfulness, so it is the office of the administrative organizer to fit administration with conditions of clear-cut responsibility which shall insure trustworthiness.

To whom is official trustworthiness to be disclosed, and by whom is it to be rewarded? Is the official to look to the public for his meed of praise and his push of promotion, or only to his superior in office? Are the people to be called in to settle administrative discipline as they are called in to settle constitutional principles? These questions evidently find their root in what is undoubtedly the fundamental problem of this whole study. That problem is: What part shall public opinion take in the conduct of administration?

The right answer seems to be, that public opinion shall play the part of authoritative critic.

But the *method* by which its authority shall be made to tell? Our peculiar American difficulty in organizing administration is not the danger of losing liberty, but the danger of not being able or willing to separate its essentials from its accidents. Our success is made doubtful by that besetting error of ours, the error of trying to do too much by vote. Self-government does not consist in having a hand in everything, any more than housekeeping consists necessarily in cooking dinner with one's own hands. The cook must be trusted with a large discretion as to the management of the fires and the ovens.

In those countries in which public opinion has yet to be instructed in its privileges, yet to be accustomed to having its own way, this question as to the province of public opinion is much more readily soluble than in this country, where public opinion is wide awake and quite intent upon having its own way anyhow. It is pathetic to see a whole book written by a German professor of political science for the purpose of saying to his countrymen, "Please try to have an opinion about national affairs"; but a public which is so modest may at least be expected to be very docile and acquiescent in learning what things it has *not* a right to think and speak about imperatively. It may be sluggish, but it will not be meddlesome. It will submit to be instructed before it tries to instruct. Its political education will come before its political activity. In trying to instruct our own public opinion, we are dealing with a pupil apt to think itself quite sufficiently instructed beforehand.

The problem is to make public opinion efficient without suffering it to be meddlesome. Directly exercised, in the oversight of the daily details and in the choice of the daily means of government, public criticism is of course a clumsy nuisance, a rustic handling delicate machinery. But as superintending the greater forces of formative policy alike in politics and administration, public criticism is altogether safe and beneficent, altogether indispensable. Let administrative study find the best means for giving public criticism this control and for shutting it out from all other interference.

But is the whole duty of administrative study done when it has taught the people what sort of administration to desire and demand, and how to get what they demand? Ought it not to go on to drill candidates for the public service?

There is an admirable movement towards universal political education now afoot in this country. The time will soon come when no college of respectability can afford to do without a well-filled chair of political science. But the education thus imparted will go but a certain length. It will multiply the number of intelligent critics of government, but it will create no competent body of administrators. It will prepare the way for the development of a sure-footed understanding of the general principles of government, but it will not necessarily foster skill in conducting government. It is an education which will equip legislators, perhaps, but not executive officials. If we are to improve public opinion, which is the motive power of government, we must prepare better officials as the *apparatus* of government. It will be necessary to organize democracy by sending up to the competitive examinations for the civil service men definitely prepared for standing liberal tests as to technical knowledge. A technically schooled civil service will presently have become indispensable.

I know that a corps of civil servants prepared by a special schooling and drilled, after appointment, into a perfected organization, with appropriate hierarchy and characteristic discipline, seems to a great many very thoughtful persons to contain elements which might combine to make an offensive official class—a distinct, semi-corporate body with sympathies divorced from those of a progressive, free-spirited people, and with hearts narrowed to the meanness of a bigoted officialism. Certainly such a class would be altogether hateful and harmful in the United States. Any measures calculated to produce it would for us be measures of reaction and of folly.

But to fear the creation of a domineering, illiberal officialism as a result of the studies I am here proposing is to miss altogether the principle upon which I wish most to insist. That principle is, that administration in the United States must be at all points sensitive to public opinion. A body of thoroughly trained officials serving during good behavior we must have in any case: that is a plain business necessity. But the apprehension that such a body will be anything un-American clears away the moment it is asked, What is to constitute good behavior? For that question obviously carries its own answer on its face. Steady, hearty allegiance to the policy of the government they serve will constitute good behavior. That *policy* will have no taint of officialism about it. It will not be the creation of permanent officials, but of statesmen whose responsibility to public opinion will be direct and inevitable. Bureaucracy can exist only where the whole service of the state is removed from the common political life of the people, its chiefs as well as its rank and file. Its motives, its objects, its policy, its standards, must be bureaucratic. It would be difficult to point out any examples of impudent exclusiveness and arbitrariness on the part of officials doing service under a chief of department who really served the people, as all our chiefs of departments must be made to do. It would be easy, on the other hand, to adduce other instances like that of the influence of Stein in Prussia, where the leadership of one statesman imbued with true public spirit transformed arrogant and perfunctory bureaux into public-spirited instruments of just government.

The ideal for us is a civil service cultured and self-sufficient enough to act with sense and vigor, and yet so intimately connected with the popular thought, by means of elections and constant public counsel, as to find arbitrariness or class spirit quite out of the question.

III.

Having thus viewed in some sort the subject matter and the objects of this study of administration, what are we to conclude as to the methods best suited to it—the points of view most advantageous for it?

Government is so near us, so much a thing of our daily familiar handling, that we can with difficulty see the need of any philosophical study of it, or the exact point of such study, should it be undertaken. We have been on our feet too long to study now the art of walking. We are a practical people, made so apt, so adept in self-government by centuries of experimental drill that we are scarcely any longer capable of perceiving the awkwardness of the particular system we may be using, just because it is so easy for us to use any system. We do not study the art of governing: we govern. But mere unschooled genius for affairs will not save us from sad blunders in administration. Though democrats by long inheritance and repeated choice, we are still rather crude democrats. Old as democracy is, its organization on a basis of modern ideas and conditions is still an unaccomplished work. The democratic state has yet to be equipped for carrying those enormous burdens of administration which the needs of this industrial and trading age are so fast accumulating. Without comparative studies in government we cannot rid ourselves of the misconception that administration stands upon an essentially different basis in a democratic state from that on which it stands in a non-democratic state.

After such study we could grant democracy the sufficient honor of ultimately determining by debate all essential questions affecting the public weal, of basing all structures of policy upon the major will; but we would have found but one rule of good administration for all governments alike. So far as administrative functions are concerned, all governments have a strong structural likeness; more than that, if they are to be uniformly useful and efficient, they *must* have a strong structural likeness. A free man has the same bodily organs, the same executive parts, as the slave, however different may be his motives, his services, his energies. Monarchies and democracies, radically different as they are in other respects, have in reality much the same business to look to.

It is necessary to see that for all governments alike the legitimate ends of administration are the same, in order not to be frightened at the idea of looking into foreign systems of administration for instruction and suggestion; in order to get rid of the apprehension that we might perchance blindly borrow something incompatible with our principles.

We can borrow the science of administration with safety and profit if only we read all fundamental differences of condition into its essential tenets. We have only to filter it through our constitutions, only to put it over a slow fire of criticism and distil away its foreign gases.

I know that there is a sneaking fear in some conscientiously patriotic minds that studies of European systems might signalize some foreign methods as better than some American methods; and the fear is easily to be understood. But it would scarcely be avowed in just any company.

It is the more necessary to insist upon thus putting away all prejudices against looking anywhere in the world but at home for suggestions in this study, because nowhere else in the whole field of politics, it would seem, can we make use of the historical, comparative method more safely than in this province of administration. Perhaps the more novel the forms we study the better. We shall the sooner learn the peculiarities of our own methods. We can never learn either our own weaknesses or our own virtues by comparing ourselves with ourselves. We are too used to the appearance and procedure of our own system to see its true significance. Perhaps even the English system is too much like our own to be used to the most profit in illustration. It is best on the whole to get entirely away from our own atmosphere and to be most careful in examining such systems as those of France and Germany. Seeing our own institutions through such *media*, we see ourselves as foreigners might see us were they to look at us without preconceptions. Of ourselves, so long as we know only ourselves, we know nothing.

Let it be noted that it is the distinction, already drawn, between administration and politics which makes the comparative method so safe in the field of administration. When we study the administrative systems of France and Germany, knowing that we are not in search of *political* principles, we need not care a peppercorn for the constitutional or political reasons which Frenchmen or Germans give for their practices when explaining them to us. If I see a murderous fellow sharpening a knife cleverly, I can borrow his way of sharpening the knife without borrowing his probable intention to commit murder with it; and so, if I see a monarchist dyed in the wool managing a public bureau well, I can learn his business methods without changing one of my republican spots. He may serve his king; I will continue to serve the people; but I should like to serve my sovereign as well as he serves his. By keeping this distinction in view—that is, by studying administration as a means of putting our own politics into convenient practice, as a means of making what is democratically politic towards all administratively possible towards each— we are on perfectly safe ground, and can learn without error what foreign systems have to teach us. We thus devise an adjusting weight for our comparative method of study. We can thus scrutinize the anatomy of foreign governments without fear of getting any of their diseases into our veins; dissect alien systems without apprehension of blood-poisoning.

Our own politics must be the touchstone for all theories. The principles on which to base a science of administration for America must be principles which have democratic policy very much at heart. And, to suit American habit, all general theories must, as theories, keep modestly in the background, not in open argument only, but even in our own minds—lest opinions satisfactory only to the standards of the library should be dogmatically used, as if they must be quite as satisfactory to the standards of practical politics as well. Doctrinaire devices must be postponed to tested practices. Arrangements not only sanctioned by conclusive experience elsewhere but also congenial to American habit must be preferred without hesitation to theoretical perfection. In a word, steady, practical statesmanship must come first, closet doctrine second. The cosmopolitan what-to-do must always be commanded by the American how-to-do-it.

Our duty is, to supply the best possible life to a *federal* organization, to systems within systems; to make town, city, county, state, and federal governments live with a like strength and an equally assured healthfulness, keeping each unquestionably its own master and yet making all interdependent and co-operative, combining independence with mutual helpfulness. The task is great and important enough to attract the best minds.

If we solve [the] problem [of public service in a federal system] we shall again pilot the world. There is a tendency—is there not?—a tendency as yet dim, but already steadily impulsive and clearly destined to prevail, towards, first the confederation of parts of empires like the British, and finally of great states themselves. Instead of centralization of power, there is to be wide union with tolerated divisions of prerogative. This is a tendency towards the American type—of governments joined with governments for the pursuit of common purposes, in honorary equality and honorable subordination. Like principles of civil liberty are everywhere fostering like methods of government; and if comparative studies of the ways and means of government should enable us to offer suggestions which will practicably combine openness and vigor in the administration of such governments with ready docility to all serious, well-sustained public criticism, they will have approved themselves worthy to be ranked among the highest and most fruitful of the great departments of political study. That they will issue in such suggestions I confidently hope.

The Idea and Forms of the State

John W. Burgess

Definitions of so comprehensive a term as the state are generally one-sided and always unsatisfactory. Nevertheless they are useful and helpful. This is primarily a question of political science. Not until the state has given itself a definite and regular form of organization, i.e., not until it has formed for itself a constitution, does it become a subject of public law. It may be said that a state cannot exist without a constitution. This is true in fact; but the state can be separated in idea from any particular form of organization, and the essential elements of its definition can be found in the principle or principles common to all forms. There are two ways of reaching the definition. The one is the process of pure philosophy, the other that of inductive logic. The one gives us an idea of the reason, the other a concept of the understanding. The two ought to coincide, but they more frequently differ. The sources of the difference are manifold. Either the speculation is colored by fancy, or the induction is not exhaustive. Either the idea is too abstract, or the concept too concrete. There is something deeper, too, than the intellectual character of the particular political scientist, which creates this disharmony between the idea and the concept of the state. The idea of the state is the state perfect and complete. The concept of the state is the state developing and approaching perfection. There is one thing, however, which modifies this divergence between the idea and the concept of the state, and that is the dependence, after all, of the speculative philosopher upon objective realities to awaken his consciousness of the idea. This brings the two nearer together. It makes the idea the pioneer of the concept, and the concept the stages in the realization of the idea. If we keep in mind the two processes followed in the formation of the definition, we shall be better able to reconcile the views of the different authors upon this subject. There is nothing more disheartening for the reader than to be dragged through a list of conflicting definitions at the beginning of a treatise, and to be required to select the principle before he knows the facts and details of the subject; still something of

Reprinted in a shortened version from *Political Science and Comparative Constitutional Law* (Boston: Ginn and Co., 1891), vol. 1, chaps. 1 and 3.

the sort must be done, briefly and tentatively at least, in order to give logical consistence to the work. The reader may take the preliminary definition upon trial at least, and accept it with a temporary faith.

From the standpoint of the idea the state is mankind viewed as an organized unit. From the standpoint of the concept it is a particular portion of mankind viewed as an organized unit. From the standpoint of the idea the territorial basis of the state is the world, and the principle of unity is humanity. From the standpoint of the concept, again, the territorial basis of the state is a particular portion of the earth's surface, and the principle of unity is that particular phase of human nature, and of human need, which, at any particular stage in the development of that nature, is predominant and commanding. The former is the real state of the perfect future. The latter is the real state of the past, the present, and the imperfect future. In a treatise, therefore, upon public law, and upon political science only as connected with public law, we have to deal only with the latter. Our definition must, therefore, be that the state is a particular portion of mankind viewed as an organized unit. This definition requires a great deal of analysis and explanation.

I. What is the principle according to which the portions of mankind forming states are to be determined?

No answer can be given to this question that will be valid for all times and conditions. In the ancient civilization the principle of common blood or a common faith, in the mediaeval that of personal allegiance, and in the modern that of territorial citizenship, have chiefly determined the political divisions of the world. We must be careful, however, not to separate these principles, as to the time of their application, too exactly from each other. Each of them reaches out beyond its proper period and, so to speak, overlaps the next, creating that confusion in regard to citizenship and alienage which every public lawyer meets and dreads. But these answers are not wholly satisfactory. They resolve the problem in part, but they raise other and more difficult questions. How far will a bond of blood, or of faith, preserve sufficient strength to serve as the principle of political organization? What are the circumstances which direct personal allegiance towards this point or that? What are the conditions which make a particular territory the home of a state? With these questions, we have again entered the domains of geography, ethnology and the history of civilization. In so far as the modern state is concerned—i.e., in so far as the question is practical—I have attempted to show what answer these sciences afford. As to the ancient and mediaeval states, we can only say that their principles of organization left their political limits and boundaries uncertain and inexact, producing continual unrest and conflict.

II. What are the peculiar characteristics of the organization which we term the state?

First, I would say that the state is all-comprehensive. Its organization embraces all persons, natural or legal, and all associations of persons. Political science and public law do not recognize in principle the existence of any stateless persons within the territory of the state.

Second, the state is exclusive. Political science and public law do not recognize the existence of an *imperium in imperio.* The state may constitute two or more governments; it may assign to each a distinct sphere of action; it may *then* require of its citizens or subjects obedience to each government thus constituted; but there cannot be two organizations of the state for the same population and within the same territory.

Third, the state is permanent. It does not lie within the power of men to create it today and destroy it tomorrow, as caprice may move them. Human nature has two sides to it—the one universal, the other particular; the one the state, the other the individual. Men can no more divest themselves of the one side than of the other; i.e., they cannot divest themselves of either. No great publicist since the days of Aristotle has dissented from this principle. Anarchy is a permanent impossibility.

Fourth and last, the state is sovereign. This is its most essential principle. An organization may be conceived which would include every member of a given population, or every inhabitant of a given territory, and which might continue with great permanence, and yet it might not be the state. If, however, it possesses the sovereignty over the population, then it is the state. What now do we mean by this all-important term and principle, the sovereignty? I understand by it original, absolute, unlimited, universal power over the individual subject and over all associations of subjects. This is a proposition from which most of the publicists, down to the most modern period, have labored hard to escape. It has appeared to them to contain the destruction of individual liberty and individual rights. The principle cannot, however, be logically or practically avoided, and it is not only not inimical to individual liberty and individual rights, but it is their only solid foundation and guaranty. A little earnest reflection will manifest the truth of this double statement.

First, power cannot be sovereign if it be limited; that which imposes the limitation is sovereign; and not until we reach the power which is unlimited, or only self-limited, have we attained the sovereignty. Those who hold to the idea of a limited sovereignty (which, I contend, is a *contradictio in adjecto*) do not, indeed, assert a real legal limitation, but a limitation by the laws of God, the laws of nature, the laws of reason, the laws between nations. But who is to interpret, in last instance, these principles, which are termed laws of God, laws of nature, laws of reason, and laws between nations, when they are invoked by anybody in justification of disobedience to a command of the state, or of the powers which the state authorizes? Is it not evident that this must be the state itself? It is conceivable, no doubt, that an individual may, upon some point or other, or at some time or other, interpret these principles more truly than does the state, but it is not at all probable, and not at all admissible in principle. It is conceivable, also, that a state may outgrow its form of organization, so that the old organization no longer contains the real sovereignty; and that an individual, or a number of individuals, may rouse the real sovereign to resist triumphantly the commands of the apparent sovereign as misinterpretations of the truths of God, nature, and reason. That would only prove that we had mistaken the point of sovereignty, and would teach the lesson that the state must always hold its form to accord with its substance. When the French National Assembly of 1789 disputed the commands of the King, it could find no ground to rest upon, either in logic or in fact, until it declared the sovereignty to be in the nation—in the nation organized in the Assembly. The common consciousness is the purest light given to men by which to interpret truth in any direction; it is the safest adviser as to when principle shall take on the form of command; and the common consciousness is the state consciousness. In the modern national state we call it the national consciousness. The so-called laws of God, of nature, of reason, and between states are legally, and for the subject, what the state declares them to be; and these declarations and commands of the state are to be presumed to contain the most truthful interpretations of these principles, which a fallible and developing human view can, at the given moment, discover. It is begging the question to appeal to the consciousness of the world or of humanity against the consciousness of the state; for the world has no form of organization for making such interpretation, or for intervening between the state and its citizens to nullify the state's interpretation. I do not ignore the fact that some great publicists think they see in the body of general agreements, positive and customary, between states, called international law, the postulates of a consciousness wider than that of a single state. This may be true; but we must not forget that these agreements and customs are not law between a state and its own subjects unless the state recognizes them as such. For instance, it is a firmly established principle of our own constitutional law that our own governmental organs, authorized thereto by the state, are the interpreters, in last instance, of international law for all persons subject to their jurisdiction. At the present stage of the world's civilization, a nearer approximation to truth seems to be attainable from the standpoint of a national state consciousness than from the standpoint of what is termed the consciousness of mankind. An appeal to the consciousness of mankind, if it bring any reply at all, will receive an answer confused, contradictory, and unintelligible. In the far-distant future it may be otherwise; but for the present and the discernible future, the national state appears to be the organ for the interpretation, in last instance, of the order of life for its subjects. Contact between states may, and undoubtedly does, clarify and harmonize the consciousness of each; but it is still the state consciousness which is the sovereign interpreter, and the state power which is the sovereign transformer of these interpretations into laws. But, it may be objected, if sovereignty must have this character of infallibility, it should be denied to the state altogether. That would mean, at once and from the start, the annihilation of the state. The state must have the power to compel the subject against his will: otherwise it is no state; it is only an anarchic society. Now the power to compel obedience and to punish for disobedience is, or originates in, sovereignty. This condition can, therefore, offer no loophole of escape from the proposition.

In the second place, the unlimited sovereignty of the state is not hostile to individual liberty, but is its source and support. Deprive the state, either wholly or in part, of the power to determine the elements and the scope of individual liberty, and the result must be that each individual will make such determination, wholly or in part, for himself; that the determinations of different individuals will come into conflict with each other; and that those individuals only who have power to help themselves will remain free, reducing the rest to personal subjection. It is true that the sovereign state may confer liberty upon some and not upon others, or more liberty upon some than upon others. But it is also true that no state has shown so little disposition to do this, and that no state has made liberty so full and general, as the modern national popular state. Now the modern national popular state is the most perfectly and undisputedly sovereign organization of the state which the world has yet attained. It exempts no class or person from its law, and no matter from its jurisdiction. It sets exact limits to the sphere in which it permits the individual to act freely. It is ever present to prevent the violation of those limits by any individual to the injury of the rights and liberties of another individual, or of the welfare of the community. It stands ever ready, if perchance the measures of prevention prove unsuccessful, to punish such violations. This fact surely indicates that the more completely and really sovereign the state is, the truer and securer is the liberty of the individual. If we go back an era in the history of political civilization, we shall find this view confirmed beyond dispute. The absolute monarchies of the fifteenth, sixteenth, and seventeenth centuries were, no one will gainsay, far more sovereign organizations of the state than the feudal system which they displaced; and yet they gave liberty to the common man at the same time that they subjected the nobles to the law of the state. In fact they gave liberty to the common man by subjecting the nobles to the law of the state. Should we continue to go backward from the absolute monarchic system to those systems in which the sovereignty of the state was less and less perfectly developed, we should find the liberty of the individual more and more uncertain and insecure, until at last the barbarism of individualism would begin to appear.

At the beginning of this argument, I assumed the state to be deprived of its unlimited power over the individual. But who or what can do this? That which can be so deprived is not the state; that which deprives is the state. Really the state cannot be conceived without sovereignty; i.e., without unlimited power over its subjects. That is its very essence. Of course the state may abuse its unlimited power over the individual, but this is never to be presumed. It is the human organ least likely to do wrong, and, therefore, we must hold to the principle that the state can do no wrong.

I think the difficulty which lies in the way of the general acceptance by publicists of the principle of the sovereignty of the state is the fact that they do not sufficiently distinguish the state from the government. They see the danger to individual liberty of recognizing an unlimited power in the government; and they immediately conclude that the same danger exists if the sovereignty of the state be recognized. This is especially true of European publicists, most especially of German publicists. They are accustomed practically to no other organization of the state than in the government; and in spite of their speculative mental character, they, as well as other men, reveal in their reflections a good deal of dependence upon the conditions of the objective world. In America we have a great advantage in regard to this subject. With us the government is not the sovereign organization of the state. Back of the government lies the constitution; and back of the constitution the original sovereign state, which ordains the constitution both of government and of liberty. We have the distinction already in objective reality; and if we only cease for a moment conning our European masters and exercise a little independent reflection, we shall be able to grasp this important distinction clearly and sharply. This is the point in which the public law of the United States has reached a far higher development than that of any state of Europe. Several of the most modern European publicists, such as Laband, Von Holst and Jellinek, have discovered this fact; and their conception of the state has, in consequence thereof, become much clearer. The European states have made great progress towards this condition since the period of the French Revolution. Europe has seen the French state several times organized in constituent convention; and in the years 1848 and 1867 something very like constituent conventions sat at Frankfort and Berlin, to say nothing of the Spanish Cortes and the less important movements of similar character. Such an organization of the state is, however, hostile to independent princely power. It tends to subject the prince to the state. It may leave the hereditary tenure, but it makes the princely power an office instead of a sovereignty. Therefore the princely government disputes the sovereignty of the constituent convention; and the political scientists become confused in their reflections by the din and smoke of the conflict in the objective world. They do not know exactly where the state is; and, therefore, they hesitate to recognize its great and essential attribute of sovereignty. The national popular state alone furnishes the objective reality upon which political science can rest in the construction of a truly scientific political system. All other forms contain in them mysteries which the scientific mind must not approach too closely.

There is no topic of political science concerning which a more copious literature is at hand than the forms of state. There is none, again, in regard to which a less satisfactory treatment has been attained than this. A careful student of what has been written upon this subject, both in Europe and America, will, I think, discover that the cause of this unsatisfactory result, upon the part of the European publicists, is the fact that they do not discriminate clearly between state and government; upon the part of the American writers, that they copy too closely the European authors.

Both of these facts are explicable. In Europe, state and government are actually more or less mingled and commingled. The publicists are confused in their reflections by the confusion in the external object. It will be profitable to dwell upon this point a moment, and inquire how this actual condition of things has come about, which has exercised such a troubling influence upon political science. I think the explanation is to be found in the consequences of the historical development of the state. No great state in Europe, except France, has cut its history into two distinct and separate parts by revolution, and founded its existing institutions directly and consciously upon revolution. We may say then, as the rule, that in the European states the form of state generated in one period of their history laps over upon that developed in the succeeding period or periods. A close scrutiny of this process will disclose the following significant facts, viz, that in the transition from one form of state to another, the point of sovereignty moves from one body to another, and the old sovereign body, i.e., the old state, becomes, in the new system, only the government, or a part of the government. Take the example of English history after 1066, to make this clearer. First, the king was the state as well as the government. Then the nobles became the state, and the king became government only. Then the commons became the state, and both king and lords became but parts of the government. Now this change from the old form of state to the new, when it works itself out gradually and impliedly, so to speak, does not mark off the boundary sharply and exactly between the old and the new systems. Naturally the old state does not perceive the change at all or, at least, not for a long time, and not until after suffering many bitter experiences. It still expresses itself in the language of sovereignty. It still struts about in the purple, unconscious that the garment is now borrowed. On the other hand, the new sovereignty comes very slowly to its organization. Moreover, it organizes itself, for the most part, in the government, and only very imperfectly outside of and supreme over the government. For a long time it has the appearance of being only a part of the government, and, at first, the less important part. For a considerable time it is uncertain where the sovereignty actually is. With such conditions and relations in the objective political world, it is not strange that the European publicists have failed, as yet, to distinguish clearly and sharply between state and government, nor that their treatment of all problems, dependent for correct solution upon this distinction, is more or less confused and unsatisfactory.

In America, on the contrary, existing conditions and relations are far more favorable to the publicists. Our state is but little more than a century old, and rests wholly and consciously upon a revolutionary basis. The organization of the state existing previous to the year 1774 was completely destroyed, and did not reappear in the succeeding organization as a part of the government, holding on to its traditions of sovereignty. We Americans have seen the state organized outside of, and supreme over, the government. We have, therefore, objective aids and supports upon which to steady our reflection and by which to guide our science. The reason why the American publicists have not written better upon this subject cannot, therefore, be the lack of the proper external occasions for the excitation of thought. It is, it seems to me, as I have already said, the fact that they still copy too closely the European authors, and have not ventured to essay independent work. America has yet to develop her own school of publicists and her own literature of political science. Down to this time, the two names which stand highest in our American literature of political science are Francis Lieber and Theodore D. Woolsey. The former was, as everybody knows, a European, educated under European institutions, and a refugee from their oppression, as he regarded it. The latter was Lieber's ardent admirer—we might almost say disciple. It is not strange that they should have suffered under the power of the old influences, and should have confounded, in some degree at least, state and government in their reflections. The new and latest generation of American students of political science have been most largely trained in European universities, under the direction of European publicists, again, and by means of European literature. It will be an effort for them to make such use of their European science as always to gain advantage. It will be of the greatest service to them if they can employ it as a stepping-stone to a higher and more independent point of view; one which will enable them to win scientific appreciation of the distinctive lessons of our own institutions. If they fail to do this, however, we can expect little help from them in the attainment of a better and more satisfying treatment of the topic of this chapter.

It is, therefore, with a good deal of misgiving that I approach this part of my subject. I know that nothing has, as yet, been written in regard to it which has commanded general assent from the political scientists. I am myself conscious of mental dissatisfaction with all that has been advanced, and I believe that the cause of the confusion of thought, clearly manifest in the different theories presented, is what I have above indicated; but when I come to the task of making clear and exact the distinction between state and government myself, I find myself involved in the same difficulties against which I have just given the word of warning. The fact is, that the organization of the state outside of, and supreme over, the government is, as yet, everywhere incomplete; and that when we assign to it this separate and supreme position, we are, in greater or less degree, confounding the subjective with the objective state, the ideal with the actual state. Nevertheless, I am resolved to make the trial upon this line; content if, upon a single point, I can bring a little more light into this discussion, and make it manifest that a better organization of the state outside of the government would be a great advance in practical politics.

The great classic authority upon this topic is Aristotle. Every student of political science is acquainted with his noted distinction of states, as to form, into monarchies, aristocracies, and democracies (*politeia*). Not every student reflects, however, that the Greek states were organized wholly in their governments; i.e., completely confounded with them. This fact made the question far more simple than it is at present. We of today have a double question instead of a single one. We must determine, first, the forms of state, and then, the forms of government. It is perhaps natural that the state and its government should harmonize in this respect; but it is not always a fact that they do, and it is not always desirable that they should completely coincide in form. It is difficult to see why the most advantageous political system, for the present, would not be a democratic state with an aristocratic government, provided only the aristocracy be that of real merit, and not of artificial qualities. If this be not the real principle of the republican form of government, then I must confess that I do not know what its principle is. Now, it seems to me that the Aristotelian proposition contains the true solution of the whole question for the Hellenic politics, and for all systems in which the state and the government are identical; and that it is the true and complete principle of distinction in regard to the forms of state, but not of government, in those systems where state and government are not identical, but exist under more or less separate organization.

My contention is, that the classification of states, as to form, into monarchies, aristocracies, and democracies, is both correct and exhaustive; that no additional forms can be made out of a combination of these, or out of a union of several states; and that the notion that there can be proceeds from the confounding of state and government in the treatment of the subject.

There remains now but a single point further to be touched under this topic. What we call the modern states are those based upon the principle of popular sovereignty; i.e., they are democracies. Not all of them appear to be such, but a close scrutiny of the facts will reveal the truth of the proposition that they are. The reason of the deceptive appearance in such cases will be found to be the fact that the state has but recently taken on its new form, and has not perfected its organization; while the old state-form, remaining as government, is still clad in the habiliments of sovereignty, shabby and thread-bare perhaps, but still recognizable. It will be highly instructive to consider, for a moment, the social conditions which precede, and make possible, the existence of the democratic state. They may be expressed in a single phrase, viz, national harmony. There can be no democratic state unless the mass of the population of a given state shall have attained a consensus of opinion in reference to rights and wrongs, in reference to government and liberty. This implies, in the first place, that they shall understand each other; i.e., that they shall have a common language and a common psychologic standpoint and habit. It implies, in the second place, that they shall have a common interest, in greater or less degree, over against the populations of other states. It implies, finally, that they shall have risen, in their mental development, to the consciousness of the state, in its essence, means and purposes; that is, the democratic state must be a national state, and the state whose population has become truly national will inevitably become democratic. There is a natural and an indissoluble connection between this condition of society and this form of state. It is this connection which has led to the interchangeable use of the terms state and nation. We must not forget, however, that they belong pri-marily to different sciences, and should not be used interchangeably without explanatory qualifications.

The American Political Science Association

W. W. Willoughby

The interests of political science, political economy, and history are so closely related that an attempt wholly to separate them, or to pursue their study as absolutely independent subjects, would be as practically impossible as it would be undesirable. Of the relation between history and political science it has been said by the late Sir John Seeley that politics without history has no root, and that history without politics has no fruit. The connection between economics and politics is, if anything, more intimate. Without the information that the study of economic principles and of economic history affords, the political scientist is unable either to explain many of the processes of political growth or wisely to determine lines of public policy. Upon the other hand, deprived of the knowledge furnished by the scientific study of the mechanism and methods of operation of governments, the economist finds himself insufficiently informed either correctly to analyze past and existing economic conditions or satisfactorily to devise the means by which the truths that he discovers may be made of practical advantage to mankind.

And yet, intimate as are these relationships, the field of political science is one that may be clearly distinguished from that of history as well as from that of economics, and the topics which the field includes, in order to be treated adequately, need to be studied as distinct subjects of inquiry.[1] It is true that to a very considerable extent the phenomena dealt with by the historian, the economist and the political scientist respectively are the same, but each examines his material from a different standpoint. The historian has for his especial aim the determination and portrayal of processes and stages of human development. With economic and political interests he is concerned only in so far as it is necessary for him to understand them in order to explain the movements he is studying. So also with the economist. His primary interest is

Reprinted from *Political Science Quarterly* 19 (1904): 107–11.

1. The establishment of this *Quarterly,* in 1886, naturally raised the same questions which are here discussed, viz., the interdependence of all the social sciences and the existence of a distinct science of politics. See Munroe Smith, "The Domain of Political Science." *Political Science Quarterly,* vol. 1, p. 7.

in the ascertainment of the principles that control the production, exchange and distribution of wealth; and he finds it necessary to enter upon political ground only in so far as government has an influence upon economic conditions, either by reason of its cost, the economic security that it gives, or the manner in which it directly interferes, or may directly interfere, in the regulation of the industrial interests of the people. Thus, since neither the historian nor the economist is primarily interested in the study of matters political, it is necessary, in order that these matters should receive adequate scientific treatment, that they should be studied by those whose special interest in them is upon their political side.

Comprehensively stated, then, political science has to deal with all that directly concerns political society, that is to say, with societies of men effectively organized under a supreme authority for the maintenance of an orderly and progressive existence. Restrictively stated, political science has to deal primarily only with those interests or phenomena that arise because of the existence of political relations.

The definite field thus marked out for the political scientists is divisible into three parts. First, there is the province of political theory or philosophy, the aim of which is the analysis and exact definition of the concepts employed in political thinking, and which thus includes the consideration of the essential nature of the state, its right to be, its ends, its proper functions and its relation to its own citizens, and the nature of law. Secondly, there is the domain of public law, including as its subdivisions constitutional, international and administrative law. Thirdly, there is the general study of government, its different forms, the distribution of its powers, its various organs—legislative, executive and judicial, central and local—and the principles governing its administration. The subdivisions of these larger subjects readily suggest themselves. Furthermore, all these topics, chief and subordinate, of course lend themselves to theoretical, descriptive, comparative or historical treatment, and nearly all involve, or at least lead up to, the discussion of practical problems of government.

The foregoing description of political science is sufficient to indicate not only the propriety, but, in the interest of scientific progress, the necessity of recognizing the study of matters political as an independent discipline. Within recent years this recognition has been increasingly extended in this country, as has been especially shown in the creation in our colleges and universities of departments and chairs of politics as distinct from those of history and economics. Not until December 30, 1903, however, did this recognition lead to the establishment of a political science association whose exclusive interests should be political in character. Upon that date there was established at New Orleans, Louisiana, at the time when the American Historical and American Economic Associations were holding their annual meetings in that city, an association whose title is "The American Political Science Association" and whose object is, as its constitution declares, "the encouragement of the scientific study of politics, public law, administration and diplomacy."

The need for such an association as this, which should do for political science what the American Economic and American Historical Associations are doing for economics and history respectively, had been felt for a number of years. Direct action leading to its establishment was not taken, however, until December 30, 1902, when, at a meeting called primarily to consider the feasibility of creating a society of comparative legislation, there was suggested and discussed the necessity for a national association that should have for its sphere of interests the entire field of political science. The outcome of this discussion was the appointment of a committee of fifteen representative political scientists which was empowered to enter into communication with such individuals and associations as should be thought likely to be interested, with a view to discovering, if possible, how general was the demand for a new association.[2] As the result of its investigation, this committee found existing, among those primarily interested in the scientific study of matters political, an almost unanimous demand for the establishment of a new national association that should take the scientific lead in all matters of political interest, encouraging research, aiding if possible in the collection and publication of valuable material, and, in general, advancing the scientific study of politics in this country. An opinion, equally general, was found to exist that the new association, if and when established, should maintain the closest and most harmonious relations possible with the American Historical and American Economic Associations, and, whenever possible, hold its annual meetings at the same times and places with them. Such a cooperation, it was declared, would be beneficial to the two older bodies and vital to the new one.

Upon these facts being presented at a meeting of those interested, in the Tilton Memorial Library of Tulane University, December 30, 1903, there was established, as has been said, the American Political Science Association. As its first president was elected Dr. Frank J. Goodnow, professor of administrative law in Columbia University. As vice-presidents were elected President Woodrow Wilson,[3] Professor Paul S. Reinsch of the University of Wisconsin, and Hon. Simeon E. Baldwin of New Haven. Professor W. W. Willoughby of Johns Hopkins University was elected as the secretary and treasurer. Associated with these officers in the government of the association there were elected

---

2. The composition of this committee was as follows: J. W. Jenks (Chairman), Cornell University; Simeon E. Baldwin, New Haven, Conn.; E. Dana Durand, Washington, D.C.; J. H. Finley, New York City; W. W. Howe, New Orleans; H. P. Judson, University of Chicago; M. A. Knapp, Washington, D.C.; C. W. Needham, Columbia University; P. S. Reinsch, University of Wisconsin; L. S. Rowe, University of Pennsylvania; F. J. Stimson, Boston; Josiah Strong, New York City; R. H. Whitten, Albany, N.Y.; Max West, San Juan, Puerto Rico; W. W. Willoughby, Johns Hopkins University.

3. Declined.

the following members of an executive council: Andrew D. White, ex-ambassador to Germany; Jesse Macy, professor of political science, Iowa College; H. P. Judson, professor of political science, University of Chicago; L. S. Rowe, professor of political science, University of Pennsylvania; Albert Shaw, editor of the *Review of Reviews;* Bernard Moses, professor of political science, University of California; J. A. Fairlie, professor of administrative law, University of Michigan; W. A. Schaper, professor of political science, University of Minnesota; C. H. Huberich, professor of political science, University of Texas; and Herbert Putnam, librarian of Congress.[4]

In order effectively to cover the whole field of political science, the association expects to distribute its work among sections, each of which will devote its especial attention, respectively, to international law and diplomacy, comparative legislation, historical and comparative jurisprudence, constitutional law, administration, politics and political theory.

The association, as such, according to a provision of its constitution, will not assume a partisan position upon any question of practical politics. This means, of course, that, though at its annual meetings and in its publications it will give the freest opportunity possible for the discussion of current questions of political interest, it will not, as an association, by a resolution or otherwise, commit itself or commit its members to any position thereupon.

Any person may, upon application to the secretary, become a member of the association. The annual dues are three dollars. By the payment of fifty dollars one may become a life member, exempt from annual dues.

By those who have been most active in its establishment, it is declared that this new association is intended and expected to attract the support not only of those engaged in academic instruction, but of public administrators, lawyers of broader culture, and, in general, of all those interested in the scientific study of the great and increasingly important questions of practical and theoretical politics. Affiliated with the American Historical and the American Economic Associations, it is asserted that a trinity of societies has been created that will be able to assume and maintain a leadership in these allied fields of thought that can be subject to no dispute. It is believed that, just as the establishment of the two older of these bodies marked the beginning of a new period in the scientific study in America of the subjects with which they are concerned, so the creation of the American Political Science Association will, in years to come, be looked back upon as at once indicating the definite recognition of the fact that political science is a department of knowledge distinct from that of the other so-called social sciences, and as marking the commencement of a new period in the scientific study and teaching of matters political in the United States.

---

4. Declined.

Political Science and the State

James Farr

A new political science is needed for a world itself quite new.
—Alexis de Tocqueville

The most perfect example of the modern state is North America.
—Karl Marx

The national popular state alone furnishes the objective reality upon which political science can rest in the construction of a truly scientific political system.
—John W. Burgess

Much remains to be done—and undone—in the study of the history of political science. This is a simple consequence of the fact that political science remembers so little of its own history, and what history it does remember is often dismissed as dead wrong, or simply dead. In this way, when it does not forget its past altogether, political science engages in that "enormous condescension of posterity."[1] Thanks to some recent labors, however, this posture of forgetfulness or condescension is beginning to give way to a more sympathetic and accurate historical stance, at least with respect to the twentieth (and the late nineteenth) century, when political science became a professional academic discipline, and with respect to certain of its concepts, like voting, public opinion, and political change.[2] But much remains to be done with

---

Reprinted in a somewhat revised and shortened version from JoAnne Brown and David van Keuren, eds., *The Estate of Social Knowledge* (Baltimore: Johns Hopkins University Press, 1991), chap. 1.

Epigraphs: Alexis de Tocqueville, *Democracy in America* (Garden City, N.Y.: Anchor Books, 1969), p. 12; Karl Marx, *German Ideology* (New York: International, 1970), p. 80; John W. Burgess, *Political Science and Comparative Constitutional Law* (Boston: Ginn and Co., 1891), 1: 58.

1. Stefan Collini, Donald Winch, and John Burrow, *That Noble Science of Politics: A Study in Nineteenth-Century Intellectual History* (Cambridge: Cambridge University Press, 1983), p. 377.

2. See works cited in the General Introduction to this volume.

respect to the predisciplinary history of political science, and much remains to be undone with respect to the concept of the state.

On the eve of discipline, political science was conceived of as the science of the state. Twelve years after the Civil War, at a time when political science was becoming a professionally recognized field of higher education, Theodore Dwight Woolsey could publish his presidential lectures at Yale quite simply as *Political Science, or the State Theoretically and Practically Considered* (1877). The closing years of the century witnessed a profusion of books about the state, and the majority of their most influential authors (like John W. Burgess, W. W. Willoughby, William Dunning, and Woodrow Wilson, among others) were identified as academic political scientists. German scholars for some time had been contributing to the view that political science was the science of the state by conceiving of it as *Staatswissenschaft*. After the American Political Science Association was formed in 1903, the state continued to command the attention of professional political scientists, especially those of Progressive leanings who sought to reform its administrative structure. Well into the New Deal, political scientists cast their works on government, parties, and policy in terms of the state. However, as revolutionary regimes spread and another world war approached, many political scientists, increasingly identified with one or another strain of liberalism, soon came to find the very idea of the state suspiciously socialist or reactionary or both. Harold Lasswell made dark references to the "garrison state."[3] Yet so strong was the identification of political science with the study of the state that it would become a principal object of attack as late as the 1950s during the opening skirmishes of the behavioral revolution. Even now, as one historian of political science regretfully acknowledges, there is "a resurrection of an older concept, that of the state" as a principal locus for the discipline of political science.[4]

This much of the story of political science and the state appears to enjoy agreement among political scientists. On other aspects of the story, however, there appears to be less agreement. At issue are questions about the predisciplinary identity and ideology of political science; the origin of its concept of the state; and the credibility and coherence of its efforts to theorize about it. It has been alleged, for example, that before the 1870s there was a "sense of statelessness" in American political thought and culture largely because of the intellectual heritage of Lockean liberalism. Political science, we are told, came to be identified as the science of the state only *after* the administrative

3. Harold Lasswell, "The Garrison State and Specialists on Violence," *American Journal of Sociology* 46 (1941): 455–68. An earlier rendition of this thesis was published in 1937.

4. David Easton, "The Political System Besieged by the State," *Political Theory* 9 (1981): 303.

and bureaucratic revolution that created the "new American state."[5] Even then, however, the state, both in theory and in practice, was to appear "alien to American experience and institutions."[6] The concept of the state, this account continues, was a German import. Under German influence, the analysis of the state—"the least American of our political words"—proved to be narrowly legalistic, not to mention "perilously figurative," "abstract and convoluted." "Far removed from the everyday talk of the people, political science even reified the state into an entity higher than the people." Consequently, political science proved to be an academic discipline whose "counterrevolution in political rhetoric" abandoned the principles of the American Revolution as it sought to "wrest political argument out of the hands of the people."[7]

In this essay, I wish to counter these particular claims and try to undo their influence. By tracing the changing concepts of *political science* and the *state* amidst the ebbing tradition of republican political discourse, we may see that Americans had a sense of the state going back to the earliest years of the Republic.[8] The language of the state was a broadly European and, then, an American one which had pervaded political discussion well before the Civil War and certainly before a number of young academics went off to Germany in the latter decades of the century in pursuit of *Staatswissenschaft*. Though abstract in the way that most complex theoretical terms are, the state provided self-styled political scientists with a framework for analyzing the organizational and ethical complexities of American political life, especially the Constitution, law, liberty, parties, public opinion, popular sovereignty, and republican government. There was, of course, considerable debate about the meaning of all this, but the concept of the state provided unity of attention amid diversity of detail and speculation. Furthermore, the self-styled political

---

5. Steven Skowronek, *Building a New American State: The Expansion of National Administrative Capacities, 1877–1920* (New York: Cambridge University Press, 1982), p. 5. Skowronek's principal concern is to address the institutional and administrative developments which constituted the process of centralized state building in the latter decades of the nineteenth century. However, he begins with an eye to theories and concepts of the state, especially those of Tocqueville, Hegel, and Marx, when he suggests that there was an "absence of a sense of the state in early America" (p. 5). It is *this* claim that concerns me here.

6. Bernard Crick, *The American Science of Politics: Its Origins and Conditions* (Berkeley: University of California Press, 1959), p. 96. Also see his remark that the United States was, late into the century, "a nation which had no sense of the state" (p. 99).

7. Daniel Rodgers, *Contested Truths: Keywords in American Politics since Independence* (New York: Basic Books, 1987), pp. 14, 145, 166, 171, 175. Political scientists, it is further claimed, "acquired the term State" from Germany because of their education there in the late nineteenth century (p. 167).

8. For the general project of conceptual history, see Terence Ball, James Farr, and Russell L. Hanson, eds., *Political Innovation and Conceptual Change* (New York: Cambridge University Press, 1989), esp. chap. 2.

scientists of the nineteenth century thought of their pedagogic task as a directly political one: to educate nascent citizens in the public virtues long associated with the republican tradition.

In what follows, I propose to investigate how and to what effect *political science* and the *state* were expressly and jointly conceptualized and reconceptualized in American political discourse during the nineteenth century. The constitutional founders, Francis Lieber, and a number of late nineteenth-century professionals are singled out for particular attention in this conceptual approach to the history of political science. Their views help constitute three moments in the history of political science, the movement of which we might characterize as the development *from discourse to discipline*. That is to say, in the course of its first century, American political science was transformed from a political discourse in the service of republican principles to a professional discipline in the service of the administrative state.

This essay's brief conceptual history of political science and the state hopes to lay the historical groundwork for an argument about the lingering republican identity and the requisite methodological pluralism of a discipline designed to educate citizens. It also admits to taking its point of departure from the efforts of political scientists and sociologists who are presently "bringing the state back in."[9] Let us, then, bring back in to the picture those statists who populated American political science from the very beginning of the Republic.

I.

The concept of the science of politics enters American political discourse in the late eighteenth century, and never more prominently than in the debates over the Constitution and the kind of republic the Constitution was to inaugurate. While most of the founders were retrospectively generous about the long history of ancient and modern contributors to this science (this "divine science of politics," as John Adams sermonized even before the Revolution), the most important and immediate influences were themselves eighteenth-century figures, especially those northern Britons credited with having ushered in a Scottish Enlightenment.[10] Like the Scots, the American founders explicitly and repeatedly used the very terms to pick out this nascent science. Thereafter, these terms—*science of politics, political science, science of government, science of legislation*, and their kin—would help reshape American

---

9. Peter Evans, Dietrich Rueschemeyer, and Theda Skocpol, eds., *Bringing the State Back In* (New York: Cambridge University Press, 1985).

10. See James Farr, "Political Science and the Enlightenment of Enthusiasm," *American Political Science Review* 82 (1988): 51–69.

political discourse and indeed the very institutions and practices of American political life.

During the Revolution, but especially during the debates over the ratification of the Constitution, the rhetoric of science was crucial. Science was invoked by all sides. Understandably, however, the methodological identity of this science was never fully specified by the various rhetoricians amid the more pressing struggles. Indeed, in the writings of the late 1780s and early 1790s, the science of politics (and its kindred sciences) seemed to range without careful methodological distinction between the rules and practical maxims that inhered naturally in American citizen-statesmen, and those laws, principles, and axioms of politics that formally resembled the generalizations of Newtonian mechanics.[11] The one drew inspiration from history and ordinary experience; the other from physics and controlled observation. But whatever its particular methods, there was a shared sense, as Alexander Hamilton pointed out, that "the science of politics, like most other sciences, has received great improvement." There were "wholly new discoveries" and even "progress towards perfection in modern times." David Ramsay thought America itself had played a foundational role in this, for the new nation had placed "the science of politics on a footing with the other sciences, by opening it to improvements from experience, and the discoveries of the future." Yet political science or the "science of government," as James Madison chimed in, had not answered all questions previously raised, especially in the matter of "the privileges and powers of the different legislative branches."[12] The American scientists of politics were there to remedy this defect, fully aware of the experimental novelty of their task.

To remedy this scientific defect was to remedy yet other defects, especially those political ones attending the postrevolutionary constitutional arrangements. In this remedial task, political science took (or, rather, was rhetorically made to take) very different sides. At stake was the nature of republicanism in general and in particular the republican arrangements

---

11. See, for example, Alexander Hamilton, James Madison, and John Jay, *Federalist* (New York: New American Library, 1961; originally 1787–88), esp. nos. 9, 31, 37, 47. For Antifederalists, see Herbert J. Storing, ed., *The Complete Antifederalist* (Chicago: University of Chicago Press, 1981), esp. vol. 2 (in the writings of "Brutus" and "The Federal Farmer"). Also see Nathaniel Chipman, *Principles of Government* (Burlington, Vt.: Edward Smith, 1833; originally 1793), pp. 3–4, 15, 45, 130, 219–20 on the science of government and the nature of its rules, maxims, and principles. Also notice the scientific tone of Chipman's discussion of the "experiment . . . first made in these United States" when he avers that "it is true, this form of government is a novelty in the political world, it cannot, it does not, appeal to history for proof of its excellence; but to present facts" (p. 152a).

12. *Federalist*, nos. 9 and 37. Ramsay's *The American Revolution*, quoted in Gordon S. Wood, *The Creation of the American Republic, 1776–1787* (Chapel Hill: University of North Carolina Press, 1969), p. 613.

thought to be necessary to an increasingly commercial society in a large territory of the new world. Indeed, the concept of political science (and its kindred sciences) should be understood as a relatively late addition to republican political discourse. Its introduction coincides with (and was conceptually party to) the demise of classical republicanism and the emergence of a new republican discourse more attuned to commerce, the balance of interests, and the institutionalization of virtue.[13] It bears underscoring that neither Federalists nor Antifederalists can or must bear the burden of liberal categories which have been placed upon them by later nineteenth- and twentieth-century interpreters who thought liberalism was somehow "given" in America. Nor, I would suggest, should the identity of political science be understood as an unproblematically liberal one, not only in the founding period but throughout the course of the nineteenth century and perhaps beyond.[14] Well into our century, political science bears the marks of its republican birth.

State was a term that came naturally to these American republicans, as indeed it had to most Western political writers of the previous two centuries upon whom the Americans readily drew.[15] Machiavelli, Bodin, Calvin, and Hobbes are particularly prominent theorists in this stretch of early modern intellectual history who helped give voice to the transformation of the earlier idea of the ruler "maintaining his estate." In its place there developed

> the idea that there is a separate legal and constitutional order, that of the State, which the ruler has a duty to maintain. One effect of this transformation was that the power of the State, not that of the ruler, came to be envisaged as the basis of government. And this in turn enabled the State to be conceptualized in distinctly modern terms—as the sole source of law and legitimate force within its own territory, and as the sole appropriate object of its citizens' allegiances.[16]

---

13. See J. G. A. Pocock, *The Machiavellian Moment: Florentine Political Thought and the Atlantic Republican Tradition* (Princeton: Princeton University Press, 1975), esp. chaps. 14–15. Also see Bernard Bailyn, *The Ideological Origins of the American Revolution* (Cambridge, Mass.: Harvard University Press, 1967); Russell L. Hanson, *The Democratic Imagination in America* (Princeton: Princeton University Press, 1985), esp. chaps. 2–3; Wood, *The Creation of the American Republic,* esp. chap. 1.

14. Wood suggests as much, as early as the end of the eighteenth century, in *The Creation of the American Republic,* esp. chap. 15. Crick even takes the methodological ideals of American political science as expressing liberal political principles in *The American Science of Politics,* p. xv. Raymond Seidelman tells a tale of disenchanted liberals in political science (in *Disenchanted Realists* [Albany: State University of New York Press, 1985]), but he also points to a variety of other traditions in political science, including the remnants of classical republicanism.

15. For the general background, see especially Quentin Skinner, "The State," in Ball, Farr, and Hanson, eds., *Political Innovation and Conceptual Change,* as well as his studies of Machiavelli and Hobbes.

16. Quentin Skinner, *Foundations of Modern Political Thought* (Cambridge: Cambridge University Press, 1978), p. x.

After the American Revolution the now-liberated colonies were conceptualized not only as republics but as states. The leaders of the new American
nation were known not only as republicans but as statesmen. Such uses of the
term *state* and its cognates were then, as now, so ordinary and taken for
granted that citizens and historians then, as now, often overlooked them.
However, the Articles of Confederation fully recognized what was at stake
with this appellation. They insured the sovereignty of the thirteen new states.
Of course, the Articles proved insufficient as an instrument of government,
which was one of the few points of agreement of the Constitutional Convention and the ratification debates which followed. But another point of agreement, at least conceptually, regarded the state.

Though Federalists and Antifederalists would disagree about whether
sovereignty could be divided and about where the state(s) did or should reside
(in the thirteen subnational territories or covering the geographical fullness of
America), the language of the state was not itself at issue. All agreed that they
were discussing the supreme power which acted through government over a
sovereign territory and to which citizens and leaders owed their allegiance.
Antifederalists (and later John C. Calhoun) meant quite literally—and without
the solecism of dual sovereignty—that the thirteen states were sovereign
states in the full-bodied European sense.[17] The Federalists denied this particular claim, but only to secure a statist identity for the nation as a whole.
Repeatedly and naturally, Federalists spoke about the state or the civil state,
including its "supreme powers," "reasons," "pride," "real interests," and
"domestic police." Hume, Montesquieu, and de Mably were all explicitly
cited in the *Federalist* as appropriate European authorities on the state whose
lessons were generally relevant (if not always directly applicable) to New
World politics. This point was reinforced (and more authorities cited and
criticized in light of the American experiment) by Nathaniel Chipman in 1793
when he repeatedly and naturally invoked the language of the state to discuss
Americans' constitutionally guaranteed rights, powers, and liberties.[18]

All parties to the debates, in short, agreed on the basic contours of the
concept. The state was the collective political agency given voice by a written
constitution and laws and expressing popular sovereignty, whatever governmental, administrative, or federal structure it assumed. Political parties were
not seen as creatures of the state, for they fanned the flames of faction rather
than channeled the competition of interests. But whatever its place or form

---

17. Herbert J. Storing, ed., as abridged by Murray Dry, *The Antifederalist* (Chicago:
University of Chicago Press, 1985), pp. 38, 281; and John C. Calhoun, *A Discourse on the
Constitution*, in *Works* (New York: Appleton, 1851).

18. *Federalist*, nos. 4, 6, 8, 15, 17, 34, 51; and Chipman, *Principles of Government*, esp.
pp. 56, 60, 119, 123–26, 137, 145, 176a, 171–79, 180–85. Hobbes, Pufendorf, Grotius, Locke,
Vattel, Beccaria, Kames, Smith, Montesquieu, Blackstone, and (especially) Paley all come in for
discussion and criticism during the course of Chipman's remarkable treatise.

and whatever its legal or federal novelties, a state it was. As should be obvious, Publius never had a dream (or Brutus a nightmare) of a Bismarckian state of the sort to emerge on the Continent within a century. But their language fully attests to their sense of stateness, not statelessness. Such was the statist discourse of the republican scientists of politics.

II.

Despite all the conceptual connections it forged and the theoretical possibilities it thereby created, this initial episode in the history of political science in America produced no sustained treatises on the state or any on the scope and methods of political science itself. And no one then explicitly conceptualized political science as the science of the state. While political science and the state would continue to animate American political discourse throughout the early nineteenth century, including making some tentative entries into the moral philosophy and moral science curriculum,[19] it would take Francis Lieber, a Prussian émigré of republican and nationalist commitments, to produce the first systematic treatises on these subjects. In the quarter-century before the Civil War, a time during which Karl Marx thought that America was already perfecting the modern state, Lieber produced a number of works which succeeded in raising the level of theoretical discourse about political science and the state, as well as securing him a chair at Columbia in 1857 as professor of history and political science, the very first of its kind in America. The title was Lieber's own creation and a point of pride he communicated to Alexis de Tocqueville, whose studies of American penitentiaries Lieber had assisted and translated.[20] Lieber himself hoped to provide for America that new political science which Tocqueville foresaw as necessary for a world itself quite new.

As early as the 1830s, the outlines of Lieber's political science were sufficiently well established, particularly in the *Manual of Political Ethics* (1838), *Legal and Political Hermeneutics* (1837), and a *Memorial Relative to Proposals for a Work on the Statistics of the United States* (1836). Later works fleshed these out, principal among them *Civil Liberty and Self-Government* (1853), *History and Political Science: Necessary Studies in a Free Country* (1858), and *The Ancient and Modern Teacher of Politics: An Introductory Discourse to a Course of Lectures on the State* (1860). Collectively, these

---

19. See Anna Haddow, *Political Science in American Colleges and Universities, 1636–1900* (New York: Appleton, 1939). Of particular importance in this literature is Francis Wayland, *The Elements of Moral Science* (New York: 1835) and Laurens P. Hickok, *A System of Moral Science* (New York: 1853).

20. Frank Freidel, *Francis Lieber: Nineteenth Century Liberal* (Baton Rouge: Louisiana State University Press, 1947), pp. 89–90, chap. 13.

works bore the marks of his German education under Niebuhr, Savigny, Humboldt, and Schleiermacher, especially the attention to philology and hermeneutics, not to mention history, law, and the state. But Lieber's works also bore the marks of his political naturalization, having lived in America since 1827 and having contributed to its first major literary effort in the New World, the *Encyclopedia Americana*. The *Encyclopedia,* and indeed all Lieber's works from the 1830s on, displayed a genuine integration of European and American sources. On its pages, Montesquieu and Jefferson, Hume and Madison, Humboldt and Calhoun, Haller and Story, Schleiermacher and Kent, Whewell and Hamilton, including the more ancient and venerable figures like Plato, Hobbes, and Pufendorf, in whose number Lieber immodestly counted himself, intermingled and provided authority for a heady brew. Much of this was a show of scholarship, of course, but much of it genuinely provided Lieber with the intellectual sources to take a new look at political science, republicanism, and the state in America.

In contrast to those who preceded him, Lieber wrote more, and more self-consciously, about the methods, objects, and educational objectives of political science. He proved to be a methodological pluralist who thought that statistics, causal generalizations, and hermeneutics all went into that "scientific treatment of politics" that "deals with man as a jural being . . . [that is,] as a citizen."[21] Hermeneutics was helpful here, for citizens as well as for political scientists, because it was "that branch of science which establishes the principles of interpretation and construction," especially for those jural texts, like the Constitution, which (literally) helped constitute American political life.[22] History was also methodologically important for political science because it provided, among other things, a wealth of facts; and Lieber himself was more historical and factual than any of his predecessors had been. In his inaugural address at Columbia, he put the point this way: "History is continuous Statistik; Statistik, history arrested at a given time." In his earlier *Memorial for Statistics* (which was read into the congressional record from the Senate floor by John C. Calhoun), he had called for "a careful collection of detailed facts, and the endeavor to arrive at general results by a comprehensive view and judicious combination of them." Statistics, in short, were "state-istics"—facts and generalizations useful for enlightened citizens and republican statesmen.[23]

---

21. *Miscellaneous Writings* (Philadelphia: J. B. Lippincott, 1880), 1: 351.

22. *Legal and Political Hermeneutics* (Boston: Little, Brown, 1839), 2d ed., p. 64. A textual and contextual analysis of this neglected work can be found in James Farr, "Francis Lieber and the Interpretation of American Political Science," *Journal of Politics* 52 (1990): 1027–49.

23. *Miscellaneous Writings,* 1: 337; *Memorial Relative to Proposals for a Work on the Statistics of the United States,* Senate Documents 314, 24th Cong., 1st sess. 1836. Serial set 282, p. 1; and Rodgers, *Contested Truths,* p. 188.

Political science was conceptually connected to the state in two further ways beyond the methodological tie of statistics. Both may be appreciated by pondering the title of an important public address given in 1859 by Columbia's professor of political science: *The Ancient and Modern Teacher of Politics: An Introductory Discourse to a Course of Lectures on the State* (published in 1860). First, Lieber was a pioneer in transforming political science into an independent course of study in higher education (a task he began as early as the late 1830s, when he assumed his first and only other academic post at South Carolina College). While it was still part of the rhetorical armory of American orators and writers through the end of the century, political science was now increasingly identified with college and university. But this was not (yet) a purely academic confinement, at least in that "the teaching of the publicist may become an element of living statesmanship."[24] Lieber was among the first self-styled political scientists to conceive of the task of higher education in political science as instilling public virtues into (potential) citizens, those "sons of republicans," who were otherwise allured by the corruptions of the age, especially perhaps its "fanatical idolatry of success." Justice, fortitude, patriotism, duty, and moderation headed a long list of public virtues for republican self-governance. And a more disinterested, general education was required for this pedagogical task of political proportions: "The future citizen, or active member of the state, is then to be included in the objects of education." Thus our professor of history and political science could praise his newly minted efforts as "the very science of nascent citizens of a republic."[25]

Second, political science was to make the state its principal object of investigation. Lieber first makes this clear well before the Civil War in the *Manual of Political Ethics*. This two-volume work, first published in 1838, should be read as the first systematic treatise on the state in American political science and perhaps in American political literature as such. In dealing with "man as a jural being," political science dealt with the state, for he conceptualized the state as a "jural society," one founded on the "relations of right" between its citizens. The state, he went on, flowed from the "sovereignty of

---

24. *The Ancient and Modern Teacher of Politics: An Introductory Discourse to a Course of Lectures on the State* (New York: Columbia College Board of Trustees, 1860), p. 10.

25. *Miscellaneous Writings*, 1: 28, 183, 343. Also see *Manual of Political Ethics* (Philadelphia: J. B. Lippincott, 1838), 1: 401, 2: 109. In a more popular, though less theoretical way, Andrew W. Young wrote with these ends in mind as well, especially in *Introduction to the Science of Government* (Rochester, N.Y.: 1842; originally 1839) and in *The Citizen's Manual of Government and Law* (New York: Derby and Miller, 1864). The former work (on pp. 3–4) singled out the massive and increasing number of immigrants as a problem, for their "education does not embrace even the first principles of political science." But common schools can remedy this and so help new and young Americans "assume the duties of citizens" of a republic increasingly the scene of "the collision of contending interests."

the people," which manifested itself not only in the law but in the governmental institutionalities of power, which best functioned when checking and balancing each other.[26] All this was best realized within a republican framework.

This much had been familiar to Americans for over half a century. But there was also some conceptual change here as well, including the very coining of the term *jural*. In calling the state a "jural *society*" he wanted to distinguish it from a mere association and thereby loosen the holds of contractarian thinking which had been influential at the founding (though not in the minds of a number of the founders' most important intellectual predecessors, in particular the enlightened Scots like Hume). This was one of the natural consequences of the historical and factual thinking with which Lieber sought to infuse political science. "Man cannot divest himself of the state," as he said in his Columbia inaugural address. "Government was never voted into existence." In contrast to the Federalists, he reunited sovereignty, thinking it incoherent to speak of a dual sovereignty. But, in contrast to the Antifederalists, he placed it in the nation as a whole over which the government ruled. In contrast to both, and in full recognition of the de facto rise and institutionalization of the American party system, Lieber confessed that "I know of no instance of a free state without parties." He heightened the theoretical importance of public opinion by making it a direct expression of popular sovereignty. These changes in the concept (or conceptual domain) of the state, once accepted, were to prove important in the subsequent history of American political science, including its veritable preoccupation with law, parties, and public opinion.[27]

None of this, I submit, merits characterization as counterrevolutionary.[28] The evident nationalist sentiments are consistent with that greater half of the country preparing to fight to maintain the Union.[29] Furthermore, none of this is incoherent or overly abstract, at least not any more so than any other complex concept which does double duty in public discourse and academic treatise. This is as true of a concept like rights, which some take to be paradigmatically American and liberal, as it is of the state. In light of the nineteenth- and twentieth-century tomes and the gyrations which they put rights through, Bentham's celebrated words are worth recalling: "Rights, nonsense; Natural and imprescriptible rights, nonsense on stilts." But yet such nonsense, if nonsense it ever was, comprised the very soul of American rhetoric. And this is as true of the state as it is of rights. In the mid-nineteenth

---

26. *Manual of Political Ethics*, 1: 152, 217.

27. *Miscellaneous Writings*, 1: 351; and *Manual of Political Ethics*, 2: 253.

28. See n. 7 above.

29. Lieber helped in this task during the Civil War by writing, at President Lincoln's and General Halleck's request, a pamphlet on *Guerilla Parties* and a set of *General Instructions for the Government of the Armies of the United States in the Field*.

century, "the state" did not sound to American ears as a Teutonic invasion against good sense, at least if we can trust the sentiments that informed the reception of the *Manual of Political Ethics* by Supreme Court Justice Joseph Story in 1838:

> It contains by far the fullest and most correct development of the true theory of what constitutes the State that I have ever seen. . . . To me many of the thoughts are new, and as striking as they are new. . . . [In] addressing itself to the wise and virtuous of all countries, it solves the question what government is best by the answer, illustrated in a thousand ways, that it is that which best promotes the substantial interests of the whole people of the nation on which it acts. Such a work is peculiarly important in these times, when so many false theories are afloat and so many disturbing doctrines are promulgated.[30]

Nullification, states' rights, and secession were indeed on the scene to disturb and frighten the new American statists who understandably had the law and the Constitution uppermost in their minds. Such were the specters haunting political science and the American state.

III.

Between the Civil War and the century's end, the varied efforts of the sort which consumed Lieber's energies came to fruition as political science moved toward discipline. Political science became increasingly self-conscious about its professional identity as a science.[31] It continued to find its site in higher education and its pedagogical purpose in fostering public virtues for nascent republican citizens.[32] This period could well be called the triumph of the state, both in fact, as well as in the self-conceptualization of the most important political scientists of the time.[33] This is made abundantly clear in Ameri-

---

30. Printed in the second, revised edition of *Manual of Political Ethics,* ed. Theodore Dwight Woolsey (Philadelphia: J. B. Lippincott and Co., 1876).

31. See Dorothy Ross in this volume and the works she cites.

32. Besides those to be discussed below, see Joseph Alden, *The Science of Government in Connection with American Institutions* (New York: Sheldon and Co., 1867), whose opening line reads: "The object of this book is to aid the young in acquiring the knowledge necessary for the discharge of their duties as citizens of the United States." The locus of higher education during this period is an important theme of both Crick, *The American Science of Politics,* and David Ricci, *The Tragedy of Political Science* (New Haven: Yale University Press, 1984).

33. Skowronek's *Building a New American State* is particularly helpful in documenting the centralizing administrative revolution in the American state during this time period—even if, as I have argued, the Americans had long had a "sense of the state." One might even say that the *state* (and its cognates) provided ready-made terminology for the new theories in political science

can works like Theodore Dwight Woolsey's *Political Science, or the State Theoretically and Practically Considered*, W. W. Willoughby's *The Nature of the State*, John W. Burgess's *Political Science and Comparative Constitutional Law*, and future president Woodrow Wilson's *The State: Elements of Historical and Practical Politics*. These works were to set the agenda for a generation of American political scientists, including those who became increasingly interested and actually involved in public administration and administrative reform. In theory, political scientists captured the state; in practice, the state captured them.

The late-nineteenth-century political scientists were increasingly methodological, if not always in actual practice, then certainly in self-presentation. The already much-used rhetoric of science and method continued to exert its pull over the American imagination. In *Political Science and Comparative Constitutional Law*, John W. Burgess, Lieber's successor at Columbia and founder of its School of Political Science in 1880, singled out his contribution to the discipline in this way: "If my book has any peculiarity, it is its method. It is a comparative study. It is an attempt to apply the method, which has been found so productive in the domain of Natural Science, to Political Science and Jurisprudence."[34] The natural scientific overtones had indeed been on the minds of self-styled political scientists for well over a century, and they would show no signs of abating well into the next. The methodological invocation of hermeneutics had not (yet) been silenced, as is understandable for a science concerned (for good historical and political reasons) with law, constitutional arrangements, and jural behavior. This was enough to temper the scientism that invariably attends the wish to make political science a natural science of politics. Beyond the scientism, however, it is true and worth underscoring that Burgess and Wilson and many of their peers were indeed more historical; thereby, they were more factual and statistical in their analyses of the state since, for them, history was a great repository of facts and events. And they were genuinely comparative in their focus, providing more or less systematic studies of American, British, French, and German institutions, practices, and laws. Thus their allegiance to the "historical-comparative" method.

This methodologically self-conscious science was to continue to conceptualize the state as its principal domain. This, too, would continue into the second quarter of the twentieth century, despite (or maybe because of) the Progressive reformers. Most of the late-nineteenth-century political scientists were conscious of the venerable conceptual materials with which they dealt,

---

which were emerging to help citizens and legislators understand and even justify national developments under way since the Civil War.

34. Burgess, *Political Science and Comparative Constitutional Law* (Boston: Ginn and Co., 1891), 1: v.

but also of the scientific novelty which they brought to bear upon them. All gave theoretical expression, as it were, to the Union victory in the Civil War. The modern constitutional state was that law-governed and liberty-protecting organization of the political community whose governmental apparatus was centered and increasingly centralized in Washington, D.C., and whose "principle of popular sovereignty" spread over the still-advancing political geography of America. Indeed, since the subnational governments were not sovereign, "it is no longer proper to call them States at all. It is in fact only a title of honor, without any corresponding substance."[35] Geography notwithstanding, the state was not (as Daniel Rodgers has recently argued) conceived of as an antonym to the people. If anything, it was a synonym, at least if we can trust Burgess's view that "the state is the people in ultimate organization" or Willoughby's view that the state was in essence "a community of people socially united."[36] Thereby the late-nineteenth-century political scientists entered into a century-old American political conversation whose terms were familiar, despite the changing theories which incorporated them and which contributed to their change of meaning. Neither abstract nor convoluted (or, at any rate, no more so than the other key words of American political thought), the state had been and would remain, as Woolsey pointed out, "a fixed political term . . . in our language."[37]

Yet these increasingly professional academics displayed considerable diversity in their theories of the state. Thus we should appreciate that the concept of the state provided them more with an intellectual framework for theoretical debate rather than some universally accepted foundation for a disputation-free science. But this was nonetheless sufficient unity amid diversity. Woolsey began to work away at some distinctions (later to be refined by Goodnow) between the political basis and the practical administration of the state. Willoughby transformed American federal principles into the language of the "composite state" and quibbled about the finer points of popular sovereignty.[38] Burgess looked for "the state made objective in institutions and laws," especially in parties and public opinion. He also pried apart a distinction between state and government, a distinction which (like the modern

<hr />

35. Ibid., 81; and John W. Burgess, "The American Commonwealth," *Political Science Quarterly* 1 (1886), as noted approvingly by Charles Merriam, *The History of American Political Theories* (New York: Macmillan, 1903), pp. 301–2.

36. Rodgers, *Contested Truths*, p. 146; Burgess, *Political Science and Comparative Constitutional Law*, 1: 88; and W. W. Willoughby, *The Nature of the State* (New York: Macmillan, 1896), p. 4. Willoughby also criticized those who would "speak of the State as . . . an entity independent of man" (p. 33).

37. Theodore Dwight Woolsey, *Political Science, or the State Theoretically and Practically Considered* (New York: Scribner, Armstrong, and Company, 1877), 1: 140.

38. Frank Goodnow, *Politics and Administration: A Study in Government* (New York: Macmillan, 1900); and Willoughby, *The Nature of the State*, esp. chaps. 10, 11.

constitution, individual liberty, and federalism) he thought had reached its greatest clarity in fact and in theory in America.

> In America we have a great advantage in regard to this subject. With us the government is not the sovereign organization of the state. Back of the government lies the constitution; and back of the constitution the original sovereign state, which ordains the constitution both of government and liberty. We have the distinction [between state and government] already in objective reality. . . . This is the point in which the public law of the United States has reached a far higher development than that of any state of Europe.[39]

Germany had hosted Burgess's postgraduate education, but his vision of the "objective reality" upon which political science rested was his own home-grown American state and its republican institutions of government. And there was nothing particularly novel or overly Germanic about this, despite the evident influence of the German academy over the structure of American higher education. From the constitutional founders, from Lieber, from count-less American publicists and orators, Burgess simply took over the concept of the state as an integral component of American political discourse. And the discipline of political science was in the process of transforming the state, both in theory and practice. Soon enough Progressive political scientists would man the administration, and soon enough an American-educated statist of this period whose principal academic work would sell in Germany in translation as *Der Staat* would become president of the United States. For good or ill, the statists of American political science would see their country's highest office go to one of their number.

Having the state as the object of one's science did not require any particu-lar partisan stance. Indeed, among the late-nineteenth-century political scien-tists there was considerable diversity in ideological orientation, though none came out explicitly against the people. Many statists were racialists and imperialists; many others were not.[40] "Conservative" is not an altogether unfair description of Burgess, at least given some of his policy recommenda-tions and given our contemporary terminology.[41] The hints of elitism are not

---

39. Burgess, *Political Science and Comparative Constitutional Law,* 1: 57, 63. Also note Burgess's judgment that "America has yet to develop . . . her own literature of political science. Down to this time, the two names which stand highest in our American literature of political science are Francis Lieber and Theodore D. Woolsey" (p. 70).

40. The racialist and even racist intimations deserve further study.

41. For this judgment, see Bernard Edward Brown, *American Conservatives: The Political Thought of Francis Lieber and John W. Burgess* (New York: Columbia University Press, 1951). Crick rightly complains of historians "reading back subsequent prejudices into a previous era"

unnoticeable (nor had they been in classical republicanism, for that matter), and these hints would be transformed into the ideology of technocratic expertise among the Progressives and statist administrators. Yet the concern with general welfare was shared by most of the nineteenth-century political scientists, and some of them thought this liberal and called it so. At least the author of the *Principia of Political Science* made this clear in his subtitle, *Upon a Reverent, Moral, Liberal and Progressive Foundation.*[42] A student of Burgess's, Frank S. Hoffman, went further still. A socialist and a Christian, he thought that the state had "not only the right but the duty . . . to abolish all private possession" and to "better promote the well-being of the people."[43] No hegemony of political judgments, in short, followed with ironclad logic from the American political scientists' concept of the state, whatever the iron chancellor was preparing for Germany.

In conclusion, the late nineteenth century proved to be a period of vitality and fertility for an American science of politics which proclaimed its unity and identity as the science of the state. In the process of educating citizens while theorizing as scientists, the discipline became more professional and thoroughly academic. Soon enough this identity, as professionals and academics, would eclipse or fundamentally transform the republican convictions which had helped to bring it about in the first place. The movement from discourse to discipline would be all but complete.

IV.

Much still remains to be done. The subsequent history of "the science of the state" needs to be told. Many political scientists continued to work under that explicitly articulated identity well into the twentieth century. They did so in the face of criticisms from authors such as Arthur Bentley and later David Easton that the concept of "the state" was formalistic, abstract, metaphysical, time-bound, or ideological. Moreover, many of the deeper categories and assumptions of American statism were preserved even when political scientists went on to embrace "actual government," "behavioral process," or the "political system" as the discipline's identifying focus. When this subsequent history of political science is joined with the earlier history of "the science of the state" (that I have tried to sketch here in broad outline), we should see just what an inheritance this American science has been and continues to be.

---

and goes on to say that "in his day Burgess was among the leading ranks of 'progress,' a conservative liberal perhaps, but in no sense himself a conservative" (*The American Science of Politics*, p. 27).

42. R. J. Wright, *Principles of Political Science* (Philadelphia: R. J. Wright, 1876).

43. Frank S. Hoffman, *The Sphere of the State; or the People as a Body-Politic* (New York: G. P. Putnam's Sons, 1894), p. 7.

Remembering this inheritance is, of course, a far cry from defending it, and much of it does not deserve defense. However, I have tried in this brief sketch to remove at least certain misunderstandings about the concept of "the state" in the early American science of politics—that it was a violation of native political experience, that it was an importation of uniquely German political thought, that it emerged as a belated consequence of late-nineteenth-century conditions, that it was egregiously nonempirical, and that it was necessarily conservative or even counterrevolutionary. Furthermore, I have tried to restore to the early political scientists of the state some of *their* principal problems and concerns—to introduce the concept of the state into modern republicanism, to educate citizens in their civic capacities, and to understand the state system of the New World. These problems and concerns are not so far removed from certain contemporary efforts to "bring the state back in," to revitalize civic education, or to understand the state system in the "new world order." If there are problems or perils in these contemporary efforts, then at the very least we should not forget their predecessors. Santayana's warning is good for disciplines, too: Those who forget their history may be condemned to repeat it.

The Development of the Social Sciences

Dorothy Ross

Let me begin by admitting that discussion of the formation of five disciplines—psychology, anthropology, economics, sociology, and political science—within the compass of a single essay and under the rubric of the "social sciences" not only lacks prudence but risks historical anachronism. At the beginning of this period in 1865, these disciplines had little independent existence in America. Although recognized traditions of thought existed in each subject, they were generally the concern of men and women of affairs debating the practical problems of government and education and of gentlemen scholars and clergymen discussing history, morals, philosophy, and natural history—the larger humanistic traditions from which these subjects branched. In American colleges, where religious considerations still controlled faculty and curriculum, many of the topics that later constituted the social sciences were treated within senior courses in moral and mental philosophy.

With the expansion of universities in the 1870s and 1880s, these five subjects began to forge separate intellectual and social identities, but they still lacked a common sense of themselves as branches of social science. Psychologists and anthropologists, for example, often felt more closely allied to biology, and political scientists to history and jurisprudence, than to any other of the five disciplines. It was only after World War I that a more common identity emerged.[1]

As before and after the 1920s, this common identity was hardly cohesive. The Social Science Research Council (SSRC), the umbrella organization formed in 1923, included history and statistics, disciplines that were linked to the social sciences yet maintained independent roots in other traditions. Even

---

Reprinted in a shortened version from Alexandra Oleson and John Voss, eds., *The Organization of Knowledge in Modern America, 1860–1920* (Baltimore: Johns Hopkins University Press, 1979), chap. 3. The original version contains another part of the paper and a fuller set of bibliographic references.

1. John Higham, *Writing American History: Essays on Modern Scholarship* (Bloomington, Ind.: Indiana University Press, 1970), pp. 3–24.

within the core subjects, diversity reigned. Both anthropology and psychology maintained strong ties with the natural sciences. A major part of psychology has never been "social." And if one attempts to find a deeper conceptual unity than the generic tag of sociality, the social sciences appear even more diverse. The focus on culture and its links to personality and social structure, which George Stocking has described as an increasingly pervasive paradigm for the social sciences since the 1920s, has had to share the field with a behavioral viewpoint, more closely linked to biology and to quantitative methods. Indeed today the five disciplines would be better described as "social and behavioral sciences" than by the former term alone. And large segments of these subjects are not essentially related to either the cultural or behavioral viewpoints, but have roots in older systematic traditions.[2]

If we keep in mind the mixed identities of the social sciences during their formative decades and still today, it is possible without anachronism to discern similarities in the way these five disciplines developed after the Civil War. All of them became separate disciplines. All became firmly established in academic institutions. All underwent a process of professionalization. And all five disciplines attempted to establish themselves as sciences.

The first three of these characteristics the social sciences shared with many other subjects in America during the post–Civil War period. The natural sciences had organized professionally in the American Association for the Advancement of Science before the Civil War. After the war, the natural sciences found new bases of support in the universities and formed separate professional organizations. Before any of the social sciences had organized,

---

2. A number of basic works on the history of the social science disciplines provide a general orientation to their institutional and intellectual development: in psychology, Gardner Murphy, *An Historical Introduction to Modern Psychology* (London: Kegan Paul, Trench, Trubner, 1929); Edwin G. Boring, *A History of Experimental Psychology* (New York: Appleton-Century-Crofts, 1957); in anthropology, George W. Stocking, Jr., *Race, Culture and Evolution: Essays in the History of Anthropology* (New York: Free Press, 1968); Regna Darnell, ed., *Readings in the History of Anthropology* (New York: Harper & Row, 1974); Frederica DeLaguna, ed., *Selected Papers from the American Anthropologist, 1888–1920* (Evanston, Ill.: Row, Peterson, 1960); in economics, Joseph Dorfman, *The Economic Mind in American Civilization*, 5 vols. (New York: The Viking Press, 1946–59); in political science, Albert Somit and Joseph Tanenhaus, *The Development of American Political Science: From Burgess to Behavioralism* (Boston: Allyn and Bacon, 1967); Bernard Crick, *The American Science of Politics: Its Origins and Conditions* (Berkeley: University of California Press, 1959); Dwight Waldo, "Political Science: Tradition, Discipline, Profession, Science, Enterprise," in *The Handbook of Political Science*, Fred I. Greenstein and Nelson W. Polsby, eds. (Reading, Mass.: Addison-Wesley, 1975), pp. 1–130; and in sociology, L. L. Bernard and Jessie Bernard, *Origins of American Sociology: The Social Science Movement in the United States* (New York: Thomas Y. Crowell, 1943); Anthony Oberschall, "The Institutionalization of American Sociology," in *The Establishment of Empirical Sociology*, Anthony Oberschall, ed. (New York: Harper & Row, 1972), pp. 187–251; Don Martindale, *The Nature and Types of Sociological Theory* (Boston: Houghton, Mifflin, 1969).

the formation of the American Philological Society in 1869, the Modern Language Association in 1883, and the American Historical Association in 1884 marked the entry into American colleges and universities of other groups of scholars with professional ideals. Four of the five social science subjects formed their first graduate departments and professional journals in the 1880s, and sociology followed in the early 1890s. Economics was the first to form a national professional association in 1885; psychology followed in 1892; and the others were organized just after the turn of the century—anthropology in 1902, political science in 1903, and sociology in 1905.

To some extent, the humanistic disciplines that emerged in the decades after the Civil War shared the scientific aspirations of the social scientists as well. Philologists and historians were also intent on making their disciplines empirical sciences. By about 1920, however, the social sciences had diverged from these older historical subjects. Social scientists focused their attention on the regularities underlying social phenomena and accepted an ideal of science that stressed objectivity of method and technical manipulation of contemporary social processes.

Several aspects of these developments have been the subject of intense investigation by recent historians.[3] Drawing heavily on this work, as well as on my own,[4] I have outlined below some of the factors that led the social sciences to take form as separate, academic, professional, and scientific disciplines. Part I below identifies a number of groups of scholars concerned with social science during the 1870s and 1880s and discusses the emergence of academic and scientific disciplines in this area. Part II describes the generation of young academics who appeared after 1880 and analyzes their impulse toward professionalization. Finally, part III deals specifically with the scientific aspirations of the social sciences and notes some of the factors that led to the appearance of a more rigorous scientism[5] after 1912.

---

3. Laurence R. Veysey, *The Emergence of the American University* (Chicago: University of Chicago Press, 1965); Mary Furner, *Advocacy and Objectivity: A Crisis in the Professionalization of American Social Science, 1865–1905* (Lexington, Ky.: University Press of Kentucky, 1975); Stocking, *Race, Culture and Evolution;* George W. Stocking, ed., *The Shaping of American Anthropology, 1883–1911: A Franz Boas Reader* (New York: Basic Books, 1974).

4. Dorothy Ross, *G. Stanley Hall: The Psychologist as Prophet* (Chicago: University of Chicago Press, 1972); idem, "James McKeen Cattell," *Dictionary of American Biography,* supp. 3, pp. 148–51; idem, "The 'New History' and the 'New Psychology': An Early Attempt at Psychohistory," in *The Hofstadter Aegis: A Memorial,* Stanley Elkins and Eric McKittrick, eds. (New York: Alfred A. Knopf, 1974); idem, "Socialism and American Liberalism: Academic Social Thought in the 1880s," *Perspectives in American History* 11 (1977–1978): 5–79.

5. By scientism I mean the belief that the objective methods of the natural sciences should be used in the study of human affairs, and that such methods are the only fruitful ones in the pursuit of knowledge. This formulation leaves open the definitions of "objective methods," "natural science," and "knowledge," which changed over time.

I.

Among social thinkers active in America during the 1870s, those with the longest heritage were the clerical professors of moral and mental philosophy in the American colleges. Since the early nineteenth century, the college curriculum had been organized to culminate in courses in mental and moral philosophy, where aspects of social life were studied as subdivisions of man's moral behavior in a natural world governed by God. Those subdivisions that rested on subjects already well-developed in British thought, like political economy and philosophical psychology, often became areas of interest and writing for these scholars. The proper principles of political action and the moral bases of social behavior were seldom given extended treatment, and topics later recognized as part of anthropology rarely appeared. Regarding themselves as preservers of the moral heritage of Protestant Christianity, these clerical professors were already fading from view in the 1870s.[6] Their place was being taken by new groups who played a more direct role in the emergence of the social sciences.

One such group were independent scholars and reformers employed in the older professions who began to take an avocational or public interest in social science reform. Such, for example, were Frank B. Sanborn, an author, abolitionist, and leader in the charity-organization movement; George W. Curtis, editor and advocate of civil service reform; and Lester Frank Ward, a government botanist whose cosmic social theory advocated the rational control of social evolution by educated experts. Others, largely self-taught, were already employed by the government in areas related to social science, among them the economist Carroll D. Wright, director of the Massachusetts Bureau of Statistics of Labor and later director of the Federal Bureau of Labor Statistics; and John Wesley Powell, geologist and ethnologist who founded and directed the Smithsonian's Bureau of Ethnology from 1880 until his death in 1902.

Except for workers in the area of anthropology, whose chief institutional tie was with the American Association for the Advancement of Science, many advocates of political, social, economic, and educational reform, like Wright, Curtis, and Sanborn, found an institutional locus in the American Social

---

6. On moral philosophy, see Wilson Smith, *Professors and Public Ethics: Studies of Northern Moral Philosophers before the Civil War* (Ithaca, N.Y.: Cornell University Press, 1956); Donald Harvey Meyer, *The Instructed Conscience* (Philadelphia: University of Pennsylvania Press, 1972); Daniel Walker Howe, *The Unitarian Conscience: Harvard Moral Philosophy, 1805–1861* (Cambridge, Mass.: Harvard University Press, 1970); Gladys Bryson, "The Emergence of the Social Sciences from Moral Philosophy," *International Journal of Ethics* 42 (April 1932): 304–8.

Science Association (ASSA). Modeled on the British National Association for Promotion of Social Science, the ASSA had been founded in 1865 to extend social knowledge and provide a more authoritative basis for dealing with contemporary social problems. Besides reformers and workers in practical social services, the ASSA drew its leadership from two important sections of the New England cultivated elite: natural scientists like Benjamin Peirce and Louis Agassiz, who had been trying for decades to raise the standard of competence in scientific investigation, and university reformers like Charles W. Eliot and Daniel Coit Gilman, who held similar goals for the American colleges and universities.

The ASSA divided its work into four departments: education, public health, social economy, and jurisprudence, a division that reflected both the definition of the older professions of education, medicine, and law and the lack of definition in the "social" category. The ASSA proved to be an important catalyst in the development of a secular social science, as both reformers and a newer generation of academic social scientists temporarily joined its ranks in the 1870s and 1880s. As each group of social investigators defined its problems and its methods more clearly, however, they seceded from the Association. The ASSA has gone down in history as the "mother of associations;" its most permanent function was to provide institutional auspices for the founding of specialized organizations like the National Conference of Charities and Corrections and the American Economic Association.[7]

For a time, however, the ASSA leadership hoped to remain at the center of social science development. As colleges adopted the elective system, members of the social science movement began to give courses to undergraduates. The courses were oriented toward social problems and took students into the cities and institutions to actually see the "delinquent, defective and dependent classes." Indeed, such "problems" courses have persisted as a feature of sociology. However, both the colleges and some leaders of the ASSA were reluctant to become too closely identified. From Ralph Waldo Emerson's rebuke of Harvard's isolation from the world in 1837 to Wendell Phillips's in 1881, American colleges had not been conspicuous for their support of reform activities. The expanding universities, with their dependence on the respectable class for students and financial support, were also wary of the social science movement. When some of the ASSA leaders urged the affiliation of

---

7. On the formation of the ASSA and the history of the social science movement, see Furner, *Advocacy and Objectivity*, intro., chaps. 1, 2, 13; Thomas L. Haskell, *The Emergence of Professional Social Science: The American Social Science Association and the Nineteenth Century Crisis of Authority* (Urbana, Ill.: University of Illinois Press, 1977); Bernard and Bernard, *Origins*, p. 8.

the association with Johns Hopkins University, President Gilman replied that the desire of the ASSA not only to study but to advocate reforms made it incompatible with university education.[8]

Meanwhile, the separate disciplines that would later constitute the social sciences were making their independent appearance in the colleges under more scholarly auspices. A number of men who had started in the older clerical or public milieus began to devote their full energies to teaching these subjects in the 1870s and to teaching them as independent subjects free from religious constraint. Under pressure from groups of trustees and alumni to introduce modern knowledge into their curricula, the colleges were beginning to make openings for this new group. William James, for example, introduced physiological psychology, and Charles Dunbar, political economy, at Harvard. William Graham Sumner taught sociology at Yale; Francis A. Walker, political economy at Yale's Sheffield Scientific School; and Andrew D. White introduced political science at Cornell. While the Philadelphia anthropologist Daniel Brinton taught briefly at the University of Pennsylvania, the main anthropological development in the 1870s occurred under Powell at Washington, or in the museums as under Frederic Ward Putnam at Harvard's Peabody Museum of American Archaeology and Ethnology.

In each of the five disciplines, the academic pioneers of the 1870s worked within systematic traditions that had been developed abroad and explored in limited ways by their clerical and secular predecessors in America. Except for classical political economy, these systematic traditions were taking form in the 1870s along evolutionary lines: British associationist psychology was being recast on evolutionary, biological assumptions; a universal theory of evolution was taking shape in anthropology; in sociology there were positivistic theories of social evolution propounded by Comte and Spencer; and in political science, theories of the historical evolution of Anglo-American political institutions. The American academics were also sometimes alert to still newer developments abroad. William James, for example, incorporated into his thinking some of the new physiology and experimental psychology. In economics, Francis Walker accepted into the classical tradition some insights from German historical economics. Simon Newcomb, an astronomer and mathematician employed in government and at the early Johns Hopkins, quickly took up the idea of marginal utility that was being formulated within the classical tradition and suggested the possibility of developing it in mathematical terms. While some members of the next generation would regard these developments in method and theory as the bases for major re-

---

8. Haskell, *Emergence of Professional Social Science*, chap. 7; Furner, *Advocacy and Objectivity*, pp. 313–20; Ralph W. Emerson, "The American Scholar" (1837) and Wendell Phillips, "The Scholar in a Republic" (1881), both delivered as Phi Beta Kappa addresses at Harvard.

orientations of their fields, for the pioneer groups of the 1870s, these developments did not so much challenge the older systematic traditions as extend
them.

The new academics tended to define science in the manner common
among humanistic subjects earlier in the nineteenth century—as a body of
systematic principles resting on empirical evidence. Consistent with this view,
the reform purpose of the new sciences was cast in the tradition of general
edification. Although influenced by the mounting evidence of conflict in the
public arena, the academics of the 1870s were unhurried in their solution.
Rational scientific principles would be disseminated in the new courses to the
future leaders of society; they would promote reasoned discourse and encourage the adoption of correct practices in the society at large. The desire to train
an expert civil service, which motivated some of the early work in political
science, and the experience of some economists in advising government and
men of affairs on economic questions were half-steps beyond this traditional
approach, related both to the concept of public leadership and the newer
concept of professional expertise.

Why this new body of interest in the social sciences emerged among
reformers and academics in the 1870s is one of the major questions facing
historical inquiry. To some extent, the appearance of the social sciences in the
1870s reflected the internal growth of knowledge in each field that had occurred in Europe over the preceding century and that had hitherto been under-
utilized in America. But it would be difficult to attribute the new attention
given these subjects to the state of intellectual development they had reached.
The advent of evolutionary concepts is one intellectual development that
occurred in several fields at roughly this period. For example, Spencer's
evolutionary theories had a galvanizing effect on American sociology, providing perspectives on historical comparative analysis that dramatically increased
the sense of scientific identity. Yet sociologists quickly discovered that beneath these broad conceptions, they had no established subject matter and few
clues as to how to analyze what subjects they addressed. In psychology, while
evolutionary concepts were providing some synthetic perspectives during the
1870s, it is arguable that the physiological psychology and laboratory experimentation developed in Germany were more central to the perception of
growth in the field held by its American practitioners and, in this case,
provided the core around which the field formed. In economics, evolutionary
concepts played virtually no role as yet in America; indeed, classical economics, though far better developed intellectually than sociological theory,
was in some quarters on the defensive, and the impact of historical methods
and marginal analysis was just beginning to be felt. The fact that these fields
all took on similar institutional identities in the 1870s, despite the varying
state of momentum, coherence and complexity in their subject matters, sug-

gests the importance of sociocultural factors in the timing of this early crystallization.

The post–Civil War decades were a time of substantial social change resulting from industrialism and the growth of cities, and sociologists have linked these social changes to profound changes in cultural attitudes. That a scientific view of the world is an essential element in the increasingly rational character of modern society has been a fundamental premise of sociological theory since it first emerged in the early nineteenth century. Historians have only recently begun to explore that linkage more carefully and to explain the particular kinds of social scientific explanations that developed in these decades by reference to the particular kinds of sociocultural needs felt at the time.

It is clear, however, that the concatenation of declining religious authority, growing urban problems, and the prolonged depression and labor conflict of the 1870s was beginning to create a sense of crisis among some intellectuals. The people who responded to the call of the ASSA and who sought to develop in the colleges a more worldly and effective kind of knowledge were particularly sensitive to the need for intelligent leadership and social order. Like many of their contemporaries in various fields, the social scientists thought of themselves as members of a social and cultural elite who represented the dominant line of American development; as the heirs of the republican tradition, they sought to assume the moral authority befitting their station. Generally the sons of native Protestant families, they had been taught in college that they constituted an elite of learning and virtue whose leadership American society should follow. Thus they regarded themselves, often quite explicitly, as a natural aristocracy generated by and in some ways identified with the "people," but yet a class apart. In the general social crisis, the authority of their class was seen as synonymous with intellectual order in the society at large—the assertion of the one being a guarantee of the other.

II.

During the 1870s, the social sciences began to take root as separate, academic, and scientific disciplines. Before we can follow these processes further and examine the professional character these disciplines displayed, we must introduce another and younger group of social scientists who appeared around 1880. The older scholars were educated and certified, if at all, in one of the traditional branches of knowledge. The younger group had received its training, and often Ph.D. degrees, from German universities or from such pioneer American universities as Johns Hopkins.[9] It was the younger generation who

---

9. Among the social scientists about whom I have thus far been able to gather data, no one in the traditional generation is born later than 1842 nor holds a Ph.D. degree. The professional

took the lead in establishing the new courses and graduate training programs and who founded the journals and national associations that ultimately defined the new professions.

Within the generation of the 1880s, we can discern two different types of scholars. In most of the disciplinary areas, there were scholars whose attitudes toward science and reform were close to that of the older, traditional generation. Although the traditionalists composed quite substantial groups in all the disciplines, there were also scholars with a different outlook and more militant professional ideals. In economics, the militant group was composed of those trained in German historical economics, like Richard T. Ely of Johns Hopkins. In psychology, it consisted of laboratory scientists trained in the new German physiological psychology, like G. Stanley Hall, founding president of Clark University. In anthropology, Franz Boas of Columbia led a group of allies and students who desired a more historical and critically scientific anthropology. In sociology, Albion W. Small, chairman of the department at Chicago, E. A. Ross of Stanford, and Franklin Giddings of Columbia spearheaded the search for theoretical and professional identity. In political science, a group of scholars oriented toward historical and administrative problems took the lead in establishing professional institutions. The pioneers in the group were John W. Burgess, who introduced political science at Amherst College in the 1870s and at Columbia College in 1880, and Herbert Baxter Adams, who established a department of history and political science at Johns Hopkins. Although enterprising advocates of political studies, Burgess and Adams shared many of the scientific and social attitudes of the older traditional scholars.[10]

---

generation, born after 1844, nearly all hold Ph.D.'s in subjects closely related to their new disciplines. Anthropology was an exception to this generalization; here there appeared to be a younger group of government- and museum-based anthropologists without professional degrees.

10. The existence of these militant groups and their early professional thrust is best seen for economics in Furner, *Advocacy and Objectivity*, chaps. 2, 3; A. W. Coats, "The First Two Decades of the American Economic Association," *American Economic Review* (hereafter cited as *AER*) 50 (September 1960): 555–74; Richard T. Ely, *Ground Under Our Feet: An Autobiography* (New York: Macmillan, 1938); for anthropology, in Stocking, *Race, Culture and Evolution*, chap. 11; idem, ed., *The Shaping of American Anthropology*, pts. 1, 2, 9; idem, "Franz Boas and the Founding of the AAA," in *American Anthropologist* (hereafter cited as *AA*) 62 (February 1960): 1–17; for political science, in R. Gordon Hoxie, *A History of the Faculty of Political Science, Columbia University* (New York: Columbia University Press, 1955); John W. Burgess, *Reminiscences of an American Scholar: The Beginnings of Columbia University* (New York: Columbia University Press, 1934); Thomas Le Duc, *Piety and Intellect at Amherst College* (New York: Columbia University Press, 1946), chap. 4; *Proceedings of the American Political Science Association* 1 (1904); Furner, *Advocacy and Objectivity*, chap. 12; for sociology, in Albion W. Small, "Fifty Years of Sociology in the United States (1865–1915)," *American Journal of Sociology* (hereafter cited as *AJS*) 31 (May 1916): 721–864; "Organization of the American Sociological Society. Official Report," *AJS* 11 (January 1906): 555–69; "The ASS," *AJS* 12 (March 1907): 579–80.

The single most striking similarity in the attitudes of these militant groups was their conception of modern science as a product of empirical investigation. The traditionalists had already felt the influence of the post–Civil War temper of realism, and their successors were even more committed to the turn to facts. Whether from their exposure to German *Wissenschaft,* then in its most empirical phase, or from the stunning achievement of Darwin in biology, and generally from both, they argued that "real" science or the "newer" science built its theories closely on empirical observation. To some extent, this empirical thrust in the social sciences may have echoed the Baconian empiricism that dominated inquiry in the natural sciences in antebellum America. But many spokesmen attempted to define a more sophisticated position. Those with philosophical inclinations and training, like Franz Boas and G. Stanley Hall, felt the need to link their empirical stance in science to contemporary epistemology. Like William James, they were under the influence of neo-Kantian idealism and worked out an empiricist epistemology that incorporated substantial elements of idealism. In all the social sciences, many spokesmen also drew support for empirical science from a new historical consciousness. If knowledge emerged only from the intimate fusion of mind and object; if social objects changed constantly over time and in complex interaction, only a social science dedicated to close and continuous observation of social objects could hope to understand them.[11]

---

11. On Baconian empiricism, see Theodore Dwight Bozeman, *Protestants in an Age of Science: The Baconian Ideal and Antebellum American Religious Thought* (Chapel Hill, N.C.: University of North Carolina Press, 1977), chaps. 1, 8. On James's revision of empiricism, see Bruce Kuklick, *The Rise of American Philosophy, Cambridge, Massachusetts: 1860–1930* (New Haven: Yale University Press, 1977). For a general account of the empirical stance and neo-Kantian and historicist roots of the militant groups, see Jürgen Herbst, *The German Historical School in American Scholarship: A Study in the Transfer of Culture* (Ithaca, N.Y.: Cornell University Press, 1965); Fritz R. Ringer, *The Decline of the German Mandarins* (Cambridge: Harvard University Press, 1969), pp. 295–315; in relation to psychology, Ross, *G. Stanley Hall,* chaps. 5, 6, 9; in relation to anthropology, Stocking, *Race, Culture and Evolution,* chap. 7. For polemical statements of the militants' empirical programs, see Richard T. Ely, "The Past and Present of Political Economy," *Johns Hopkins University Studies in Historical and Political Science,* 2d ser., no. 3 (March 1884); the debate between the historical school and the classical economists in *Science,* reprinted as Henry C. Adams, et al., *Science Economic Discussion* (New York: Science Co., 1886); Ross, *G. Stanley Hall,* chaps. 9, 10, 13; James McKeen Cattell, "Mental Tests and Measurements," *Mind* 15 (1890): 373–81; "The Progress of Psychology," *Popular Science Monthly* 43 (1893): 779–85; Boas's early programmatic statements in *Science* and his address at the St. Louis Congress in 1904; "The History of Anthropology," reprinted in Stocking, ed., *Shaping of American Anthropology;* Albion Small and George E. Vincent, *An Introduction to the Study of Society* (New York: American Book, 1894); Small, "The Era of Sociology," pp. 1, 15; idem, "Free Investigation," pp. 212–13; idem, reviews, pp. 219–28, *AJS* 1; Burgess, "The Study of the Political Sciences in Columbia College," *International Review* 12 (April 1882): 346–51; "Political Science and History," *American Historical Review* 2 (April 1897): 401–8.

Besides their empirical conception of science, the militant groups also generally shared a desire to use their knowledge more directly in the solution of social problems than had their academic precursors. Their sense of urgency undoubtedly arose from the fact that they grew to maturity during the 1870s and 1880s, when industrialization had generated the first major wave of depression and labor violence in America. During that period, the revival of democratic sentiment and the appearance of socialism as an alternative course for modern industrial society accentuated their sense of social crisis. Many of them also came from family backgrounds in which the Protestant evangelical tradition had been a powerful influence. In part the failure to believe literally in Christianity any longer, or the failure to achieve the religious experience some evangelical sects demanded, led them to pour their energy into the fervor for moral betterment. The organic religious values and idealistic world-view of the evangelical social scientists made the social conflict they saw around them particularly painful and led them to seek ways to use their scientific knowledge to restore social harmony.[12]

The active reform concern of these scholars was expressed in social values that were generally different from the values of their traditional precursors and contemporaries, in most cases further left on the political spectrum toward greater social equality and governmental responsibility. The conflict in social values was particularly fierce in economics, where the historical economists were influenced by socialism and desired to expand the role of the state in economic activity as a means of moderating the harsh consequences of industrialization. Militants took a more liberal or radical position on such issues as government ownership or regulation of the economy, support of labor unions, labor's claim to a greater share of profits and control of industry, and government welfare legislation. Their overtly ethical conception of economics conflicted sharply with that of the traditionalists, who had been trying to separate their subject from moral philosophy by asserting that economics, as a science, had nothing to do with ethics.

In political science the difference in social values was much less severe than in economics. While the political scientists agreed on the need for a more positive role for the state in modern society, their views occupied a more conservative range on the political spectrum, probably because scholars concerned with pressing social issues of the day naturally gravitated to economics and sociology. Burgess's interest in the state had emerged from Civil War

---

12. Ross, "Socialism and American Liberalism"; A. W. Coats, "Henry Carter Adams: A Case Study in the Emergence of the Social Sciences in the United States, 1850–1900," *Journal of American Studies* 2 (October 1968): 177–97; William R. Hutchison, "Cultural Strain and Protestant Liberalism," *American Historical Review* 75 (April 1971): 386–411; Richard T. Ely, *Ground Under Our Feet*, pp. 16, 65, 72.

nationalism and conservative concern for order; in the context of the new economic and social issues, he advocated a limited role for the state as protector of property rights. Most others in the group, and their students who moved into professional leadership at the turn of the century, saw the state as an agent of liberal, stabilizing reform.

In psychology, the conflict in values was again sharply drawn. Far more than their traditional precursors, the new experimental psychologists wanted to divorce themselves altogether from religion and metaphysics and to shift the ground on which moral and existential issues were to be solved. These secular values involved them from the start in conflicts over religious belief and educational practice, with the new psychologists siding generally against the soul and with some form of progressive education.

Thus, during the 1880s many of the new generation of social scientists turned to professionalization. They recognized that professional development—in the form of graduate programs, journals, and national associations—was the means by which they could force entry for their new programs into the American colleges and universities.[13]

In political science and sociology—as opposed to economics and psychology—the efforts toward professionalization did not result in clear-cut conflicts between militants and traditionalists. Burgess's program of political science based on history and law was not at first sharply differentiated from the aspirations of a traditional figure like White, or from the study of history. Given his position at the still unreformed Columbia College, Burgess's aggressive professional efforts were initially directed against the conception of the older college and narrow legal training rather than against history per se, which he usurped by appointment. In the course of the 1880s and 1890s, however, the distinctly scientific aims and contemporary statist concern of Burgess's program became more sharply delineated from the historians, while the institutional development Burgess secured at Columbia grew through the efforts of such students as Frank Goodnow into a professional journal and association for the whole discipline.

In sociology, professional organization came late, when the range of political conflict and institutional rivalry had narrowed. The new sociologists quickly found that they had laid claim to the true science of society through the development of professional institutions before they could make good

---

13. While these social scientists had the components of the concept of professionalization clearly in mind, they sometimes spoke of their aims as being specifically "professional," and other times, reacting to the narrower practical connotations of the term, defined their aims as "non-professional specializations." For an example of the former, see Ely, "American Colleges and German Universities," *Harper's New Monthly Magazine* 61 (July 1880): 253–60; for the latter, see John W. Burgess, *The American University* (Boston: Ginn, Heath, 1884), reprinted in idem, *Reminiscences,* p. 365.

on the promise. Instead of facing a sharp-edged enemy in the traditional camps, the professionalizing sociologists were surrounded by a sea of academic doubters who questioned the substance of their new field.[14]

The social scientists of the 1880s had to exert their authority not only against other academics but also against popular claimants to science and social usefulness. This second front was not very important where disciplinary expertise was already well developed, as in economics, or where popular practitioners made no claim to science, as in politics. But the new psychologists had to counter popular spiritualists and psychic researchers, and the sociologists tried to displace the growing number of clerical and lay social reformers. For the insecure and amorphous subject of sociology, popular counterclaims were a major threat, particularly since popular reformers often advocated more radical reforms than the academic sociologists could approve. In the 1890s, Small and his colleagues regarded the reformers as their chief competitors, and Small apparently rushed to start his *American Journal of Sociology* to prevent the formation of a reformist journal for "Christian sociology."[15]

The conditions and motives behind the professionalizing activity of the 1880s is a major question for historical inquiry. We have seen that the younger militant social scientists had a powerful motive for the formation of professional institutions: they lacked a firm footing in the colleges and educated communities for their new conceptions of social science, and thereby for themselves. But their turn to professionalism also reflected fundamental changes in modern society.

Sociologists and historians have long seen the development of industrialism in the nineteenth century, with its increased specialization of labor, as the seedbed for professionalism.[16] Professionalism can be defined as a form of occupational control, one form among others (guilds, patronage, state regulation) that historically have attempted to regulate the problematical relationship between producer and consumer arising from the specialization of labor. Two aspects of that relationship create the possibility of professionalization. One is the degree of uncertainty in the relationship, which increases with the degree of specialization in production; the other is the potential for autonomy that an occupational group has—the degree to which it can exert its power over the producer-consumer relation. Professionalism is a form of collegial occupa-

---

14. Ely, *Ground Under Our Feet*, p. 132; Ross, *G. Stanley Hall*, pt. 2; Stocking, *The Shaping of American Anthropology*, pp. 283–86; Burgess, *Reminiscences*, chap. 5; Somit and Tanenhaus, *Development of Political Science*, pp. 34–48; Furner, *Advocacy and Objectivity*, pp. 278–91; Small, "Fifty Years," pp. 781, 796–804.

15. Ross, *G. Stanley Hall*, pp. 162–64, 170–71.

16. See, for example, Haskell, *Emergence of Professional Social Science*, chaps. 1, 2; Robert Wiebe, *The Search for Order, 1877–1920* (New York: Hill and Wang, 1967), chap. 5.

tional control in which the producer's expert knowledge creates a high degree of uncertainty in the relationship and thus a high need for control, and in which the historically high status of its practitioners and the fragmentation of its consumers has enabled the occupation to press and enforce its claims for collegial autonomy.[17]

All the groups of social scientists we have discussed here—the reformers of the ASSA, the academic pioneers of the 1870s, and the younger generation of the 1880s—were subject alike to the underlying process of modernization, and all showed some interest in professional development. As industrialization proceeded and society became more complex, a greater degree of uncertainty entered into the relationship between the producers and consumers of social knowledge, an uncertainty that increased as thinkers and reformers began to propound unfamiliar explanations. In addition, the social base of many of the social scientists in the patrician class or in the genteel professions—and the claim they made to scientific expertise at a time when the authority of science was rising dramatically—augmented the power of the social scientists to enforce their claims to autonomy.

The tempo of professionalizing activities, however, was markedly quickened by the generation of the 1880s and the kind of professionalism they espoused came to dominate their disciplines. There appears to have been at least three professional ideals at work among the early social scientists—that of the practitioner, that of the college-based teacher-scholar, and that of the research-oriented scholar-scientist. If we examine more closely the differing claims to professional status put forward by these early social scientists, we can see why the attitudes of the academics of the 1880s led more directly toward professionalizing activity and why the institutions and norms they established prevailed.

There were a number of groups of practitioners in the area of social science, many of them active in the ASSA, who felt the need to develop expert knowledge, vocational careers, and organizational bases for professional advancement; these included particularly workers in the area of charity and corrections, and government workers in the areas of labor and statistics. Carroll D. Wright is perhaps the best example of such a practitioner who attempted to develop a scientific professional base in government civil service. Had American social science developed in that mold, as it did partially in Britain, it might have fallen heir to the large amount of private funding for

---

17. My understanding of professionalism is drawn primarily from Terence J. Johnson, *Professions and Power* (London: Macmillan, 1972); Henrika Kuklick, "The Organization of Social Science in the United States," *American Quarterly* 28 (Spring 1976): 124–41; Magali Sarfatti Larson, *The Rise of Professionalism: A Sociological Analysis* (Berkeley: University of California Press, 1977).

social welfare activities available after 1900 and particularly after 1920. The ASSA, as some academics and practitioners originally contemplated, might then have served as a bridge between expert practitioners and academics, bringing together both theory and practice in the investigation of social problems.[18]

However, in late-nineteenth-century America, the practical vocations offered limited opportunities for people interested in developing social scientific knowledge. Government service offered very few jobs above a routine level. The Social Gospel, Chautauqua, and urban reform movements that supported some of the early economists, sociologists, and political scientists offered equally meager support for a career, as did the politically influenced and erratically funded public school systems. Only in anthropology did museums and government seem to provide any basis for a sustained career. Moreover, neither charity work nor government service offered the kind of status that could support claims to professional autonomy. The younger social scientists therefore saw more opportunity in the scholarly vocation and semi-patrician status of the college professor than in the practical vocations.[19]

The academic pioneers in social science subjects during the 1870s also had professional goals, but they were already members of a profession, that of college teacher, which had generally been in America a marginal adjunct to the clerical profession. Their professional aims were oriented toward strengthening the traditional conception of the college professor as a teacher and as a member of an elite community. In that multifaceted ideal, competence and scholarship in a special field were important but remained imbedded in duties to the community and the institution that related to personal character and class status. Traditional scholars, like William Graham Sumner and William James, were joined by university reformers based in the ASSA, such as Charles W. Eliot and Andrew D. White, in this desire to establish academic careers for teacher-scholars who could speak with authority to the problems and anxieties of the respectable community.

Rooted in a long-standing genteel and community-based professional culture, the teacher-scholars believed that their systematic knowledge could be shared with an enlightened public, its principles taught and grasped in classrooms and public journals alike. Thus they felt less strongly the growing uncertainty in the relationship between producers and consumers of social

18. James Leiby, *Carroll Wright and Labor Reform: The Origin of Labor Statistics* (Cambridge, Mass.: Harvard University Press, 1969); Abrams, *The Origins of British Sociology,* chap. 7; Barry D. Karl, *Charles E. Merriam and the Study of Politics* (Chicago: University of Chicago Press, 1974).

19. Burgess, *Reminiscences;* E. A. Ross, *Seventy Years of It* (New York: D. Appleton-Century, 1936), p. 90; Ross, *G. Stanley Hall,* p. 136; Ely, *Ground Under Our Feet,* pp. 35, 41, 60, 124; Higham, *History,* pp. 6–25, 64.

knowledge. Moreover, they enjoyed a firm base in their institutional communities through personal, family, or class ties and could hope to strengthen their professional roles through the kinds of alliances with trustees, alumni, journalists, and philanthropic capitalists through which they had already begun to reform the colleges.

Finally, there was the professional ideal the younger social scientists of the 1880s learned chiefly in Germany: that of the university professor whose prime commitment was to the advancement of knowledge in his own discipline. While the example of the flourishing German universities had influenced American intellectuals intermittently throughout the nineteenth century, the social scientists of the 1880s participated in the upsurge of migration to German universities. Many of them, impressed by the scientific success and the relatively high status of German university professors, adopted the German ideal of the research-oriented professor.[20] The first professional institutions the Americans so quickly fashioned, from graduate seminars and Doctor of Philosophy degrees to journals and associations, were adaptations of the institutional framework of their respected German models. These institutions were at once professional and research-oriented. Their research function—to provide the kind of exchange of information and peer review that was necessary to stimulate and monitor advanced scholarship—was itself a collegial exercise of autonomy.

Moreover, in Germany, the younger social scientists studied at first hand the specialized bodies of knowledge that had developed in the universities during the nineteenth century. In degree of technical elaboration as well as in language, these scholarly traditions offered a kind of social knowledge more esoteric and distant than the social scientists possessed before and thus increased the need and opportunity for professional control. While to some extent the German model of professional status and specialized knowledge influenced all the new social scientists of the 1880s, it appeared to influence those in the militant groups most strongly. Many of the younger traditionalists either studied only in this country or were critical of their German mentors. But the militants were more impressed by their German hosts and more immersed in German scholarship. They thus sought entrance to the university in a manner that utilized the collegiality of their German-based research ideal and gave maximum power to the professional credentials attached to that ideal.

The desire of these academics of the 1880s to establish their disciplines as academic professions would not have met with success, however, had it not been for one timely development—the modernization and expansion of the

---

20. Herbst, *The German Historical School*, chap. 1; Veysey, *Emergence of the American University*, pp. 125–33; Ringer, *Decline of the German Mandarins*.

universities. There were already by the early 1880s more social science aspirants than there were academic jobs for them. Ely and Hall, for example, had been nearly destitute for a time on their return from Germany. Hall and Burgess had rushed at the chance to teach at their unreformed collegiate alma maters, and had university reform not allowed them to move to more promising institutions, they may well have remained where they were and been forced to modify their aims.

The social scientists followed in a long line of scholars who had tried to establish an ideal of scholarly research in American colleges. Earlier in the nineteenth century some of the natural science fields, and then philology and modern languages, had felt the impact of the research ideal. Intermittently scholars in these fields had forced the colleges to accept their demands for less elementary teaching and more time and facilities for research. But in a few cases in the 1870s and increasingly in the 1880s, college presidents and trustees became willing partners in this process.

Thus the professional ideal of the young research-oriented scholars gained prominence in American universities as the position of the cultivated elite gradually weakened, even in its locus of greatest strength—the college community. In England, the traditional ideal of the teacher as moral guide and member of a broadly literate community of gentlemen commanded far greater resources, in the nation and the universities, and thus was able to subordinate the demand for specialized research-oriented disciplinary communities. In American academe, however, the professional ideal of the genteel culture could not withstand the inroads made by the aggressive, competitive, professionalizing activities of the research-oriented newcomers.

Connected to the rise of the new university, and stretching out from it, was the power of a respectable and literate middle class. Ultimately, the ability of the militant social scientists to sustain their claims for a place in the universities and for professional standing rested on the willingness of the educated public to accept those claims. It may be that their functional orientation, their empirical scientific stance, and the specific vocabularies they applied to the problems of industrial society carried greater credibility and authority in the new industrial world than did the genteel norms and knowledge. But once established in the universities, the professionals fell heir to an important source of authority. As Veblen showed, the democratization of culture resulted in wide acceptance through the middle class of genteel respectability and its canons of intellectual and moral hierarchy. Although the professional academics had to fend off popular rivals, what is perhaps most striking is the rapidity with which their role was accepted and their knowledge sought. With relative ease—and sometimes hearing little change in content—the middle class public turned from the moral advice of the clergy to the expert advice of the university social scientists, from the old elite's conception of society as hierarchically ordered by virtue to the new elite's conception of society as a meritocracy, hierarchically ordered by competence.[21]

III.

The basic conditions that led to the development of separate, academic professions provided the basis for their scientism as well. The social sciences formed under the banner of science. The competitive university and professional contexts in which they grew required that they constantly prove and solidify their status as sciences. Given these underlying factors and the failure of the social sciences actually to achieve the kind of agreement that characterized the natural sciences, it is understandable that social scientists would continually try to reformulate and strengthen their methodological programs.[22]

The social scientists began, however, with very diverse conceptions of science. Methods and models continued to be drawn from parent humanistic disciplines as well as from natural science. The natural sciences themselves presented different models of scientific authority ranging from astronomy and physics, the reigning natural sciences of the eighteenth century, to physiology and biology, the rising sciences of life during the nineteenth century. Moreover, the heavy influence of German historicism on the social scientists of the 1880s led to the definition of scientific method as much in historical as in natural-science terms. Among the historically oriented economists, sociologists, and political scientists—like Ely, Small and Burgess—scientific method meant in large part historical method. However, many of them were methodologically unsophisticated (Small was an exception) and rhetorically linked their conception of social science methodology to the more scientifically prestigious fields of physiology or physics. Members of these idealistic historical schools, recognizing that their reformist goals involved not only scientific determination of facts but ethical judgments regarding values, believed it possible to include both those functions within the domain of science. Thus when Veblen asked in 1898, "Why Is Economics Not a Darwinian

---

21. The degree to which the new language of social science harbored the old concepts of Protestant village culture needs considerably more exploration. Ross, *G. Stanley Hall*, chaps. 7, 15–18; C. Wright Mills, "The Professional Ideology of Social Pathologists," *AJS* 49 (September 1943): 165–80.

22. Speaking for the militants in sociology, Small later remarked: "It was strategically necessary for these innovators . . . to gain ground by playing the academic game under the existing rules. Their instincts . . . prompted them to speak for a 'science' in the old uncritical sense, and having announced themselves as the exponents of a 'science,' they were under bonds to make good. . . . I have certain persuasive reasons for believing that the academic beginnings of all social sciences in this country were in this respect substantially like those of sociology." Small, "Fifty Years," pp. 801–2 n.

Science?" he was not only urging a more rigorous scientism on his colleagues but a Darwinian model of economics whose scientific authority neither the ethical historical school nor the classical market economists would accept.[23]

The first generation of professional social scientists also had rather loose conceptions of empirical scientific method. In psychology, for example, empiricism initially denoted laboratory experimentation and direct observation but specified little else regarding how these procedures were to be carried out. In the other social sciences, little distinction was initially made between empiricism as the gathering of historical evidence from books and documents and empiricism as direct observation under systematic conditions.[24] From the 1890s onward, however, efforts were made to achieve more rigorous scientific methods. Psychologists showed an increasing concern for rigor in laboratory investigation, and economists were attracted to statistical methods and theories capable of mathematical formulation, such as marginal utility theory. After the turn of the century, political scientists and sociologists displayed increasing concern over the development of techniques of observation that would enable them to understand the actual functioning of social and political processes.

Around 1912, however, a distinctly new voice appeared in the social science literature, and it swelled to a powerful chorus after World War I. Social scientists began to call for a more objective version of empiricism and social intervention. The new program was more quantitative and behavioristic and urged that social science eschew ethical judgments altogether in favor of more explicit methodology and objective examination of facts. While the call for objectivity sometimes expressed itself as a renewed commitment to empiricism, it also was apparent in efforts to revise general theory.

In psychology, the subject with the deepest roots in American collegiate philosophy, and therefore the strongest impulse to disengage from it, this scientistic impulse was profound and far-reaching. Enunciated first in 1912 and 1913 by John B. Watson, behaviorism sought to eliminate from psychology any dealings with subjective consciousness. Psychology was to observe and record only objective behavior, behavior that could be seen in, and understood entirely as, biological response. Although few followed Watson's attempt to reduce thought wholly to muscular behavior, his theory, his objectivist attitude, and his emphasis on achieving total prediction and control deeply influenced psychology and, more superficially, the other social sciences.[25]

23. *Quarterly Journal of Economics* 12 (1898): 373–97.

24. For discussions of early methods, see Albrecht, "The New Psychology"; Ross, *G. Stanley Hall*, chap. 9; Somit and Tanenhaus, *Development of Political Science*, pp. 69, 76; Small and Vincent, *Introduction to the Study of Society*, chap. 3.

25. John C. Burnham, "On the Origins of Behaviorism," *Journal of the History of the Behavioral Sciences* (hereafter cited as *JHBS*) 4 (April 1968): 143–51; Thomas M. Camfield, "The Professionalization of American Psychology, 1870–1917," *JHBS* 9 (January 1973): 71–73.

In economics, the interest in basic statistical data was augmented after the war by a more self-conscious group of younger institutionalists, such as Wesley C. Mitchell of Columbia. They were successors to the old historical school, but they were influenced by Veblen's scientific stance and behaviorist psychology to call for a closer empirical study of the actual working of the economic institutions of capitalism.[26] In sociology, Robert Park, who had early been disillusioned with reformers and attracted to direct investigation of social facts, dominated Chicago sociology during the 1920s with his program of urban research seen as basic science. More radical than Park was a group of objectivist sociologists, including Luther Lee Bernard and William F. Ogburn, who called for a behaviorist attitude and research program.[27] In political science, Charles Merriam led the movement for a more systematic collection of data, exact methods, and the incorporation of the advances of neighboring sciences. Merriam also had in his camp younger colleagues who urged a more stringently behavioristic approach to the study of political processes.[28] All of these groups hoped that the development of an objective science would eventually provide social scientists with the tools to exercise "social control."

The conditions that led to the emergence of this more rigorous scientism have only begun to be investigated by historians. One factor appears to have been the increasingly aggressive influence of biology, and then of behaviorist psychology, on the other social sciences after about 1905. From about 1880 to 1905 the social sciences did not appear to feel that their free borrowings placed them under threat, either institutional or intellectual, from the natural sciences or from the more rapidly advancing psychology. After 1905, however, there is evidence of greater sensitivity to, and defensiveness against, both biology and psychology in the face of new currents within these subjects—Mendelian genetics, the mechanistic philosophy of Jacques Loeb, behaviorism. The social sciences thus had to disengage from their old roots in

26. Dorfman, *Economic Mind*, 4: 133–35, chap. 13; Paul T. Homan, "An Appraisal of Institutional Economics," *AER* 22 (March 1932): 10–17; Charleton H. Parker, "Motives in Economic Life," and "Discussion," *AER* 8, supp. (March 1918): 212–38, reprinted in *Proceedings of the ASS* 12 (1918): 131–57; J. M. Clark, "Economic Theory in an Era of Social Readjustment," and Walton H. Hamilton, "The Institutional Approach to Economic Theory," and "Discussion," *AER* 9, supp. (March 1919): 280–99, 309–24.

27. Faris, *Chicago Sociology*, chaps. 2, 3; Fred H. Matthews, "Robert E. Park and the Development of American Sociology" (Ph.D. diss., Harvard University, 1973), p. 163; L. L. Bernard, "The Objective Viewpoint in Sociology," *AJS* 25 (November 1919): 298–325; J. L. Gillin, "Report of the Committee on the Standardization of Research of the ASS," *Proceedings of the ASS* 15 (1920): 231–41; idem, "Report of the Research Committee of ASS," *Proceedings of the ASS* 16 (1921): 243–48.

28. Somit and Tanenhaus, *Development of Political Science*, chap. 9; Crick, *American Science of Politics*, chap. 8; Karl, *Charles E. Merriam*, chaps. 6–8; "The Present State of the Study of Politics," *American Political Science Review* 15 (May 1921): 173–85.

an outmoded biology, protect their social spheres from total absorption by a mechanistic biology or behavioristic psychology, and prove by the more rigorous standards of these schools the genuine character of their own sciences.

Another level of explanation for the particular kind of scientism espoused by American social science lies in the political-institutional context. The political and professional pressures that had pushed social scientists toward a centrist political stance from 1880 to 1905 could feed into scientism. When Richard Ely and E. A. Ross were attacked for their political heterodoxy, they made it clear to their colleagues that they would henceforth do only genuinely scientific work. Many in the growing political center of Progressive reform appeared to believe that in accepting the goals set by the society at large they were eschewing ethics for science. The later cycle of political heterodoxy and postwar reaction appeared to produce similar results. Whether social scientists wished to retreat from the public arena altogether or only to hide the political implications of their work, a program of basic quantitative or behavioral science and such scientistic euphemisms as "social control," "adjustment," or "social reconstruction" were appropriate shields.[29]

Not only on a political level did conflicts in values lead toward scientism. In late-nineteenth-century America, the breakup of Protestant village culture by the industrial economy and the rise of the heterogeneous city precipitated a profound crisis in values. While there had been different and competing value systems in America before, there had not been a large class of educated people whose allegiance was so deeply divided. The division of intellectual authority itself between village and religious sources on the one hand and more modern and scientific sources on the other created, in the minds of people shaped by both, severe conflicts in values.[30]

In the waning light of natural law conceptions, science could appear to resolve these conflicts by making value decisions itself. The most popular solutions in late-nineteenth-century America were attempts to root values directly in scientific evolutionary laws. Within an evolutionary framework, the disparate ideals of the older, agrarian and commercial society and the newer heterogeneous, urban one, and the countercurrents of emotional expression and rational control that the Victorian culture had organized into

---

29. The scientism induced by the war needs considerable research. The motives expressed in Merriam, "Present State of the Study of Politics," suggest that for him, science served as a kind of liberal detour that would avoid the violent ideological conflict that had overrun political discourse, make good the defeat of Progressivism, and lead back ultimately to greater social usefulness. For evidence of concern with the political advantages of an objective scientific stance, see Karl, *Charles E. Merriam.*

30. See Vernon Dibble, *The Legacy of Albion Small* (Chicago: University of Chicago Press, 1975), pp. 73–74.

sexual and class roles—all these could be hierarchically arranged and pinned down on a scale of races, classes, sexes, and historical stages, rooted in nature itself and organized to display the future triumph of traditional virtues.

Explicitly or implicitly many of the new social scientists shared all or part of this evolutionary viewpoint. Yet for many, the empiricist program and its reformist values implied contrary hierarchies. Exposure to the complex life of modern society and the insistent exploration of irrationality in human nature led many to grapple more directly with the problem of values. No one described the resulting sense of crisis more tellingly than Albion Small in 1902. The problem, he said, was the breakdown of the older Protestant standard of values, the fragmentation of society into a multiplicity of ethnic groups and functional roles, each of which provided a different framework of values and viewpoints from which to understand the world. More than that, these conflicting values had polarized around a set of fundamental problems:

> We are dealing in modern society with certain radical questions; e.g., Shall we aim for physical enjoyment, or for extinction of sensuous desire? Shall we posit an ideal of government or no government? Shall we plan for private property or communism, for monopoly or competition, for freedom of thought or for perpetual social chaperoning of mind and conscience? These are not questions of biology, or civics, or economics, or theology. They are not questions of ways and means. They are not problems of how to do things. They are questions of what is fit to do.[31]

Small, rooted as he was in the older moral philosophy, argued that the only solution was for sociology to discover the totality of relations that composed modern society and, on the basis of that scientific knowledge, to construct a hierarchy of values.

Other social scientists, perhaps those less deeply and personally rooted in the older morality, could not face that task with equanimity. For these people science offered an alternative solution to the conflict of values: it enabled value decisions to be avoided altogether. For example, Robert Park, Small's successor at Chicago, was early immobilized by the painful problem of value judgment and sought to escape in the distance of objective science. "There is only one thing I can do," Park had concluded, "understand." The program for sociology he developed urged scientists not to make value judgments but only to exercise their insight and empathy in understanding the values of their subjects.[32] Some behaviorists went further. John B. Watson, raised and edu-

31. Small, *The Significance of Sociology for Ethics*, University of Chicago Decennial Publications no. 4 (Chicago: University of Chicago Press, 1902), pp. 5–6, 23–24.

32. Matthews, "Robert E. Park," pp. 55–56, 59, 216–18, 258–60.

cated in a rural, provincial, and religious South Carolina milieu, was thrown suddenly into the midst of Chicago, the subtleties of philosophy, and the power of the irrational exposed by Freud, and he reacted violently. Watson apparently escaped the strange and threatening panoply of conflicting values by urging scientists to avoid the consciousness of their subjects altogether, to deal with them wholly externally, as objects.

It may be that the emergence of this fiercely objective social science reflected in part the appearance of a distinctly new generation of social scientists. Among the leadership, at least, Watson, Mitchell, and Merriam were all born in the 1870s and had received their training in the United States, under the first professional generation. Imbued with the scientific hopes of their teachers, they could nonetheless easily perceive—as each new generation has been able to do—the values that lay just below the surface of their mentors' claimed objectivity.[33] Yet the accelerating crisis in values affected them as sharply as their elders, indeed more so, for they were without the unconscious legacy of the old moral idealism. Such a generational experience could have been involved in the attempt of these social scientists to form an objective, value-free social science.

Finally, from an institutional point of view, the war and the greater centralization of science it inaugurated augmented the contacts between the social sciences and the natural sciences and increased the vulnerability of the social sciences to their standards. The federal government's organization of science and its control of research funds were still meager during this period, but in the following years they constituted an ever more powerful magnet, drawing the social sciences toward the development of their disciplines along apolitical and value-free scientific lines acceptable to the natural sciences and to the government.[34]

The wave of scientism launched before and after World War I did not wholly prevail. Older methods and models persisted and scientific aspirations considerably outran scientific capabilities. Moreover, scientism set in motion substantial countercurrents in defense of social science methods that took into account the uniquely human attributes of subjectivity and choice. And when reformist attitudes arose in the society at large, as they did again in the 1930s

---

33. Charles Merriam recalled how as a graduate student he had surprised his mentor at Columbia, William A. Dunning, by telling him that h⸗ could detect beneath Dunning's studied objective prose, his preference in political philosopl.⸗. Merriam, "Dunning," in *American Masters of Social Science*, Howard W. Odum, ed. (Port Washington, N.Y.: Kennikat Press, 1965), p. 137.

34. Stocking, *Race, Culture and Evolution*, chap. 11. On the post-1945 trend toward behaviorism influenced by foundation and government control of research money, see Somit and Tanenhaus, *Development of Political Science*, p. 185; James G. Miller, "Toward a General Theory for the Behavioral Sciences," in *The State of the Social Sciences*, Leonard D. White, ed. (Chicago: University of Chicago Press, 1956), pp. 29–30.

and 1960s, they stimulated reactions against scientism in the name of a more explicitly value-oriented social science.

The result of these interacting processes is the imposition of a cyclical pattern upon the search for more sophisticated methods, as waves of scientism recede under the impact of political activism and the failure of scientific results to match scientistic rhetoric, and as conservative political pressures and the recognition of scientific inadequacy send social scientists again into a renewed commitment to the development of an objective science. These recurrent cycles of scientism appear to be rooted in the political and institutional contexts and bifurcated aims of the social sciences—contexts and purposes that were firmly established during the formative decades of the social sciences in America.

Part 2
Developments/1903–1945

Introduction

In the nearly half-century between the formation of the American Political Science Association and the end of World War II, political science in the United States came into its own as a distinct professional academic discipline. Advanced degrees became increasingly commonplace as entry certificates to the profession, and amateurs were increasingly replaced by professors and graduate students on the APSA's membership rolls. Dozens of graduate schools and undergraduate departments were established. Annual APSA meetings had to be held in something larger than the average lecture room. In short, what we know today as the modern profession took shape.

Yet what gave intellectual and disciplinary integrity to the institutional growth? For many political scientists these days, political science before the 1950s is often remembered—if it is remembered at all—as a rather unsophisticated prelude to the succeeding behavioral and postbehavioral eras. There are, however, distinctive intellectual and political features of political science between 1903 and 1945, or at least distinctive enough to think of these four decades as something more than a mere prelude to what came later.

The most important intellectual characteristic of the developing discipline was what it took to be its "revolt against formalism." The concerns of Lieber and Burgess were reduced in the minds of their successors to statist, institutional, and legal ones; and these were then derided as so much "soul stuff" by the likes of Arthur Bentley. Bentley urged that political science detail only the "process" or "pure activity" of "groups" in competition for power and political resources.[1] The comparative history of institutions was labeled as "dogmatic" by Charles Beard because it was alleged to mystify and sanctify the power of elites under a mound of abstractions and speculation. Even Woodrow Wilson, who had self-consciously tried to distance himself from any institutional formalism, was nonetheless said to lean too far in its direction.

---

1. Arthur Bentley, *The Process of Government: A Study of Social Pressures* (Chicago: University of Chicago Press, 1908), chap. 1 and passim. Bentley's classic was particularly important when its intellectual orientation was recovered and revitalized later by E. Pendleton Herring, David Truman, and others. In its own day, however, it was harshly criticized, if it was not ignored, by many disciplinary leaders who nonetheless shared much of Bentley's criticism of late nineteenth-century political science.

The urge to discover, if not to unmask, the "real behavior" of people and groups acting within institutions helped to germinate a new research agenda for political science. At three Conferences on the Scientific Study of Politics held in the early 1920s, the study of "attitudes" was heralded as the fundamental task of new research. In what might be categorized as the "first behavioral revolution," political scientists stalked "attitudes" by initiating studies of public opinion and propaganda, voting and nonvoting, political socialization and the psychological bases of participation. While the distinctiveness of the discipline's mission was trumpeted, emulation of the techniques, methods, and approaches of other social science disciplines—most notably psychology, sociology, and economics—undergirded the new "realistic" studies.

As critical as they were of formal theories of the state, political scientists of this era remained quite interested in what might be called the study of "democratic state-building" in the American context. Emphasis on the study of attitudes, far from abandoning the study of the state, could help to bring about what Charles Beard called (as printed below) a "democratic state where the rule of the majority is frankly recognized" and "where government . . . is emancipated from formal limitations and charged with direct responsibility to the source of power."

A new realism thus blended with a concern to develop a science of democracy that would support and even help create a positive and purposive government at the helm of the liberal democratic American state. Before World War I, and later as well, political scientists were actively engaged in the establishment of legislative reference bureaus, fact-gathering commissions, and civil-service training institutes at all levels of government.

The optimism in liberal democratic processes that these activities generated was dramatically tempered by World War I and its aftermath. In the next thirty years, optimism—if not America's brand of liberal democracy itself—was put to the test both by events and by the results of the studies initiated by political scientists themselves. Psychological tests conducted during World War I, for example, revealed that the ordinary American soldier was hardly the rational, critical citizen that was supposed to be at the source of democracy. Books published somewhat later, most notably Harold Lasswell's *Psychopathology and Politics* (1930), created real doubts about the long-term viability of democracy. The rise of fascism and communism abroad raised further questions about the safety of liberal democracy in the West, while the Great Depression undermined confidence at home that American democracy, much less the American way of life, was "given" or uniquely exempted from the economic forces of the modern world.

In their responses to the perceived crisis of democratic liberalism, political scientists made many serious contributions of theory and practice. The conscious construction of the social, political, and economic conditions that would fully realize or secure liberal democracy in the American context became a central concern. More sophisticated techniques and methods to study attitudes promoted not only better theories about democratic politics but provided a scientific basis for "social control" and thus the means to change American politics for the better. The election of Franklin Roosevelt as president seemed to make it possible for political scientists to have an enormous impact through public positions. A few, such as Charles Merriam, served directly as advisers to Roosevelt, operating under the belief, as Merriam himself had put it earlier (as printed below), that "unless a higher degree of science can be brought into the operations of government, civilization is in the greatest peril from the caprice of ignorance and passion." Many others served more generally as consultants to commissions on administrative management or on economic planning, or as authors of studies advocating the reform and democratization of political parties. Civic education sparked renewed interest in political scientists who hoped to alter the rather disappointing findings of public opinion research about the citizenry's lack of genuinely democratic attitudes.[2]

Of the six essays included below, those by Charles A. Beard and Charles E. Merriam are particularly instructive examples of the blend of politics and method that animated political scientists in these years. They also provide very forthright treatments of political science's origins and purposes, even though they were written fifteen years apart and from rather different points of view. Remembered more frequently these days as a historian and especially as the author of *An Economic Interpretation of the Constitution of the United States* (1913), Beard was nonetheless the virtual archetype of the reform political scientist of his generation. Beard's essay was originally delivered as an address at Columbia University in 1908, well before his subsequent fame or his presidency of both the American Historical Association and the American Political Science Association. Under the simple title "Politics," it is a judicious but frank attack on what he calls the "axioms" of past politics. It is as clear a defense of the nexus of new forms of study with the rise of Progressive politics as can be found. In Beard's essay, calls for political reform and for a new political science are virtually identical.

Merriam's essay was originally the first part of a progress report issued in

---

2. See, for example, Charles Merriam's *Civic Education in the United States* (New York: Charles Scribner's Sons, 1934), which was part of the American Historical Association's broader Report of the Commission on the Social Studies in the Schools. More generally on the political activities and values during the period, see Barry Karl, *Executive Reorganization and the New Deal* (Cambridge, MA: Harvard University Press, 1963); John Diggins, *Mussolini and Fascism: The View from America* (Princeton: Princeton University Press, 1972); and Barry Karl, *Charles Merriam and the Study of Politics* (Chicago: University of Chicago Press, 1974).

1923 by the Committee on Political Research, which had been established by the APSA two years earlier. The progress report may be understood as one of the defining documents of the "first behavioral revolution" in the years following World War I, and Merriam's essay in the report should be read as one of the discipline's most synoptic overviews of its methodological history. The committee's purpose was to "scrutinize the scope and method of political research in the field of government, with a view to obtaining a clearer view of the actual situation and of offering certain constructive suggestions."[3] In contrast to Beard, with whom he often disagreed, Merriam in his essay emphasizes the necessity for an impartial science of politics, one whose history should be understood in terms of the upward struggle to achieve objectivity, comprehensiveness, and methodological sophistication. In his view, political science ought to follow the lead of more mature scientific disciplines, especially psychology. Indeed, Merriam dates the last of four periods in the development of the discipline with "the beginnings of the psychological treatment of politics." Although impartial in its methods, political science practiced in this way could best serve democracy and achieve its "highest form" in America by developing "more precise methods of political and social control than mankind has hitherto possessed."

The essays by Benjamin E. Lippincott and Harold D. Lasswell present the reflections of two political scientists at the end of the New Deal and on the eve of World War II. Both echo certain of the themes of the Progressive era, at least in their methodological criticism of the discipline and their hopes for its democratic contributions. Surveying the discipline's growth, Lippincott complains that the profession has sinned against reason and courage. Its empiricism (in part, the product of Merriam's efforts) has ignored the systematic study of economics and politics, especially the influence of the upper classes on American politics. Bias, Lippincott argues, is also built into the discipline because its very categories issue from a middle-class professionalism. Foreshadowing later forms of dissent in political science, Lippincott nonetheless stops well short of rejecting the scientific ideal as such. His is an effort to unmask bias but also to urge political scientists to undertake more controversial and democratically relevant research on the role of economic factors in political life.

Lasswell in his essay directly addresses the practical relationship between political science and democracy. A brilliant student of Merriam's at Chicago who, like his teacher, later served as an APSA president, Lasswell gained fame for introducing or popularizing Marxian, Freudian, and Weberian categories in American political science. His research on power, propaganda,

---

3. "Progress Report of the Committee on Political Research," *American Political Science Review* 17 (1923): 274.

public opinion, psychopathology, revolution, and the policy sciences represented an extraordinarily wide range of scholarly achievements. The essay chosen here comes not from his well-known scientific works—most notably *Psychopathology and Politics* (1930) and *Politics: Who Gets What, When, How* (1936)—but from *Democracy through Public Opinion* (1941), which was published just before the American entry into the war and was addressed to a more popular audience. Lasswell's chapter outlines why political scientists and other experts are indispensable to democratic society. While much of Lasswell's pioneering work fostered considerable skepticism about the prospects of democracy, Lasswell here holds that in a world where publics are subject to constant manipulation by elites, political science "experts" and "specialists" can be depended upon, as he puts it below, "to give eyes, ears, hands and feet to morality." Contrary to mere "moralists," researchers have a defined "method of observation" that can provide the means "to discover how democratic attitudes can be guided by proper insight." Here, then, is a classic expression of an argument for scientific expertise and social control as indispensable for modern democracy in mass society.

The section concludes with essays by two contemporary disciplinary historians, David M. Ricci and John G. Gunnell. In different ways, both are concerned with the interplay of political science and democratic liberalism during the prewar period. To Ricci, there is irony, even tragedy, in the political science of the 1920s and 1930s. Throughout the period, scientific evidence mounted against the cherished view that liberal democratic values were ensconced in the citizenry or in American institutions. Indeed, an irrational citizenry, an unresponsive government, and an incipient authoritarianism were political facts of life. Yet, political scientists could not forego defending liberalism because the liberal value of open inquiry helped to make science possible. The consequence, Ricci argues, was that political science wound up defending liberalism not with scientific facts about American political life but with little else than "enthusiasm for the home team."

Gunnell explores what he calls the contemporary "estrangement" of political theory from political science. His vehicle for doing so is an investigation of the origins of the conflict up to and through the 1940s. Gunnell finds that the source of the estrangement was the arrival of émigré scholars from Nazi Germany in the 1930s. Both from the Left (especially the Frankfurt school of critical theorists) and from the Right (including Leo Strauss, Eric Voegelin, and others) the émigrés shocked political scientists by their claims that both liberalism and science were complicit in the rise of totalitarianism. As can be seen by the other essays in this section, most American political scientists of the period took liberal and scientific values for granted. But the émigré attack challenged these values at their core. Gunnell finds that the traditions of political science as they were understood in the prewar period left the discipline undefended. A revolution in the discipline's self-understanding was needed. Thus Gunnell turns our attention to the postwar period and especially to the second, better-known "behavioral revolution," viewing it in good part as a rebellion launched in response to the émigrés' attack.

Politics

Charles A. Beard

Every science begins by laying hold of some definite and tangible facts, and advances by tracing their myriad relations until they are lost in the great complex of things. So politics starts with the government which, in final analysis, is a determinate number of persons in a political community charged with certain public duties, and it advances to a consideration of the phenomena which condition the organization and operations of the government.

It is evident at a casual glance that official performances are not really separable from other actions of the governmental agents themselves or from many of the actions of citizens at large. For instance, the declaration of war against Spain was a political act, but clearly it was only an incident in the sum total of events which led up to the armed conflict. For months before the official proceeding, social forces had been gathering strength, and impinging on the minds of persons charged with transmuting the feeling and will of the nation into the legal state of war. It was by a mere formal process that social realities passed over into political facts.

It is apparent that the jural test of what constitutes a political action draws a dividing line where none exists in fact, and consequently any study of government that neglects the disciplines of history, economics, and sociology will lack in reality what it gains in precision. Man as a political animal acting upon political, as distinguished from more vital and powerful motives, is the most unsubstantial of all abstractions.

It is, however, to my way of thinking a false notion that the ancient and honorable discipline of politics has been overthrown or absorbed by the dissolution of the subject into history, economics, and sociology. Rather does it seem that solid foundations are being laid in reality in place of in the shifting sands of speculation. We are coming to realize that a science dealing with man has no special field of data all to itself, but is rather merely a way of looking at

Reprinted in a somewhat shortened version from "A Lecture Delivered at Columbia University in the Series on Science, Philosophy, and Art, February 12, 1908" (New York: Columbia University Press, 1908).

113

the same thing—a view of a certain aspect of human action. The human being is not essentially different when he is depositing his ballot from what he is in the counting house or at the work bench. In place of a "natural" man, an "economic" man, a "religious" man, or a "political" man, we now observe the whole man participating in the work of government. Politics starts with the observation of such of his acts as may be juristically tested, passes to the acts most nearly related, and then works out into the general field of human conduct. In describing the forms of government, in seeking the historical and social reasons why government in Germany differs from that in France; in explaining the elaborate details of administration; in endeavoring to penetrate the sources of party organization and operation; in comparing the political experiences of different nations, politics has a definite field of its own, even if it does not meet the approval of the high priests of the mathematical and the exact.

It may be conceded at the outset that politics does not possess a single piece of literature as substantial as a table of logarithms or an engineer's handbook, nor a body of doctrine to be applied with celerity as a form of first aid to the injured. And after all, the men of pure science must admit that politicians are scarcely more disputatious over the best form of a primary law than are consulting engineers over the problem of ventilating the subway. In fact all knowledge, when applied to specific problems, even in many branches of natural science, is often at best a dim light, and political knowledge suffers from this general limitation on the human intellect. In spite of the many troubles that beset him, however, the student of politics may rejoice in an ever growing body of sound material, historical on one side, descriptive and statistical on the other.

Archaeologists and anthropologists are disclosing to us primitive types of society which were unknown to Aristotle, Hobbes, and Locke. Vast collections of laws, documents, chronicles, and miscellaneous papers, revealing step by step the processes in the origin and development of the state, have been edited with scientific care by historical investigators. Great treatises like those of Stubbs, Maitland, Gierke, Brunner, Coulanges and Spencer have put the student of politics further in advance of Montesquieu than he was ahead of Marsilius of Padua of the fourteenth century. Governments are now taking censuses on an ever larger scale and on more scientific principles; bureaus are obtaining and arranging data on political experiments of every sort. Private persons, like Charles Booth in his survey of London, are laying bare realities once the subject of futile speculation and thus outside the range of effective political action. From this vast heterogeneous mass of materials are coming an ever sounder notion of the origin, functions, and tendencies of the state, a higher view of its possibilities as the experiments of each nation are placed at the disposal of all, and finally a more scientific theory of causation in politics.

One of the most salutary results of this vast accumulation of data on politics has been to discredit the older speculative theorists and the utopia makers. Even their very interests and presuppositions are being rudely brushed aside. For example, Locke devoted about one half of his famous "Treatises on Government" to rejecting the Adamite source of political authority. Locke proceeded to base his reasoning on an equally unhistorical proposition that "to understand political power aright and derive it from its original we must consider what estate all men are naturally in and that is a state of perfect freedom to order their actions and dispose of their possessions and persons as they think fit within the bounds of the law of nature without asking leave or depending upon the will of any other man."

Quite different from this is the procedure of the student today. If he wants to discover how government originated, how its forms have changed, the tendencies of its evolution, and the forces modifying its structure and functions, he knows that there is no hope for real knowledge except in the painstaking examination of the materials that are left to us—records of past politics, statistical materials on races, groups and classes, and descriptions of the bewildering types of society gathered from the past and from the four corners of the earth.

The influence of the historical school on correct thinking in politics has been splendidly supplemented by that of the Darwinians. They have given us as the political unit not a typical man with typical faculties, but a man infinite in variety and capacity, ranging from the dog-faced cannibals of the Andaman islands to the highest type of modern citizen who surrenders the hope of private gain that he may serve the state. The eighteenth-century philosophers were wrong. We have not been driven from a political paradise; we have not fallen from a high estate, nor is there any final mold into which society is to be cast. On the contrary, society has come from crude and formless associations beginning in a dim and dateless past and moves outward into an illimitable future, which many of us believe will not be hideous and mean, but beautiful and magnificent. In this dynamic society, the citizen becomes the co-worker in that great and indivisible natural process which draws down granite hills and upbuilds great nations.

Some very profound scholars, among them Sir Henry Sumner Maine, have thought that, in spite of this persistency of change, society has arrived at two fundamental notions of permanent validity, namely, freedom of contract and private property. Nevertheless, beyond agreeing that a certain freedom of contract is indispensable to the working of natural selection and that pure communism is a device for angels and not for men, recent writers seem unable to find an abiding place for contract or property. Under feudalism, as we know, some of the most elemental matters of a political nature now fixed in public law were the subjects of free arrangement between sovereign and vassal, while many other matters then determined by status are now left to private agreement. Thus contract like other institutions falls into the flow of things; we are never compelled to choose between status or contract; but we shall have perennial questions as to the positive limits on the kinds of things which men may agree to do.

It is the same with private property. If we trace its evolution from the quasi-communism of primitive times to the age of intangible securities, we find that men's ideas have differed fundamentally as to what particular things should constitute private property. Thus some forms of property have disappeared altogether; the public has laid hold of domains once reserved to the individual; and private rights are becoming more and more penetrated with notions of public welfare. The great question of any age, therefore, is not shall private property as such be abolished, for the nature of man demonstrates that it cannot be, but what forms of property shall be permitted, and to what public uses shall they be subjected. Here politics confronts not axioms of law or polity set like the hills, but complicated social questions to be settled, not in the closet with the philosophers, but amid the multitudinous experiences of the market place where society daily meets the pressing needs of life.

It is not only in possessing sound historical and evolutionary notions that the student of politics lays claim to being more scientific than his predecessors in the eighteenth century. He endeavors more and more to subject his own thinking to the very disciplines of history and evolution. He is convinced of what Professor Dunning has so amply and admirably demonstrated, that political philosophy is the product of the surrounding political system rather than of pure reason. The older philosophers naïvely gave expression to the opinions which logically fitted their respective environments and then apparently unconsciously assigned universal validity to their cogitations. The modern scholar solemnly warned by the fate of the older doctrinaires is on his guard against formulating into a transcendental philosophy either the emotions connected with the status quo, or the ecstatic delight derived from contemplating a perfected humanity. He has a strong suspicion that when his attention is sustained to the highest point and his so-called reasoning faculties are hardest at work, there are welling up within him and finding articulation, forces connected with his own life history and of the race and nation from which he sprang. He knows that it is an almost superhuman doctor who can set the norm for a sound mental eye.

These personal or subjective forces which distort the vision even when we would see straight are both gross and subtle, and they may be divided roughly for practical purposes into three groups—religious, class, and patriotic biases.

Now all of these biases, and many more, are dangerous foes to the ascertainment of truth concerning any set of political facts—which is the real aim of scientific politics and which we have learned from the natural sciences is the best way in the long run to acquire that wisdom which exalts a nation. I hold that it is not the function of the student of politics to praise or condemn institutions or theories, but to understand and expound them; and thus for scientific purposes it is separated from theology, ethics, and patriotism. I know there is high contempt on the part of many persons for the pursuit of learning that does not end in the vindication of their preconceptions, just as, until quite recently, no American history was acceptable in the North that did not charge the South with moral depravity in addition to treason. I believe that on mature deliberation, thoughtful persons, contemplating the ruins which indiscriminate hate and fierce dogmatism have helped to make, will agree that the introduction of a little philosophic calm will not work corruption in the minds of men or undermine the foundations of society. The data secured by scientific investigation may be used by the theologian, the teacher of ethics, and the patriot for their several devices, and the student of politics will rejoice if they will use real facts in the place of pseudo-facts which are too often found in the armory of their arguments.

It is accordingly in the spirit of modern science that the student of politics turns to the great divisions of his subject, namely, the state, government, the limits of government action, political parties, and international relations. No apology need be made for placing the state first, for it is the unit in world politics; it is the highest form of human association yet devised; and with fundamental notions concerning it are connected both ideal impulses and practical policies. In common usage the word *State* is indiscriminately confused with the term nation or political community, but, as Professor Burgess has so clearly and definitively demonstrated, there can be no approach to a science of politics unless we have at the outset a somewhat precise concept of what is meant by the state.

The surface of the earth, at least of the civilized world, is now sharply divided into geographical areas inhabited by distinct political communities produced by ethnological, economic, and other factors. It is apparent to the most casual observer that not all the persons within any particular group—men, women, and children—share in the making of laws or the conduct of government. Moreover, as Sir William Markby urges, the lawyer in dealing with legal questions must always be prepared to prove, if it is denied, that there is a determinate and supreme sovereign or sovereign body whose intentions as regards the matter under consideration are capable of being ascertained and that the commands of this person or body will be obeyed. It is undoubtedly difficult, and sometimes almost impossible, to determine precisely the person or body within a nation which possesses unlimited underived authority over all the others and is capable, under ordinary circumstances and in last resort, of enforcing its authority. Nevertheless for juristic and political purposes such a body must exist, and in many instances it is possible rather sharply to distinguish the state from the nation, especially where there is a recognized ruling class or absolute monarch.

The origin of this sovereign power in the political society is an ancient question and four answers have been made to it. The theologians, in times past, have attributed to the state a divine origin. This theory is now rejected because it does not explain the exact process by which the state came into existence, and if literally accepted would close the doors to research and understanding.

The second theory, which is generally connected with the name of Rousseau, not because he originated it but because it became such a powerful instrument of agitation in his hands, is that the state originated in a compact made in prehistoric times by free individuals. Even Rousseau did not believe the original compact to have been an actual historic fact, but it afforded him the semblance of a natural philosophy as the basis of an attack on the theologians who had a monopoly of the divine right doctrine. The third explanation of the origin of the state, associated with the name of Sir Henry Sumner Maine, views the state as the product of gradual evolution out of patriarchal authority—the original form of domination among human beings. The state is only the enlarged family. This is now rejected on the simple ground that not a single one of the states of Western Europe of whose origin we have tolerable records can be traced genetically to the extension of patriarchal authority.

The real origin of the state, in Western Europe at least, is to be found in conquest, although it must be admitted that power-bearing individuals were previously rising within the older patriarchal groups as a result of the economic discipline they were able to impose on their slaves and semi-free kinsmen. A military leader and his war band, in search of plunder and sources of steady income, conquer and fuse settled communities loosely united by kinship, and settle down upon the subject population as the ruling authority, absorbing surrounding areas by diverse processes. In the beginning, the power of the leader is checked by his war band, but the threads of dominion are slowly gathered into his hands, especially after he becomes king and receives religious sanction, though in the exercise of his battle-born authority he may be always thwarted or swayed on many policies by his warrior aristocracy and the Church Militant.

War thus begets the king; in time the king becomes the prime source of political authority. The strong king proves acceptable in spite of his sometimes cruel despotism and irresponsible actions. His peace protects merchants and cities against robber barons; his courts afford justice—rude and curious—but more certain in principle and more effective in action than the justice of the feudal castle. At his palace learning is cherished; arts and commerce flourish; a middle class of smaller landed proprietors and men of trade is created; it seeks to standardize the king by the strict rules of business. Its members ask the king not to tax them without their consent, not to seize their person or property without observing some regular public forms, not to make laws without asking their opinions. Thus constitutional government is born and thus political authority passes from the king to a portion of his nation. It is sometimes a painful process for the sovereign. If he resists encroachments on his consecrated rights, refuses to conciliate, mistakes the inevitable process for temporary insubordination, then there is a cataclysm and the new form of state is created in the throes of revolution. If the king is wise he contents himself with the insignia of office and continues to symbolize the nation's unity and power. Such in brief is the story of the rise and diffusion of political authority—i.e., sovereignty. It rests not on vacuous speculation, but upon the results of laborious research and patient winnowing on the part of innumerable historical scholars.

It is evident that in this diffusion of political power among the masses the state has lost its ancient definiteness of form, for it is difficult to discover not only who compose the state from the standpoint of law, but also where among those enjoying nominal sovereignty is the real power. It is clear that these thousands of units making up the state are not all equal in intelligence or influence. It is also evident that a great portion of them do not exercise the power which they lawfully have, that another portion has no very lively consciousness of the motives on which it acts, and that the actual will of the state in any one instance is merely that of a majority at best. This problem has received very little attention from students of power, but it would seem that the real state is not the juristic state but is that group of persons able to work together effectively for the accomplishment of their joint aims, and overcome all opposition on the particular point at issue at a particular period of time.

Since the essence of the state is the exercise of sovereign authority by some person or group of persons, it is evident that from the standpoint of jurisprudence there can be only three forms of state—monarchical, aristocratic, and democratic—the rule of the one, the few, or the many. Changes in the form of the state have been caused primarily by the demand of groups for power, and in general these groups have coincided with economic classes which have arisen within the political society.

Corresponding with these three principal stages in the evolution of the forms of state, there have been three general types of government, considered in their fundamental nature rather than their accidental structural aspects. In the absolute monarchy we find the unlimited rule of the sovereign. In the use of the instruments of government, even where they are taken from primitive popular institutions, the absolute monarch is, in law and fact, irresponsible and unrestricted, save by the limitations of nature and the possibilities of revolt on the part of his subjects. In the aristocratic state, where the prerogatives of the sovereign are in reality shared by a portion of his subjects, the agents of government are positively limited by the effective will of the minority thus admitted to power. The result is a balancing of the titular sovereign against the interests of those who divide dominion with him, and the establishment of a disjointed government, inefficient for positive action on a large scale and characterized by that irresponsibility which division of power inevitably engenders. In the democratic state, where the rule of the majority is frankly recognized (a condition of affairs gravely feared by the framers of our Constitution), government tends toward a type, unified in internal structure, emancipated from formal limitations, and charged with direct responsibility to the source of power.

This tendency in the evolution of state and government has been fully grasped by many students in the United States who have broken away from the familiar notion that we are living under a peculiar dispensation in the matter of political institutions. President Woodrow Wilson opened the way a few years ago by his splendid study of Congressional Government, in which he protested against further belief in "political witchcraft" [and] urged a frank consideration of the defects of the Constitution. Two other American scholars, Mr. Henry Jones Ford and Professor Goodnow, have further advanced clear thinking on American politics by revealing the intimate character of the relation between our democratic society and the framework of government built upon eighteenth-century ideas, which were misunderstood by their formulators and have been abandoned by the nation from which they were originally drawn. These scholars have conclusively shown the unreality of the doctrine of divided powers, and the positive fashion in which our democratic political society seeks through extra-legal party organization to overcome the friction of a disjointed machine. They urge that a separation of powers is in practice impossible, claiming that the function of government is two-fold—the expression and execution of popular will—and that the body that wills must, in the nature of things, control the body that executes, if government is to be efficient. Following out this contention, these writers maintain that our strong party machinery is the extra-legal instrument with which democracy strives to obtain that coordination of legislative and executive functions. They admit, however, that this attempt to control through powerful party engines is fraught with serious evils, that the confusion and division of authority among the organs of government render direct and transparent responsibility impossible, and that an element of uncertainty and distraction is added by our practice of submitting complex social and economic questions to the juristic tests of the Courts.

Since radical changes in the framework of government are outside the field of practical politics at present, there has been a decided tendency recently to attempt the establishment of responsible government by securing, through primary legislation, the responsibility of the party organization which operates the government. Provision for popular control of party has gone so far in Wisconsin as to require the nomination of practically all candidates by direct vote. Other states have gone farther and sought more effective supervision in the form of direct legislation, placing the popular will above all governmental instruments. To some this seems to be adding only cumbersome complications to our politics, but to others it appears to be only our circuitous way of achieving legislative responsibility.

In thus coming to recognize in clear and direct responsibility the essence of democratic government, American students are changing many of their earlier notions about the details of administrative organization. They no longer believe that democracy requires the election of every officer from the street sweeper to the state health commissioner, and they are now advocating centralization of administration (once regarded as a species of original sin) and secure tenure for technical officials as the primary necessities of efficient government. Where responsibility can be firmly and unequivocably secured, power may be safely entrusted to the agents of government, and to meet the great centralizing tendency in our economic institutions (the basis of all political institutions) power must be so entrusted, in order to administer effectively the very laws upon which the permanence of popular government depends.

The enormous burden which maintenance of this extra-legal responsibility has thrown upon the political party in the United States has given it a peculiar position in our political system, though its operations were almost neglected by our students until Mr. Bryce called attention to them. Now we are becoming alive to the fact that juristic descriptions of the forms of government incur the danger of being mere abstractions when party customs are left out of account. For example, the jurist in describing the Federal government will say that the House of Representatives elects the speaker, but as a matter of plain fact the speaker is really selected by a caucus of the majority party held after many dinners and political tempests. Constitutional law has nothing to say about committees, but everybody knows that our laws are made by the committees and log-rolling. Examples might be multiplied indefinitely and the story pushed so far that a practical treatise on government would give party organization and methods the text, and reduce the formal law to the footnotes.

Patent and important as this fact is, the student of politics is compelled to admit that we have no scientific descriptive works on the formal organization of parties or their real practices. We have, it is true, many works purporting to relate the history of parties, a few excellent studies such as the beginnings made by Ostrogorski and Bryce, and no little theorizing on the functions of parties, but we have no account of the actual historical processes by which the party has arisen and, as an extra-legal institution, controls the legal forms of government. Rich as are our political and social statistics, we have made no considerable attempts to discover inductively the precise composition of parties or their relation to surrounding social and economic phenomena. We have no philosophical treatise on the process by which the party becomes an institution commanding allegiance and punishing for treason. Under these circumstances it seems to me that the party in general and particular, as a centre of power and a working institution, offers the richest field of investigation now open to the student of politics, and the results of really scientific investigation would have the highest theoretical and practical value.

The work of the student of politics is by no means complete when he has described the forms of state and government and the operations of the latter through party control, for underlying all problems of politics is the fundamental question of the limits on government interference with individual activity. During the early part of the nineteenth century it was thought in certain quarters that this problem was settled for all time by the solution advanced by the laissez-faire school who proposed to limit the functions of government to the maintenance of peace, the protection of property, and the enforcement of contracts—"anarchy plus the police constable."

Nevertheless, like all other political philosophies, the doctrine of laissez-faire has been compelled to submit to the limitations imposed by theoretic criticism and the march of events. On one hand, it was pushed to extremes by that type of anarchist, conscious or unconscious of the nature of his philosophy, who agreed with the laissez-faire school that the government was a necessary evil. This rebel against the institution of government went to the logical extremity of declaring that governmental intervention to protect private property, especially in the form of inheritance, was a violation of the first principles of competition—the struggle of all against each and each against all, resulting in the survival of the fittest.

On the other hand, the beneficent results of buying in the cheapest market and selling in the dearest, regardless of all human considerations and the waste it entailed, were not realized in the social life of England during the period in which the doctrines of laissez-faire were at their height. Indisputable evidence of the distressing state of affairs is to be found in the bulky volumes of the parliamentary reports, in the memoirs of the enlightened men who investigated the conditions in the factory centres, and in the dry pages of the statutes revealing the wrongs which parliament sought to remedy. After considerable time had elapsed the scholars came to see the palpable untruth in the statement that the government has no concern in economic matters. The government defines what shall be the subjects of private property, provides the laws of inheritance, places burdens in the form of taxation, prescribes the terms on which corporations are formed, in short fixes the entire juridical framework in which economic laws operate—a fact too often neglected by political economists. In time men came to learn that society is no more a fortuitous collection of warring individuals than one of Beethoven's symphonies is a mere chance assemblage of individual notes. Evolution in the business world also rendered obsolete the abstract propositions of laissez-faire which were tenable enough before the universal extension of the factory process and the organization of business in national and international forms. As a result of philosophic considerations and the pressure of fact no student of politics today will attempt to lay down dogmatically what government in all times and places should undertake to do, for he realizes that what the government does in practice depends not upon any theory about its proper functions, but upon the will of the group of persons actually in control at any one time or upon the equilibrium that is established through conflicts among groups seeking to control the government.

Turning from the field of theory to practice, we find that three powerful forces are now at work pressing for an increase in the functions of government. First in order of historical importance is paternalism or the effort of the upper classes (through sympathy or fear) to advance the interests and security of the working class. This form of state interference is less popular among the more purely individualistic industrial nations where the cash nexus has more fully supplanted the personal relation.

A second group of advocates of increased government activity is fundamentally individualistic in the old sense of the word, insomuch as its members seek to use the arm of the law to destroy, or closely restrict, large corporations in order to encourage the diffusion of real property and the intensification of competition. Thus we have the paradox of extreme individualists calling on the government to interfere in economic matters to a certain degree for the purpose of forestalling the possibility of a future intervention on a larger scale.

A third force working for state interference is the constant increase in the huge industrial army that inevitably accompanies the advance of mechanical revolution in production and distribution. The mediaeval system in which each worker owned and controlled his simple implements and conducted his business in his own fashion has disappeared forever and in place of it has come a divorce of the laborer from his tools—the ownership and management of which have passed largely into the hands of a relatively small proportion of the population. It is demonstrable, of course, that there are gradations of fortune in modern industrial communities and that persons are constantly passing from the working class into other ranks, but this should not be permitted to obscure the permanence of that class itself as an inevitable concomitant of the industrial revolution. There is therefore in every Western nation a vast class of persons without land, tools, or homes, dependent for a livelihood upon the sale of their labor power, and subject to the fluctuations of modern business.

As the doctrines of divine right formerly had no permanent validity for the rising middle class, so the doctrines of individual liberty—trial and indictment by jury and due process of law—do not have the same reality to the workingman that they have to members of the possessing group. Freedom of contract between an employer and an employe with a few days' supplies behind him obviously cannot have the same meaning that it has between persons similarly situated as far as economic goods are concerned. To discourse on the liberty afforded by jury trial to a man who has never appeared in a court but often suffers from considerable periods of unemployment is to overlook the patent fact that liberty has economic as well as legal elements.

Quite naturally this new industrial democracy is evolving a political philosophy of its own, confused and inarticulate in diverse ways, but containing many positive elements ranging from minor modifications of the labor contract to the socialist doctrine that the passive ownership of property is merely a special privilege to be eliminated by the use of the government as the collective instrument for the administration of all important forms of concrete capital. With the large implications of this new philosophy, the student of politics need not tarry unless he is of a speculative turn of mind, but its concrete manifestations in the form of labor parties, and the precise nature and points of their pressure on existing governmental functions constitute a new and important branch of research and exposition.

As a result of all these forces and the growing complexity of our civilization, along with the increasing possibilities of effective collective action, the burdens of our governments tend to multiply, and the stress once laid on individual liberty in the juristic sense is being diminished. Our own Congress, in obedience to these new economic forces, seems willing to stretch to its utmost its powers of regulating industrial operations and protecting the working class; and in its extension of the notions of the police power, the Supreme Court reveals the existence of this new pressure in our political jurisprudence.

A fifth and, in certain aspects, almost new division of political research may be denominated world politics. Of course we have long had treatises on the history and forms of diplomacy and also upon international law as a system of rules recognized and enforced by the tribunals of enlightened nations. But the marvelous expansion of trade and commerce which have refashioned the map of Africa in our own day, awakened the slumbering nations of the East and the islands of the seas, has brought new problems of universal interest which we have scarcely begun to analyze. They embrace such questions as the meaning and tendency of race conflicts, the control of the tropics, the attitude of imperial nations toward subject races, the best forms of colonial administration. The shuttle of trade and intercourse flies ever faster and it may be weaving the web for a world state. It may be that steam and electricity are to achieve what neither the armies, nor the law, nor the faith of Rome could accomplish—that unity of mankind which rests on the expansion of a common consciousness of rights and wrongs through the extension of identical modes of economic activity.

In closing this lecture, it seems desirable that I should indicate more precisely some of the tendencies in the scientific literature of politics. In comparing the political writings of the last twenty-five years with earlier treatises one is struck with decreasing reference to the doctrine of natural rights as a basis for political practice. The theory has been rejected for the reason that it really furnishes no guide to the problems of our time and because we have come to recognize since Darwin's day that the nature of things, once supposed to be eternal, is itself a stream of tendency.

Along with decreasing references to natural rights there has gone an increasing hesitation to ascribe political events to Providential causes. As in history, scholars are seeking natural and approximate causes; they treat politics as a branch of sociology; and leave to the theologian and philosopher the ascertainment of the ultimate rationale of the whole complex.

Closely related in spirit to the tendency to elucidate political questions by reference to divine will was the somewhat later notion that divergences in the history and institutions of different peoples were to be explained on the ground of racial characteristics. Now, it is not to be denied that there are such things as race characteristics, but as Seeley warns us "we should be slow to allege mere national character in explanation of great historical phenomena. No explanation is so obvious or suggests itself so easily. No explanation is so vague, cheap, and so difficult to verify. Why did the English gain freedom so early? Anyone can answer, because they are English and it is the nature of Englishmen to love liberty. I call this a cheap explanation. It is easily given and almost impossible to verify. It is the more suspicious because it gratifies national vanity." Wherever Hegel, with his *Patriotismus* reduced to a science, has been dethroned there is a decided tendency to look to economic and material facts rather than to race psychology as the most reliable sources of institutional differences.

The practical outcome of this rejection of the divine and racial theory of institutions is a persistent attempt to get more precise notions about causation in politics, and this is destined to have a high practical value. The heat with which the politicians cite the fate of the Roman empire as evidence of what will happen to the United States if the Philippines are retained and a thousand experiences of political life bear witness that a treatise on causation in politics would be the most welcome contribution which a scholar of scientific training and temper could make.

After all I have said about the fields of political research and the intensely human and practical nature of the questions which students of politics have to consider, it may seem a work of supererogation to refer to the actual service of the science of the nation. Nevertheless, I believe a word of defence should be spoken, for in this world of ours we are turning keen and troubled faces to the instant need of things, and it is wise that we should. Decidedly real as are the subjects with which the student of politics deals, it must be admitted that he suffers many disadvantages when he endeavors to meet the call for practical receipts guaranteed to cure quickly. The nation as a whole is a high abstraction; it seldom demands remedies; it is groups within the state that demand remedies. Shipbuilders want ship subsidies; workingmen want labor legislation. The desirability of their demands cannot be referred to eternal standards; what they will probably get will depend more on the power and effectiveness of their organization than upon sweet political reasonableness. If the student of politics prescribes a remedy which pleases the group that applies, he will probably be hailed as a scientist; if his suggestion is unpalatable, he is only a professor anyhow.

Notwithstanding this fact, politics renders a high service in general and in details. Statesmen have gained in breadth and firmness of perspective in proportion as they have deliberated upon one or all of the great subjects which fall within the domain of politics. The origin, tendencies, and destiny of human society politically organized are subjects, moreover, which appeal to the highest type of a citizen. The ideals arising from the contemplation of experience and the potentialities of the future, more than anything else differentiate human from animal societies. Mature consideration of the problems of state in the grand outlines helps to transform petty politicians into statesmen, and inspires them to press on even when in the midst of party squabbles they lament with Machiavelli the "fickleness and folly of a vain world." The discipline that comes from deliberating upon great things, even though we see through the glass darkly, has a real value though it cannot be weighed in scales or sold over the counter.

To speak more modestly of politics, I shall descend into particulars. Politics renders a service by the collection and classification of data, by the description of institutions and experiments, and this service alone justifies it in claiming a high place in the university. The recent sane tendencies of legislative bodies to construct laws on reports of expert commissions rather than on impulse and high notions of popular prerogative, however legitimate, is only an application of the scientific method and spirit of politics as a university subject. Such action is not infallible, but surely we may agree with Diderot that the use of such reason as we have is not indecent. As I view it, accordingly, it is the function of the university research in politics to seek the truth concerning special problems simply in the spirit of science.

It is the duty of the teacher to say to his pupils: Observe these facts, consider these varying explanations, ponder upon these theories, study the most impartial records of political operations, look to the future as well as the past, and as a citizen of this great nation build this discipline of the mind into the thought and action of afterlife. Book-learning cannot make a wise man of a fool nor a great statesman out of a village politician; it cannot correct nature's mistakes, but it may open highways to her potentialities. Technical information is the necessary part of the equipment of the person who intends entering the actual service of the state, and the wisdom that comes from a wide and deep and sympathetic study of the political experiences of men is the true foundation of that invisible government, described by Ruskin, which wears no outward trappings of law, diplomacy, or war, but is exercised by all energetic and intelligent persons, each in his own sphere, regulating the inner will and secret ways of the people, essentially forming its character and preparing its fate.

Recent Advances in Political Methods

Charles E. Merriam

Recent History of Political Thinking

The purpose of this survey was to examine the development of methods of inquiry in recent years in the field of political science and of the related social sciences. It was also proposed to examine specifically the advance made in methods of the study of government in the United States. And finally it was proposed to sum up the principal advances in method in the study of government and the chief remaining obstacles.

An adequate analysis of recent political thought requires at the outset a look at the fundamental factors conditioning the intellectual processes of the time. Here if time permitted we might sketch the outlines of the larger social forces of the time, such as industrialism, nationalism, urbanism, feminism. We might examine the larger group interpretations as seen in the theories of the middle class, of the business group, or of the labor group, and we might scrutinize the rationalizations of the several race groupings of the time. Any thorough inquiry would necessitate some such wide-sweeping view of the forces that so profoundly affect the character and method of political thought. For present purposes it will be assumed, however, that such an inquiry has been made and that its results are fresh in the mind of the inquirer. It would also be desirable and necessary to examine the general intellectual technique of the time as reflected in philosophy, in religion, and in science. Obviously it is necessary for the purposes of such a paper as this to assume that this survey has already been made. We may then advance to a more minute inquiry into the methods of political thought in the narrower sense of the term. It will be necessary to advance with great rapidity in order to cover the ground within reasonable limits of space, but it is hoped that it may prove possible to sketch the main outlines of the development of political thinking in recent times adequately for the purposes of considering what methods are now open to the

Reprinted in a somewhat shortened version from *American Political Science Review* 17 (1923): 274–95. Also published in Merriam, *New Aspects of Politics* (Chicago: University of Chicago Press, 1925), pp. 107–48. Copyright 1925, 1931 by The University of Chicago.

use of political scientists, and what the relative advantages of these methods may be.

Methods in Related Fields

The development of methods of inquiry in related fields of social science is so intimately associated with progress in the study of government that advances in the various social disciplines will be briefly sketched at this point.

Politics has been placed under obligations to economics during the recent period of development. The classical and historical schools of the first part of the nineteenth century were continued and expanded, but new forms of economic speculation came into vogue. The climax of the classical school was found in the writings of the famous British economist, Alfred Marshall, who while in many ways eclectic in his theory may perhaps most accurately be characterized as a neo-classicist. The historical school found noted expounders, particularly among the German thinkers, in the writings of Wagner, Schmoller, and others. In the main, however, these thinkers continued the development of the classical and historical types of economic reasoning already begun in the first half of the nineteenth century.

In the meantime there appeared the Austrian school of economics evolving the doctrine of subjective value, or what might loosely be called psychological values. In the writings of Wieser, Menger, and Böhm-Bawerk, emphasis was shifted from the earlier forms of analysis to another aspect of the economic process which they called the subjective and which some others term psychological. Here we have an attempt to interpret economic values in terms of mental attitudes, suggesting but by no means realizing, the later developments of psychology.

Following the Austrian school came the study of economic motives, instincts, tendencies or traits, in short the inquiry into economic behavior. These inquiries were by no means complete, in fact they were characteristically inchoate. Their chief significance thus far is the emphasis laid upon another aspect of economic thinking. These scattered inquiries mark, as in the political field, the beginnings of another line of observation and reasoning.

The doctrine of the economic interpretation of history, developed in the middle of the nineteenth century by historians and economists was a subject of further analysis and application.[1] Loria, following Marx, undertook an interpretation of institutions in terms of economic interests and forces which, while not very skillfully executed, was symptomatic of general tendencies. The socialist group in general utilized the doctrine of the economic basis of politics for purposes of class propaganda. Generally speaking this emphasis

---

1. See E. R. A. Seligman, *The Economic Interpretation of History.*

upon the economic factor in social life found wider and wider acceptance among the students of politics.

There was a pronounced tendency, however, to inquire into the social and psychological causes of events as well as the more strictly economic. It became evident that unless "economic" was used as an all-inclusive term covering the whole material environment it would be inadequate as an explanation of human behavior in all instances. While it was frequently asserted that men reason in terms of their economic interests, seldom was the question raised as to what determined their precise type of thought. Obviously the interpretation of the same economic interests might differ and even conflict, in which case the reason for the variation must be sought elsewhere than in the economic force itself and must lie in the forms or types of thinking. If out of exactly similar economic situations diametrically opposed conclusions or widely varying types of reasons were developed, it is clear that some other factor than the economic interest must have entered into the forces that produced the result.

The study of history during this period developed materials of great significance to political science, although its influence is not as notable as in the second and third quarters of the nineteenth century. At that time the historical method had swept the field both in jurisprudence and in economics. The German historical jurisprudence and the German national economics had illustrated in a striking fashion the influence of the historical method of inquiry. In this period the historical influence was unquestionably dominant, although toward the end of the era it tended to weaken and decline where it was supplanted by processes of actual observation and of psychological and statistical analysis.

History itself was profoundly influenced by the same set of forces that were gradually changing the character of the study of government.[2] The conflict between romanticism and positivism in this period was vigorously conducted but on the whole the idealists seemed to yield to the attacks of the historical realists or materialists. Buckle, Ranke, Lamprecht, and in America writers of the type of Turner, recognized the influence of mass, races, societies, economic and social tendencies in determining the course of historical events and they reached out with great avidity for illustrative material of different types. History ceased to be purely military or political, and tended to become either economic or social history, while in some instances historical materialism triumphed completely and the course of events was interpreted altogether in terms of the action and interaction of environmental influences.

From the point of view of political science, however, an immense

---

2. See G. P. Gooch, *History and Historians in the Nineteenth Century;* Croce, *Theory and History of Historiography,* especially chap. 7 on the "Historiography of Positivism."

amount of institutional political history was uncovered and made available, and in the absence of a more definite technique on the part of the students of politics and in the absence of an adequate number of observers and students of government, the boundary lines between government and history were blurred, as indeed they must always overlap, and the technical writing of the history of politics was still in the hands of the historical group. Economists, however, tended to take over the evolution of economic thought and institutions as did the workers in the field of material science. The review of the scientific processes and forms was completely taken over by the technicians in the various scientific disciplines, as in the case of the history of mathematics, the history of chemistry, and the history of physics.

Significant advances were made in the last generation by the sociologists, who began the study of social organization and process in systematic fashion. While much of the work of Comte and Spencer was abandoned, there remained an inpulse toward the development of a science of society, which enlisted the sympathy of many students.[3] The work of Gumplowicz, Ratzenhofer, Simmel, Durkheim, Tarde, LeBon and, in America, Small, Ross, and Giddings, was a notable contribution to the understanding of the social process. For the sociologists a central problem was that of social control, to which political control was incidental and collateral, but inevitably the study of the one subject threw light upon the other. Of special significance was the attention directed by these students to the importance of social forces and social groups in the development and functioning of political forces, purposes, and institutions. Political scientists of the type of Bodin in the sixteenth and Gierke in the nineteenth century had directed attention to these factors, but they had been somewhat neglected and new interest and study of them was imperatively needed.

The sociologists did not arrive at a very definite social technology, but they struggled hard with the problem and made certain advances of note. The use of the social survey was an achievement of value in the understanding of the social process and tended to introduce more exact methods into the task of social measurement. The frequent use of the case method was also an accomplishment of great utility in the development of the more accurate study of social phenomena.

Of great significance in the methods of political science were the inquiries in the fields of anthropology, ethnology, and archaeology. Here were opened out wide vistas in the early development of the race and in the study of the characteristics of the various groups of mankind. In the field of quantitative measurement, anthropology made material progress, endeavoring to work

---

3. See H. A. Barnes, "The Contribution of Sociology to Political Science," *American Political Science Review* (15): 487; Albion W. Small, "Sociology," in *Encyclopaedia Americana.*

out the characteristics of groups by means of physical standards and tests. Even anthropology, however, was often overlaid with race prejudice or with national influence or propaganda of an absurdly transparent type.

In the field of psychology progress was rapid. Advancing from purely philosophical inquiry to the standardized and comparable methods of observation, psychology tended to become an instrument of relative precision and uniformity in its application. It was no longer introspective and meditative alone, but developed instruments for making observation standardizable and comparable, and began to make possible a clearer understanding of human behavior, and of what had hitherto been charted as the great unknown in human nature. The significance of psychology for political inquiry was not at first fully appreciated, but in time the results of the psychologists began to be appreciated by the student of government and of social science. Political psychology began to be a subject of discussion and the terminology of psychology came into common although not accurate use in political inquiry. Psychology began also to find practical application to the problems of government.

In still broader fashion social psychology tried to solve the problem, dealing not merely with individuals but with the group, or with the intricate interrelations between groups. Here we approach closely the work of some of the sociologists who were interested in the same problem and undertook somewhat the same type of examination.

Methods of Political Inquiry

The philosophical treatment of politics, firmly established in the seventeenth and eighteenth centuries, continued in recent time, but with less notable examples of logical method than in the eighteenth or earlier nineteenth century. John Stuart Mill's type of political and social reasoning had marked the end of an epoch of speculation among English thinkers, as had that of Hegel among the German philosophers.[4] Bosanquet was an apostle of neo-Hegelianism, while Hobhouse discussed the metaphysical theory of the state. Sorel, an engineer, and Cole, a mediaevalist, discussed political problems in philosophical style, while Bertrand Russell, the brilliant mathematician, essayed a theory of politics. The pragmatists, best represented by Dewey, definitely set about to effect a reconciliation between philosophy and affairs, and to develop a type of logic adequate to the demands of the situation. In the main, however, it is clear that the a priori speculation upon political questions was on the decline as compared with the thinking of the eighteenth and nineteenth centuries.

Many thinkers approached the problem of government from the juristic

---

4. See Mill's *Logic;* William Dunning, *A History of Political Theories,* part 3, chap. 4.

point of view, and primarily their method was the logic of the law. But in many of the leading instances, this attitude was modified by other forms of inquiry. Thus Gierke was essentially a student of the genesis of political ideas. Maitland and Pollock were also deeply interested in the genetic processes of legal development. Von Jhering, with his far-reaching doctrine of social interests, the protection of which is the chief concern of the law, was deeply affected by the social studies of his time, and showed the profound influence of the social science of his day. Berolzheimer was imbued with the influence of social and economic forces in shaping the course of law and government. Duguit was likewise fundamentally affected by the rising study of social forces and of sociology in systematic form. Pound with his sociological jurisprudence is a modern illustration of the same general tendency. Jellinek with the theory of subjective public law and Wurzel with his projection theory are conspicuous examples of legal logic modified by psychology and by the consideration of social forces.

The study of criminology followed another line of advance, proceeding with Lombroso and his more conservative followers to adopt methods of measurement, to consider the influence of the environment and statistical analysis foreign to the speculations of the stricter juristic group, but enormously fruitful in ultimate result upon the nature of penology. In this respect these studies differed widely from the current type of legal speculation, placing itself upon the basis of scientific inquiry rather than upon precedent or the logic of the law.

A frequent way of approach to the study of politics has been the historical inquiry into the development of political institutions. The modern historical movement began as a reaction against the doctrinaire theories of the French revolutionary period, and swept through the domain of law and government. In recent times it has been a well-traveled road toward political conclusions and much of the energy in political research has been expended in this field. A survey of the literature of the time shows that the bulk of the output falls under this category. The process of development is employed for the purpose of illustrating broad movements and tendencies of political and social forces, and perhaps deducing certain lessons, morals, or laws from the examination of the past. Thus the previous development of the institution or the people is used to explain its present status or its probable future tendency. In these situations the history of political ideas or customs or forms or institutions becomes the background for the consideration of its present situation.

Another method has been that of comparison of various types of institutions, with a view of classifying, analyzing, discovering similarities and dissimilarities in them. Here we have a study of comparative government or law which, while using historical material, is not confined to an inspection of the genetic process, but employs contemporary material as a basis for political reasoning. Industrious researches of this type have been carried on in recent years both by jurists and by students of government. Kohler is a conspicuous example of this juristic group and Bryce of the other. Freeman, Seeley, Sidgwick, Hasbach, Laband, and many others have employed similar methods. In general, description and classification are developed in this way and certain useful comparisons and analogies are set up.

With the comparison of types there came to be a body of political science centering around the observation and description of actual processes of government, as distinguished from historical development or from comparisons of existing types of organization and structure. Much of Bryce's work fell under this head, as did that of Ostrogorski, Redlich, and Lowell. Bryce's *Modern Democracies*, Ostrogorski's *Democracy and the Organization of the Party System*, Lowell's *Government of England*, and Redlich's *Local Government in England* are examples of this method of studying government. Many monographic studies of the workings of particular institutions were made in various parts of the world, some decidedly descriptive and structural and some more noticeably analytical. Many of these studies were of course combined with historical inquiries and comparative and analogical researches.

Closely associated with the development of comparison of types and observation of processes was the form of investigation which came to be called the survey. This method of investigation appeared almost simultaneously in economics, government, and sociology. The essence of the survey was the actual observation of forces in operation, with an effort to measure these forces and to standardize some system of measurement. The survey owed much to the engineers and the accountants who contributed materially to its development. The engineer was of course the original surveyor laying out his lines and conducting his measurements with great accuracy and precision. Surveys of human behavior were also taken up by the industrial engineers especially in the form of the time and motion studies of the Taylor-Emerson type. Here we have an effort at precise measurement of human behavior in the shape of what was commonly called scientific management. At the outset these studies omitted the basic factor of psychology, but later on they reinstated this essential element in their calculations although not achieving complete success in this undertaking. The accountant also aided through the analysis of financial data leading to the creation of cost accounting, a process which led to an objective appraisal of human behavior or human services rendered for specific purposes. Thus the accountant and the engineer have given a sharper point to the observation of political forces and processes than it had ever had before.

The social survey was developed by the sociologists approaching the inquiry from another point of view. Much was undoubtedly due to the efforts of city workers of the type of Booth in London and many other scattered students. The classic type of large-scale survey employing modern methods was the Pittsburgh Survey, followed by many others, usually upon a smaller scale. The survey of course contained elements of advertising, or publicity, or even propaganda, as well as an element of scientific analysis, and sometimes the advertising features overtopped the scientific analysis, but in the main it directed attention specifically toward concrete factors which were observed objectively and as far as possible measured accurately, analyzed, and compared carefully.

The political survey developed most rapidly in the United States and especially in the urban communities. The large-scale losses and wastes in the expenditures in cities challenged attention, and specialized grafting was met by specialized analysis and inquiry for the purposes of community protection. These investigations while carried on by trained students of political science were usually conducted outside of the academic walls. The leader in this movement was the New York Bureau of Municipal Research followed by the many other similar agencies in Chicago, Philadelphia, Cleveland, and elsewhere. The political survey was the immediate observation of the operations of government combined with the effort to measure these operations as precisely as possible and to organize methods of comparison and conduct analysis of facts observed. This method was distinct from the juristic method or the historical method or the historical-comparative method in that it substituted actual observations of government in operation and made strenuous efforts toward precise measurement. These efforts were not always wholly successful, but at any rate they were movements in the direction of precision. Later, similar undertakings were set on foot by state governments and by the United States government. In England also national inquiries of the same character have been carried through on a considerable scale.

Another group of thinkers approached the study of government from the point of view of psychology, or of social psychology, bordering upon what might be called political psychology. Of these by far the most conspicuous was the English thinker, Graham Wallas, whose *Human Nature in Politics,* and the later and more systematic study, *The Great Society,* started a new line of political investigation and opened up new avenues of research. It is interesting to compare Wallas's chapters on material and method of political reasoning with the famous chapters in Mill's *Logic* on the logic of the moral sciences.

Wallas, originally a student of the classics, later interested in practical political activity, reacted against the consideration of government in terms of form and structure and undertook an interpretation in terms of human nature. This method of inquiry seemed to involve the development of a type of political psychology. In his *Great Society* Wallas considered political forces as organized around the three fundamental factors of intelligence, love, and happiness, on the basis of which he endeavored to rebuild a political theory and a political structure. In *Our Social Heritage* he opened out still other forms of subtle analysis of political processes, hitherto unexplored.

Wallas's work was brilliant, stimulating, and suggestive, rather than systematic. While he discussed the influence and importance of quantitative measurement of political phenomena, he did not make elaborate use of statistical data in his work; and while he continually emphasized the significance of a psychology of politics, he did not advance far in that direction. But on the whole his work was a decided variation from that of his predecessors or contemporaries, and his impetus to a new method was a notable one. An interesting comparison might be made between the method of John Stuart Mill, that of Lord Bryce, and that of Graham Wallas, all significant figures in the shaping of English political thought.

Walter Lippmann followed much the same method as his early instructor, Wallas, notably in his *Preface to Politics* and in his *Public Opinion*. Lippmann made wider use of contemporary psychological advances than did Wallas, however. A significant phase of his discussion is the analysis of organized intelligence in the concluding chapters of *Public Opinion*. This is a plea for the establishment of an intelligence bureau in the several departments of the government, and for a central clearing house of intelligence centers. Accompanying this is the suggestion for the articulation of these intelligence centers with the work of the professional students of government in the development of the problems of "terminology, of definition, of statistical technic, of logic."

There were also eclectic types of thinkers employing several of the methods just described. There was no writer who did not employ logic and history and comparison and analogy at various times. Even the most dogmatic lapsed into statistics at times, and the most statistically inclined developed philosophical attitudes somewhat inconsistent with the general position of the statistician. Differences in method were often differences in emphasis and in degree rather than in kind. Nevertheless the differences were appreciable and significant evidences of the general tendency in methods of political theory. Broadly speaking they indicate the following to be the chief lines of development of the study of political processes:

1. The a priori and deductive method down to 1850
2. The historical and comparative method, 1850–1900
3. The present tendency toward observation, survey, measurement, 1900–
4. The beginnings of the psychological treatment of politics

Summary of Advances and Difficulties

From another point of view we may summarize the advances in the study of politics in the period since the vogue of the natural-law philosophy, roughly speaking during the last one hundred years, as:

1. The tendency toward comparison of varying types of political ideas, institutions, processes; toward analyzing similarities and dissimilarities.
2. The tendency toward closer scrutiny of economic forces in their relation to political processes, in some cases extending to the economic interpretation of all political phenomena. In this, the relative ease of quantitative measurement of certain economic facts greatly aided the process, in fact tending to an extension of economic beyond the ordinary usage of the term.
3. The tendency toward the consideration of social forces in their relation to political processes. At times this took the form of a social interpretation of all political facts.
4. The tendency toward closer examination of the geographical environment, and its influence upon political phenomena and processes.
5. The tendency toward closer consideration of a body of ethnic and biological facts, in their relation to political forces.
6. These influences taken together set up another relationship between political phenomena and the whole environment, both social and physical. Crude analogies of this kind had already been made by Bodin and Montesquieu, but these were by no means as fully developed as the later and far more minute and searching inquiries.
7. The tendency to examine the genetics of political ideas and institutions. This was the joint product of history and biology with their joint emphasis on the significance of historical growth and development and of the evolutionary theory of life. Since the middle of the nineteenth century, it has operated powerfully upon all political thought.
8. The joint tendency to combine a view of the environment (economic, social, physical) as a whole, with the genetic or evolutionary point of view may be said to have effected a profound and indeed almost revolutionary change in political thinking. Certainly this is true in comparison with the static doctrine of scholasticism, or with the absolutistic tendencies of the *Naturrecht* school of thought.
9. The tendency toward more general use of quantitative measurement of political phenomena. On the one side this took the form of statis-

tics or the mathematical analysis of political processes. The great agency through which this was brought about was the census, which prepared great masses of material, for the use of the observer and the analyst. Two disciplines in particular were able to apply the quantitative methods with especial success. These were anthropology and psychology, in which domains notable advances were made in the direction of measurement.

10. Political psychology was foreshadowed but not at all adequately developed during this time.

These tendencies taken together may be said to constitute the most significant changes in the character of political thought down to the present day. Significant defects in the scientific development of the study of government are as follows:

1. Lack of comprehensive collections of data regarding political phenomena, with adequate classification and analysis
2. Tendency toward race, class, nationalistic bias in the interpretation of data available
3. Lack of sufficiently precise standards of measurement and of precise knowledge of the sequence of processes

Some fundamental difficulties in the scientific study of political processes are readily discerned:

1. The paradox of politics is that group discipline must be maintained in order to preserve the life of the group against internal and external foes; but that rigid discipline itself tends to destroy those vital forces of initiative, criticism, and reconstruction without which the authority of the group must die. There must be general conformity with the general body of rules and regulations laid down by the state, otherwise there is no advance upon anarchy; but there must also be reasonable room for freedom of criticism, for protest, for suggestion and invention within the group.
2. The difficulty of isolating political phenomena sufficiently to determine precisely the causal relations between them. We know that events occur, but we find so many alternate causes that we are not always able to indicate a specific cause. For the same reason we are unable to reach an expert agreement upon the proper or scientific policy to pursue and by the same logic we are unable to predict the course of events in future situations.
3. The difficulty of separating the personality of the observer from the

social situation of which he is a part; of obtaining an objective attitude toward the phenomena he desires to interpret. This has been perhaps the chief stumbling block in the evaluation of the political process. Classes and races and all other types of groupings put forward as authoritative the so-called principles which are the outgrowths of their special interests, unconsciously perhaps interpreting their own interests in general terms of universal application. Thus the greater part of political theorizing on close analysis proves to be more or less thinly veiled propaganda of particular social interests. A theory may contain an element of truth or science in it, but the truth will be so colored by the interests of those who advance the particular theory that it has little genuine or permanent value. The opinions of the most eminent philosophers of a given race or nation regarding the merits of that race or nation are subject to heavy discount, almost without exception. The same thing may be said of the defenders of economic classes or of other types of groups. In the last hundred years, progress has been made in separating the student of politics from his local situation; but the livid propaganda of the war period and the attitude of nationalistic scientists toward each other indicates that after all relatively little progress has been made. Not only were political scientists often made propagandists, but they subordinated the work of all other scientists to their purpose, namely the advocacy and advancement of nationalistic claims.

4. The difficulty of obtaining the mechanism for accurate measurement of the phenomena of politics. Until relatively recent times, most estimates had been rough and uncritical. It is only since the development of modern statistics that anything like accuracy or precision in political fact material was possible. Even now obstacles apparently insuperable are commonly encountered. The development of adequate machinery for the survey of political forces is still ahead of us. Yet the development of mechanical devices for observation of facts and their analysis do not present difficulties that cannot be overcome with sufficient persistence, ingenuity, and imagination.

5. A fourth difficulty lies in the absence of what in natural science is called the controlled experiment. The student of physical science constructs a temporary hypothesis which he proceeds to verify if possible by processes of experiment, performed under his direction and control. These experiments he may reproduce at will until he is satisfied of the truth or error of his hypothesis. Such experiments, however, have seemed to lie beyond the reach of the student of political or social science. On the other hand, the living processes of politics are constantly going on, reproduced countless times at various

points, and in various stages of the world's political activity. It is possible to draw inferences and to verify these inferences by repeated observation in the case of recurring processes. This requires, however, the setting up of more subtle and precise machinery than has yet been invented. It is possible that the mechanism for this process may be found in the development of modern psychology or social psychology, which seems to hold the key to the study of types of conduct or behavior, or in statistical measurement of processes recurring over and over again in much the same form, and apparently in sequences that may be ferreted out, given sufficient acuteness and persistence.

These are not presented as final objectives or as insuperable difficulties. They present obstacles, but that they cannot be overcome we do not know; neither do we know that they can be overcome. We only know that we do not know whether it is possible or impossible to ascertain with scientific precision the laws that govern human behavior in the political field or in the social field.

Political Science in the United States

With reference to the development of political science in the United States, we may say that down to the middle of the nineteenth century there was no effort to systematize the study of government. There was the shrewdest kind of practical political wisdom or prudence exhibited by men of the type of Hamilton, Madison, Adams, and Jefferson, and on the juristic side by such masters as Marshall, Story, Webster, and Calhoun. But of organized scientific study there was little trace. To this we may make exception in John Adams's *Defense of the Constitutions of Government of the United States,* and Calhoun's *Disquisitions on Government.*[5]

The founder of the systematic study of government was Francis Lieber, a German refugee who came to America in 1827. His *Manual of Political Ethics* (1838–39) and his *Civil Liberty and Self Government* (1853) were the first systematic treatises on political science that appeared in the United States, and their influence was widespread. Lieber was a pupil of Niebuhr, the famous German historian, and was familiar with the German and continental developments of this period. After many vicissitudes, he became professor of politics in Columbia University. His characteristic achievement was the introduction of a form of historical and comparative method of inquiry into the field of political study.

---

5. Explanation of current types of political theory are seen in Nathaniel Chipman, *Principles of Government* (1793); F. Grimke, *Considerations on the Nature and Tendency of Free Institutions* (1848); Richard Hildreth, *The Theory of Politics* (1853).

The next great impetus to organized political inquiry came with the foundation of the Johns Hopkins and Columbia schools of history and political science. The moving spirit in the Johns Hopkins movement for the scientific study of history was Herbert B. Adams, while the founder of the Columbia school of political science (1880) was John W. Burgess. Both of these men were trained in the German universities and transplanted into American soil the characteristic methods of their time. These groups laid the foundation for the modern system of historical and political research, basing them in large measure upon the development of what in Germany was called *Staatswissenschaft*. Out of this movement has grown a long series of monographic studies in the field of government and politics. The establishment of these research institutions was epoch-making in the evolution of the scientific attitude toward political inquiry in this country. They undertook the examination of comparative types of institutions, and also undertook inquiry into the genesis of political forms and types. They brought to the study of government for the first time an impartial and objective attitude, and they began the construction of certain mechanisms of inquiry. It may be said that they did not reckon sufficiently at the outset at least with economic and social forces underlying the evolution of political institutions, and that they did not fully appreciate the importance of what has come to be called political and social psychology. These developments were reserved indeed for a later period, in which there came to be a fuller understanding of economic and social influences, and of the more subtle psychological processes underlying and conditioning them.

In the meantime, a great forward step had been taken in the direction of scientific attainment through the expansion of the work of the United States census bureau, notably under the direction of the well-known economist, General Walker.[6] This work of governmental observation and reporting had been begun with the foundation of the government itself, or shortly thereafter, but for the first half century it made comparatively little progress. Under Walker, the dignity and importance of this highly significant type of large-scale observation was very greatly increased. Large masses of comparable facts assembled with some degree of precision were now attainable for students of government, and of the allied social sciences. The American Statistical Society, first established in 1839, was reorganized and rejuvenated in 1888, and gradually increased in numbers and in information. The statistical development in this country remained in a relatively undeveloped state, however, as is the case down to the present time. One of the major tasks of our political science is the survey of the possibilities of political statistics and the development of schedules for extending the domain of statistical information.

---

6. See John Koren, *History of Statistics.*

The historical and comparative studies remained the dominant types in the United States for many years, and may be said to be in the ascendency at the present time. In this group belongs the bulk of the output of the scientific world.

At the end of the period came the beginning of the study of forces behind government as well as the forms and rules of government. The work of Lowell in this field was notable, but was interrupted by his transfer to another realm of activity. Like Bryce and Dicey he pointed the way to a different type and spirit of inquiry, involving the study of the forces conditioning governmental activity. Like Bryce he avowed his lack of faith in political principles of universal validity, but like Bryce he alluded on many occasions to the possibilities of political psychology, a domain however into which neither of them entered.

The work of Lippman, a pupil of Wallas, in the approach to a study of political psychology has already been discussed, but may be again considered in its local, American setting. Advancing from the side of government, he approaches the psychologist, moving forward for the position of the technical analyst of human traits. On the practical side, this is well illustrated by the recent establishment of the bureau of personnel research in the Institute of Government Research, with the union there of the psychologist and the expert in civil service.

Some notable developments are discussed in further detail in this report. Both of them deal with the modus operandi of fact collection and analysis. One of them was undertaken in connection with the work of the law-makers of the state of Wisconsin, under the leadership of Charles H. McCarthy.[7] Another developed in connection with the activities of municipal government, beginning with the work of the New York Bureau of Municipal Research, but later taken up in many other municipalities, and lately to the establishment of the Institute for Government Research, the Institute of Public Administration, and the Institute for Public Service. These movements are of very great significance, however, in the technical development of the study of government, in that they mark the beginning of an effort to collect fresh material regarding the actual operation of political forces, and also the beginning of a more specific relationship between the theory and the practice of government.

An acute English observer recently expressed the belief that in such projects as these the United States might be expected to blaze the trail toward the development of scientific social research in its highest form. The development of the survey, the tendency to observe and analyze political forces, the increasing appreciation of the statistical method, the faint beginnings of politi-

---

7. See *The Wisconsin Idea.*

cal psychology, are all significant advances in the development of political technique.

A notable variation in the general style of study was the application of the doctrine of the economic interpretation of history to certain phases of American political development. This was seen notably in Beard's work on the *Economic Interpretation of the Constitution,* and *Economic Origins of Jeffersonian Democracy.* Seligman's penetrating critique of the economic interpretation of history was a notable contribution to the methodology of the time. The significance of these studies lies in the fact that they indicated a tendency to go below the surface of the forms of government and politics, and to examine more ultimate factors and forces influencing the situation.

Another notable development was the study of the American frontier by Turner, in which the influence of the pioneer environment upon the course of history was portrayed. The spirit of revolt against the current methods of historical writing was most effectively represented by James H. Robinson, who broke through the conventional lines of historical inquiry, first in his volume on *The New History,* later in his *The Mind in the Making.* Robinson challenged the traditional purposes of history, writing with particular reference to the undue attention given to political and governmental institutions. In his later work, he advanced a step farther and challenged the validity of the current methods of historical and social research. These protests seem to mark the beginnings of a new type of historiography similar to the earlier one in its emphasis upon documentation but leading out into broader ranges of what may be termed for lack of a better phrase, social inquiry. Of deep significance was Shotwell's *History of History* (1922).

The beginning of the study of sociology in the United States also influenced the course of the systematic study of government.[8] The sociological studies seemed at first somewhat vague and sentimental, but as time went on became more specific, concrete, and more methodical. In the works of Lester F. Ward, the pioneer of sociology in this country, and later Giddings, Small, Ross, Cooley, and others, the sociological point of view and the sociological method became more and more widely influential. Small emphasized particularly the importance of what he called the "social point of view," by which he meant the consideration of all the social factors in a given situation, as distinguished from the isolated or exclusive consideration of economic factors or political factors alone. Ross, particularly in his work on social control, seemed to veer over toward the study which came to be called social psychology. Giddings was at first interested in the development of the fundamental factor which he called "consciousness of kind" and later in efforts to introduce a degree of mathematical accuracy and precision into the measurement of social phenomena.

---

8. See Albion W. Small, *Fifty Years of Sociology in the United States.*

The development of political economy was also of significance in relation to political science. Its chief types of inquiry followed the direction of the classical political economy and the lines of inquiry laid down by the historical school. There were notable evidences, however, of the development of statistical method in economics, even taking the shape of mathematical economics; and there were the beginnings of the study of the psychology underlying economic activities. There was also seen as in the study of government the tendency toward actual observation of economic processes, developing into types of surveys of sets of economic phenomena. Toward the end of the period came the powerful tendency toward vocational training for industry, and toward the development of business or industrial research. Broadly speaking, economics and politics seemed to follow parallel lines of advance, from the a priori method of the classical political economy and the natural law school, to historical and comparative studies of economics or of politics, to statistical inquiries and actual surveys, and on to the study of the psychological bases of economic or political activity as the case might be.

It is needless to say that the question of the development of methods will not be settled merely by discussion of the ideally best way of approaching the subject, but rather by the diffusion of the spirit of systematic, intensive, protracted, and sustained inquiry. We are still very far from exact political science, and there must be many experiments and probably many failures before there are many signal successes. The willingness of many men and women to devote long years of arduous and unremitting toil to the detailed study of political problems is a prerequisite to achievement, and even industry and devotion alone will not prove adequate if they slip into the ruts of scholasticism and only wear deeper the grooves of traditional thought. Experience shows that it is easy to fall into industrious but sterile scholarship. Imagination on the one hand and precision on the other, are essential to advancement in this field as in other departments of science. We must have both enthusiasm and tools, often a difficult combination, since the toolmakers may lack vision and the visionaries ignore the precise mechanisms or specific attainment. The political scientist must be something of a utopian in his prophetic view and something of a statesman in his practical methods.

Methods of approach to politics may easily be the most sterile subject of inquiry, if not followed by actual trials and tests. The discussion of methods has its greatest value as a by-product of specific undertakings, as an analysis of the strength and weakness of various going tasks of scientific political inquiry, in connection with actual pieces of investigation. Methodological discussion alone will not develop much in the way of scientific advance.

On the other hand scientific progress is not likely to be realized without persistent scrutiny and searching examination of fundamental methods. Like all other sciences, politics constantly faces the necessity of reviewing and revising its methods. Human nature may not change or may change only slowly, but the knowledge of human nature is advancing swiftly, and the understanding of its processes is developing with great rapidity. The political side of human nature is equally capable of more acute analysis and its processes may likewise be made the subject of more scientific study than ever before in the history of government. Never were there greater possibilities than now in the direction of accurate and scientific knowledge of the processes of political control; and never was the student's responsibility greater for the development of objective and analytical methods of observation of these processes, and for the minute understanding of the nature of the laws that govern their action and must control their adaptation and reconstruction.

It is easy to scoff at the possibilities of scientific research in the field of government, but unless a higher degree of science can be brought into the operations of government civilization is in the very gravest peril from the caprice of ignorance and passion, playing with the high explosives of modern scientific invention. Without the development of a higher type of political science in the fields of secondary education, in the organization of public intelligence, and of the technical knowledge of human nature, we may drift at the mercy of wind and waves or of the storm when we might steer an intelligent course. Social science and political science are urgently needed for the next great stage in the advancement of the human race. As custodians of the political science of our time, the responsibility rests upon us to exhaust every effort to bring the study of government in its various stages to the highest possible degree of perfection, to exhaust every effort to obtain effective knowledge of political forces, to bring to bear every resource of science and prudence at our command.

The Bias of American Political Science

Benjamin E. Lippincott

Political problems, as Aristotle observed, are at bottom psychological and moral. It is equally true, however, that the political activities of men, as Aristotle also pointed out, are affected in a fundamental way, often crucially, by economic factors. Yet curiously American political scientists,[1] so far as their writings are concerned, have been all but oblivious of this elementary truth. Since the Civil War only two political scientists, J. Allen Smith and Charles A. Beard, have given us special studies of the economic factor in politics. If Smith led the way with his *Spirit of American Government* (1907), Beard followed with his *Economic Interpretation of the Constitution* (1913) and his *Economic Origins of Jeffersonian Democracy* (1915), and showed conclusively the penetrating light such studies could throw.[2]

To be sure, a number of political scientists, such as Arthur N. Holcombe, E. Pendleton Herring, Frederick L. Schuman, Peter Odegard, Max Lerner, and Brooks Emeny, have introduced an economic interpretation into their writings, and have shown the bearing it can have. But only Smith and Beard have given us special studies, studies that attempt in some detail and systematically to bring out the economic relationships of politics. For American political science to have produced only two writers who have dealt intensively with the economics of politics in a period of seventy-five years is little short of astonishing.[3]

Reprinted from *The Journal of Politics* 12 (1940): 125–39. By permission of the University of Texas Press.

1. The term *political scientist* refers to members of the academic profession.

2. In *The Idea of the National Interest* (New York, 1934) Beard has given us another intensive study in the economic relations of politics. His *Open Door at Home* (New York, 1934) interprets the facts brought forward in his study of the national interest and formulates a program for the United States. *The Economic Basis of Politics* (New York, 1921) is a general discussion.

3. This record is essentially the same when tested by the journal of our profession. From November, 1906, when the *American Political Science Review* first appeared, to 1940, a period of approximately thirty-three years, only four out of five hundred main articles (notes excluded) were written by American political scientists that attempt to show systematically and in some detail economic relations of politics. This record would suggest that the official mind of political science has been all but immune to economic events in the real world. Not until the fifth year of

Our failure to probe into the economics of politics is surprising when we consider the great influence exerted by economic forces in the modern world. Living under a machine economy which has raised our standard of living, but which alternates between "prosperity" and depression, which gives men jobs and takes them away, we are more dependent than ever before upon economic activity. Material values penetrate deeply into our lives. Material welfare has become an end in itself, as such writers as Sinclair Lewis, Theodore Dreiser, and Eugene O'Neil have shown, rather than a means to an end. We work in a system of acquisitive economics; profit is the chief incentive; and the accumulation of wealth is the test of success. It is obvious that in such a system economic interests profoundly affect the state; it is a truism to say that those who own property can bend the will of the state to their will, and create a system of privilege. These facts are all plain and clear, and have been so for many years. But American political science has not seen fit to study intensively facts which could throw a penetrating light on the process of government.

We have neglected the study of economic factors, furthermore, in spite of the importance attributed to them by classical writers. We have apparently forgotten that both Plato and Aristotle, writing in the fifth century, B.C., showed that a consideration of economic factors is indispensable to a study of politics. We have apparently forgotten that Harrington and Locke, writing in the seventeenth century, showed that a realistic view of politics includes a view of economics. Nor do we seem to remember that Madison, Hamilton, and John Adams, in the eighteenth century, showed the same thing. Nor do we seem to be aware that Marx, in the nineteenth century, showed with great force and insight the connections between economics and politics.

The question is, why have American political scientists given so little attention to the economic aspect of politics? The answer is to be found, I suggest, in our notion of the scope of political science, in our conception of scientific method, in certain American conditions, in our middle-class assumptions, and in certain conditions of academic life. Of all these factors, our conception of scientific method and our middle-class assumptions seem to be the most significant factors.

Scope of Political Science

Since the Civil War we have looked at political science very largely as the study of constitutional law and of the organization, functions, and machinery of government.[4] Political science has been for the most part a formal study;

---

the Great Depression was a special study brought forward dealing with the economic relations of American politics.

4. See Anna Haddow, *Political Science in American Colleges and Universities, 1636–1900* (New York, 1939), chap. 13.

government has been considered rather as a mechanical institution working apart from society, apart from the social, psychological, moral, and economic factors. To be sure, political scientists have been intellectually aware that these factors are involved in the problem of government, and they have given some attention to the psychological and social side, but the profession as a whole has not been vitally aware of them.

It is indeed true that Francis Lieber, in his *Political Ethics* (1838), which was the first systematic political treatise from the pen of an American, looked upon man as a many-sided animal. He derived his politics from morals and showed that the problem of government involved a view of psychology and religion and a conception of economic and social institutions as well. But his formal analysis, supported by a wealth of information, revealed no new relationships, nor did it bring to light any new order of facts. Woolsey's *Political Science* (1878), which was the first systematic study of politics to make its appearance in the Gilded Age, continued the formal analysis of Lieber, but did not go beyond him in any important way. In fact, it was characterized neither by insight nor by thorough knowledge. It was left to Woodrow Wilson to strike a fresh note in his *Congressional Government* (1884); this book was the first in America really to show the working of party government. But Bryce's *American Commonwealth* (1888) "opened up a whole new world of understanding of the actual processes of politics."[5]

Although Bryce looked behind the legal forms, the organization, and the structure, and saw government in terms of the human equation, his work was largely a work of description. The criteria he brought to bear for testing government in action were limited to those of the nineteenth-century liberal. Standards of honesty, efficiency, and intelligence in government were more important, for example, than the quality of rights afforded the mass of men, and the extent of social and economic opportunity. He was aware, of course, of the power of great wealth; he saw that it made for privilege and that it corrupted public officials, but he considered these things rather as incidental phenomena. He made no attempt to probe them, nor did he question whether they were really incidental. In short, Bryce wrote from an uncritical middle-class point of view.

A year after Bryce's work appeared, Wilson, in *The State* (1889), showed that much was to be learned by a historical and comparative study of government in the ancient and modern world. John W. Burgess, in a still more scholarly work, *Political Science and Comparative Constitutional Law* (1890–91), demonstrated the merits of the historical and comparative method by an intensive study of the constitutions and constitutional law of the leading nations of the modern world. But both Wilson and Burgess worked in tradi-

---

5. Walter J. Shepard, "Recent Tendencies in American Political Science," *Politica* (February 1934): 2.

tional disciplines. It remained for Frank J. Goodnow to strike out in a new direction. Best known for his *Politics and Administration* (1900), he extended the boundaries of political science to include a study of the operations and techniques of the governmental mechanism. He was the first scholar, Charles A. Beard has said, in the United States to recognize the immense importance of administration in modern society and to sketch the outlines of the field. It is clear that by the end of the century political science was turning to an intensive study of law, and of the institutions and machinery of government.

With the organization of the American Political Science Association in 1903, the scientific study of politics really began. Yet it can hardly be said that since 1903 we have greatly expanded the scope of our studies beyond what it was at the end of the nineteenth century.

It is true that we have widened the province of political science to some extent by studies in public administration and local government, but our researches here have been mainly concerned with techniques and the improvement of governmental machinery. We have deepened—and this is certainly a contribution—rather than broadened our view of the functioning of government. It is also true that we have widened our boundaries to some extent by studies in the psychology of politics—in public opinion, propaganda, and ideologies—which has enriched our understanding. We have done something, too, on the social side of politics in our studies of pressure groups, which have given us a more realistic grasp of the operation of government. Yet we have only begun to break through on the social and psychological frontiers, and the economic has been all but overlooked and the moral has not been considered seriously to exist. If the scientific study of a subject includes the study of its relevant aspects, we have yet to study politics scientifically; that is, we have been biased, especially against the economic aspect, not to mention the moral.[6]

Scientific Method—Empiricism

In view of our conception of scientific method, it is hardly surprising that political science has restricted its scope so largely to the study of law, organization, structure, and machinery of government. Most political scientists have been exponents in some degree or other of empiricism, and empiricism leads to a concentration on these aspects. Empiricism worships two doctrines: first, that if you collect all the relevant facts and classify them, they will speak for

---

6. In taking stock of the progress of American political science in 1925, Charles E. Merriam said that the field of economic interpretation struck out by Beard is still incomplete. See his presidential address before the American Political Science Association, "The Progress of Political Research," *American Political Science Review* 20 (1926): 2.

themselves (i.e., laws or principles will emerge somehow automatically); second, that preconceived theories or ideas about the facts are not only unnecessary but positively dangerous.

Emphasizing the great importance of collecting facts, it is only natural that political scientists have turned to sources where they are easily available. Holding that preconceived theories about the facts should be shunned like poison, because they represent a bias, the empiricist searches for facts that are neutral, facts that are beyond dispute. These can best be found, of course, in the fields of law, organization, structure, and machinery of government. Because empiricism assumes the nominalist view of knowledge, that the particular alone is real, still another emphasis is placed on facts in the legal and institutional fields, for here facts are tangible and concrete.

Hostility to theory has meant that political scientists would describe our legal and political arrangements rather than explain them. Yet it is when we attempt to explain the character of government and of law that economics vitally enters in; when we attempt to explain, for example, why Congress passed the Smoot-Hawley tariff act. Hostility to theory has also meant that we would describe political ideas instead of seeking their relationships, for a relationship is an abstraction, and what is abstract, according to the empiricist, is unreal and can hardly be expected to exist. Yet only by thinking of political ideas in terms of their relationships can connections with other ideas be seen.

Aversion to theory has meant, still further, that we would write histories of political thought instead of producing political theory. During the thirty-seven years American political science has been organized as a profession, we have produced only one writer, W. W. Willoughby, who has attempted a systematic political theory.[7] To describe the ideas of dead writers and to relate them in a time sequence enables the empiricist, of course, to maintain an "impartial" scholarship but does not enable him really to advance political theory. To treat theory only historically and not to treat it as theory is to abandon the very aim of science. For the chief and ultimate aim of science is the formulation of a consistent and systematic body of principles. The great advances in physics have not been achieved by writing the history of physics.

The truth is the empiricist is a victim of the illusion of objectivity, which must prevent him from being a thoroughgoing scientist. Empiricism says to put away preconceived theories, and collect the relevant facts, and a law, principle, tendency, or probability will emerge. But how are we to determine the relevant facts? It is obvious that a notion of what to select, which is a

---

7. MacIver wrote *The Modern State* (London, 1926) before he came to this country. Willoughby presented his political theory in *The Fundamental Concepts of Public Law* (New York, 1924) and *The Ethical Basis of Political Authority* (New York, 1930).

theory, must precede the act of selection. And how can a law, which is universal and general, emerge from what is particular? Brute facts obviously cannot arrange themselves into a law, nor is this their function; the function of the facts is to confirm or to invalidate a theory which has been put forward tentatively as a law.

By banishing theory from scientific method, the empiricist must believe that all facts are free and equal, for he has no means of evaluation. The result is that he is unable to distinguish important from unimportant facts. He will give an elaborate description of the organization, powers, and machinery of government, but tells us very little of the principles for which these things were instituted, or how they work in practice. He will describe our democratic machinery with a full account of how to vote, but will leave us in the dark as to the meaning of democracy. He will describe the check and balance system in American government, but he will not tell us that the checks go to the politicians and the balances to private interests. He will tell us the dimensions of the Senate chamber, but will not point out that the Supreme Court has been biased in favor of wealth. He will give us a full description of the Italian corporate state without telling us that it exists chiefly on paper. But the empiricist has no difficulty in defending his lack of realism; he will say, when pressed, that after all these things are a matter of opinion. He will retreat, in other words, to the swamps of nominalism where all trees are stumps and look alike.

It is impossible, however, as we saw above, for the empiricist to avoid a point of view, a bias. Not only does he assume a theory and a scheme of values when he selects his facts, but also when he writes about them and tells us what they mean. Although he may think his objectivity is simon-pure, nevertheless, there will be found in his text, in the lines and in between the lines, all sorts of conclusions—in fact, a whole philosophy. If he believes that he has been completely objective, then he will have introduced a scheme of values unconsciously. To be unaware of the play of theory is to become the unwitting accomplice of one's own bias.[8] The bias which most political scientists have introduced, whether unconsciously or not, into their writings has been that of the middle-class point of view. Whether they will or no, their writings are in the main an acceptance and a justification of the status quo.

Inquiry into the economics of politics is hampered no less by empiricism's distrust of reason; that is, of logic and of reflection. Placing so great an emphasis on facts, expecting them to perform a miracle—to produce a law or

---

8. This discussion does not mean, of course, that a scientist should not be as objective as he can, for obviously he should. But the most objective scientist is one who is aware of the limits of objectivity, who knows where his own values and bias enter into his judgment.

generalization by themselves—the empiricist is suspicious of logic and skeptical of reflection. Logic, he is convinced, cannot prove anything. This is true, but neither can the facts by themselves prove anything; at best the facts along with the theory can only confirm or not confirm a proposition. But logic, too, has its place. It can make the premises of our theories explicit and thereby further explanation; it can show inconsistency between propositions; and, as an instrument of analysis, it can aid in increasing the number of hypotheses or possible explanations of our facts.

Reflection is equally important. It enables us to find meaning in our propositions; it enables us to consider alternative hypotheses; and it enables us to find the explanation best suited to the facts. Science advances by doubting accepted explanations in the search for one still more penetrating. Wonder, indeed, lies at the root of truth. The ideas that lie at the base of our great scientific discoveries seem to have come to men's minds as a hunch or as a flash of intuition. The history of science indicates that fruitful hypotheses have generally come to certain gifted minds as musical themes or great poetic expressions have come to others.

By minimizing the importance of logic, reflection, and imagination, the empiricist represses the play of thought and originality. He diminishes the possibility of creative explanation, and lessens the chance of discovering new causes and more profound truth. He becomes a kind of stooge of common sense. Certainly great contributions to science are not made by those who go to nature innocent of all preconceptions, but rather by those who have acquired the most knowledge and fruitful ideas on the subject of their inquiry. To emphasize the role of reason does not minimize the importance of facts, but makes the latter more significant.

American Conditions

Certain characteristics of American life and politics have undoubtedly played a part in turning the minds of political scientists to formal study and away from realistic inquiry. Our government with its complicated structure—a federal system with separation of powers and judicial review—has been a paradise for the empiricist. With constitutions, legislatures, courts, administrative agencies, and political parties in the nation and the forty-eight states, not to mention local government, it is obvious that there are thousands of facts to describe. So imposing an array of data must have a strong attraction for the political scientist.

To live, moreover, in a technical and industrial civilization must also stimulate an interest in structure and the mechanism of government. Our pride in being practical and our general suspicion of theory, which are products of our English inheritance, the frontier, and acquisitive economics, lend support to this interest. Perhaps, too, in a world of rapid change, we tend to cling to external things, for they appear secure, established, and solid.

The prosperity we have enjoyed from the end of the Civil War to the Great Depression, has hardly been a stimulus to social thought. An expanding economy, bringing ever more material comfort, has apparently acted as a check rather than a spur to original inquiry. Nor is the fact that there has been no critical challenge to authority since the Civil War without its bearing. For over half a century the American ship of state has sailed on calm seas. With most men accepting the assumptions of the middle-class state, there has been little clash of ideas regarding the purpose of the state, there has been little criticism of the state as it now exists, there has been little discussion of what the American state ought to be and how such a state might be attained. It seems that when there are vital issues to be fought for and defended, men are more apt to write creatively, with a sense of the presence of things, to deal with ideas. There is undoubtedly a connection between revolutionary America and the writings of Madison, Hamilton, John Adams, and Jefferson, as there is between the ferment of ideas before the Civil War and Calhoun. The want in America until late years of any serious conflict or dissent over fundamentals is not unrelated to the want of a penetrating inquiry by political scientists into the basis of authority and the nature of control.

Middle-Class Assumptions

As members of the middle class, especially as important members, political scientists have been content to think almost entirely in terms of its framework. They have accepted as all but final the assumptions of capitalist democracy. They have stood for economic individualism and a laissez-faire state. They have held that the primary function of government was to maintain law and order and a few indispensable social services. They have contended that the function of government, so far as industry was concerned, was to act as a policeman. Men, according to the individualist, were made to compete and government was a necessary evil. If government intervened in the affairs of business, the presumption was that government was acting arbitrarily, irrationally, and against the rules of the game. The proper function of government was to govern. The function of industry was to produce. Industry was industry, and presented no problem in government, although the corporation was a little state in itself and acted politically. The view of government entertained by laissez-faire individualism could hardly be very sympathetic to an intensive study of politico-economic relationships.

The truth is that political scientists have not questioned the foundations of the capitalist order. They have not asked whether the profit-gain system, which is the basis of middle-class supremacy and which today permits ten million men to be unemployed, is the final solution of the economic problem. They have not sought to discover the effects upon government of great concentrations of wealth. They have not brought forward an intensive study of the effects of corporate power upon the lawmaking process and upon administration. They have not asked whether the assumptions of the middle-class state make for privilege for the middle class and an abrogation of rights for the working class. They have not asked whether the assumptions of the middle-class state represent a narrow ideal; or whether assumptions different from those of the middle class might constitute a superior order. They have shown little capacity, in short, to doubt familiar facts and accepted values, yet the beginning of wisdom and the beginning of science lay in doubt. Political scientists, whether they have been conscious of it or not, have in fact served the interests of the middle class.

If the acceptance of middle-class political and economic assumptions has discouraged inquiry into the economic aspect of politics, the fact that they have been members in a very real sense of a dominant and prosperous class seems to have had the same effect. To participate, if only indirectly, in control, and to share the benefits of supremacy, does not engender doubt in the basis of these things but, on the contrary, establishes their excellence. Men who have experienced rapid advancement in their career and have found that life is good are hardly inclined to question a system that so quickly discovered their talents. The acceptance, furthermore, by political scientists of what is probably the chief social idea of the middle class, the idea of progress, has scarcely sharpened their critical sense. The belief in progress has meant that there was no need to question our political and economic arrangements, for American institutions were better than those in any other country, and would continue to be better. Dominance, prosperity, and the idea of progress, it would seem, have all played a part in developing among political scientists a willingness to believe in things as they are.

Academic Life

The political scientist lives in a college or university community whose organization hardly inspires a search into the economic causes of things. Most universities and colleges are governed on the autocratic principle, that is, the teacher is responsible to an authority which he has had little or no part in creating. He is immediately responsible to a dean and a president. He is ultimately responsible to a board of trustees. The board of trustees, which in the last analysis determines his career and way of life, is usually composed of successful men from the business and professional world, men of property, controlling individuals.

An autocratic arrangement of authority, however benevolent, fosters timidity and caution, not independence and a critical spirit. The knowledge that most administrators and trustees believe in the middle-class state, or a modified form of it, does not encourage doubt as to its assumptions, especially its economic assumptions, for these touch the heart of middle-class power. Nor does the knowledge, in private institutions, that pertinent questions may interfere with endowments promote unorthodox research. Nor do charges of radicalism and threats of investigation by patrioteers, by vested interests, and by legislators who desire to make a name, promote courageous thinking in our institutions of higher learning.

If timidity and caution are fostered by the fact that faculty men are members of a profession which, unlike law and medicine, has little voice in determining the rules under which it lives, indeed, is ruled in the last analysis by men from other walks of life, timidity and caution are also fostered by the faculty man's economic position. Salaries of most teachers are not large enough to make them economically independent. Most faculty men, whether of the rank of full professor or instructor, do not possess a real sense of independence. Men in the higher ranks who are on "permanent" appointment may say that this is not the case, but they will generally be found to act as if it were.

Men who possess neither the security of property nor the protection that comes through organization, as in a union, will be slow to risk their positions by novel speculation. Men who have families to support on inadequate incomes will think twice before they criticize views that lie deep in the emotions, such as views on private property. Life and vigorous inquiry into established verities is not likely to flourish when there is a contingent possibility that unpopular ideas may cost the academic man his position, or interfere with his promotion—and from past experience he knows that this is more than a mere possibility. He is impressed by the record of dismissals published in the *Bulletin of the American Association of University Professors*. He knows that in recent years men have lost their positions at Ohio State, Pittsburgh, Rensselaer, Yale, Harvard, Montana, and St. Louis University. Whatever may be the facts in these cases, the opinion is widespread, either from the evidence of the case or from the way in which the case was handled, that men were dismissed from these institutions for their ideas.

Experience has taught the social scientist that the road of the dissenter is hard and rough. He is conscious of the classic example of Veblen; he sees in him an original and brilliant mind who criticized the reigning social and economic dogmas of his time only to go unrecognized in our leading universities. When at the height of his powers, and in need of a position, no bid was made for his services by our great institutions of higher learning. Surely Parrington was not far from the mark when he said that "provocative social thought and the American university seem never to have got on well together."[9]

Nor, finally, is the usual test by which men are promoted to the top ranks unrelated to the poverty of economic thinking in politics. The test is "productive" scholarship, and too often this is identical with sterile empirical studies that resemble the compilation of a telephone directory, or that consist, as has been said, in the counting of manhole covers. A premium is placed in large universities upon "productive" scholarship because it is difficult for the administrator to know his faculty and their talents at first hand; in the circumstances, and in the absence of an adequate personnel policy, quantity of writing seems to furnish the most objective test. A large volume, furthermore, or a long list of publications is more impressive to trustees and to the public than critical work which may occupy a small space. The pressure to turn out quantity production is hardly conducive to critical reflection.

If the analysis in this essay is correct, the American political scientist has failed to cross the border into the economics of politics fundamentally because of his conception of scientific method, empiricism, and his middle-class scheme of values. His bias, then, against an intensive study of the economic relations of politics is at bottom very largely the result of a bias still more fundamental, a bias against a well-rounded conception of scientific method, one which is followed in physical science, and a bias against a broad view of the community's interest.

The political scientist, to speak in more general terms, is guilty of two sins: a sin against reason and imagination, and a sin against courage. His sin against reason and imagination explains his failure to search beyond empiricism to a more creative scientific method, it explains his failure to widen the scope of his inquiries, and it explains his failure to transcend his middle-class assumptions. His sin against courage explains his easy acceptance of an autocratic system of government in his own bailiwick, although such government is contrary to the best thought of his science.

---

9. Parrington, *The Beginnings of Critical Realism in America* (New York, 1930), p. 124.

Specialists on Intelligence

Harold D. Lasswell

Public opinion in the public interest depends upon the general level of intelligence in society, and upon the degree of successful specialization upon intelligence. No matter how high the general level, the community cannot act intelligently unless needed data are supplied by specialists. The democratic citizen may be well equipped to think about what he reads, sees, and hears; or to observe himself and discount the effect of his own biases. But the result of his thinking may be absurd unless he has the proper raw materials of thought; and these come chiefly from specialists upon intelligence. There are specialists on truth to make original observations; there are specialists on clarity to make them lucid; there are specialists on interest to make them vivid. Unless these specialists are properly trained and articulated with one another and the public, we cannot reasonably hope for public opinion in the public interest.

In a democracy the chief function of the specialist on intelligence is to contribute to the discovery of justice. Democracy is bound by its own principles to take the thoughts and feelings of others into account; hence a democratic society must be equipped with specialists who communicate the truth about others with clarity and emphasis. For sympathetic observation of others, modern society has social and psychological scientists; for clarification and emphasis, there are specialists in every channel of communication.

Our civilization has witnessed an unparalleled growth of the total stream of communication, and of specialists upon communication. Some of this work of communication presents us with charts that show how the nonsymbolic parts of the world have grown in recent times. However, a comparable job has not been done in presenting curves that show the volume of our symbolic world—curves that depict the soaring total of new words introduced into the dictionaries and lexicons of the last hundred years, or the increase in the number of words that are shot every day through the presses or over the wires or over the long and short waves of the world. Yet the fact is that the expansion of the material environment is more than outstripped by the symbolic

Reprinted from *Democracy through Public Opinion* (New York: Banta, 1941), chap. 5.

world. The volume and variety of the stream of communication surpasses even the gadgets of modern science and technology.

Little wonder in the light of this general growth that the specialists on communication have multiplied in number and variety. They range all the way from austere specialists on experimental psychology to boisterous wise-crackers on the stage. All who specialize in symbols (words or their sub-stitutes) contribute to the flow of communication. There are sociologists who devote a lifetime to the study of one American community. There are an-thropologists who live for years among people of alien culture on the fringe of civilization. Such specialists rarely contribute to press, radio and motion picture; yet from their occasional reports may come new themes and anec-dotes, or even new attitudes toward life. Some specialists perfect new instru-ments of measurement to describe the skills and attitudes of others.

At first glance, the highly specialized social scientist, psychologist, or physician seems to have little in common with the staff of the media of mass communication. There are bustling reporters and exacting copyreaders, pon-tifical editors and temperamental feature writers, serious-minded news com-mentators and harum-scarum "gag-men." There are scores of distinctive skill groups in the field of publication, radio and motion picture; and few of them operate with the care or leisure of the social scientist. The production cycle of the news commentator may be the split second; an idea comes into his mind, and rolls off his tongue into the ears of the listening audience. The scientific specialists on tests may spend months or years in the perfecting of a scale of measurement; although he knows in a general way that he must eventually "produce," his methods and results may be withheld for years.

It would be easy, however, to exaggerate the difference between the life of the scientist and of other specialists on the flow of intelligence. The produc-tion cycle of the novelist, dramatist or poet may equal or exceed the scientist; and it is not to be assumed that the scientist is under no pressure to publish his results.

Even when proper allowance is made for the similarities between scien-tist and nonscientist, wide differences of emphasis remain, differences that greatly complicate the task of unifying the intellectual skills of society in the discovery of justice. The scientist is, above all, a specialist on the systematic expression of new truth. Whatever his working methods, he hopes to systema-tize his observations according to an elaborate set of postulates, definitions, and propositions. The disciplined scientist looks forward to the day when he can find a mathematical formula that unifies the observations that are made.

As you pass from the intellectual who is specialized on the discovery of truth, you come to those who clarify. Their task is to make new truth lucid to the beginning student, or the inquisitive layman. In some respects they touch shoulders with specialists on interest; for most of them seek to enliven what they do in the hope of reaching an ever-broadening public. In some ways the writer of textbooks carries the heaviest burden of all; he is caught between the ever-expanding territory of the specialist on truth, and the ever-inviting audience of all who might be interested in truth, once it is simplified and vivified.

There are specialists on interest who are cheerfully unconcerned about truth or clarity; they seek only plausibility and applause. They are impatient of restriction in the interest of truth, morals or taste; yet they often hit upon devices of communication that widen the potential audience of truth.

Every distinctive skill has something to contribute to the task of improving the stream of communication. We need specialists on truth, clarity, and interest; we need to harness them to the discovery of justice. In a just society, the channels of communication must focus attention upon the clear presentation of truth about the thoughts and feelings of others.

It cannot be successfully maintained that in the recent history of American society our specialists on intelligence have performed a satisfactory job. We need go no further back than the catastrophic depression after 1929. Specialists did not quickly enough sense the human significance of what was happening to Americans who lost employment. Everyone was able to see the threat of starvation and to be properly horrified by it. All were impressed by the crippling effects of material loss upon the health and comfort of the jobless. And presently the jobless were provided with bread; and this was humane and sound. But the specialists did not make it clear to themselves— nor to others—that a more subtle blow was inflicted upon the jobless. They might be given bread; but they were provided with no reason for living. Millions of jobless were allowed to continue in a state of suspended animation, stigmatized as useless members of society.

If our society had been thoroughly respectful of human personality, our specialists would have been quick to sense the violation of human dignity that was perpetuated in our treatment of the jobless. They would have sensed the true proportions of the tragedy in the declaration of uselessness that was implied in the word, "the unemployed."

Why this comparative insensitivity to the democratic values? No doubt this obtuseness is connected with the exaggerated amount of attention that has been given to economic activity and economic phraseology. The business man is accustomed to think in terms of profit and loss, to translate every alternative in terms of the dollar. He is a specialist on profits. He is not accustomed to translate what he does in terms of increased or diminished self-respect of workers, customers, investors, or any other group of society; or even of himself. The business man is accustomed to take these outcomes for granted. And the tax gatherers, even in a democratic government, think in dollars.

Neither business nor government makes up a balance sheet of what it contributes to the self-respect of human beings.

We must rely upon the specialists on intelligence to provide us with a picture of human reality that is true, clear, and vivid. The primary responsibility for truth rests with two groups of specialists; researchers and reporters. Researchers study events until they can describe them in a way that contributes new data to the fundamental propositions of the human sciences. For the most part, we depend upon social scientists, psychologists, and physicians for the basic data that we need. But we cannot wait until events are described by the eye of science; we need to know what happened yesterday, today, or even a few moments ago. The cursory look is the special skill of the competent reporter. His job is to see as much of the truth as he can at a glance, for he must act against a "deadline."

Although it is customary in some circles to contrast the researcher with the reporter to the disparagement of the latter, this judgment is quite unjustified. Researchers and reporters are engaged upon a common task, and as our society learns more about itself, there will be closer contact between them. Researchers will contribute more to the fundamental education of the reporters, and in this way improve the skill with which they appraise the meaning of what they see. This process has already begun; the newer generation of reporters is often trained in the social and psychological sciences. Schools of journalism are changing their scope, sloughing off their superabundant "tool courses," and adding the human sciences.

It need not be supposed that the relation between researcher and reporter is entirely one-sided. Modern reporters have already begun to contribute in greater volume than before to the description and the interpretation of recent events.

One result of closer contact between reporter and researcher is that the results of research are clarified and vivified for a wider public. A rising generation of specialists has come into existence for the reporting of scientific research.

Any well-balanced picture of human reality must be selective, and this calls for a clear conception of the whole. What is the structure of American society as a whole, and in different regions? Fortunately recent research has provided us with far better knowledge of the basic facts about America than we have ever had before. Among metropolitan areas, basic data are perhaps best for Chicago, thanks to the work of the Social Science Committee of the University of Chicago.[1] One of the best known regional areas is the twin cities, thanks to studies at the University of Minnesota. The National Resources Board has provided basic data for several component areas of the entire nation.

Research has already given us valuable cross-sectional descriptions of

---

1. Organized at the instigation of Charles E. Merriam, who was also the prime mover of the national Social Science Research Council.

life at recurring intervals in some American communities. The most famous example is *Middletown,* which was described by the Lynds on the eve of the Great Depression, and again several years later. There is much current interest in the systematic study of local communities, and the human realities of American life are becoming better known. We have fuller pictures of what it means to belong to a particular income group in a specific area of the country; we are learning, too, of the position of the low deference groups (Negroes, Mexicans, Japanese, for example). Our studies include the casual laborer, the youth, the women, and many other components of the nation.

Because the makers and executors of policy are so rushed, the record-taking function must go into the hands of a specialist on that particular skill. Researchers and reporters must be motivated and then outfitted with proper equipment before they can wisely be entrusted with the record-making function.

The specialized observer of interpersonal relations is always attracted into two opposite directions: to spend a very short time observing a great many people; to spend a very long time observing a few.

The well-equipped observer of human relations makes a record of more than the literal words that people use. He pays attention to what people know they are saying, and also to what they do not know they are saying.

Researchers and reporters are alike in that they have the same basic contribution to make to the achievement of democracy. They are the specialists upon whom we must depend for the facts which are needed before it is possible to achieve public opinion in the public interest. From these specialists we need above all to obtain a clear, truthful, and vivid picture of the degree of mutual respect that obtains throughout society. We depend upon these observers to supply us with the facts about the degree of present justice.

The moralists have been at a disadvantage in comparison with "materialists" because the moralists have no method of observation. For the most part the professional devotees of the good have been less well equipped than their rivals. The moralists have been specialists in reading what other moralists have said in the past, and in the logical analysis of this literary inheritance. They have often delivered secular sermons on morality. But they were incapable of discovering which events in society were just and which were not. They had no technique of describing such "intangible" relationships as "mutual respect." The "materialist" could point to his charts of goods and prices; he could dismiss the sermonizing of the moralist who talked about the primacy of "human" values. When the moralist was asked to say which events were "just" or "unjust," he often discredited himself by giving voice to the simple preferences of his social class or income group. It was too often obvious that majestic rhetoric in celebration of justice was an imposing cloak for petty prejudice.

Our problem is to give eyes, ears, hands and feet to morality. We cannot specialize indefinitely upon the cry for justice divorced from the means appropriate to the end of increasing the frequency of just events. Men and women who grow up in our civilization share many democratic aspirations; and our problem is to discover how democratic attitudes can be guided by proper insight into the conditions and requirements of justice. This is the primary function of the researcher and the reporter, for they specialize upon the observing of events; and what we need to know the truth about is the state of mutual respect throughout society. The channels of communication in a democratic society must be flooded with communications that show us the truth about deference. Public knowledge of the state of justice is itself a means to a just society.

Contradictions of a Political Discipline

David M. Ricci

The Theory and Practice of Democracy

The first generation of political scientists worked from 1880 to 1900, mainly after the fashion of comparative history, and succeeded in firmly establishing the early programs of political studies, such as these were. The second generation pressed forward from 1900 to 1920, setting up the APSA, consolidating collegial departments, and working out a sense of collective identity quite distinct from that of all other disciplines, such as history, economics, and sociology. In the third generation, from 1920 to 1940, the emphasis on science finally came of age, with aspiration turning more and more to practice, as older political scientists gave way to younger men better trained in the techniques of modern research. In America at large, this was an age of disillusionment, of realization that World War I signaled a loosing of forces, both domestic and international, that would make human progress less than automatic and more an objective to be obtained only by extraordinary efforts, if at all. For those interested in politics, it seemed time for taking stock, for seeing where the nation presently stood, where things were going well and where they were not. This they felt after decades of political invention and reform that produced the referendum, the initiative, the recall, nonpartisan elections, city managers, direct election of senators, suffrage for women, and considerable substantive legislation.

Many political scientists, such as Charles Merriam, were active in reform circles prior to 1920.[1] Their commitment to the liberal tradition thereafter persisted, but it was tempered by skepticism concerning the outcome of that tradition in practice. The mood was summed up, in retrospect, by Bernard Crick when he observed that political scholars, together with many other

Reprinted in a shortened version from *The Tragedy of Political Science: Politics, Scholarship, and Democracy* (New Haven: Yale University Press, 1984), chap. 3. Copyright © 1984 by Yale University.

1. On Merriam, see Barry D. Karl, *Charles E. Merriam and the Study of Politics* (Chicago: University of Chicago Press, 1974).

Progressive intellectuals, "had worked hard to return politics to the people, and the people had returned Harding."[2] Under the circumstances, there seemed good reason for academics to involve themselves less directly in politics than before the war, and to discharge their civic responsibilities instead by emphasizing scholarly research within the university. By studying political phenomena closely, they said, scientific knowledge would emerge and contribute to improving the quality of public life in America. This renewed dedication to scientific inquiry found formal expression in the APSA's sponsorship of three National Conferences on the Science of Politics, in 1923, 1924, and 1925. It also appeared in the Association's strong support for the creation of a Social Science Research Council in 1923, with the Association entering as one of several founding disciplines.

The 1920s and 1930s came to be marked, then, by a steady flow of empirical research and descriptive studies, designed to enlighten first political scientists, and then their students and the public, as to the condition of American politics and the way in which all citizens might maintain and improve the nation's democracy. A brief survey of some salient points in the literature will suffice to show that, as the years passed, political scientists found themselves confronting the contradictions between scientific form and professional substance; that is, the danger that practitioners might, in a scientifically acceptable way, produce a research product whose effect would be to undermine the very object which the discipline was professionally committed to support, namely, the democratic polity. In uneasy awareness of what their prewar writings had already revealed, and with growing concern for the mounting evidence displayed in their postwar research, political scientists were eventually forced to admit that liberalism's postulates about individual rationality, political groups, and responsible government—matters of common expectation concerning human and institutional behavior in politics— were strongly challenged by the facts.

The Postulate of Rational Men

Liberalism's "most fundamental assumption," as Edward S. Corwin put it in 1929, was the notion "that man is primarily a rational creature, and that his acts are governed by rational considerations." Indeed, upon this assumption rests "the doctrine that the people should rule."[3] Yet the political behavior of real people, when closely analyzed, did not seem rational enough to fit the bill.

---

2. *The New Science of Politics* (Chicago: University of Chicago Press, 1925), p. 134.
3. "The Democratic Dogma and the Future of Political Science," *American Political Science Review* (August 1929): 570–71.

On this point, the findings of psychology could not be overlooked. Sigmund Freud had long claimed that human personality is a complicated alloy of id, ego, and superego, with the id and the ego driven by elemental forces of instinct only weakly constrained by reason and the superego's injunctions of conscience. Political scientists did not always endorse Freudian categories of analysis, but they did more and more conclude that if human beings were largely irrational, politics could not be far behind. Thus Graham Wallas observed that "representative democracy is generally accepted as the best form of government; but those who have had most experience of its actual working are often disappointed and apprehensive." For Wallas, the assumption of rationality in politics amounted to what he called the "intellectualist fallacy," which held "that all motives result from the idea of some preconceived end." To the contrary, he argued, the "empirical art of politics consists largely in the creation of opinion by the deliberate exploitation of subconscious non-rational inference." Using the art of advertisement to illustrate his point, Wallas held that both the commercial and the political worlds of persuasion rely on deliberate manipulation of "entities"—like "country" or "party" or "justice" or "right"—which constitute our images of the world but which are in fact complicated mixtures of fact, instincts, and emotions that do not permit orderly and accurate thinking.[4]

Irrational men, those who respond to manipulation of their instincts and emotions, willful men: what did such people in politics imply for the liberal notion of informed public opinion, which was supposed to instruct government and to hold it in check? A. Lawrence Lowell, in his major work on public opinion, began by noting that "the elder breed of political and economic philosophers erred in regarding man as a purely rational being." Rather, he said, men act in accordance with their traditions and a weltanschauung, which together mix up opinion, knowledge, beliefs, and so forth, even though the consequent ideas in our heads may be "inconsistent with actual facts or wholly foreign to the real benefits received." One result, according to Lowell, is that their nature causes citizens to be so ill-informed on most political issues that after an election it is difficult, from the returns, to know which interests they thought to advance; or, as he made the point, "it is often impossible to ascertain on which of the issues involved the people have rendered their verdict."[5] But if the people do not express a clear sense of their interests, for whatever reason, how can representative government be possible, in the traditional sense? This was precisely the question raised by Mer-

---

4. *Human Nature in Politics* (London: Archibald Constable, 1908), pp. ix, xi, 23–25, 59–97.

5. *Public Opinion and Popular Government* (New York: Longmans, Green, and Co., 1913), pp. 16, 18–19, 25.

riam and Harold Gosnell in their classic work on nonvoting, when they studied the reasons why more than 50 percent of the potential electorate in Chicago's municipal elections of 1923 either did not register to vote or, once registered, did not cast their ballot on election day. Confronted by the fact that 44 percent of the nonvoters gave "general indifference or some form of inertia" as their reason for ignoring election day, Merriam and Gosnell concluded that every effort must be made to bring more voters to the polls, else the country would be ruled, in effect undemocratically, by the minority who voted regularly but only in order to advance interests narrower than those of the citizenry as a whole.[6]

In all, the literature on voters and rationality revealed two problems: the first was irrational action spurred by observable impulse, and the second was a failure to act due to patent indifference. To both of these manifestations of behavior as revealed in research, the most comforting reaction was to claim that with enough additional research the situation might improve. And thus, while conceding that psychological evidence shows human behavior to flow from an amalgam of reason and passion, Merriam argued that intelligence is rooted partly in genetic abilities and partly in environmental influences. We need not be entirely pessimistic, according to him, concerning future political behavior, for scientists may eventually improve intelligence through genetic selection or via the right sort of education, in sufficient quantities.[7]

This response to revelations of political irrationality was not entirely satisfactory because, apart from its reliance on genetic solutions that have still not materialized, the plea for more education, though natural to educators, too easily slid over into a prescription for offering citizens constant help in order to fulfill their democratic responsibilities—in which case, how much democracy is left? The dilemma was highlighted in Harold Lasswell's work. "The findings of personality research show that the individual is a poor judge of his own interest," said Lasswell,[8] and he proceeded to study not just voters but also political leaders as irrational individuals. From Lasswell's psychoanalytic viewpoint, it was logical to conclude that the quality of public life will improve when political activists are guided and advised by social-science professionals, presumably those trained in psychology. It seemed the scientific thing to say, but there was no clear link between this sort of process and that of democracy itself, a matter of free interplay between opinions expressed by men and women from all regions and walks of life. In fact, Lasswell was

6. Charles E. Merriam and Harold F. Gosnell, *Non-Voting: Causes and Methods of Control* (Chicago: University of Chicago Press, 1924), p. 158, 232–49.

7. "The Significance of Psychology for the Study of Politics," *American Political Science Review* (August 1924): 476–77ff.

8. *Psychopathology and Politics* (orig., 1930; Chicago: University of Chicago Press, 1977), p. 183.

both explicit and scientific concerning open discussion of public affairs: he opposed it, charging that such discussion endangered society by expressing interests in such a way as to expose personal problems—irrational fixations and compulsions—and thereby complicate political confrontations unnecessarily. Oddly enough, in his recommendations for overcoming irrationality in the political process, Lasswell came very close to advocating the same sort of techniques for manipulating public opinion that he, among others, had condemned when they were used by propagandists in World War I. After the war, Lasswell deplored the way in which governments on both sides had created consensus by controlling the minds of their peoples, when truth and reason were casualties of a public relations effort unrestrained by "the canons of critical veracity."[9] But concerning the cause of peace he was quick to suggest that, in a world of irrational men, stable order must rely on a "universal body of symbols and practices sustaining an elite which propagates itself by peaceful methods and wields a monopoly of coercion which it is rarely necessary to apply to the uttermost.[10] At that point, science had come a long way from democracy, no matter how admirable the intent.

The Unreason of Groups

What science said about irrational men bore directly upon the role of groups within a democratic society since, after all, such groups are but composites of individuals. In contrast to what liberals had long expected from groups in the way of concerted but rational action, observers were struck by the fact that group activity could be as irrational as that of individuals. Robert Michels was a European student of collective unreason who was widely read by American social scientists, and he, arguing from the data of research into political parties, held that there is an "iron law of oligarchy" that works in all organizations. As Michels explained this law, administrative necessity and unequally distributed political talents assure that when men come together to advance their interests, the assemblage will invariably fall under the control of leaders who may, and often do, act against the joint interests of the group's members in order to protect narrower interests instead, that is, their own.[11]

Intrigued by such theoretical "laws," students of American politics turned their attention to political groups of various kinds and discovered many

---

9. *Propaganda Technique in the World War* (New York: Knopf, 1972), p. 206.

10. *World Politics and Personal Insecurity* (New York: McGraw-Hill, 1935), p. 181.

11. On the law, see Michels, *Political Parties: A Sociological Study of the Oligarchical Tendencies of Modern Democracy* (orig., 1915; New York: Dover, 1959), pp. 377–92. In "Some Reflections on the Sociological Character of Political Parties," *American Political Science Review* (November 1927): 753–72, Michels summarized his overall view of oligarchical tendencies in political organizations.

manifestations of group irrationality or, at the least, failure to serve clearly defined collective interests. Parties, for example, were persistently disappointing.[12] Thus Frank Kent, who described most voters as knowing little of public affairs, wrote of people and party machines who play "the great game of politics." Unfortunately for democracy, machines and their boss leaders played the game for money, rather than on behalf of the public welfare.[13] They could do this—selling offices and legislative favors—precisely because voters, instead of thinking for themselves, responded to political slogans rather than facts, thereby leaving the party in control of a small elite, as Michels had predicted.

Beyond parties, a particular set of groups caused special difficulty for political scientists intent on reconciling liberal theory with democratic reality, and these were the groups advancing special interests, perhaps benign but certainly not as broad as the public interest itself, whatever that might be. Thus Frank Kent observed that party leaders were not able to formulate issues out of rational consideration and then discuss them with the voters, but instead were forced to consider an agenda of needs created by powerful special interest groups whose desires had to be placated in order to assure reelection. And just how many of these powerful groups there were, at the national level alone, was described by E. Pendleton Herring, in a study of more than one hundred lobbying organizations with offices in Washington, D.C.[14] Herring made it clear that such groups, with their offices, public relations experts, contacts with the mass media, experienced witnesses before congressional committees, and well-heeled masters of Washington entertaining, were in the nation's political life to stay. Exactly where they fit into the liberal notion of democracy, in an era when mass irrationality and voter indifference were widely recognized, was not so clear.

A final body of political analysis concerning groups centered on the concept of "publics," which were less organized than parties and formal interest groups, but which nevertheless played an important role in democratic theory. Walter Lippmann, who did influential work along these lines, started from the fact that people tend to think in terms of "stereotypes"—such as the "wily Oriental," the "Georgian redneck," and the "pedantic professor." These building blocks of inference convey a simplified picture of our social surroundings, because men cannot acquire and assimilate all the facts available

---

12. See Charles E. Merriam, *The American Party System*, rev. ed. (New York: Macmillan, 1929), p. 456, for the standard charges against parties in this era.

13. *The Great Game of Politics: An Effort to Present the Elementary Human Facts About Politics, Politicians, and Political Machines, Candidates and Their Ways, for the Benefit of the Average Citizen* (Garden City, N.Y.: Doubleday, Page, and Co., 1924), p. 79.

14. *Group Representation Before Congress* (Baltimore: Johns Hopkins University Press, 1929).

on public matters. But because by their very nature stereotypes are incomplete, "democracy in its original form never seriously faced the problem which arises because the pictures inside people's heads do not automatically correspond with the world outside."[15] What happens, in fact, is that when matters of collective import are considered by the polity, various "publics" will arise, some already organized and long interested, others temporary and only lately concerned. Among these publics, opinions will be expressed and, via political pressures and electoral decisions, leaders will eventually be induced to take one action or another. For Lippmann, the problem was that, given their habit of thinking in stereotypes, most people who belong to publics will not really know what the facts of an issue are. Must we then leave the fate of a democratic society in the hands of these ignorant publics, assuming that the right to vote and act politically cannot be withdrawn because it is an inviolable part of American life? All Lippmann could conclude was that publics should not seek to make government behave according to preconceived plans but should instead vote and thereby express a judgment as to policies and decisions proposed by various small and more knowledgeable groups—elites, really—who have enough of a grasp on the facts to propose some course of action but too much of a stake in the outcome that they might safely be left unrestrained by the larger body of citizens.[16] In other words, Lippmann held that America's common men could not chart the nation's path by themselves but should leave the job of conceiving and initiating policy to some other force. It was a realistic theory, firmly rooted in the latest research, but far from the expectation of a liberal tradition.

Responsive Government

Another liberal postulate had to do with democratic government, and with the conviction that even where political power must, of social necessity, be exercised by the nation's leaders, they could, by employing various devices, be held responsible to public opinion and the people's interests. Political science as a discipline thus strongly supported the existing institutions and practices of liberalism. With only an occasional intimation that some individual political scientist might favor an avowedly nondemocratic reform,[17] most practitioners continued to write books and journal articles praising constitutional rights, frequent elections, federalism, competitive parties, and so forth. However, as the evidence on individual and group irrationality mounted,

---

15. *Public Opinion* (New York: Harcourt, Brace, 1922), pp. 30–31.

16. *The Phantom Public* (New York: Harcourt, Brace, 1925), pp. 54–62.

17. For example, see Walter J. Shepard, "Democracy in Transition," *American Political Science Review* (February 1935): 18–19.

many members of the discipline felt constrained to advocate an approach to American politics designed to compensate for some of democracy's perceived shortcomings, and here they virtually admitted the impossibility of democracy's functioning according to the liberal vision. Specifically, it became commonplace among political scholars to recommend setting aside a certain realm of public activity and, in the name of efficiency, maintaining it beyond the range of day-to-day democratic control.

Woodrow Wilson, in the classic statement of this position, wrote as early as 1887 that political thinkers had spent two thousand years addressing the problem of who should make basic decisions for society. Democrats, of course, had decided in favor of the people. The time had come, Wilson argued, to think more about how the same decisions might be executed well, for it was actually "getting to be harder to *run* a constitution than to frame one." As he put it, "Administrative questions are not political questions. Although politics sets the tasks of administration, it should not be suffered to manipulate its offices." To make the new concept even clearer, Wilson suggested that "Politics is . . . the special province of the statesman, administration of the technical official."[18] In Wilson's scheme of things, it is right that electorates and the elected will exercise ultimate control over America's administrative officials, but not every day and not with direct impact on every conceivable administrative function. Formal democracy aside, his intention was to expound the notion that some specially trained people are necessary for government to operate smoothly, although to the extent that these people and their work come to embody and reflect expertise and specialization, actual democracy is surely attenuated.

Frank Goodnow foreshadowed this eventuality in his book *Politics and Administration*. Following Wilson's lead, Goodnow encouraged the public to play a democratic role by electing many officials and by expressing its will via referenda and initiatives. But he, too, defined administration as an activity requiring people of special training and competence, almost as if they would substitute for the rationality that seemed lacking in democratic practice. As Goodnow put it, government needed "a force of agents" that would be "free from the influence of politics because of the fact that their mission is the exercise of foresight and discretion, the pursuit of truth, the gathering of information, the maintenance of a strictly impartial attitude toward the individuals with whom they have dealings."[19]

The idea of a realm of administration standing next to that of politics now seems a natural outgrowth of those general trends described by Mary Furner

---

18. "The Study of Administration," *Political Science Quarterly* 2 (June 1887):197–222.

19. *Politics and Administration: A Study in Government* (New York: Macmillan, 1900), p. 85.

and Thomas Haskell,[20] whereby developing professions in the late nineteenth century created specialized knowledge and offered it to society in exchange for status and authority. In the specific case of political science, as we have seen, the discipline committed itself to promoting good citizenship, broadly conceived, and that mission entailed training young people for ordinary political participation and/or government service. What evolved was a program of studies serving two ends, not always entirely compatible with each other. Political science professors taught courses to instruct students in the principles of good citizenship, that is, to believe in democracy's great institutions and to fulfill their expected role in public life. However, the same professors, or their departmental colleagues, also taught courses in which students learned the principles of administration, or how to run government agencies expertly. As Dwight Waldo has shown, right up to World War II this two-track notion reigned almost unchallenged in the discipline.[21] It eventually collapsed not because the contradiction between democracy and expertise became intolerable, but when political scientists realized that real-life administration was as political as politics can be.

When political scientists recommended expertise and administrative skill as an antidote to some of democracy's ills, their specific suggestions reflected the discipline's persistent and deepening commitment to science itself, which we have already noted as a postwar phenomenon. The reports of the three National Conferences on the Science of Politics, held from 1923 to 1925, were full of exhortations to produce scientific knowledge that would help to improve the quality of political life in America. As Merriam wrote, "unless a higher degree of science can be brought into the operations of government, civilization is in the very gravest peril from the caprice of ignorance and passion."[22] Or, "The whole scheme of governmental activity requires a body of scientific political principles for even reasonable efficiency and success. It is the function of political science to provide this science of politics."[23]

The general idea, which political scholars shared with other social scientists of the age, was that what Lippmann called "organized intelligence,"[24] wielded by experts, would help Americans stop "muddling through" and

---

20. Mary O. Furner, *Advocacy and Objectivity* (Lexington: University of Kentucky Press, 1975); and Thomas Haskell, *The Emergence of Professional Social Science* (Urbana: University of Illinois Press, 1977).

21. *The Administrative State* (New York: Ronald Press, 1948), passim, esp. pp. 12–21, 159–66.

22. "Progress Report of the Committee on Political Research," *American Political Science Review* (May 1923): 295.

23. "Reports of the National Conference on the Science of Politics," ibid. (February 1924): 119.

24. See Lippmann, *Public Opinion*, part 8, "Organized Intelligence," pp. 369–418.

finally "apply scientific methods to the management of society as we have been learning to apply them in the natural world."[25] In the vocabulary of political science, familiar since Plato used the same concepts under other names, the goal was to let knowledge, rather than mere opinion, rule the realm of public affairs. Many advocates of the new approach seem not to have realized how seriously their clamor for scientific expertise denied the validity of liberalism's postulates about rationality, groups, and government. And if their enthusiasm for knowledge over opinion implicitly raised the question of who, in the modern era, might serve as latter-day Platonic philosopher kings—or who Lasswell's "political psychiatrists" might be—they did not see fit to discuss this question at great length. But it was being asked and answered, with stunning effect, in the world at large, and with consequences that American political science could hardly ignore.

The Challenge of Authoritarianism

In 1933, William F. Willoughby, twenty-seventh APSA president, addressed his colleagues and spoke of the weakness of democracy, of "the tendency of the voters . . . to demand or approve the reckless occurrence of debt and extravagance in the expenditure of public funds; . . . of blocs in our legislative bodies to put special or class interests above those of the general welfare. To these may be added the difficulty encountered in making popular government a reality . . . in the sense of preventing real political powers from becoming vested in self-seeking, and often corrupt, political rings."[26] Willoughby touched upon, albeit unintentionally, the failure of liberal democracy in exactly those three areas—of individual citizenship, political groups, and responsible government—where it was not supposed to fail, according to America's most fundamental expectations. His remarks indicated, then, that by the early 1930s the discipline as a whole had reached a point where its scientific findings could not be discounted as separate curiosities but constituted, instead, a coherent body of testimony to the notion that something in democracy either needed radical repair or—always a possibility when old faiths are challenged—a new and reassuring explanation.

The Political Scene

The liberal faith certainly was challenged, and severely so, throughout the 1920s and 1930s. Authoritarian governments seemed everywhere on the

---

25. James T. Shotwell, *Intelligence and Politics* (New York: Century, 1921), p. 26.
26. "A Program for Research in Political Science," *American Political Science Review* (February 1933): 3–4.

march, and Americans were unprepared to confront them, either in theory or in practice.

The existence of modern authoritarianism embarrassed American liberals in two ways. On the one hand, it impressed upon them the fact that democracy had failed almost entirely to take hold in Europe after World War I. This was especially disturbing where it had been established in Eastern Europe after Woodrow Wilson's calls to make the world safe for democracy and self-determination, although the plague of repression was not confined there. By the mid-1930s, authoritarian regimes held sway in Italy, Germany, Turkey, Austria, Bulgaria, Greece, Portugal, Hungary, Poland, Romania, Yugoslavia, Latvia, Lithuania, Russia, and Japan. All this led many Americans to conclude that democracy was not a viable form of government except under special circumstances, or with a development period measured in generations if not centuries. More significantly, this political reality, when considered soberly, suggested that men are not naturally created with a capacity, or even a desire, for self-rule. In consequence, Americans increasingly wondered whether, contrary to their liberal faith, the nation's institutions might be artificial rather than the model of a natural order for mankind.

On the other hand, not only authoritarian circumstances but also their attendant ideologies, such as Marxism and National Socialism, argued directly against the notion that America's democratic institutions and procedures were appropriate for modern man. The fundamental rationale for dictatorship, on both the Left and the Right, was that people are not rational, that they are swayed by their emotions, that individuals have no right to congregate in groups such as independent churches or free labor unions in order to express their private interests but must subordinate those as against the nation's destiny, that parliamentary representation with multiple parties can only lead to confusion and a perversion of the national will, and that countries must therefore be ruled undemocratically either by a single and exclusive party or by a dominant and charismatic leader. In fact, the whole point of authoritarian ideology, as Karl Loewenstein explained, was to claim that people lack sufficient reason to rule themselves temperately with laws and constitutions, wherefore they must be led, on the basis of intoxicating sentiment, by some agent—either party or dictator—who will address them with emotional propaganda and primitive symbols in order to create consent that is apparently spontaneous but actually imposed.[27]

When liberal, democratic scholars were confronted by these notions, they found, in Brecht's terms, that "science was unable to define Western civilization by reference to fundamental principle," for the scientific method

---

27. "Militant Democracy and Fundamental Rights," *American Political Science Review* (June 1937): 418.

"does not enable us to state, in absolute terms, whether the purpose pursued by us or by others is good or bad, right or wrong, just or unjust, nor which of several conflicting purposes is more valuable than the other. It only enables us to answer those questions in relative terms."[28]

In a way, it was the triumph of professional creed over liberal context, where the entire corpus of scientific knowledge seemed unable to provide a course for society to follow, and where in 1939 Robert S. Lynd called into question the scientific enterprise itself in the very title of his book, *Knowledge for What?*[29] Nevertheless, many political scientists seemed unable to refrain from persisting in their commitment to the scientific approach, almost as if its shortcomings were irrelevant to their professional objectives. For example, William Munro argued in 1928 that his colleagues' "immediate goal . . . should be to release political science from the old metaphysical and juristic concepts upon which it has traditionally been based." We should, he said, "discard our allegiance to the absolute, for nothing would seem to be more truly self-evident than the proposition that all civic rights and duties, all forms and methods of government, are relative to one another, as well as to time and place and circumstance."[30] Did he really think that, for Americans, loyalty to the Constitution was relative, a matter of fleeting taste? George E. G. Catlin expounded the case for science very plainly when he suggested that "the business of the scientist is to study those methods which a man must adopt to attain this or that end *if* he happen to choose it."[31] Was he really ready to let political scientists choose to inquire into the most efficient ways to overthrow America's government, and then publish the results?

Triumph and Tragedy

Consider for a moment how far political science had come by the late 1930s, and what it had done in order to get there. Seeking to work scientifically, so as to acquire a share in the authority generated by the new professions, political scientists organized, did their research, published the results, and generally did what universities expected them to do. It was a triumph of successful adaptation to new circumstances in the world of higher education. This is not to say that every political scholar worked in the approved scientific fashion, but the trend was clear.

---

28. *Political Theory: The Foundations of Twentieth-Century Political Thought* (Princeton: Princeton University Press, 1959), pp. 8, 124.

29. *Knowledge for What? The Place of Social Science in American Culture* (Princeton: Princeton University Press, 1939).

30. "Physics and Politics," pp. 8, 10.

31. "Appendix: Commentary," in Stuart A. Rice, ed., *Methods in Social Science* (Chicago: University of Chicago Press, 1931), p. 93.

All along, as the discipline's members in effect strove to fulfill liberalism's further postulate, on the efficacy of science, they knew that the substance of their work was to bolster democratic goals widely endorsed by America's citizens. Yet, as the commitment to science translated itself into research practice, its results made liberalism's postulates with regard to expected political behavior seem less and less true. At that point only one liberal tenet, on moral equality, could be considered beyond empirical disproof. Yet as to that precept, even though nothing compellingly persuasive could be said against the moral equality of men, neither could the same proposition be professionally expounded in conclusive fashion. In short, faced with a crisis in the real world, political science had little constructive to say because there was little interface between the enterprise of scientific scholarship and the realm of old-fashioned virtue. And here was the tragic condition—a matter, in literary terms, of pursuing one good end so single-mindedly as to lose out on another.

Thus the conjunction of triumph and tragedy contained a historical irony. The difficulty was not, after all, due to any idiosyncrasy of individual political scholars, since most of them were wholeheartedly committed to American democracy. In fact, the difficulty flowed from success, for, throughout the universities, teachers of all sorts were together consummating their collective victory over the college system of administrative control for curriculum and teaching, whereupon political scholars, along with the rest, finally gained the right to profess what they thought should be professed. Almost immediately, however, political scientists discovered that they did not know where they should stand collectively with regard to some of the most important questions being addressed to their field.

Of course there were many political scientists who responded energetically to the multiple crises of American democracy in the 1930s, to the economic failures at home and the strategic confusions abroad. But what cannot be denied is that, for all their enthusiasm and genuine commitment to liberal values and devices, they were not professionally persuasive in support of democracy in its hour of need. For example, Charles Beard called upon American educators to instruct young people in the ideals and practice of democracy. He admitted, however, that "our democracy rests upon the assumption that all human beings have a moral worth in themselves that cannot be used for ends alien to humanity. This is an assumption and cannot be proved."[32] Carl Friedrich conceded that academic freedom, when "vindicated in terms of neutral truth" in an age of ideological confrontation, can only be farcical. But he could offer, in place of such truth, only "faith in the develop-

---

32. "Democracy and Education in the United States," *Social Research* (September 1937): 394.

ment of the free personality as the ultimate ideal of humanity."[33] For Charles Merriam, there were four principal "assumptions" of democracy, including "the essential dignity of man" and the "perfectability of mankind."[34] It is clear from his exposition of the subject that he supported every sort of common decency and deplored its absence. But he never explained whether his "assumptions" referred to fact or to aspiration, and what compelling reasons there might be to adopt those assumptions if they were, after all, only aspirations.

In their enthusiasm for the home team, political scientists who supported a free society during the 1930s may have been effective cheerleaders. As professionals, however, in an age so thoroughly committed to science, they advocated the right objectives in terms that carried very little weight. Some members of the discipline recognized the problem and feared that insufficient attention to values would somehow undermine both American patriotism and commitment to democracy. They therefore urged their colleagues to remember that political science must always retain a "normative" character, that it must teach values as well as the facts of political life.[35] Arguments of this sort had some emotional appeal, but the Cassandras were not noticeably effective in changing the discipline's professional course. Their more forward-looking associates preferred to await a new theory of democracy that could assimilate the results of scientific political research while continuing to find strength in science itself rather than in traditional morals.

---

33. "Education and Propaganda," *The Atlantic Monthly* (June 1937): 693, 701.

34. "The Assumptions of Democracy," *Political Science Quarterly* (September 1938): 329.

35. One persistent critic of the trend toward a scientific political science was William Y. Elliot. See his *The Pragmatic Revolt in Politics* (New York: Macmillan, 1928); and "The Pragmatic Revolt in Politics: Twenty Years in Retrospect," *Review of Politics* (January 1940): 1–11.

American Political Science, Liberalism, and the Invention of Political Theory

John G. Gunnell

Only that which has not history is definable.

—Nietzsche

This essay, most narrowly specified, is part of an account of the discoursive history of academic political theory in the United States. It can, however, for at least two reasons, be construed as a study in the history of political science. First, the period under consideration, 1940–50, was a crucial one in the development of this discipline, and the issues that arose in the subfield of political theory were determinative with respect to its subsequent evolution. Second, the discourse of political theory was also the basic vehicle for reflection on the state of the discipline, its past, and its future prospects. But the relationship between political science and political theory has, since the beginning of the period in question, been an uneasy one. The principal purpose of this essay is to explain that relationship and to explore the origins of a controversy that fundamentally shaped the structure and content of contemporary academic political theory.

Political theory today has little to say to or about its parent field, and much of political theory is of marginal interest and intelligibility to many political scientists. This estrangement cannot be explained merely in terms of normal trends in professional differentiation. It is in part the legacy of an old quarrel that was one of the principal factors in the emergence of the independent interdisciplinary field of political theory. Since the early 1970s, the subfield of political theory in political science, once understood to be the core of the discipline, has tended to reflect concerns generated within the wider, more autonomous field that has evolved its own institutional structure, issue nexus, and self-image.

Reprinted in a somewhat shortened version from *American Political Science Review* 82 (1988): 71–87.

This situation has sometimes been perceived as a problem, but it has seldom occasioned great concern among either political theorists or political scientists as a whole. In some quarters, both in political theory and mainstream political science, there is a sense of relief that the tension between field and subfield that had characterized the behavioral era has been ameliorated by intellectual distance. There are narrow but weighty professional pressures that tend to lead to the validation of separation but that are rationalized in terms of notions of intellectual pluralism. Often the problem is depreciated by noting that it is more apparent than real if one takes into account the manner in which the policy turn of the postbehavioral era has produced a convergence between normative and empirical research. But the propensity to confront the issue on a superficial level conceals both the historical source of the problem and some very basic difficulties that cannot easily be dismissed.

A readily accessible and familiar explanation of the alienation of political theory from political science locates the cause in the conflict that arose in the course of the behavioral revolution and its attack on the study of the history of political theory as antiquarian and inimical to the development of empirical theory and a scientific study of politics. This explanation is not incorrect, but it is incomplete. It is necessary to reach a deeper historical sense of the genealogy of political theory and to recover some of the more fundamental issues that occasioned the controversy we associate with behavioralism and its aftermath. By the early 1950s some of these issues had already been submerged in the rhetoric and legitimating philosophies that characterized the debate between "traditional" and "scientific" theory. A pivotal transformation in the discourse of political theory, which occurred during the 1940s, was obscured. An understanding of that transformation is also important for exploring the general problem of the relationship between academic political inquiry and politics—a problem that was at the heart of the controversy about political theory as it originally developed.

The Real History of Political Theory

The basic images of political theory of and by which we are now possessed, images of theory as both a product and activity and as both a subject matter and mode of inquiry, have been generated within, and have little meaning outside, the language of political theory as an academic field. Attempts to endow political theory with world-historical significance by seeking its past in a great tradition from Plato to the present, by categorically defining it as the reflective and critical dimension of political life, by understanding it as a tributary of theory in the natural sciences, or by creating other putative identities that would enhance the authority of this professional field and provide foundations for its claim to knowledge, cannot withstand much analytical scrutiny (Gunnell 1986). Although we have become accustomed to thinking of the history of political theory as the chronologically ordered canon of classic texts, such history is in fact largely a reified analytical construct. What we might call the "real history of political theory" is the history of the academic field that created this image as its subject matter and projected it as its past. Furthermore, despite the current distance between political theory and political science, these images, and the field of political theory itself, were largely an invention of U.S. political science.

Although it is important to investigate the early development of the concept of political theory as well as the academic practice that gave rise to it (Gunnell 1983), the current species of both essentially came into existence after 1940 in the wake of the emigration of refugee scholars from Germany. Although the émigrés did not, for the most part, come to the United States understanding themselves as political theorists, this eventually became their identity. The adoption, appropriation, or discovery of this identity and the propagation of their image of, and concerns about, liberalism, as well as a related conceptual cluster including positivism and relativism, precipitated a scholarly and ideological conflict within political science that was manifest in a debate about political theory. Although the behavioral revolution was hardly one-dimensional, it was in an important respect initially a conservative rebellion catalyzed by, and directed against, the encroachment of a vision that was hostile to the traditional values of U.S. political science.

Notions of theory as the history of political ideas and as part of empirical social-scientific inquiry had, through the 1930s, been consistently understood as either complementary or even merely diachronic and synchronic modes of the same endeavor, which involved explaining politics by linking behavior and ideas. Charles Merriam, despite his emphasis on jettisoning or surpassing history as a form of inquiry, neither disparaged the paradigmatic studies of the history of political theories associated with his mentor, William Dunning, nor perceived any serious discontinuity between such studies—in which he himself participated significantly—and the advancement of social scientific theory. But a more significant factor in explaining the lack of tension was an underlying intellectual consensus that transcended various scholarly and ideological divisions between empiricism and idealism, history and science, and statism and laissez-faire. The history of political theory was understood by all as the history of the development of scientific knowledge about politics and as a story of the progress of the symbiotic relationship between such knowledge and the evolution of liberal democratic thought and institutions.

The notions of political theory and the disciplinary practices that developed between the late 1800s and the 1930s were, to be sure, the receptacle for the discourse that emerged in the 1940s. The arguments, for example, of someone such as Leo Strauss about the rise and decline of the great tradition would not have taken hold if the basic idea of the tradition had not already gained conventional acceptance in the work of George Sabine and his predecessors, and there was nothing in the behavioral credo that had not been already articulated as an ideal to which political science should aspire. But the transformation was dramatic. The dominant consensus was frontally challenged for the first time, and political theory, as the focus of controversy, became an essentially contested concept.

The great change began almost unnoticed, or at least uncomprehended, as the claims of Strauss, Hannah Arendt, Hans Morgenthau, Theodor Adorno, Eric Voegelin, Franz Neumann, Arnold Brecht, Max Horkheimer, Herbert Marcuse, and others, in varying ways and degrees but inexorably, reshaped the discourse of political theory. Despite some very great differences in ideological and philosophical perspective, they looked much alike to the successors of Merriam as they uniformly and on very similar bases challenged the liberal, scientific, relativistic, historicist perspective that dominated political theory and political science. What might be taken as the politically conservative arguments of individuals such as Voegelin were initially more professionally visible than those on the Left associated with the Institute for Social Research, but they all propagated the thesis that liberalism, either inherently or because of its degenerate condition, was at the core of a modern crisis and implicated in the rise of totalitarianism.

It would be far too simplistic to suggest that the behavioral revolution should be understood exclusively as a reaction to this challenge, but we have lost sight of the degree to which its arguments were originally formed in response to it. The attack on liberalism and science and the rejection of the progressive-pragmatic vision of history were too basic to allow any syncretic resolution. The sense of liberal givenness, which characteristically allowed U.S. theorists to embrace relativism and the idea of the separation of facts and values while remaining totally committed to definite political ideals, was incompatible with the transcendental speculation and philosophies of history, whether of the Marxist or natural-law variety, that marked the new literature. Since at least the turn of the century, such ideas had traditionally been specifically what most U.S. political theorists had understood themselves as rejecting.

I seek to specify as precisely as possible how the controversy commenced and how it shaped the discourse of political theory. The situation as it first emerged was not clear to many of the participants. The new ideas had often not taken distinct and published form when the conflict began, and some of those involved in the controversy were at first truly perplexed. Individuals such as Sabine, whose influential analysis of political theory was not significantly different from that of those devoted to empirical political science, found himself the target of those whose ideas he largely shared simply because he represented the history of political theory. Similarly, protobehavioralists and the founders of the behavioral movement, such as David Easton, saw not only a growing tendency toward historical and evaluative analysis that was pointedly at the expense of the idea of a scientific study of politics and liberal values but one that was being mounted within the genre of political theory, which had heretofore reflected the constitutive conventions of the discipline of political science.

The Transformation of Political Theory

Apart from textbooks, there was at the beginning of the 1940s a dearth of literature distinctly understood as political theory, and institutionally, as a subfield of political science, it had all but disappeared. The revitalization of discourse could be construed as beginning with the publication of Sabine's 1939 article, "What is Political Theory?" in the first issue of the *Journal of Politics* and with the appearance, in the same year, of the *Review of Politics* (which became a principle vehicle for the work of the émigrés). The resumption of discussion about political theory and its place in political science was in part prompted by an increasing concern about the status of the scientific study of politics which, despite the work of Harold Lasswell and others connected with the Chicago school during the 1930s, had received limited attention after Merriam's enthusiastic claims in the 1920s. More than a decade before the behavioral revolution, Benjamin Lippincott (1940) argued that in practice the discipline of political science was much as it had been at the turn of the century and that the greatest deficiency was theoretical. What passed as political theory had been devoted to the recounting of past ideas, and even among those committed to science, there was an "aversion" and "hostility" to theory (p. 130). But most important was the renewed reflection on liberal political values and the beginning of the impact of newly arrived European scholars who severely questioned the scientific faith and liberalism as well as the historical vision that united them.

A pointed "challenge" to political scientists was advanced by William Foote Whyte in an article published in 1943. This piece (quite accidentally) served as the principal catalyst for the incipient controversy. Whyte was a social anthropologist who had been studying political organization in a slum district, and there is no indication that he had any notion of the nerve endings that would be agitated by his comments. He suggested that the war had occasioned a concern about democratic values that had led political scientists to "write political philosophy and ethics" and neglect the study of "plain politics." He argued that "a scientific study of politics" required "the discovery of certain uniformities or laws" and that political scientists should direct their attention to "the description and analysis of political behavior" (pp. 692–93).

The most immediate response to Whyte was by John Hallowell (1944a) whose work would become one of the principal conduits through which the ideas of the émigrés entered political theory and whose voice would come to represent the new mood in the field. The response, however, moved the discussion to a very different context. Whyte, much like Lippincott, was writing from the perspective of traditional American social science, but Hallowell identified this critique, as well as the general commitment to science in the discipline, with an intellectual position that was not only alien but unfamiliar to most U.S. political scientists. Hallowell suggested that Whyte's views reflected "increasingly positivistic" trends that threatened to undermine "all belief in transcendental truth and value" that could serve as a barrier to intellectual and political "nihilism" (pp. 642–43).

The political-theory research committee of the American Political Science Association had been largely inactive in the early years of the war, but in 1943 it met, under the chairmanship of Francis G. Wilson, and attempted to sort out the issues that were beginning to surface. Wilson noted that there was now a "deep cleavage among political theorists in the area of primary ideas" on an "ultimate issue" (Wilson et al. 1944, 726–27). The exact nature of this issue and cleavage was something that he had some difficulty in specifying. One facet of the issue, or one way of stating it, involved a conflict between those who, like the "great political thinkers," took metaphysics seriously and those who believed that philosophy was relevant only as "logical thought." Was scientific "detachment" from traditional philosophy a sign of "progress" or "ineptitude"? Another definition of the problem was in terms of a clash between the "theological approach" and the "empirical" or "'positivistic,' scientific, or liberal technique of social study." A theological perspective was considered by some as necessary for understanding both the past and contemporary society, but there was a question of what constituted such a perspective and the manner in which it might conflict with the "approaches of idealistic and rationalistic liberalism" that were more characteristic of political science (p. 727).

There was also a recognition of a conflict between those who stressed "value-free discussions in political science" and those who believed that there was "more in politics than simply clinical observation." All agreed that it was important to "formulate and criticize values" and that there should be "a frontal attack" on the problem of "value in American political society," and many believed that in some sense it was necessary and possible to arrive at "valid social and political principles." There was much the same kind of discussion about knowledge of regularities regarding "political behavior." Most were willing to compromise at some point and acknowledge that both "utopia" and the "facts" should be given consideration (pp. 727–28, 730), but it was clear that the consensus in political theory was breaking down.

Some believed, Wilson reported, that the fundamental cleavage was manifest in the differences between the thought of the Middle Ages and that of the modern age, between natural law and natural rights. There was also a division between those who argued that the United States needed a consciousness of history and that an examination of our philosophy of history was in order and those who wanted to concentrate on practical questions of political choice and the "ends-means relationship." There was also a general, but maybe less than enthusiastic, agreement that there was a need for a greater availability of the "texts of the great thinkers" and that "the political tradition of the West must be subjected to close scrutiny."

Wilson, who was a specialist in American political thought and a consistent spokesman for a U.S. brand of conservatism, did his best to report and make sense of the various and sometimes novel notions of theory that surfaced in these discussions and to reconcile them. Neither task was easy. The issues being formulated were radically different from those that had been characteristic of American political science and political theory.

In the symposium, Benjamin Wright (who had written on the American tradition of natural law) claimed that the greatest need of the period was for a statement of objectives in terms of ideals, since there was no "clear conception of what we are fighting for, what goals we should seek to attain, even in this country, after the war" (739–40). Ernest S. Griffith, on the other hand, argued that "research in political theory hitherto has been largely synonymous with searches for the origin, growth, and decline in ideas, principles, and doctrines," while what was required, if there was to be "precision" in the field, was more attention to "the basic concepts that underlie all theory" and to the definition of these concepts. Such research, he cautioned, should not be understood as a search for "*correct*" concepts, since theorists have too long looked for absolute principles and failed to recognize that principles are subjective and historically relative to various institutional arrangements (pp. 740–42).

The claims of Wright and Griffith could easily be situated within the characteristic discourse of the field and did not necessarily represent sharply conflicting attitudes. The increasing tension between such positions, however, indicated a different kind of influence. Voegelin, who had fled to the United States in 1938, was beginning to make his mark on professional discussions of political theory during this period, and in this symposium he presented at some length the basic research scheme and thesis regarding the derailment of modern political thought that would inform his *New Science of Politics* (1952)—a book that would epitomize one of the poles of political theory during the 1950s and 1960s.

Voegelin suggested that the study of the history of political ideas had been represented with distinction by individuals like Dunning and Sabine and was of particular importance to U.S. scholars who had done the most to develop this field, over which they had held a "monopoly." He claimed, however, that it was now necessary to rethink the field in light of the vast new historical knowledge available and in terms of the general philosophy of history.

The increasingly pivotal issue of relativism was, at this time, grounded in a concrete concern about the defense of liberal democratic principles. The war and the domestic political crises of the 1930s that preceded it had prompted an uneasiness about the lack of an articulate and philosophically grounded democratic ideology. And the work of individuals like Charles Beard and John Dewey had already incited a controversy about historicism and relativism as a threat to both political values and scientific objectivity. The concern about relativism, then, was not without precedent. But as the issue entered the literature of political theory, it took on a reconstituted identity based on new claims about the origins of totalitarianism. The assessment advanced by émigré scholars, and by Hallowell, was that the problem of totalitarianism was at root a problem of science, liberalism, and relativism and that it was susceptible in large part to a philosophical or religious solution.

If we want to understand fully the behavioral animus toward "traditional" political theory, it is necessary to take account of the extent to which what had actually been traditional in American political theory was being fundamentally challenged. The unhappiness with liberalism and science that would mark much of the major work in the history of political theory by the 1960s (Strauss, Voegelin, Arendt, and others) was already taking shape. And it propagated the image of a crisis and decline in Western political history and thought. Hallowell, in reviewing Brecht's account of the decline of the German republic, argued (1944b) that Brecht did not sufficiently stress the degree to which that decline was "a direct consequence of the liberal's lack of conviction in his own philosophy." The solution, for Hallowell, was a renewal of what he believed were the religious and spiritual foundations of liberal democracy.

Hallowell's attack on liberalism became strident (1947), and the substance of his argument was hardly congenial to American political science. Merriam, for example, had stressed the danger of theology to liberalism while Hallowell was suggesting that secular liberalism, with the disintegration of religious conscience, led to anarchy and tyranny. Much of the tradition of U.S. social science had grown out of an attempt to replace religion as a cohesive social force with a science of social control and public policy that would realize liberal values, but now "political theorists" were claiming that liberalism and "the liberal science of politics" were a failure and the breeding ground of totalitarianism.

It would be a mistake to assume that political scientists committed to the scientific study of politics were unconcerned with values—either as an object of study or as premises and goals of empirical inquiry. As Herman Finer put it (1945), "the need was for an ideology that would accomplish for democracy what Marxism had done for Soviet Communism" (p. 239). These claims would be overshadowed by the renewed commitment to scientific inquiry by the end of the decade, but the "value-free" stance of behavioralism did not entail a rejection or neglect of what it understood as liberal democratic values. Gabriel Almond, for instance, even argued that the "chief challenge" of the day was to seek "a valid theory of natural law" (Almond et al. 1946). The problem was not that the new influences in political theory stressed values but that behavioralism could not countenance the idea that science and liberalism exemplified social and intellectual decline.

The symposium, "Politics and Ethics," in which Almond participated was conceived as an attempt to explore further the issues that had been raised by Whyte. But, for the most part, the participants talked past one another, and the arguments were by now far removed from Whyte's actual concern and understanding. Whyte claimed that he did not recognize the target of Hallowell's criticism—that he had never even met anyone who represented the position attributed to him. He stated that he was not interested in the "philosophy of science" and "positivism" and that Hallowell had gone off on a "tangent" and created a "straw man" (p. 301). Hallowell was caught up in a realm of ideas and issues that were distinctly European and closely related to the arguments of individuals such as Arnold Brecht.

Brecht had been a political actor and administrator who did not enter academia, or what he understood as the pursuit of "science," until he came to the United States and the New School of Social Research in 1933 after a period of Nazi harassment. Around the turn of the decade, he published several articles dealing with the question of relativism, absolutism, and science that eventually became the basis of his book, *Political Theory: The Foundations of Twentieth-Century Political Thought* (1959). Brecht did not directly attribute the rise of national socialism to a philosophical context, but, like many others, he was concerned about the influence of legal positivism and relativism on judges and lawyers who applied laws that were morally reprehensible. He believed, however, that it was impossible to seek a form of "scientific" proof or some rationalistic equivalent for moral principles and natural law. Moral judgment was a matter of human volition even though no less lacking in validity. Brecht argued that scientific value relativism, as expounded by Max Weber, Hans Kelsen, Gustav Radbruch, and Lasswell, had once seemed a liberating philosophy, but in the face of Nazism it became a paralyzing one. In a search for intellectual authority to combat totalitarianism, intellectuals, however mistakenly, "turned from being political scientists to becoming ethical philosophers or theologians (if not simply bad logicians) and *they called this science*" (1970, pp. 434, 490). For Brecht, the great dilemma of modern political theory was that there was no scientific knowledge of values. His solution was to teach "the *limits* of science" and urge other ways to bridge the *is* and *ought* (p. 494).

In 1947, Brecht reported on a roundtable ("Beyond Relativism in Political Theory") that included Francis Coker, Roland Pennock, Lippincott, Wright, Voegelin, Hallowell, and Almond. Kelsen was unable to attend, but he sent a message indicating that despite the growing unpopularity of value relativism in the United States, he was still an adherent and remained a critic of moral "absolutism." For Kelsen, as well as for most U.S. political scientists and theorists, value skepticism and relativism were understood as the foundations of liberal democratic theory. Only on this basis, they believed, could liberal democracy be justified. Moral absolutism signaled political absolutism for émigrés like Kelsen, while for Kelsen's erstwhile student, Voegelin, relativism abetted and reflected the decline of the West.

Brecht suggested that the paradox of modernity was that "modern science and modern scientific methods, with all their splendor of achievement, have led to an ethical vacuum, a religious vacuum, and a philosophical vacuum." He argued that the situation had come to a point where social science found it impossible to distinguish between right and wrong, good and evil, and justice and injustice. Political science was particularly affected by this dilemma, because it dealt most directly with the phenomena of nazism, fascism, and communism, which had "settled down" in this vacuum. Brecht claimed that "no political theorist can honestly avoid the issue" posed by "scientific relativism" (pp. 470–71). Most participants in the symposium offered little in the way of a concrete recommendation for getting "beyond relativism."

There has not been sufficient recognition of the degree to which the transcendental urge and historical pessimism manifest in the émigré literature affected political theory. It contributed to the split between political theory and political science during the behavioral era and to the eventual constitution of political theory as an independent field. Although the behavioral revolution, or counterrevolution, in many ways transformed the mainstream practice of the discipline, it was, at least theoretically, a reaffirmation of past ideals— ideals that did not rest easily alongside the arguments that characterized the new literature of political theory. Although the behavioralists singled out the study of the history of political theory as requiring displacement, transformation, or supercession, this was more because it was the genre to which most of the offending arguments happened to belong than because the literature characteristic of the field before 1940 actually embodied the problems with which behavioralists were concerned.

By 1950, there was an antiscientific, antiliberal sentiment in political theory even though neither the medium nor the message were always entirely clear. Although, for example, Arendt had published widely during the 1940s in a variety of journals, her first major work in English, *The Origins of Totalitarianism,* did not appear until 1951. Much of Strauss's *Natural Right and History* was originally presented as Walgren lectures at the University of Chicago in 1949, a year after his appointment, but the book was not published until 1953. Strauss had already announced in his work on Hobbes (1936) some of his distinctive themes, including the depreciation of both liberalism and the new science of politics, but the book received little attention and surely not much comprehension.

Although these attacks on science, liberalism, and the legitimacy of the modern age had not yet coalesced into a definite oppositional force in political science, they were at least engendering an alien mood that had a considerable professional impact. There were all sorts of reasons to reassert the scientific image of political science in the postwar years, and the new voices in political theory were not only failing to do so but were inimical to such an image. The need for scientific theory was the theme of William Anderson's survey of political science in 1949. What was required, he argued, was an "established body of tested propositions concerning the political nature and activities of man that are applicable throughout the world and presumably at all times" (p. 309). It was, he claimed, necessary to distinguish between politics and science and pursue the latter, and the way to do this was to study individual "human political behavior" or the "political atom" and produce knowledge in the "field of scientific method" (pp. 312–14).

Behavioralists, beginning in the 1950s, would increasingly emphasize their dedication to a vision of pure science, but the underlying concern at the end of the decade was still the articulation and realization of a science of *liberal* politics. In two articles, on Bagehot (1949) and Lasswell (1950), that closely preceded his analysis of the "decline of political theory" (1951), Easton made clear that the pursuit of science was a means and not an end and that the belief in the complementarity of scientific realism and liberal democracy was still alive. The ultimate purpose remained political rationality, but the immediate goal was to create a theoretically grounded science of politics equal to this task.

The individuals most responsible for affecting and sustaining the behavioral revolution had almost without exception been primarily trained in the field of historical and normative political theory, as traditionally conceived. While the debate within the discipline would eventually often be understood as a conflict between political *scientists* and political *theorists,* it really signified a split between different conceptions of theory. Few of the early behavioralists understood themselves as antitheoretical, and probably very few initially understood their concern with scientific political theory as a rejection of their earlier education. To some extent, what was involved was a lag between the graduate educational establishment and the new literature and mood of political theory. The theorists trained in the 1930s and 1940s had, for the most part, not been exposed to the arguments of the new wave of European thought that was appearing in political theory, and they felt a good deal more at home with the traditional goals of the field than with the perspective that characterized this literature. Ultimately they felt compelled to choose between political theory and political science, and the choice was as much ideological as professional. But by the mid-1950s, the behavioral critique of political theory was forcing the same polarizing choice on theorists concerned with historical and normative issues.

In 1950, Lippincott attempted, as he had a decade earlier, to make sense of what constituted political theory in the United States and to provide a critical analysis of the field. He suggested that political theory was at least potentially—and as correctly understood—the "most scientific branch" of political science. It was, however, an area in which political scientists had "produced little," if theory were defined, as he believed it should be, "as the systematic analysis of political relations." It should, he argued, be concerned with "general" claims about the "actions and behavior of men" and with particular events and institutions only as objects for testing its principles (pp. 208–9). Up to this point, Lippincott argued, "the greatest effort has been devoted to writing the history of political ideas" and "defining and classifying terms and principles of politics." The methods in political theory had been basically historical, and the "emphasis placed on the history of political ideas has meant very largely the abandonment of the aim of science" (pp. 209, 211, 214).

The call for science was increasingly accompanied by an attack on the existing practice of political theory. Theory was often described as historical, teleological, utopian, moralistic, ethical, and generally obscurantist. There was more going on in these critiques than was readily visible, and the exact target of the criticism was often not clearly or easily specified. By 1950, however, Hallowell had brought together his arguments in a comprehensive work (*The Main Currents of Modern Political Thought*). It reflected and summarized claims that had emerged in the discourse of political theory during the 1940s, and it initiated a genre that would find its classic expression in the work of Strauss, Voegelin, and others during the next decade. Even a work such as Sheldon Wolin's *Politics and Vision* (1960), which ideologically and philosophically was far removed from the positions of Hallowell, Voegelin, and Strauss, was still a story of liberalism and the decline of modern politics. The imprint of the 1940s was fundamental for the future of political theory.

Although Hallowell's book was about "modern political thought," a large portion was devoted to a synoptic reconstruction of the development of political ideas from ancient times up through the emergence of what he designated as "integral liberalism," which he claimed was an outgrowth of the ideas of individuals like Grotius and Locke. The image projected was one of a seamless web of history that moved from the classical world through the evolution of modern science, the Renaissance, and Hobbes to the rise of liberalism. However, the story of modern political thought was now a story of decline—a decline as organic as the upward slope of the past and one that was offered as an explanation of modern political problems and "the crisis of our times" exemplified in socialism, Marxism, the Soviet Union, fascism, and the theory and practice of totalitarianism in general. But the most basic problem was the decadence of contemporary liberalism and its inability to defend and maintain itself.

In Hallowell's saga, the main villain was positivism, which in turn he viewed as a direct outgrowth of the Enlightenment, utilitarianism, and German idealism. His notion of positivism was the very general one of an "attempt to transfer to the study of social and human phenomena the methods and concepts of the natural sciences," and he believed that it was represented by the work of Comte, J. S. Mill, Herbert Spencer, Lester Frank Ward, and Gumplowicz. Positivism, with its attendant separation of fact and value, and relativism undermined liberalism and allowed the rise of antiliberal political movements.

Some émigrés like Kelsen (1948) and Felix Oppenheim (1950) would continue to argue, like U.S. liberals, that relativism and empiricism were more conducive to democracy than moral absolutism. They claimed that there was a root connection between democracy and the spirit embodied in the scientific method. The imminent debate between "scientific" and "traditional" political theory would be far from simply a debate about method and political inquiry or even about an emphasis on values as opposed to facts. It was, in the end, a debate about liberalism, its foundation, and its fate—and about the relationship between political theory and politics.

There was an increasingly extravagant dimension to the rhetoric on both sides of the debate. Actual research and publication in the field hardly matched the picture of "positivism" that was painted by the critics of scientism, and the image of moralistic political theory on which the protobehavioralists focused was equally unreflective of the literature. To claim that political science was "mostly history and ethics" was simply counterfactual, and to argue that "the propositions of political theory have a character of 'unreality' and futility that bars out any serious interest in their discussion" (Perry 1950, 399, 401) was clearly to speak generically on the basis of a narrow and unspecified body of literature. But there was, ironically, a sense in which each faction was now beginning to fulfill the image conjured up by its opponents.

Herbert Simon, George A. Lundberg, and Lasswell participated in the discussion and pressed, as they would in many forums, for making the language of social science scientific. Although they did not specify their sources, they were clearly no longer strangers to the positivist philosophy of science. Simon enunciated a model of science as a system of predictive-cum-explanatory general propositions from which could be deduced other propositions about concrete observables that were therefore testable. Science was conceived methodologically as a unity, and human action as an object of inquiry was viewed as requiring no departure from the methods of natural science.

For Simon, it was essential that political science adopt what he considered to be the more advanced methods of the other social sciences, and he insisted that central to this task was a *transformation and redefinition of political theory* that would entail "consistent distinctions between political theory (i.e., scientific statements about the phenomena of politics) and the history of political thought (i.e., statements about what people have said about political theory and political ethics)" (p. 411).

Lasswell warned against getting too involved in the question of what "science" means and neglecting the practical end toward which scientific inquiry was ultimately directed, that is, "to decrease the indeterminacy of important political judgments," but he advocated "more attention to the construction of theoretical models" that would guide research (pp. 423, 425). Exactly what was entailed by the commitment, or recommitment, to science was not very clearly defined, but there definitely was a new philosophic dimension to the argument. Lasswell's collaboration with Kaplan, who had been a student of Carnap's, was one obvious point of intersection. And they had stated in the introduction to their book (1950) that it reflected a new scientific outlook informed by "a thorough-going empiricist philosophy of the sciences" based on "logical positivism, operationalism, instrumentalism" (pp. xiii–xiv). Maybe their position was actually more justified than informed by this philosophy, but in the face of new philosophical challenges, political scientists attempted more self-consciously to ground and articulate their scientific faith.

By 1950, some mainstream political scientists were becoming uneasy about the implications of the new scientism. Paul Appleby (1950), speculating on the direction of political science during the next twenty-five years, argued that a much broader value-oriented vision was required than the one that was then developing in the discipline, and for many the concern was still to link science to problems of practical politics (White 1950). Easton's call for the reconstruction of political theory has quite reasonably often been construed as the first shot fired in the behavioral revolution. But although *The Political System* (1953) was, to be sure, a critique of the study of the history of political theory and a plea for the creation of scientific theory, it is sometimes forgotten that it was an explicit challenge to the new "mood" in political theory and an attempt to find a basis for the reconciliation of political science and political theory that would at the same time sustain and advance liberal democratic values (chap. 1). By mid-decade such mediative integrating efforts had largely given way to the alienating forces that pushed political theory and political science along different paths. And in an important sense the language and agenda of political theory, for at least a generation, had already been set.

Conclusion

The literature of political theory is, and since the late 1930s has been, saturated with discussions about liberalism and its tradition, rise and decline, faith, dangers, limits, collapse, challenges, agony, paradox, irony, spirit, development, end, poverty, and crisis and its relation to innumerable things, individuals, and other political concepts. Even when the concept is not specifically a focus of discussion, the concern about liberalism significantly structures the discursive universe of political theory. An understanding of this situation requires a grasp of those initiating issues that informed the invention of political theory and that fundamentally shaped its real history. The enthusiastic reception of European thought in recent years, such as that associated with Habermas, is directly related to its perpetuation of the critique of liberalism, and surely some of the literature that has had the greatest impact on the field has been devoted to attempts, such as that of John Rawls, to provide new foundations for liberal theory.

Although the tension between political science and political theory was, and in large part has remained, the product of a disagreement about liberalism, the controversy quite early on became detached from concrete political issues. From the beginning, there was a tendency for the debates about liberalism to escape the political concerns that had given rise to them. For the émigrés, the experience of Weimar and totalitarianism was determinative and came close to confirming the idea that in Germany, as in Athens and Rome, liberalism was the manifestation of political decline and the threshold of tyranny. No matter how much individuals like Strauss and Marcuse might disagree on various grounds, they were at one in extending the analogy to contemporary politics in the United States. And even their specific critiques of liberalism were not all that different. For U.S. political scientists also, the rise of totalitarianism and its attendant ideologies during the 1930s, as well as the domestic problem of rationalizing the conflict between government and the economic enterprise, indicated a need to rearticulate and ground the principles of liberal democracy. If a sense of crisis regarding liberalism, in theory and practice, had not been part of the world of political science, the arguments of the émigrés would likely not have carried the weight that they did.

On both sides of the controversy, however, there continued to be an alienating displacement of the issues. In the case of the émigrés, there was a philosophization of their experience and a projection of the analysis onto recalcitrant political circumstances in the United States as well as the ambiguous screen of world history. This produced an estrangement between academic political theory and politics that has plagued the subsequent evolution of the field. The defense of liberalism among political scientists also became oblique. Either it became the validation of an image that was not easily related to political realities, or it took the form of a philosophy of science, conceptual frameworks, and empirical findings that often seemed to confirm the existence and efficacy of liberal society.

The debate about relativism was also originally grounded in a practical issue that was eventually obscured by the philosophical formulation of the problem. This was the problem of the relationship between academic and public discourse or between philosophy, political theory, and political science on the one hand and politics on the other. This concern about the authority of political inquiry and the intellectuals who engaged in it was equally prominent in the work of both the émigrés and the practitioners of traditional American political science, but the responses were different.

Although relativism, as a philosophical problem, may arise in reaction to crises in substantive practices such as science and politics, it more basically and frequently reflects a crisis in the understanding of the relationship between first- and second-order discourses, that is, between, for example, academic political theory and politics. It is a problem in part because second-order inquiry conceives its mission as the proprietary one of discovering, validating, or explicating the grounds of judgment in the activity it has appropriated as its subject matter. But the problem is often only tangentially one of the possibility and integrity of practical judgment. The pursuit of a solution to the problem of relativism is a quest for a comprehensive answer to the infinitely complex and contextually diverse questions attending the nexus between theory and practice. It most essentially reflects a crisis in the self-image of political theory and the foundations of its claims to knowledge.

The world of the émigrés was one of not only political but intellectual and professional insecurity, and the problem of relativism was a philosophical expression of their anxiety. The question of the authority of academic inquiry was an important concern for political science, but there were several reasons why the discipline tended not to perceive relativism as a threat. Easton's remedy for the decline of political theory, for example, called for the reconstitution of value theory without jettisoning the liberal belief in the relativity of values and their emotive nontranscendental basis. One reason that political science was able to absorb the issue of relativism was because it was an essential part of the pragmatic liberal creed of fallibility and progress in both scientific inquiry and politics. But the liberal science of politics had its own grounds of certainty.

There was, first of all, the belief that history validated liberalism and that liberal values were embedded in the basic institutions of U.S. politics. Relativism never was taken as implying that one value was as good as another but only that values reflected contexts and perspectives. Furthermore, certainty was to be achieved through science. Although science could not yield values as such, it seemed to select, confirm, and discredit them in various ways, and, again, there was the belief that the logic and procedures of science and liberal democracy were inherently mutually supportive and that both rested on a pragmatic notion of truth and the eschewal of absolutist speculation. Finally, political science was, much more than the emerging autonomous enterprise of political theory, an established disciplinary practice with its substantive criteria of judgment and, despite continuing concern about its public role and possibilities, a sense of practical efficacy and professional identity. It was, consequently, less daunted by the philosophical phantom of relativism that haunted émigré political theorists.

The discipline of political science constituted a context that profoundly and singularly shaped the institutional form and ideational content of political theory. Political theory, in turn, was deeply implicated in some of the most fundamental changes that took place in political science, including both the behavioral and postbehavioral revolutions. Today, political theory has largely retreated from an involvement with, let alone critique of, political science, and political science has, for the most part, afforded political theory the ultimate disdain of pure tolerance. This situation has allowed many important issues, both explicit and implicit, to slide into obscurity or to become, as in the case of liberalism and relativism, detached from the practical concerns that originally generated them. Professional pressures, under the guise of intellectual principle, continue to push in the direction of separatism, but the results are debilitating. Both political science and political theory have been diminished. The former has lost its most important critical and reflective dimension, and the latter has lost its congenital and maybe most authentic field of action.

REFERENCES

Almond, Gabriel, Lewis Dexter, William Whyte, and John Hallowell. 1946. "Politics and Ethics—A Symposium." *American Political Science Review* 40: 283–312.
Anderson, William. 1949. "Political Science North and South." *Journal of Politics* 11: 298–317.
Appleby, Paul. 1950. "Political Science, the Next Twenty-five Years." *American Political Science Review* 44: 924–32.

Arendt, Hannah. 1951. *The Origins of Totalitarianism.* New York: Harcourt, Brace.

Brecht, Arnold. 1947. "Beyond Relativism in Political Theory." *American Political Science Review* 41: 470–88.

Brecht, Arnold. 1959. *Political Theory.* Princeton, NJ: Princeton University Press.

Brecht, Arnold. 1970. *The Political Education of Arnold Brecht.* Princeton, NJ: Princeton University Press.

Easton, David. 1949. "Walter Bagehot and Liberal Realism." *American Political Science Review* 43: 17–37.

Easton, David. 1950. "Harold Lasswell: Political Scientist for a Democratic Society." *Journal of Politics* 12: 450–77.

Easton, David. 1951. "The Decline of Political Theory." *Journal of Politics* 13: 36–58.

Easton, David. 1953. *The Political System.* Chicago: University of Chicago Press.

Finer, Herman. 1945. "Towards a Democratic Theory." *American Political Science Review* 49: 249–68.

Gunnell, John G. 1983. "Political Theory: The Evolution of a Subfield." In *Political Science: The State of the Discipline,* ed. Ada W. Finifter. Washington: American Political Science Association.

Gunnell, John. 1986. *Between Philosophy and Politics: The Alienation of Political Theory.* Amherst: University of Massachusetts Press.

Hallowell, John H. 1942. "The Decline of Liberalism." *Ethics* 52: 323–49.

Hallowell, John. 1943. *The Decline of Liberalism as an Ideology.* Berkeley: University of California Press.

Hallowell, John. 1944a. "Politics and Ethics." *American Political Science Review* 38: 639–55.

Hallowell, John. 1944b. "Review of Arnold Brecht, *Prelude to Silence: The End of the German Republic.*" *Journal of Politics* 6: 466–69.

Hallowell, John. 1947. "Modern Liberalism: An Invitation to Suicide." *South Atlantic Quarterly* 46: 453–66.

Hallowell, John. 1950. *The Main Currents of Modern Political Thought.* New York: Holt, Rinehart & Winston.

Horkheimer, Max. 1947. *Eclipse of Reason.* New York: Oxford.

Kelsen, Hans. 1948. "Absolutism and Relativism in Philosophy and Politics." *American Political Science Review* 42: 906–14.

Lasswell, Harold, and Abraham Kaplan. 1950. *Power and Society.* New Haven: Yale University Press.

Lippincott, Benjamin. 1940. "The Bias of American Political Science." *Journal of Politics* 2: 125–39.

Lippincott, Benjamin. 1950. "Political Theory in the United States." In *Contemporary Political Science,* ed. W. Ebenstein. Paris: UNESCO.

Marcuse, Herbert. 1941. *Reason and Revolution.* New York: Oxford University Press.

Oppenheim, Felix. 1950. "Relativism, Absolutism, and Democracy." *American Political Science Review* 44: 951–60.

Perry, Charles. 1950. "The Semantics of Social Science: Discussions by Max Radin, George Lucás, Harold Lasswell, and Herberg Simon." *American Political Science Review* 44:394–425.

Sabine, George H. 1939. "What is Political Theory?" *Journal of Politics* 1: 1–16.

Strauss, Leo. 1936. *The Political Philosophy of Thomas Hobbes: Its Basis and Genesis*. Chicago: University of Chicago Press.

Voegelin, Eric. 1952. *The New Science of Politics*. Chicago: University of Chicago Press.

Voegelin, Eric. 1975. *From Enlightenment to Revolution*. John H. Hallowell, ed. Durham, NC: Duke University Press.

White, Leonard D. 1950. "Political Science, Mid-Century." *Journal of Politics* 12: 13–19.

Whyte, William F. 1943. "A Challenge to Political Scientists." *American Political Science Review* 37: 692–97.

Wilson, Francis G., Benjamin F. Wright, Ernest S. Griffith, and Eric Voegelin. 1944. "Research in Political Theory: A Symposium." *American Political Science Review* 38: 726–54.

Wolin, Sheldon. 1960. *Politics and Vision*. Boston: Little, Brown.

Part 3
Debates/1945–1970

Introduction

From the end of World War II to the beginning of the end of the Vietnam War, political science in the United States experienced dramatic changes. Many of these changes were institutional and professional. In the period between 1946 and 1966, for example, membership in the American Political Science Association rose from 4,000 to 14,000, and for the first time the majority of these members were professional academics with doctoral degrees.[1] New regional associations and journals were founded, and departments and graduate programs burgeoned across the country. In these and other measurable ways, political science took part in the most rapid expansion of higher education in American history. It was also a party to the creation of a network of inter- and extra-university research institutes, committees, and centers, prominently including the Survey Research Center, the Institute for Social Research, the National Opinion Research Center, the Social Science Research Council's Committee on Political Behavior, and the Center for Advanced Study in the Behavioral Sciences. As it shifted its war work—from World War II to the Cold War to the Vietnam War—the United States government assisted these various developments in and outside the universities, both by grants and employment. Large, well-endowed philanthropic foundations—such as Carnegie, Rockefeller, and Ford—were also of inestimable importance for the growth of the discipline during this period. At the level of these institutional and professional changes—before the mid-sixties at least—it was a period of considerable optimism and forward-looking. With an eye toward the century's end, Leonard D. White could say to an assembled group of peers in 1950 (printed below) that "we are, organically speaking, immortal."

Other changes in the discipline were intellectual and scholarly, and optimism about them was palpable if somewhat more guarded. Leading political scientists during this period continued the process inaugurated by Merriam and the earlier "Chicago school" to ally their inquiries to those of the other social sciences and to distance them from history, moral philosophy, studies of the state, and the historical-comparative method. There were, of course,

---

1. Albert Somit and Joseph Tanenhaus, *The Development of American Political Science: From Burgess to Behavioralism* (Boston: Allyn and Bacon, 1967), chap. 11.

many political scientists who resisted these moves and were soon labeled "traditionalists." (Looking over the ocean as well as his own island, one British commentator even declared that "for the moment, anyway, political philosophy is dead,"[2] so tradition bound did it seem to be.) The concepts of political behavior, public opinion, pressure groups, and the political system increasingly came to fill the pages and the titles of the most influential political science texts. With these concepts, political scientists tried to understand and explain not only politics in some generic sense, but also current developments in the United States and the liberal democracies of the West, as well as the appeals of communism in the East and the *realpolitik* governing nations during the Cold War. The great profusion of works during this period helped to fix an agenda for upcoming generations of new political scientists; and they catapulted their authors into positions of intellectual and professional leadership. Among works on a much larger list, we might number Hans J. Morgenthau, *Scientific Man versus Power Politics* (1946), Herbert A. Simon, *Administrative Behavior* (1947), E. E. Schattschneider, *Toward a More Responsible Two-Party System* (1950), David B. Truman, *The Governmental Process* (1951), David Easton, *The Political System* (1953), Gabriel A. Almond, *The Appeals of Communism* (1954), Samuel Stouffer, *Communism, Conformity, and Civil Liberties* (1955), Heinz Eulau, ed., *Political Behavior* (1956), Anthony Downs, *An Economic Theory of Democracy* (1957), Seymour Martin Lipset, *Political Man* (1959), Angus Campbell, Philip E. Converse, Warren E. Miller, and Donald E. Stokes, *The American Voter* (1960), Daniel Bell, *The End of Ideology* (1960), V. O. Key, *Public Opinion and American Democracy* (1961), Robert A. Dahl, *Who Governs?* (1961), Gabriel A. Almond and Sidney Verba, *The Civic Culture* (1963), Heinz Eulau, *The Behavioral Persuasion in Politics* (1963), and David Easton, *A Systems Analysis of Political Life* (1965).

These works, and many others as well, displayed considerable intellectual diversity and spawned a series of new debates over the proper objects, theories, and methods of political science. Debates over systems theory, structural functionalism, community power, pluralism, game theory, survey research, and quantitative methods ranged widely over various books and journals, and drew in political scientists with very different substantive interests. However, the most important debate, one that subsumed the rest, was over "behavioralism." To this day, behavioralism is difficult to describe in a way that would please all those who took themselves to be (or not to be) behavioralists. Even in the heyday of debate, it was ambiguously characterized as a revolution, a protest, a movement, a tendency, a persuasion, even a mood. Yet for all that, behavioralism captured the appellative imagination of numerous

---

2. Peter Laslett, ed., *Philosophy, Politics, and Society* (Oxford: Basil Blackwell, 1956), p. vii.

political scientists (and their critics) who were wont to underscore (or to criticize) the *scientific* aspirations of the discipline. Science, they argued, required the observation, description, explanation, and prediction of the empirical regularities consequent to the actual behavior of individuals in social and political systems. The development of reliable measurement techniques and various methods of quantification was taken to be essential to this task. So, too, was the attempt to segregate normative values, much less political ideologies, from the actual practice of science.[3]

It would be hard to overestimate the importance of the debates over behavioralism in the development of twentieth-century political science. Although it was distantly preceded by the nineteenth-century desire for a "science of politics" and more immediately preceded by the "first behavioral revolution" of the Progressive Era, behavioralism at mid-century galvanized the discipline. Political scientists with significantly different substantive and theoretical interests found behavioralism a convenient rubric under which to work. And behavioralism proved to be as crucial for critics as for proponents. The debates over it became increasingly heated as questions about the political identity of the discipline became inextricably intertwined with those about its methodological identity. Critics seized upon the behavioralist claim to value-freedom, finding in it either an "apolitical politics" or the quite value-laden assumptions of American liberalism.[4] Regarding the crises of liberal democracy, the political philosopher Leo Strauss could even contend in 1962 that political science "fiddles while Rome burns" and then facetiously go on to "excuse [it] by two facts: it does not know that it fiddles, and it does not know that Rome burns."[5] During the later sixties, the behavioralists' anticipation of the "end of ideology" was shattered by urban riots and Vietnam War protests.

---

3. For a powerful, short statement of the tenets of behavioralism, see David Easton, "The Current Meaning of Behavioralism," in James C. Charlesworth, ed., *The Limits of Behavioralism in Political Science* (Philadelphia: American Academy of Science, 1962). The other essays in that volume are helpful in giving a sense of the nature of behavioralism as well as proving to be a harbinger of the intensity of debates that would rage over behavioralism. On behavioralism in general, see Austin Ranney, ed., *Essays in the Behavioral Study of Politics* (Urbana: University of Illinois Press, 1962); Heinz Eulau, *The Behavioral Persuasion in Politics* (New York: Random House, 1963); Heinz Eulau, ed., *Behavioralism in Political Science* (New York: Atherton, 1969); and David Ricci, *The Tragedy of Political Science* (New Haven: Yale University Press, 1984), especially chap. 5.

4. Charles McCoy and John Playford, eds., *Apolitical Politics* (New York: Crowell, 1967); and Bernard Crick, *The American Science of Politics: Its Origins and Conditions* (Berkeley: University of California Press, 1959). For other volumes critical of behavioralism, see, among others, William Connolly, ed., *The Bias of Pluralism* (New York: Atherton, 1969); and Marvin Surkin and Alan Wolfe, eds., *An End to Political Science* (New York: Basic Books, 1970).

5. In Herbert J. Storing, ed., *Essays on the Scientific Study of Politics* (New York: Holt, Rinehart, and Winston, 1962), p. 327. For a spirited critique, see John Schaar and Sheldon Wolin, "Essays on the Scientific Study of Politics: A Critique," *American Political Science Review* 57 (1963): 125–50.

Dissidents within the discipline formed a Caucus for a New Political Science, in large measure to protest what they took to be the quiescence or status-quo orientation of the behavioral mainstream. These various events were to mark the days of behavioralism and to date what came after it as a "postbehavioral" era.

In a word, the political identity of political science was as prominent as its scholarly or institutional identity during this period. This does not itself distinguish the discipline, as the selections in the previous two sections clearly show. But the particular combination of a quick succession of wartime contexts, the massive increase of governmental and philanthropic support for research, and the debates about behavioralism certainly does. In the first essay below, Terence Ball brings these various elements together in a selective overview of the period under inspection, with special attention to the institutional dynamics influencing the development of political science. Among other things, he documents certain of the political aspects and consequences of the unprecedented research support provided by the government and philanthropic foundations at the end of World War II. The Cold War, he goes on, exacted a particular price in the public presentation of the social and political sciences. When citizens and senators could confuse "social science" with "socialism"—or think of social scientists as meddling academics with cross-gender haircuts—the invocation of "behavioral science" was a timely conceptual innovation that helped avoid further overt criticism. (Relatedly, David Easton points out in his essay in part 4 below that avoiding the slanders of McCarthyism was partly responsible for the "value-neutrality" that the greater number of behavioralists publicly espoused.) More importantly, behavioral scientists could—and did—emphasize to the public and to their benefactors that the payoff of their research was in terms of social engineering and the development of the policy sciences. Political leaders could thereby draw upon and apply forms of behavioral knowledge that political scientists would supply.

On the scene, as it were, Leonard D. White expressed the point in grander terms: "There is always the unfinished business of perfecting the American system of democracy" as well as "advising our fellow citizens" and carrying out "the enormous task of enlightenment." As one of the wartime presidents of the APSA and a member of the Chicago department of political science, White surveys political science at mid-century in generally optimistic and praiseworthy terms. He underscores the institutional and professional strides that political science has made in the immediate postwar years, but is a trifle more skeptical about its intellectual foundations. Even though the replacement of Burgess's "science of the state" with Merriam's "social science" is a genuine improvement, he allows, many things remain to be done. In particular, political science must help develop "a new philosophy for the new world" and "a more profound understanding of political behavior." Here in 1950, in short, the concept of political behavior that was destined to dominate the lexicon of behavioral political science is incorporated into the "ancient American faith in our capacity to deal with whatever may lie before us."

The concept of political behavior and the call for an improvement in behavioral data helped characterize David Easton's phenomenally influential book, *The Political System: An Inquiry into the State of Political Science,* published in 1953. In the selection from that book, presented below, Easton displays the critical capacities not only of a programmatic political scientist but of a disciplinary historian as well, one intent on sweeping away what he took to be the intellectual debris of an earlier era and orienting the conceptual compasses of a new generation of political scientists. The "political system" and the "authoritative allocation of value," he argues, should replace the "state" (as in Burgess) and even "power" (as in Catlin and Lasswell). The consequences are significant for defining the special objectives and contributions of political science. They are equally significant, he argues, for developing empirical political theory in the face of the future and for ending "the malaise of political science since the Civil War," as he puts it elsewhere in *The Political System.* Systems theory, as it was subsequently developed, provided one of the most highly touted research agendas of the 1950s and 1960s, as well as one of the most influential articulations of the theoretical shape that behavioralism would take in American political science.

Behavioralism is the demonstrable object of Robert A. Dahl's "epitaph." In the 1950s and 1960s, Dahl's own substantive work on democracy fit more comfortably under the label of "pluralism." But in the essay printed below, he memorializes and admonishes the behavioral "movement" as a whole. His explanatory sketch of its development is intriguing, in part, for its causal diversity. He gives equal billing to Merriam, World War II, the SSRC Committee on Political Behavior, survey methods, and philanthropic foundations. These historical sensibilities are complemented by textual ones, particularly in the case of an important but rather neglected 1951 essay on behavioralism by David B. Truman from which Dahl extensively cites. Behavioralism will "gradually disappear," Dahl concludes, but only because it will have "succeeded" and been "incorporated into the main body of the discipline." Yet there are still important tasks ahead—those which, as it turned out, the critics of behavioralism would emphasize as well—including addressing "what ought to be," avoiding "ahistorical theory," abandoning the "search for mere trivialities," and finding a place for "speculation."

Engaging in speculation is precisely what the political theorist Norman Jacobson claims to be doing in his 1963 essay, "Political Science and Political Education." What if Paine, not Madison, had succeeded as the exemplar of political science and its form of political education? he asks. In imagining an answer to this counterfactual question, Jacobson reveals the importance of historical inquiry, as much as speculation, for questions of contemporary identity. Indeed he finds the assumptions in *Federalist 10*—as mediated, somewhat surprisingly, by Arthur Bentley—as establishing an "affinity between political education and political science existing in America today" and as demonstrating that "political science in America has been the rational outcome of an established political system." Political education could have been or still be different inasmuch as "political behavior is no synonym for human nature." In any case, political scientists must accept responsibility for the education of citizens in the United States *and* abroad, an activity in which they ineluctably engage. Jacobson's reminder of responsibility was and remains a very important one to those who acknowledged and continue to acknowledge, as Leonard D. White puts the point in his essay, that "we have a practical task of world education in the American way of life and in the spirit of American government, made in its image."

American Political Science in Its Postwar Political Context

Terence Ball

The history of political science may be written in a number of ways. One is through interviews or "oral histories" featuring firsthand accounts by participants.[1] Another way—and the approach adopted by several contributors to this volume—is to trace the history of political science as an intellectual enterprise. Illuminating as these approaches are, I shall take a third route. Mine is less an intellectual than an "institutional" history. That is, instead of emphasizing the ideas and theories that have constituted political science, I propose to focus on the political contexts and institutional matrices that have helped to shape and direct the discipline.

My thesis, simply stated, is that the development of American political science cannot be understood apart from the changing historical and political contexts in which it has found itself and to which it has responded. Such developments as the behavioral revolution and the turn toward "science," in something like a positivistic sense, can accordingly be viewed politically as that discipline's rational and self-interested response to the climate and temper of the times. My aim in what follows is to clarify, qualify, and substantiate this thesis by highlighting a number of important episodes in the development of political science in the postwar period.

My essay proceeds in four stages. In the first, I sketch several features of the social and political landscape on which political science in the 1940s found itself and which it, in turn, tried to help shape. Second, I recount the rhetorical stratagems and arguments employed by political scientists to garner public recognition, financial resources, and political legitimacy for their discipline. Third, I try to trace some of the sources and consequences of

---

Previously unpublished essay.

1. See *Political Science in America: Oral Histories of a Discipline*, Michael A. Baer, Malcolm E. Jewell, and Lee Sigelman, eds. (Lexington, KY: University Press of Kentucky, 1991).

political science's success in this endeavor. Finally, I recount the reasons for the failure of political science to fulfill its postwar promise.

I.

The social sciences, and political science in particular, became increasingly prominent in the wake of World War II. The discipline owed its growing prestige to a number of developments. The creation of the welfare state during the Great Depression of the 1930s, American hegemony following the allies' successful prosecution of World War II, and the political climate of the Cold War created an atmosphere in which the claims of political scientists came to have a certain appeal. Thus it is in the postwar period that we see for the first time the creation of an institutional infrastructure—governmental granting agencies, private foundations, the modern multiversity, and the increasing professionalization of the social sciences themselves—for supporting social science research and training. Through this combination of circumstances, the social sciences—and the so-called 'policy sciences' in particular—came into their own.

The New Deal, and the birth of the American welfare state, helped to alter popular attitudes about the proper relation between citizens and their government. These include changing beliefs about government's responsibility for alleviating social ills, for engaging in limited economic planning (by, among other things, regulating the money supply, bolstering the banking system by regulating banking practices, insuring individual deposits, and the like), for mediating between the interests of capital and labor, and generally checking the worst social and economic excesses of an otherwise untrammelled laissez-faire market economy.

But, important as the New Deal was in changing the political climate in which American political science became ever more prominent, it pales in comparison with World War II. The war greatly increased opportunities and resources for research and disciplinary advancement. Before 1940, most social science research was funded from private sources. Even during the Depression, government monies allocated for social science research were spent mainly on gathering and publishing statistical information. The war changed all that. "World War II," as Harry Alpert of the National Science Foundation notes, "was undoubtedly the major catalytic event leading to the expansion of the federal government's programs in [the social science] field." Indeed, he adds, the present-day prominence of the social sciences in America

is a product of World War II and of the postwar era and represents novel developments both with respect to the magnitude of the funds involved and the types of problems and disciplines supported. The events of the war on both the military and civil fronts, and the problems of postwar readjustment . . . provided the social sciences with dramatic opportunities to demonstrate their practical value and essential role in modern society. As a result, social science research firmly established its legitimacy as a fundamental contributor to our national life.[2]

A report released by the Russell Sage Foundation in 1950 noted that in "the prosecution of World War II . . . social scientists were converted into social practitioners. Their services were comparable to the function of engineers and other specialized technologists in applying knowledge of the physical scientists [sic]."[3] Physicists might say how atoms behaved and engineers how weapons worked, but social scientists could explain, predict, and, possibly, help to control the behavior of those who pulled the triggers and dropped the bombs.

A good deal of effort was accordingly devoted to studying the attitudes and behavior of wartime GIs. One of the now classic studies—*The American Soldier,* by Samuel Stouffer and his associates—was originally undertaken for the very practical purpose of improving the selection, training, and performance of military personnel.[4] The "policy sciences" (as Harold Lasswell was later to term them)—political science, public administration, and allied disciplines—were called upon to analyze the effects and assess the effectiveness of various wartime policies.[5] They studied farm subsidy programs, recycling schemes, ad campaigns for war bonds, the draft-registration system, the beliefs and behavior of the American soldier, the determinants of military morale, race relations in the military, the social effects of the bombing and shelling of civilians, the effectiveness of different kinds of propaganda, the social causes of the spread of venereal diseases, and dozens of other war-related phenomena. So much in demand were political and social scientists that finding, recruiting, and training them became a considerable problem.[6]

2. Harry Alpert, "The Growth of Social Research in the United States," in Daniel Lerner, ed., *The Human Meaning of the Social Sciences* (New York and Cleveland: World Publishing Co., 1959), p. 79.

3. Russell Sage Foundation, *Effective Use of Social Science Research in the Federal Services* (New York: Russell Sage Foundation, 1950), p. 42.

4. Samuel Stouffer et al., *The American Soldier,* vols. 1 and 2 (Princeton, NJ: Princeton University Press, 1949).

5. Harold D. Lasswell, "The Policy Orientation," in Daniel Lerner and Harold D. Lasswell, eds., *The Policy Sciences* (Stanford, CA: Stanford University Press, 1951), pp. 3–15.

6. John McDiarmid, "The Mobilization of Social Scientists," in Leonard D. White, ed., *Civil Service in Wartime* (Chicago: University of Chicago Press, 1945), pp. 73–96.

II.

At the end of the war, most political scientists returned to the academy from whence they had come. But if they had helped to change the course of the war, the war had also helped to change them. No longer "ivory tower" academics, many political scientists became, by their own account, harder-headed realists with a soberer sense of political possibilities and limitations. During the war, as Robert Dahl was later to observe,

> a great many American political scientists temporarily vacated their ivory towers and came to grips with day-to-day political and administrative realities in Washington and elsewhere: a whole generation of American political science [*sic*] later drew on these experiences. The confrontation of theory and reality provoked . . . a strong sense of the inadequacies of the conventional approaches of political science for describing reality, much less for predicting . . . what was likely to happen.[7]

The new sobriety took a number of forms. One was a turn away from the formal and legal analysis of institutions to a deliberate and self-conscious focus on actual political behavior. Another was a decided preference for "scientific" modes of inquiry and a suspicion bordering on hostility towards "traditional" concepts (e.g., "the state") and approaches (especially political theory or philosophy). Thus began the "behavioral revolution," which picked up steam and influence through the 1950s and peaked in the decade that followed. And, like all modern revolutions, this one had its manifestoes and its own program for reforming and indeed remaking an ostensibly backward and dormant discipline.

These developments did not, of course, occur in a political vacuum but took shape and color within the complex political context of postwar America. Although one war was over, another had begun. If World War II had been a war of weapons—including, toward its end, the most fearsome weapon of all—the Cold War was above all a war of ideas and ideologies, of psychology and propaganda. It was, in a phrase not yet coined, a struggle for the hearts and minds of men. In this long twilight struggle, political scientists had, or purported to have, something special to contribute. Before making that contribution, however, political scientists had to receive a greater measure of public recognition and acceptance, not to say pecuniary support. And this

---

7. Robert A. Dahl, "The Behavioral Approach in Political Science: Epitaph for a Monument to a Successful Protest," *American Political Science Review* 60 (December 1961): 763–72, 764.

required that they allay the suspicions still harbored by many members of the public and their political representatives.

This postwar battle was joined in the attempt to persuade the federal government to fund peacetime research and to support the education of future social scientists. Of the several skirmishes fought at the time, one was especially noteworthy. The Magnuson-Kilgore bill for the establishment of a National Science Foundation, introduced into the Congress in 1945, contained a provision for establishing a social science division. This proposal occasioned considerable debate in the Congress and prompted prolonged hearings, at which a parade of prominent political scientists made the case for an intimate connection between funding their disciplines and serving the national interest.

To look back to those encounters is to see something of the suspicions still harbored by the public and its representatives toward political science and its sister disciplines. It also helps explain the discipline's emphasis on "science" and its vaunted value-neutrality. Among the several themes that emerge from these hearings, the following were particularly prominent. The first goes something like this: We politicians know, and are awed by, what the natural sciences can do. A short time ago they gave us the atomic bomb and victory in the Pacific. We are therefore willing, and even eager, to support their researches. We are less certain about the social sciences, and perhaps political science in particular. What have they done for us lately, or ever, for that matter? A second theme, with variations aplenty, is that political science and the other social sciences are not really scientific, after all; they are really only common sense, disguised in an uncommonly arcane jargon designed to confuse and mislead laymen and legislators. A third theme is that the social sciences, far from being normatively neutral or value-free, embody or represent values that are somehow inimical to those that Americans hold dear. The cherished values of personal privacy and freedom seem somehow threatened by social scientists intent upon probing and analyzing our attitudes, beliefs, and innermost secrets. A fourth theme concerns costs and benefits. How are Americans to know whether, or to what degree, their tax dollars are being well spent by social scientists, and spent in ways that promote the national interest instead of the interest of individual academics? I shall touch briefly upon each of these themes.

One after another, social scientists and their allies in government and the military attested to the important role played by their respective disciplines in World War II. They noted, for example, that wars are not fought with weapons only but by, and against, human beings. In order to wage a successful war, we need to know about more than the number of soldiers our adversary has in uniform, the size of their coal and ore stockpiles, their oil reserves, refinery capacities, and the number and types of weapons at their disposal. We need to know about our enemy's culture, national character, political system, class structure, history, and traditions. We benefit by knowing something about the psychological makeup of their leaders and the morale of their citizenry. These matters, which are outside the ken and competence of natural scientists and military men alike, are quite properly the province of political science and the other social sciences. Appearing on behalf of the War (later the Defense) Department, General John Magruder of the Office of Strategic Services (OSS)—the wartime forerunner of the CIA—put it this way: "In all of the intelligence that enters into the waging of war soundly and the waging of peace soundly, it is the social scientists who make a huge contribution in the field in which they are the professionals and the soldiers are the laymen." The general went on to suggest that World War II could scarcely have been waged, much less won, without the aid of sociologists, anthropologists, economists, and others. It was they, as much as the spies behind enemy lines, who supplied the "intelligence" that aided the allied victory in the European and Pacific theaters. And what was true of World War II would, he concluded, be even truer of future wars.[8]

The way in which General Magruder was thanked by the chairman of the committee tells us a good deal about how the war had helped to change popular attitudes toward the social sciences. Since "there is a sad lack of public understanding of the social sciences and what they do," said the chairman, "statements like this are badly needed." Because "we had to utilize the social scientific facilities of the country to the utmost during the depression, trying to pull out of it," he continued, "the general impression was out that it was sort of a playground of welfare workers and things of that kind alone." Now that we know that the social sciences have proven themselves to be militarily useful, he averred, this mistaken impression can be corrected.[9]

Without exception, the social scientists testifying before congressional committees stressed the "scientific" character of their disciplines. All the sciences, natural and social, were said to subscribe to a single method—the "scientific method" of objective observation and controlled inquiry. The only differences between the natural and social sciences were ones of degree. They studied different subject matters and dealt in different degrees of probability; otherwise they were essentially identical. Thus, for example, Dr. E. G. Nourse, the vice president of the Brookings Foundation, assured the senators that "formal divisions between natural, biologic, and social science are arbi-

---

8. Testimony of General John Magruder, 31 October 1945, in Senate Committee on Military Affairs, *Hearings on Science Legislation, S. 1297 and Related Bills,* 79th Cong., 1st sess. (Washington, DC: U.S. Government Printing Office, 1946), pp. 899–901.

9. Ibid., pp. 901–2.

trary." Useful as they are in some respects, these formal divisions run the danger of obscuring "the inherent unity of science. The basic problem of all science is to get fuller and more accurate knowledge as to the materials to be found and the forces which operate in our world. . . ." Far from being wholly disinterested and academic, research into these forces is undertaken "in order that they may be so controlled and utilized that mankind may have a safer and more satisfying existence."[10]

Not content simply to assert the methodological similarities between the natural and the social sciences, some chose to go on the offensive. William F. Ogburn of the University of Chicago pressed a pincer attack. He began by noting that the innovations introduced by the natural sciences—the steam engine and the atomic bomb among them—create unintended social consequences. To understand and to find ways of dealing with these consequences is the task of the social sciences. Ogburn then advanced a second argument about the social sciences' ability to "aid in national defense." The advent of the atomic bomb has made all-out war obsolete and unthinkable. Modern warfare, he maintained, is "total war [which] must be fought not only with munitions but also with institutions." Social science research, he testified, "is just as necessary for national defense as is research in radar or jet propulsion" because "modern wars are total wars. Hence we need the mobilization of our social resources as well as our mechanical ones." The "obligation of the natural scientist . . . is to work on the weapons. The groups to whom the Nation should look are the social scientists whose function is to study social institutions."[11] Inefficient or malfunctioning social institutions are as bad, if not worse, than malfunctioning weapons. Nay more: the Cold War being more a contest of ideas and institutions than of weapons, the social sciences were arguably more indispensable than the physical sciences.

Political scientists went to great lengths to assure the senators that they were not ideologues or reformers but scientists devoted to the disinterested pursuit of truth. Dr. John M. Gaus, president of the American Political Science Association, worried aloud about "those who sneer at the social sciences, and research in such fields, as too greatly influenced by the prejudices of their participants to constitute true sciences, presumably characterized by dispassionate inquiry."[12] Nothing, he assured his audience, could be further from the truth. Political science and the other social sciences were genuine sciences, and as objective as any of the natural sciences. Others agreed.

10. Testimony of Dr. E. G. Nourse, 29 October 1945, in *Hearings on Science Legislation*, p. 757.
11. Testimony of Professor William F. Ogburn, in *Hearings on Science Legislation*, pp. 765, 767.
12. Testimony of Dr. John M. Gaus, 29 October 1945, in *Hearings on Science Legislation*, p. 747.

Ogburn, for example, insisted upon "a differentiation between . . . knowledge and ethics." To illustrate his point, he likened the social scientist to a natural scientist charged with the task of inventing a poison gas. Just as "it is not in his province as a scientist . . . to say whether that gas shall be used for spraying fruit trees or for killing human beings," so it is not the business of the social scientist, qua scientist, to ask how social-scientific knowledge is to be used. The social sciences would be "greatly confused by the mixing in of values with the consideration of knowledge. I think if that distinction is kept clear, the role of the social scientist is seen very much better." As far as ethical ends and political interests are concerned, then, social-scientific knowledge is—or at least ought to be—normatively neutral.[13]

Despite these assurances, several senators and congressmen remained openly skeptical. Some even saw in the social sciences the specter of scientific socialism of the Soviet variety.[14] This piece of semantic confusion later led some social scientists to refer to themselves as "behavioral scientists," in hopes of avoiding the socialist stigmata. But if this stigma was easily scotched, others were not. The image of social scientists as nosey "welfare workers and other things of that kind" persisted in the popular imagination. This suspicion was voiced succinctly by the irrepressible Congressman Clarence Brown of Ohio:

> Outside of myself, I think everyone else thinks he is a social scientist. I am sure that I am not, but I think everyone else seems to believe that he has some particular God-given right to decide what other people ought to do. The average American does not want some expert running around prying into his life and his personal affairs and deciding for him how he should live, and if the impression becomes prevalent in Congress that this legislation [to establish a social science division within the National Science Foundation] is to establish some sort of an organization in which there would be a lot of short-haired women and long-haired men messing into everybody's personal affairs and lives, inquiring whether they love their wives or do not love them and so forth, you are not going to get your legislation.[15]

---

13. Ogburn testimony, in *Hearings on Science Legislation*, pp. 768–69. See the similar claim in George A. Lundberg's postwar polemic, *Can Science Save Us?* (New York: Longmans, Green & Co., 1947), especially pp. 48–50.

14. This charge was aired and denied in the 1952 report of the House of Representatives Select Committee (Cox Committee) investigating tax-exempt foundations. "Many of our citizens," the report said, "confuse the term 'social,' as applied to the discipline of the social sciences, with the term 'socialism.'" Quoted in Harry Alpert, "The Knowledge We Need Most," *Saturday Review*, 1 February 1958, p. 38.

15. Testimony before Committee on Interstate and Foreign Commerce, House of Representatives, 79th Congress, 28–29 May 1946 (Washington, DC: U.S. Government Printing Office, 1946), pp. 11–13.

The congressman's words proved prophetic. The social sciences did not get their legislation, less because of the specter of socialism and the fear of short-haired women than because of other considerations. When at last the National Science Foundation (NSF) was created by Public Law 507, passed by the 81st Congress and signed by President Truman on May 10, 1950, it did not include a social science division. The prestige of the natural sciences, along with the residual suspicions surrounding the social sciences and assorted considerations of fiscal economy, proved to be too great an obstacle to the passage of legislation for which social scientists had lobbied long and hard.

The setback was, however, only temporary, and more apparent than real. Not only had private foundation support for social science research increased apace after the war; the federal government, in both military and civilian sectors, relied increasingly upon the research and advice of political scientists and other social scientists. So marked was this trend, indeed, that by 1950, the Russell Sage Foundation could report that

> the federal government has become the outstanding employer of social scientists and consumer of social science materials in the conduct of practical affairs. Expenditures of the federal government for social science research projects, either under direct governmental auspices or under contract with private agencies, and for personnel in administrative capacities having command of social science knowledge far exceeded the amount given by all the philanthropic foundations for similar purposes.[16]

When in 1953 the NSF studied the possibility of, and in 1954 unanimously approved the creation of, a Social Science Division, it did not so much create something new as it regularized the funding for a phenomenon already well established.

In attempting to counter the popular image of social scientists as nosey welfare workers or socialists or short-haired women and long-haired men, political scientists were wont to emphasize not only their discipline's practical usefulness but their own professionalism. In the in-house literature and public pronouncements of the postwar period, political scientists are likened repeatedly to technicians, to engineers, and even to physicians concerned with the "health" of American society. In 1947, the Social Science Research Council's Pendleton Herring put it this way:

> One of the greatest needs in the social sciences is for the development of skilled practitioners who can use social data for the cure of social ills as doctors use scientific data to cure bodily ills. . . . The term social sci-

---

16. Russell Sage Foundation, *Social Science Research,* p. 5; cf. also p. 42.

ence technician [refers to] an individual who has been professionally trained to apply to practical situations the facts, generalizations, principles, rules, laws, or formulae uncovered by social science research. . . . Social engineering [is] the application of knowledge of social phenomena to specific problems.

"Social engineering," he concluded, "is a meaningful conception, worthy of considerable expansion."[17]

And expand it did. Measured in almost any terms—monies allocated, scope and size of foundation funding, professorships endowed and filled, fellowships awarded, surveys conducted, number of books and articles published, dissertations written, degrees granted, and so on—the postwar years proved a bountiful period for political science. These developments also set the stage for the emergence of a new but by now thoroughly familiar figure in the American academy: the academic entrepreneur or grantsman skilled in the art of securing governmental and foundation funding. Little wonder, then, that this new figure on the academic scene was soon to be singled out for special censure by C. Wright Mills and other critics.[18]

It is tempting and altogether too easy to follow in the footsteps of C. Wright Mills and the New Left, detecting in these developments a massive conspiracy to co-opt and corrupt American academicians. That there was, and is, some measure of co-optation and corruption would be difficult to deny. But these developments doubtless had more to do with functional imperatives than with the conscious conspiratorial designs of a power elite. In conclusion, one of these imperatives and its implications are worth considering.

III.

By and large, behaviorally oriented research tends to be more costly than an individual scholar or a small institution can afford. The funding for such research has therefore come, more often than not, either from federal agencies or private or public foundations. One might suppose that here, as elsewhere, the old adage applies: He who pays the piper calls the tune. If so, it is not called consciously and directly but unconsciously and indirectly. That is, these agencies and foundations by no means predetermine the specific outcomes or findings of scholarly research. They do, however, help to shape the

---

17. E. Pendleton Herring, "The Social Sciences in Modern Society," Social Science Research Council *Items* (March 1947): 5–6. See, further, the "oral history" interview with Herring in Baer, Jewell, and Sigelman, *Political Science in America*, pp. 22–39.

18. See C. Wright Mills, *The Sociological Imagination* (New York: Grove Press, 1959), chaps. 4 and 5.

kinds of questions that researchers ask and answer, and the kinds of inquiries and investigations deemed worthy of support and thereby, less directly, of reporting via conferences, symposia, publications and even, eventually, pedagogy. In the 1950s, as Somit and Tanenhaus note,

> An unprecedented flow of foundation funds helped further ease the rigors of scholarly life. Whereas a $10,000 grant was a major event in the 1930's or even 1940's, so modest an amount barely occasioned mention by the late 1950's. Carnegie and Rockefeller multiplied manyfold their support of political science. Of even greater moment was the appearance of a new giant—the Ford Foundation. The lavish beneficence of this leviathan late-comer dwarfed the combined giving of the older agencies. Taking the twenty years as a whole, it would be conservative to say that the Ford complex provided 90 percent of the money channeled to political science by American philanthropic institutions.

"Under these circumstances," they continue, "political scientists would have been less than human were they not tempted to manifest a deep interest in the kinds of research known to be favored by Ford Foundation staff and advisers."[19] And what was true of the Ford Foundation was no less true of other granting agencies, public and private alike.

But this is only the less interesting and important half of the story. Other costs—less tangible but no less real—are also incurred by political scientists doing research of this kind. We might even couch this in terms of a lawlike generalization to the effect that the more expensive the researches, the less independent the researcher. As Marian Irish remarks, rather matter-of-factly: "There is an understandable tendency in university circles to direct one's research where the money is available rather than into independent research. Even the most scientific research—for example, basic research in comparative politics, cross-national studies, the politics of violence, or the politics of race relations—may be mission-supporting."[20] Translated into plain English, "mission-supporting" means that such knowledge may be useful in one group's efforts to control, coerce, repress, suppress, or subvert other, rival groups.

One's scholarly integrity and independence may also be compromised in another way. To the extent that political scientists are dependent upon govern-

---

19. Albert Somit and Joseph Tanenhaus, *The Development of American Political Science* (Boston: Allyn and Bacon, 1967), p. 167. Cf. also Dahl, "The Behavioral Approach," p. 765.

20. Marian D. Irish, "Advance of the Discipline?" in *Political Science: Advance of the Discipline,* Marian D. Irish, ed. (Englewood Cliffs, NJ: Prentice-Hall, 1968), p. 19. Cf. her "oral history" interview in Baer, Jewell, and Sigelman, *Political Science in America,* pp. 82–106.

mental or foundation funding, they are less likely to ask certain kinds of questions. And foremost among these are questions about the locus, distribution, and uses of power. As David Easton observed in 1953, "entrenched power groups . . . are prone to stimulate research of a kind that does not inquire into the fundamentals of the existing arrangement of things. . . . History has yet to show us empowered groups who welcomed investigation into the roots and distribution of their strength."[21]

Yet, while many books and articles published during the postwar period reported on research funded by corporate or governmental agencies, few, if any, exhibit overt ideological or political bias either in their methods or in their conclusions. If there are biases, they tend to be of a more subtle sort, having to do with the kinds of issues addressed, the unarticulated premises from which they begin, and the questions that remain unasked. This can be seen even in the most distinguished work. Consider, for example, the seminal studies of prejudice, tolerance, and intolerance conducted during the postwar period. Two of the most important and influential of these—Adorno, Frenkl-Brunswick, and Levinson's *The Authoritarian Personality* (1949) and Samuel Stouffer's *Communism, Conformity, and Civil Liberties* (1955)—share as their fundamental guiding assumption the belief that tolerance is the preeminent political virtue. That tolerance may well be a virtue in a diverse and pluralistic society such as the United States would be hard to deny. But two points are worth noting. The first is that the issue is never framed in the "normative" language of virtue. And the second is that (the virtue of) tolerance is predicated upon a particular political theory—interest group liberalism—whose practices (and prejudices) these studies of (in)tolerance then serve to legitimize if not insulate from criticism.

The postwar period also saw the publication of numerous studies of the theory, practice, and psychological appeals of communism. One of the most important of these—Gabriel Almond's *The Appeals of Communism*, sponsored by the Carnegie Corporation—attempted to discover the sources of communism's appeal, in hopes that effective psychological and propagandistic means might be found to counter it.[22] In these and other ways political science became a valued and welcome addition to America's Cold War arsenal.

It is surely ironic that during the postwar period that old staple of political description and analysis—"the state"—virtually disappeared from the social scientists' vocabulary, even as the American state was becoming more powerful than ever. Structuralists, functionalists, and structural-functional

---

21. David Easton, *The Political System* (New York: Knopf, 1953), pp. 50–51.
22. Gabriel A. Almond, *The Appeals of Communism* (Princeton, NJ: Princeton University Press, 1954).

"systems" theorists such as David Easton preferred to speak instead of "the political system" as a "subsystem" of a larger and more benign entity, "the social system." Characterized by widespread normative consensus and the virtual absence of protracted conflict (especially class conflict), the social system looked a lot like an abstract version of the America being portrayed by the consensus historians and by social scientists who in the late 1950s announced "the end of ideology."

Much of "mainstream" political science in the postwar period tended to be more celebratory than critical. No need to search for the good society, said a future president of the APSA, since it is already here. American-style democracy, wrote Seymour Martin Lipset, is "the good society itself in operation."[23] Even our defects turned out, upon closer examination, to be virtues. For example, survey researchers discovered that most Americans are politically ill-informed, inactive, and apathetic. By "traditional" democratic lights, this was cause for considerable alarm. Yet according to the newly emergent "elite theory" of democracy, it is widespread political participation that poses the greatest danger to democracy. Fortunately an antidote is readily available. That antidote is apathy. Widespread apathy allows well-educated and affluent "democratic elites" to have a disproportionate say in the shaping of political possibilities.[24] In these and many other ways, the groundwork was being laid for a post-Progressive vision of a "consultative commonwealth," a "knowledge society" guided by the "epistemocratic authority" of experts.[25]

IV.

While many political scientists educated in the postwar years stayed in the academy, some went to work for government agencies and corporations. Sometimes, however, it seemed difficult to tell the difference between them. For even those remaining within the professional departments within the multiversity often worked under contract on "mission-supporting" projects. Called "the new Mandarins" by their critics and "the defense intellectuals" or "policy scientists" by their defenders, they attempted to contract a marriage between knowledge and power. From that marriage came numerous offspring,

---

23. Seymour Martin Lipset, *Political Man* (Garden City, NY: Doubleday and Co., 1959), p. 439.

24. See Bernard Berelson's concluding chapter, "Democratic Practice and Democratic Theory," in Bernard Berelson et al., *Voting* (Chicago: University of Chicago Press, 1954).

25. See, respectively, Heinz Eulau, "Skill Revolution and Consultative Commonwealth," 1972 APSA Presidential Address, *American Political Science Review* 67 (March 1973): 169–91; and Daniel Bell, *The Coming of Post-Industrial Society* (New York: Basic Books, 1973), especially chap. 6. For a critique of these and other visions of "epistemocratic authority," see Terence Ball, *Transforming Political Discourse* (Oxford: Blackwell, 1988), chap. 5.

some benign and some not. Project Camelot and the Vietnam War were arguably among the most notorious and visible of these progeny.[26] Under the guise of objectivity and value-freedom, some political scientists sold their skills and services without asking any hard moral questions, either of themselves or their sponsors. The Cold War, threats of communist expansionism, America's new preeminence as a world power, the coming of the welfare-warfare state, the rise of the multiversity, and the largess of the large philanthropic foundations were among the conditions that created the climate in which a positivistic vision of an instrumentally useful and normatively neutral social science could take root and flourish.

By the late 1960s, however, this vision had begun to come under considerable strain. Not only was the lustre of the policy sciences tarnished by the Vietnam War and earlier "counterinsurgency" research programs like Project Camelot, but their demonstrable lack of explanatory and predictive power was becoming increasingly obvious. Thus, for example, ideology, far from ending as predicted in the late fifties, enjoyed a resurgence in the sixties and afterward; economic forecasts have proved particularly unreliable; all the theories of revolution have come a cropper; theories of modernization and secularization have proved singularly unsuccessful in explaining or predicting developments in the Middle East and elsewhere; and assertions about the longevity and durability of totalitarianism have proved false. And while there have doubtless been some successes, these seem in retrospect to have been few and far between.

Ironically, the present predicament of the social sciences, and political science in particular, may well have been brought about less by the failure of their theories and explanations than by their unparalleled political success in securing support from foundations and government. And as we have seen, this support stemmed in no small part from their enormously successful self-promotion during the postwar period. Promises were made, or at least implied, and credit was extended. From the relative penury of the late forties and early fifties, the social sciences came to enjoy unprecedented prosperity in the sixties. If federal and foundation funding is any index of support, political science was well supported during the 1960s.[27] A war abroad and the Great Society at home proved to be a profitable combination of circumstances.

---

26. See Noam Chomsky, *American Power and the New Mandarins* (New York: Pantheon, 1967); and the essays in Irving Louis Horowitz, ed., *The Rise and Fall of Project Camelot* (Cambridge, MA: MIT Press, 1967).

27. Between 1960 and 1967, federal funding for social science research increased fivefold, from less than $73 million to more than $380 million. This figure, however, covers only federal expenditures for domestic programs. See *The Use of Social Research in Federal Domestic Programs*, a Staff Study for the Research and Technical Programs Subcommittee of the Committee on Government Operations, U.S. House of Representatives (Washington, DC: U.S. Government Printing Office, 1967), part 1.

The boom did not, and perhaps could not, last. If the 1960s were the halcyon days, the decade of the 1980s was not an altogether happy one for political science. Losing much of its funding was a serious setback, to be sure; but losing its way, and perhaps its identity, is more serious still. If political science is to have a bright future, or indeed any future at all, we shall have to look to our discipline's past—not to live in it but to learn from it. It was, I believe, Bismarck who once quipped that "the truly wise man [*sic*] does not learn from his own mistakes. He learns from other people's mistakes." Political scientists could do worse than applying Bismarck's maxim to the historical study of their discipline.

Political Science, Mid-Century

Leonard D. White

Exactly fifty days from today the first fifty years of the twentieth century will have expired. Many of you present this evening will witness the end of this troubled century and will greet the twenty-first at midnight, December 31, 1999. It is not my function tonight to wish you a happy return of this mid-century a half-century hence. Since I shall not be among the guests on that occasion, I may, however, express the hope that you may then praise the achievement of what political scientists of the first fifty years have left undone.

Toward the end of his long life one of the first and most respectable members of our profession, James Madison, wrote to a friend, "Much may be expected from the progress and diffusion of political science. . . ." While the first half of the twentieth century certainly has left much undone, we may perhaps claim that political scientists have justified Madison's faith in substantial degree. It is with some gratification that we can measure our present resources against those that our predecessors in 1900 possessed, and, if we must assess our work with due modesty, as we should, we may nevertheless assert that we have made a contribution to the Republic.

The resources of political scientists are measured first in terms of manpower and facilities, and second in terms of the intellectual structures that we establish as the foundations on which to penetrate deeper into the mysteries of man, the political animal. May we examine these matters in succession.

Our present resources in manpower are far beyond those that Frank J. Goodnow and his associates at Columbia could count as the nineteenth century came to an end. A rough calculation indicates that in 1900 there were in the United States not more than 100 men and women who would recognize themselves professionally as political scientists. Another rough calculation suggests that in 1950 there will be probably 4,000 men and women who are professional political scientists, practising the art in academic halls, govern-

"An Address Delivered before the Southern Political Science Association, November 11, 1949, Knoxville, Tennessee." Reprinted from *Journal of Politics* 12 (February 1950): 13–19. By permission of the University of Texas Press.

ment offices, and research institutes. This is the largest body of political scientists in the world.

In 1900 the subject matter of political science was recognized only in the larger endowed and state universities. Elsewhere it was a not too welcome camp follower of history, public law, or moral philosophy. By 1950 it had become a recognized member of the social science curriculum in almost every college and university in the country and was widely taught in the more progressive secondary schools.

In 1900 the political science teacher had indeed the immense asset of Bryce's *American Commonwealth,* but for the rest he was forced to take his students through such works as President Woolsey's *The State,* or Professor Burgess's *Political Science and Constitutional Law.* The hand of German scholarship was still heavy upon our "infant industry."

By 1950 American scholars had created a body of professional writing not only large in volume but penetrating in analysis. Our unsolved problem now is to find time to read what our colleagues write while we write what our colleagues ought to read. Our facilities of the written word are rich beyond measure, and have greatly expanded our horizons since 1900. In 1924 Charles E. Merriam published his *New Aspects of Politics,* reminding us that we were still one of the social sciences and that we advanced hand in hand with psychology, sociology, economics, statistics, and anthropology, not to mention history, law, ethics, and philosophy, our earlier associates. Others pushed forward ingenious types of statistical analysis; psychopathology was brought to bear on politics, and the administrative art came in for its first inspection.

Out of our own problems, which were certainly serious enough, we thus gradually began to build our own political science. Like good Americans we also began to organize. First we created the American Political Science Association in 1904, and later set up regional associations. The South led the way in 1929 by organizing the Southern Political Science Association, in whose eighteenth annual meeting we are participating. Nine more regional associations have since sprung into existence, and the attendance at their conferences often well exceeds the number I can remember in earlier years at the national meetings.

We also organized a number of associations based on our special fields. The international lawyers set up housekeeping in 1906 in the American Society of International Law. Many political scientists took an active part in the affairs of the National Municipal League, and in other associations designed to improve American government. The students and practitioners of public administration organized the American Society for Public Administration in 1939. Not content with a merely American pattern of organization, our political scientists moved across the seas, taking an active share in the affairs of the Institute of Pacific Relations, the International Union of Local Authorities, and the International Institute of the Administrative Sciences, to symbolize a spacious participation by only three examples. Most recently, indeed only two months ago, our national president, Quincy Wright, participated in Paris in the formation of the International Political Science Association, and himself was elected chairman of the organizing committee.

It would be fruitless to follow political scientists into all their professional societies and all the "reform" groups through which they work. Suffice it to say that where good works are to be done on the body politic, there political scientists are to be found.

Looking backward over a half-century we cannot assert that we have fulfilled Edward Bellamy's prophecy of a well-organized world. We *can* switch on music from a distant source—one of Bellamy's lucky guesses—and fortunately we can switch off most of it. We are no nearer Bellamy's placid order now than when his hero began his long nap in 1887, and perhaps it is just as well. We have, however, improved our governmental machine and made it capable of achievement that would have been impossible in 1900. We have endowed it with standards of integrity and responsibility, lacking in 1900, of which we may be proud. Political scientists have had a special share in these affairs.

Political scientists took a major responsibility for the reconstruction of municipal government, the hottest of our governmental problems in the first decade of the century. They led the way in the reorganization of state governments in the second and third decades. They were influential in the drive for a short ballot and better election procedures. They were chiefly responsible for educating the American public to the necessity of a budget system. They began the long process of discussion that finally, with the powerful help of circumstances, reversed the historical direction of American foreign policy.

All this, and much more that could be added, demonstrates how mistaken is the old stereotype of the professor in his ivory tower, bent over an ancient parchment and occasionally wiping the dust from his steel-rimmed spectacles. American political scientists are participant-observers of the governmental scene—sometimes even more participants than observers. Wherever the political pot boils we can find a political scientist stirring the broth, or putting wood on the fire. At one moment, he or she may be spending a hot summer in Washington with congressmen and their committees; at another he or she may be speaking before the League of Women Voters, or activating a local chapter of the American Society for Public Administration. At another, he or she may be selling civil service reform to a governor or a legislative committee, and in the twinkling of an eye turn to the technical problems of a public employee retirement plan. We can find him or her talking to vice-presidents, senators, governors, representatives, county commissioners, mayors, school boards, employee organizations, and citizens, as well as to the students who still provide us with our principal constituents.

We ought not to underestimate our influence. We are often frustrated and defeated on particular issues and on particular occasions. We are seldom defeated on major issues or in the long run. We have assets that perhaps no other group possesses in our status as staff assistants to the American people. We have trained capacity to forecast the morrow and to concentrate on what is important in the emerging future. We have means of communication among ourselves that are adequate to bind us into a homogeneous task force, with due recognition of our domestic differences. We are, organically speaking, immortal. We multiply ourselves over and over again tenfold, a hundredfold, as we send our graduates into the world of American citizens. Through them we project on the American scene not our various personal views on public issues, but capacity for analysis, character, and integrity, and a sense of responsibility for participation in the affairs of the world.

Our growing resources in manpower and facilities have thus borne much fruit. Can we claim as much progress in building a strong intellectual foundation for the field of knowledge for which we are responsible?

It can be argued that we have succeeded more amply in making an impress upon our times than we have in laying adequate foundations for our subject matter. When we examine our intellectual situation we may well become uneasy. Our intellectual substructure is feeble. On it we have erected an imposing, but very heterogeneous superstructure, the various parts of which we identify as international law, public law, political theory, parties, politics and propaganda, public opinion, public administration, comparative government, state government, municipal government, rural government, regional organization, valley authorities, public corporations, government and business, and so on at much length. What then is political science? Is it anything but a collective name descriptive of a large number of interesting matters that no other social scientists claim as their special territory? Has it a coherent central structure of its own?

At mid-century it is not easy to give a satisfactory answer to such questions. We are more vulnerable as members of a learned profession than our colleagues in economics, sociology, or anthropology, all of whom have established an accepted and reasonably satisfactory concept of the special aspects of human experience that they are concerned with.

The formula with which we started this century, that political science studies the state, merely tells us the object of our attention. The sociologists also study the state; so do the students of ethics and philosophy; and the economists often view it with alarm. Another formula, renewed and put to use during the last twenty years, asserts that the political scientist studies the phenomena of power. This proposition does set the stage for the formulation of hypotheses, for observation of a framework of related propositions that tend to give form to what still remains substantially formless. But political scientists are equally interested in the phenomena of cooperation, an aspect of our public life that is of obvious importance, if often overlooked. Much hard thinking is required of us on this professional front.

Standing on the edge of the mid-century, political scientists can hardly refrain from speculating about their future tasks. The new generation of political scientists that may now properly prepare to greet the twenty-first century—just around the corner—may ask us what unfinished business they inherit. Everyone will make his own answer. There is always the unfinished business of perfecting the American system of democracy. There is always the unfinished business of advising our fellow citizens as best we can on their municipal, county, state, national, and international problems. There is always the major task of informing each oncoming generation of their democratic inheritance and their public responsibility.

As a political scientist I would propose four tasks which seem worthy of our mettle. One I have suggested: the better formulation of the intellectual foundations of our own subject matter. This task carries with it a broader one, in which many besides ourselves will participate—the formulation of a new philosophy for the new world which obviously lies before us; new in a special sense, new as never before, full of potential terror, but also full of unparalleled prospects for good.

A second task, now on our doorstep, is to reach a more profound understanding of political behavior, with help from the anthropologists, psychologists, sociologists, and the medical profession. We need some men and women holding doctor's degrees in political science and medicine, political science and psychology, political science and anthropology.

Third, we have a practical task of world education in the American way of life and in the spirit of American government, made in its image. We cannot and ought not impose our special democratic forms on other people; we can and ought to borrow something from the spirit and practice of our democratic sister nations as we learn from them while they become acquainted with us. But in a world that derives its understanding of America from the movies and newspaper headlines there is an enormous task of enlightenment in which we must carry a part.

Finally we need to take our share of the responsibility for lessening the tensions which harass the world and those who live upon it. National hostility, race conflict, economic strife are only three of many horsemen who ride us hard. As political scientists and as citizens we have a half-century of work ahead of us on this front alone.

To enumerate our problems is a ready and endless occupation. They are many and they are grave. Less easy is it to maintain perspective in the midst of perplexities. It is useful to recall that our age is not the only one that has groaned under its burdens. It is well to reassert that ancient American faith in our capacity to deal with whatever may lie before us. It is good, at mid-century, to repeat the stout words written at a dark moment of Federalist history by one of the greatest of the Federalists, Alexander Hamilton: "I anticipate with you that this country will, erelong, assume an attitude correspondent with its great destinies—majestic, efficient, and operative of great things. A noble career lies before it."

The Idea of a Political System and the Orientation of Political Research

David Easton

Essentially, in defining political science, what we are seeking are concepts to describe the most obvious and encompassing properties of the political system. The idea of a political *system* proves to be an appropriate and indeed unavoidable starting point in this search. Although there is often uncertainty about the unity of political science as a discipline, most students of political life do feel quite instinctively that research into the political aspects of life does differ from inquiry into any other, sufficiently so to constitute a separate intellectual enterprise. These students have been acting on the unexpressed premise that the phenomena of politics tend to cohere and to be mutually related. Such phenomena form, in other words, a system which is part of the total social system and yet which, for purposes of analysis and research, is temporarily set apart.

In the concrete world of reality not everything is significantly or closely related to what we call political life; certain kinds of activity are more prominently associated with it than others. These elements of political activity, such as governmental organizations, pressure groups, voting, parties, and other social elements related to them, such as classes, regional groupings, and so forth, all show close enough interaction to be considered part of the political process. They are, of course, part of the whole social process and therefore are part of analytical systems other than the political. But they do show a marked political relevance that is more than purely accidental or random. If they were accidental there would be little point in searching for regularities in political activity. The search for recurrent relationships suggests that the elements of political life have some form of determinate relation. The task of research is to discover what these are. In short, political life constitutes a concrete political system which is an aspect of the whole social system.

Reprinted in a shortened version from *The Political System: An Inquiry into the State of Political Science* (New York: Knopf, 1953 and 1971; Chicago: University of Chicago Press, second edition, 1981), chaps. 4 and 5. Copyright 1953, © 1971 by David Easton.

We must recognize, as I have intimated, that ultimately all social life is interdependent and, as a result, that it is artificial to isolate any set of social relations from the whole for special attention. But this artificiality is imposed upon political scientists by the need for simplification of their data. Since everything is related to everything else, the task of pursuing the determinants of any given relation would be so vast and ramifying that it would defy any tools of investigation available either to the social or physical sciences. Instead, political science is compelled to abstract from the whole social system some variables which seem to cohere more closely than others, much as price, supply, demand, and choice among wants do in economics, and to look upon them as a subsystem which can be profitably examined, temporarily, apart from the whole social system. The analytic or mental tool for this purpose is the theoretical system (systematic theory). It consists, first, of a set of concepts corresponding to the important political variables and, second, of statements about the relations among these concepts. Systematic theory corresponds at the level of thought to the concrete empirical political system of daily life.

It is now clear why an initial step in developing systematic theory must be an inquiry into the orienting concepts of the system under investigation. If the object of such theory is to identify all the important variables, some criteria are required to determine relevance or importance. We require some knowledge at the outset about the kind of activity in general that we describe as political before we can examine political life more closely to identify its components. Without some guide to the investigator to indicate when a variable is politically relevant, social life would simply be an incoherent wilderness of activities.

At first sight, to be sure, and, for that matter, even upon closer examination, political science does not seem to possess this systemic coherence. There seem to be no broad variables common to the whole discipline; instead there seems to be a large number of heterogeneous fields. For the sake of illustration we might notice that the list of doctoral dissertations in progress at any one time seems to be made up of a fantastic agglomeration of subjects.

A search for unity out of this variegated manifold does indeed tax one's ingenuity. Throwing up their hands in defeat when confronted with such heterogeneity, some political scientists have ventured the opinion that this is the great weakness of their discipline: it lacks the intrinsic unity necessary to make a science.

One thing, however, is certain. Political scientists are not interested in all kinds of facts in the world. Some process of selection does take place. Quite instinctively, if only as a result of slavish adherence to their training, they turn their attention to a kind of fact that differs radically from the kind other social scientists usually study. For example, a political scientist, if he is wise, does not attempt to voice a professional or authoritative opinion on the relation of the breakdown of family life to personal insecurity common in modern society, or on the relation of fluctuating price levels to depressions. His interest leads him to focus on other matters related to these and yet distinctively apart. However diffuse political science may appear to be, there can be no doubt that "political" refers to a separable dimension of human activity.

The origins of this separable interest lie buried in the differences that distinguish all the social sciences, each from the other. This means that in order to appreciate fully the individuality of political science, and its systemic character, we must turn for a moment to the broader question of the historical and logical reasons for the separation of the various social sciences into independent fields of study. This will provide the clue essential for the discovery of the major orienting concepts implicit within political research.

The Divisions among the Social Sciences

To telescope into a few brief phrases the evolution of the social sciences towards their present excessively specialized state cannot do justice to its complicated, tortuous nature. Over the past twenty-five hundred years the central body of knowledge about social matters has undergone a complete transformation. At one time this knowledge was unified and largely undifferentiated, and it was the proper topic for discussion by any articulate person who wished to contribute his share to an understanding of society. Today, in contrast, the original body of unspecialized knowledge has gradually been reduced in quantity and scope by the divorce from it of the separately organized contemporary social sciences. From an era, several centuries ago, of integrated, unified knowledge, we have today arrived at a period of extreme specialization. The weight of all empirical knowledge has become too heavy for any one person to carry and too intensive for any one scholar to digest and develop in creative research.

In no small degree this trend towards specialization has been imposed by the historical accumulation of knowledge to which we are heirs. Until the eighteenth century, the moral sciences, as the social sciences were then known, possessed greater unity than diversity. So broad was the range of subject matter with which the moral philosopher dealt that he was truly a universal student of society. But with the increase in the rate of research by the beginning of the nineteenth century, economics, through the efforts of Adam Smith, and sociology, in the work of Auguste Comte, began to pry themselves loose from the main body of social thinking. Psychology, too, had by that time made some progress in separating itself from philosophy. And by the end of the century, anthropology, inspired by the work of the Scottish school at an earlier period, emerged from its swaddling clothes.

Of all the areas of social life, politics was the first to win the concentrated attention of men. The overwhelming interest of the ancient Greeks centered in the nature of the political system; Plato's interest in human nature, for example, and in problems of education and other matters stemmed from his concern for the *polis* as a whole. Since an understanding of political life was thus the source of inspiration for the study of society, it might have been expected that political science would be one of the first to break away from the main body of moral philosophy. But the truth is that it was the last. Only after the other well-recognized social sciences had drifted away from the general body of knowledge, leaving a residue composed essentially of politics and general philosophy, did the growing weight of political data finally force political science as well to branch out on its own.

Thus the purely physical need for a division of labor helps to account for the distinctions among the social sciences. This fact, however, cannot be used as a means for explaining the genuine deep-going differences in the data of these sciences.

It is in the logic of the situation that each separate, distinct, and vital set of questions posed leads to the discovery that the answer involves the pursuit of ramifying paths of related knowledge. All the social sciences may well have a common body of theory,[1] and the paths of the social sciences may cross and may be the same at some points for short distances. But each social discipline works out its own pattern or system since its motivating questions lead it to a different proximate goal, although the ultimate purposes to serve human needs are the same.

Political science, too, arose in this way. The body of data which compose it grew up in response to some key questions, the answers to which men thought would help in the amelioration of their collective lives. These key questions set the initial orientation of political research. The knowledge, therefore, that it is the motivating questions that distinguish the social sciences helps us to understand the subject matter of political science itself. It leads us to search for these questions, which, strangely enough, are not easily discovered. Although men who are political scientists have no doubt about the fact that they are political scientists—after all, they were trained as political scientists or they are paid by political science departments, a matter of no small importance—there is some doubt about why the congeries of subjects they discuss properly fall within the scope of politics or constitute variables within a concrete political system.

Lack of awareness, and where awareness does exist, of agreement, about the major orienting concepts of political research is an index of the fact that this discipline is coming late into the field as a social science. Men will always

---

1. T. Parsons, *Essays in Sociological Theory Pure and Applied,* chap. 3.

differ about the reasons for their activity, but there does seem to be less agreement in political science than in most of the other social sciences. The task of the rest of this section and the next will be to identify the basic questions in search of an answer to which men have turned to the study of the distinctively political aspects of human activity. In this way we may be able to unearth a few integrative concepts that serve to identify the major characteristics of the political system.

The Concept of the State

Although there is little agreement on the key questions which orient political research, in the course of history two main schools of thought have developed. One directs itself to the study of political life by asking what are the nature and characteristics of the state; the other, by asking what can be understood about the distribution and use of power. We must examine the extent to which the question of either school leads to a gross frame of reference revealing the most general and characteristic properties of political life.

The weight of the discussion here will be that neither the state nor power is a concept that serves to bind together political research. Each has some merit but also has distinct shortcomings. It could be argued, of course, that political science ought to confine itself to something called the state or it ought to display an exclusive interest in power. To do this, however, would be to attempt to create a new field in the pattern of its designer. No such attempt will be made here since there is no evidence that political science shows any inherent limitations in its present focus to prevent it from answering the kind of question it really asks. In the next section I shall suggest that this question is: How are values authoritatively allocated for a society? Hence, an attempt at total revision would be needless and gratuitous.

The opinion is broadly held that what draws the various divisions of political science together is the fact that they all deal with the state. "The phenomena of the state," reads an elementary text, "in its varied aspects and relationships, as distinct from the family, the tribe, the nation, and from all private associations or groups, though not unconnected with them, constitute the subject of political science. In short, political science begins and ends with the state."[2]

This description is deceptively simple. The truth is that it achieves greater success in confusing than in clarifying since it immediately begs the

---

2. W. Garner, *Political Science and Government* (New York: American Book, 1928), p. 9. See also R. G. Gettell, *Political Science* (rev. ed., New York: Ginn, 1949), p. 19: "Since political science is the science of the state, a clear understanding of what is meant by the term 'state' is important."

question as to the characteristics of the state. And to anyone who is familiar with the infinite diversity of responses to this question, the suspicion must indubitably arise that it succeeds in substituting one unknown for another; for the unknown of "political science" we now have the unknown of the "state."

What is the state? One author claims to have collected one hundred and forty-five separate definitions.[3] Seldom have men disagreed so markedly about a term. The confusion and variety of meanings is so vast that it is almost unbelievable that over the last twenty-five hundred years in which the question has recurringly been discussed in one form or another, some kind of uniformity has not been achieved. One person sees the state as the embodiment of the moral spirit, its concrete expression; another, as the instrument of exploitation used by one class against others. One author defines it as simply an aspect of society, distinguishable from it only analytically; another, as simply a synonym for government; and still another, as a separate and unique association among a large number of other associations such as the church, trade unions, and similar voluntary groups. For those who ascribe to the state ultimate power or sovereignty within constitutional or customary limits, there are corresponding thinkers who insist upon the limited authority of the state whenever a conflict of allegiance to it and to other associations arises. There is clearly little hope that out of this welter of differences anyone today can hammer out a meaning upon which the majority of men will genuinely, consistently, and constantly agree. When general agreement has sometimes arisen, small differences have usually become magnified and have laid the basis for new and forbidding disagreement. Hence it seems pointless to add a favored definition of my own to those already listed.

After the examination of the variety of meanings a critical mind might conclude that the word ought to be abandoned entirely. If the argument is raised that it would be impossible to find a substitute to convey the meaning of this term, intangible and imprecise as it is, the reply can be offered that after this section the word will be avoided scrupulously and no severe hardship in expression will result. In fact, clarity of expression demands this abstinence. There is a good reason for this. At this stage of our discussion we are interested in concepts that pick out the major properties of the concrete political system. If we were to use the concept of the state with its most widely adopted meaning today, we would find that it has a number of obvious shortcomings for an understanding of the political system. It describes the properties not of all political phenomena but of only certain kinds, excluding, for example, the study of pre-state societies; it stands overshadowed as a tool of analysis by its social utility as a myth; and it constitutes at best a poor formal definition. Let us look at these three defects in this order.

---

3. C. H. Titus, "A Nomenclature in Political Science," *American Political Science Review* 25 (1931): 45–60.

If political science is defined as the study of the state, can there be said to be any political life to understand in those communities in which the state has not yet appeared? Among the varied conceptions of the state today, the most generally acceptable view accords most closely with that offered by R. M. MacIver. In *The Modern State* he sees the state, in modified pluralist vein, as one association among many with the special characteristic that it acts "through law as promulgated by a government endowed to this end with coercive power, [and] maintains within a community territorially demarcated the universal external conditions of social order."[4] The state is different, then, from other kinds of associations in that it embraces the whole of the people on a specific territory and it has the special function of maintaining social order. This it does through its agent, the government, which speaks with the voice of law. Expressed in most general terms, the state comes into existence when there is a fixed territory, a stable government, and a settled population. In the United States this view, with incidental modifications, prevails in a major part of empirical political research that turns to the state as its focus of attention. The territorial state as we have known it since the Treaty of Westphalia has thus become the prototype from which the criteria for all political systems are derived.

But prior to the seventeenth century, for the vast span of time in which men lived and governed one another, according to this interpretation of the state at least, no state was in existence. At most there was a truncated form of political life. Greece had its city-community, mistranslated today as the city-state; the Middle Ages had its system of feudalities; contemporary exotic communities have their councils, leaders, and headmen. But, by definition, this modified pluralism denies that in these communities there is a fully formed political system. These are transitional political forms, pre-states, or nascent states, and therefore of only passing interest to political scientists since their main concern is presumably with states fully developed.[5]

Not all scholars would agree when or where the state in this sense appears. But whatever the time and place, all preceding kinds of social life are

---

4. R. M. MacIver, *The Modern State* (London: Oxford University Press, 1926), p. 22.

5. "Of all the multifarious projects for fixing the boundary which marks off political from the more general social science, that seems most satisfactory which bases the distinction on the existence of a political consciousness. Without stopping to inquire too curiously into the precise connotation of this term, it may safely be laid down that as a rule primitive communities do not and advanced communities do manifest the political consciousness. Hence, the opportunity to leave to sociology the entire field of primitive institutions, and to regard as truly political only those institutions and those theories which are closely associated with such manifestation. A history of political theories, then, would begin at the point at which the idea of the state, as distinct from the family and the clan, becomes a determining factor in the life of the community." W. A. Dunning, *A History of Political Theories* (New York: Macmillan, 1902), pp. xvi–xvii. See also MacIver, *The Modern State*, p. 338.

considered to have been devoid of identifiable political aspects. One student, for example, pushes back the appearance of the state to a very early period in human history. "The shift to agriculture," he writes, "may have taken place first in the alluvial valleys of the Nile and Euphrates, or of the Chinese rivers. While these rich river-bottoms were enormously productive when cultivated, the surrounding regions afforded meager pasturage. When a pastoral kinship group settled on the land, the State began. The group had already set up a government; it now acquired territoriality."[6] In this view, clearly, it took the establishment of a fixed territory to convert mere social life into political life. Not even the existence of government could inform the social existence of the pastoral kinship group with a political quality. The state being nonexistent in pastoral groups, there could be little subject matter for political research.

Common sense alone, however, would compel us to deny this restriction upon political inquiry. The literature on contemporary nomadic groups, for example, suggests that the strife within a migratory tribe for control of its movement and resources is exactly similar to what we would consider political struggle. Similarly, the investiture conflict in the Middle Ages was as highly charged with politics as any dispute today. And there is also a growing awareness that too little attention has been paid to the anthropological data about political life among primitive and nonliterate peoples. Where there is any kind of organized activity, incipient as it may be, there, what we would normally call political situations, abound. Thus even if we could reach agreement to adopt as our meaning for empirical research the most general definition today given to the concept of the state, it must still fall short of providing an adequate description of the limits of political research. By definition it excludes social systems in which there can be no question that political interaction is an essential aspect.

The historical origins of the term further help to explain both the difficulties we have with its meaning today and its unsatisfactory nature as an orienting concept. The truth is that the concept was originally less an analytical tool than a symbol for unity. It offered a myth which could offset the emotional attractiveness of the church and which later could counteract the myths of internationalism and of opposing national units.[7]

As a concept the state came into frequent use during the sixteenth and seventeenth centuries. It appears in Machiavelli's *The Prince* although at that

6. E. M. Sait, *Political Institutions* (New York: Appleton-Century, 1938), p. 131.

7. Ibid., pp. 88–89; George H. Sabine, "State," *Encyclopaedia of the Social Sciences* (New York: Macmillan, 1930), vol. 14, pp. 328–32; R. Kranenburg (transl. by R. Borregaard), *Political Theory* (London: Oxford University Press, 1939), pp. 76–77; C. J. Friedrich, *Constitutional Government and Democracy* (Boston: Little, Brown, 1941), chap. 1; F. Watkins, *The State as a Concept of Political Science* (New York: Harper, 1934); H. Finer, *The Theory and Practice of Modern Government* (London: Methuen, 1932), 2 vols., vol. 1, chap. 1.

time it usually referred to officials of government or to the government itself, not to the political aspects of the whole community. Although it was not until the nineteenth century that the term developed its full mythical qualities, in the interval it served the growing needs of nationalism as against the universal claims of the medieval church and the particularistic competition of the local feudal powers. It was especially vital as a symbol to combat the emotional appeal of the church. The varied ecclesiastical institutions, officials, and governing bodies could be personified and crystalized in two words, the church. The growing national territorial governments required a similar emotionally imbued concept, and they found it in the happy notion of the state. Men need not serve a government, a king, or an oligarchy; they could pledge their loyalties to a unity as transcendental and eternal as the church itself. Leaders and rulers may come and go, but the state is everlasting and above mundane dispute. Secular authority could thus hope to draw men's allegiance with all the force of religion without depending wholly upon religion for its emotional appeal.

The state concept became a crucial myth in the struggle for national unity and sovereignty. Its very vagueness and imprecision allowed it to serve its purposes well. Each man, each group, and each age could fill the myth with its own content; the state stood for whatever one wanted from life. But however diverse the purposes imputed to the state, it symbolized the inescapable unity of one people on one soil. By the nineteenth century the struggle of nation against church had been largely resolved in favor of the former, but new problems in the form of international conflict arose. In giving an ideological basis for the kind of national sovereignty with which we are familiar, the concept of the state now reaches the height of its political utility. Each state can claim the ultimate loyalty of its members as against a class or an international society because it, the state, in some mystical way now represents the supreme virtues.[8]

Bearing in mind the actual history of the political use of the concept, it is difficult to understand how it could ever prove to be fruitful for empirical work; its importance lies largely in the field of practical politics as an instrument to achieve national cohesion rather than in the area of thoughtful analysis. We can, therefore, appreciate the difficulty into which we must fall if we attempt to treat the concept as a serious theoretical tool. And yet, for want of a superior set of guiding concepts, this is exactly what large numbers of practicing political scientists do attempt.

This brings us to the last of the three shortcomings mentioned earlier: the inadequacy of the state concept for depicting in general terms what it is the political scientist studies that distinguishes him from other social scientists.

---

8. C. J. Friedrich, "Deification of the State," *Review of Politics* 1 (1939): 18–30.

The concept falls short of a satisfactory kind of definition. It defines by specifying instances of political phenomena rather than by describing their general properties.

Basically the inadequacy of the state concept as a definition of subject matter stems from the fact that it implies that political science is interested in studying a particular kind of institution or organization of life, not a kind of activity that may express itself through a variety of institutions. For this reason, the use of the state concept, as we saw, could not explain why political scientists ought to be interested in forms of social life, such as nonliterate and exotic societies, in which the state, at least as defined by modified pluralism, does not exist. No one could deny that political science is indeed interested in the state, as defined here, as one type of political institution. But it is equally apparent that political research today, stimulated by the knowledge made available by social anthropology, has begun to accept the fact that societies in which the so-called state institution is nonexistent afford excellent material for a general understanding of political life.

The major drawback of the state concept is thus revealed. It does not serve to identify the properties of a phenomenon that give the latter a political quality. At most, the state concept is usually just an illustration of one kind of political phenomenon, a comprehensive political institution. However, since there are periods in history when such states did not exist, and perhaps the same may be true in the unknown future, the state is revealed as a political institution peculiar to certain historical conditions. Presumably in order to understand the full scope of political research, it would be necessary to specify in equal detail the kind of institutions to be studied in social systems from which the state is absent. The point here is that in practice the field of political science is usually described by the least desirable and least meaningful kind of definition, denotation.

As long as political science is characterized as the study of the state, it must remain at the level of enumerating or denoting the various kinds of institutions which it examines. Once we ask, however, just why political science studies the kind of institution often called the state together with other institutions in societies where states are acknowledged to be nonexistent, we have a means of discovering the connotative meaning, that is, the general properties of any political phenomenon. We find that we are looking for a kind of activity which can express itself through a variety of institutional patterns. Since new social conditions call forth new kinds of structures and practices for the expression of this activity, the precise mechanism, whether it be an organizational pattern called a state or some other kind, is always a matter for empirical investigation. A general description of this activity, for the moment indifferent to its particular institutional pattern, would indicate the properties that an event must have to make it relevant for political science. To say, therefore, that in asking "what is the nature of the state?" political science is drawing attention to the core of its subject matter, is at best to mistake a part for the whole and to attempt to describe the properties of an activity by a single, even if important, instance.

The Concept of Power

Although the state concept as such has seldom been directly attacked or rejected, it has come in for oblique criticism from a long line of writers who see that the characteristic of political activity, the property that distinguishes the political from the economic or other aspect of a situation, is the attempt to control others. In this view the motivating question behind political research is "who holds power and how is it used?" It is true that most political scientists who adopt the power concept continue to speak of the state and seldom go so far as to argue that there is an intrinsic hostility between the two ideas in an empirical context. Nevertheless, the idea of the state usually recedes into the shadows of their empirical research and plays little part in their conclusions.

The obvious merit of the power approach is that it identifies an activity, the effort to influence others. *Prima facie* this makes it superior to the institutional description of political life as the state. Any activity that is characterized by the general property of being able to influence others immediately acquires political relevance. Therefore, we have here at least a connotative definition. In spite of this and in spite of the prevalence today of the conviction that power lies at the heart of political research, my conclusion will nevertheless be that the idea of power, as it has been employed until quite recently, has failed to provide a rounded description of the gross subject matter of political science.

Because the power concept has in the past been associated with doctrines that asserted the limitless power of government, students have traditionally adopted a deep suspicion towards this approach. Where a social philosopher has adopted the idea of power as central to his thinking, as in the case of Machiavelli or Hobbes, it has usually seemed to imply abusive coercion on behalf of the coercer. It has therefore appeared that this view of the central problem of politics must always carry with it a certain misanthropy towards life. Where political life seemed to be reduced to a mere struggle for power, all the noble aims which the philosophers have depicted as the matrix of life seemed to crumble.

In spite of these unhappy associations of the power approach, however, some contemporary students of political science have succeeded in rehabilitating it as an orienting concept. They have discerned in it an activity which would lend itself to scientific study and which might cover the whole field of political life. Their great merit has been that they have made the power approach more respectable in the United States than it ever had been. They have converted it from a street urchin to an irreproachable child of the age. Indeed, it has become respectable enough today for courses on power to be offered in the universities and for widely used texts, such as *Politics Among Nations* by H. J. Morgenthau, *American Politics* by P. H. Odegard and E. A. Helms, *Politics, Parties and Pressure Groups* by V. O. Key, and *A Study of the Principles of Politics* by George Catlin, to use power as the central theme around which to weave their facts about political life.

Despite this latter-day, hard-earned popularity, however, for a reason not difficult to find, the power approach must fail to convince us of its merits as an adequate, initial identification of the boundaries of political research. The reason for this is that power is only one of the significant variables. It omits an equally vital aspect of political life, its orientation towards goals other than power itself. Political life does not consist exclusively of a struggle for control; this struggle stems from and relates to conflict over the direction of social life, over public policy, as we say today in a somewhat legal formulation. Some attention to the work of Harold D. Lasswell,[9] one of the most articulate architects of power theories, will point up the merits, inadequacies, and necessary modifications of an attempt to describe the limits of political science predominantly in terms of power relations.

Lasswell is a serious student of power relations, and perhaps in recent times, together with other members of the so-called Chicago School, he has contributed more than any other individual to the popular diffusion of this approach in the United States. He sees political science as an "autonomous" discipline and "not merely applied psychology or applied economics."[10] He describes it initially, not as the power process, but as "the study of changes in the shape and composition of the value patterns of society."[11] However, since the distribution of values must depend upon the influence of the members of society, political science must deal with influence and the influential. Integral to his thinking, therefore, is the conclusion that the major concepts guiding political research must be values and power. In its broadest perspective the task of political research is to show the interdependence between the two: how our values affect the distribution and use of power and how our location and use of power act on the distribution of values. Or as he phrased it in the happy title of his well-read little book, political science concerns *Politics: Who Gets What, When, How.*

---

9. Particularly in H. D. Lasswell, *Politics: Who Gets What, When, How* (New York: McGraw-Hill, 1936), and with A. Kaplan in *Power and Society.*

10. Lasswell and Kaplan, *Power and Society,* p. xviii.

11. H. D. Lasswell, *World Politics and Personal Insecurity* (New York: McGraw-Hill, 1935), p. 3; see also Lasswell, *Politics: Who Gets What, When, How,* chap. 1; *Power and Society,* pp. xii and 240.

The title of this book represents his most general conception of the subject matter of political science and was offered as such by the author himself. "Those who accept the frame of reference here proposed," he wrote in his preface to this book, "will share common standards to guide future intellectual effort." In terms of the actual problems that were explored in this work, however, the title appears somewhat overambitious. It does not really mirror the contents lying between its covers. It bears the promise that the author will discuss how social values are distributed in society—when it is and how it is that certain groups get more or less of socially valuable things. In fact, however, it is devoted to exploring the sources of power held by a political elite. Its focus therefore is not on the way values are distributed but on the way the elite, which has power, uses it to acquire the desirable things of society, such as safety, income, and deference. The book is primarily an inquiry into the means the elite uses to arrive at and survive in the seat of power. If political science is devoted to the study of changing value patterns, as Lasswell maintains, this study must be interpreted as describing only a small part of the whole process. It is restricted to revealing the role of the minority that holds power.

Contrary to general belief, therefore, this work on *Politics: Who Gets What, When, How* does not in itself provide a general framework for the study of political life. It is a vehicle not for the investigation of the whole political system but only for determining the power and characteristics of one social formation, the elite. The book is devoted, therefore, to an examination of the composition of the elite and the conditions and techniques of its existence. The fact is that under exactly the same title one could write a volume making the antithetical assumption—that the masses dominate over policy—and then go on to explore historically the composition of the various masses and the conditions and techniques surrounding their survival and change. Such a work would provide no more comprehensive a framework than a study of the variables influencing the power of the elite.

In short, the elitist theory is only a partial scheme of analysis helping us to discern the sources of power over values of certain groups but presenting us with little data about the power of others. It centers only on one problem, however crucial it is today: the tendency in mass societies for power to concentrate in the hands of a minority. It assumes that this oligarchic tendency in the political system eternally prevents the diffusion of power beyond the governing group. Aside from the validity of such a theory and its insight, the point here is that all it provides is a narrow-gauge synthetic theory.

This narrow-gauge theory, however, has been interpreted by most political scientists to mean that Lasswell conceived the whole subject matter of political science to be the struggle for power. And, in fact, until the publication of *Power and Society,* the emphasis of Lasswell's research was weighted so heavily on the power side, that it was justifiable to draw the inference that he thought power stood alone at the heart of political research. In *Power and Society*, however, Lasswell and his collaborator undertake the broader task suggested in *Politics: Who Gets What, When, How* of exploring the total configuration of power in relation to values. The authors write that "the political act takes its origin in a situation in which the actor strives for the attainment of various values for which power is a necessary (and perhaps also sufficient) condition."[12]

We shall see in the next section that even this attempt, unique with Lasswell, to describe political science as the study of the distribution of values is unsatisfactory. It describes all social science rather than political science alone; this helps to explain why in recent years he has broadened the scope of his own research to cover all the social sciences, the policy sciences, as he is fond of calling them.[13] However, from the nature of his early work and of his influence as a teacher and author, power appeared to be the central datum of political science. In retrospect we can see this to be a misconstruction of his conception of the nature of political life, but in terms of his impact on American political research, we can say that until recently he appeared to have adopted an exclusively power orientation.

In contrast to Catlin's and others' use of the power concept, Lasswell's yielded immediate and promising results within the limits of his elitist interpretation of the location of power. It offered greater opportunity for fruitful empirical research largely because he consciously defined the field so as to invite concrete investigations. It stimulated an interest in the characteristics of governing groups, their skills, class origin, subjective attitudes and personality traits, and the instruments, such as goods, practices, violence, and symbols, that they use in arriving at and surviving in the seat of power. It led Lasswell to inquire, from a concurrent interest in psychoanalysis, into the personality types that arrive, an inquiry that brings out sharply the emphasis in our culture on power as a driving motive. It thereby broke new ground in the study of political leadership. The use of the power concept helped to tie together what seemed like miscellaneous data about the operation of various political pressure groups and about the tactics of politicians. These data could now be viewed as contributing towards a theory of power.

But in spite of these obvious merits, Lasswell does not provide us with a satisfactory minimal orientation to political phenomena. He argues that all power relations, wherever they may exist, are automatically an index of the

---

12. Lasswell and Kaplan, *Power and Society*, p. 240.

13. See, for example, his *Power and Personality* (New York: Norton, 1948), esp. chap. 6; and D. Lerner and H. D. Lasswell, *The Policy Sciences* (Stanford: Stanford University Press, 1951), esp. chap. 1.

presence of a political situation. For him the hierarchical arrangement of relationships within a criminal band or in a respectable fraternal club both testify to the existence of political life there. The realization of this implication when politics is described as power, pure and simple, reveals the excessive breadth of the definition. Not that Lasswell was wrong in maintaining that political science is and ought to be interested in these phenomena, but he was misleading when he failed to point out that political scientists are not concerned with them for their own sake. The definition is too broad, for political science is not interested in the power relations of a gang or a family or church group simply because in them one man or group controls the actions of another. It might be necessary, to be sure, to devote time to such a comprehensive examination of power situations in order to develop a generalized theory of power. This theory would be very helpful to the political scientist, but by the nature of his task he directs his attention not to power in general but to political power.

What Lasswell and, in fact, many power theorists neglect to clarify is the distinction between power in general and power in a political context. In fact, even though they do not distinguish verbally between these two different aspects of power and insist upon power in general as the central phenomenon of politics, in their practical research their natural predisposition toward political questions quite logically leads them to emphasize the political aspects of power. An inquiry into the characteristics of this aspect will compel us to modify their conception of the limits of political science.

Neither the concept of the state nor that of power in general offers a useful gross description of the central theme of political research. The task of the next section therefore, will be to explore suitable concepts for identifying in broad outline the major political variables.

The Authoritative Allocation of Values for a Society

Because political science has historically set for itself the task of understanding what social policy ought to be, how it is set and put into effect, its general objective must be to understand the functioning of the political system. We have in the concept of authoritative policy for a society a convenient and rough approximation to a set of orienting concepts for political research. It provides us with the essential property of that complex of activity, called political, that over the years men have sought to understand.

But this is only the first step on the way to discovering the focus of political research. We must inquire into the meaning of the three concepts used in this description: policy, authority, and society. We shall examine them in this order and in the process we shall be led to rephrase the description slightly. In the end, I shall suggest, convenience for purposes of actual research dictates that political science be described as the study of the authoritative allocation of values for a society.

To look at the first of the three concepts just mentioned, what do we mean when we talk about policy? The essence of a policy lies in the fact that through it certain things are denied to some people and made accessible to others. A policy, in other words, whether for a society, for a narrow association, or for any other group, consists of a web of decisions and actions that allocates values. A decision alone is of course not a policy; to decide what to do does not mean that the thing is done. A decision is only a selection among alternatives that expresses the intention of the person or group making the choice. Arriving at a decision is the formal phase of establishing a policy; it is not the whole policy in relation to a particular problem. A legislature can decide to punish monopolists; this is the intention. But an administrator can destroy or reformulate the decision by failing either to discover offenders or to prosecute them vigorously. The failure is as much a part of the policy with regard to monopoly as the formal law. When we act to implement a decision, therefore, we enter the second or effective phase of a policy. In this phase the decision is expressed or interpreted in a series of actions and narrower decisions which may in effect establish new policy.[14]

If the law directs that all prices shall be subject to a specified form of control but black markets take root and the appropriate officials and the society as a whole accept their existence, the actual policy is not one of price control alone. It also includes the acceptance of black markets. The study of policy here includes an examination of the functioning and the determinants of both the legal and the actual policy practices. Similarly, if the formal policy of an educational system forbids discrimination against Negroes but local school boards or administrators so zone school attendance that Negroes are segregated in a few schools, both the impartial law and the discriminatory practices must be considered part of the policy.

If we are to orient ourselves properly to the subject matter of political research, therefore, it is important that we do not narrowly construe social policy by viewing it only as a formal, that is, legal, decision. It is possible, of course, to interpret policy as the "apportionment of rights and privileges"[15] by law. But this is only one of the ways in which a policy expresses itself, and from the point of view of empirical research, the legal description of policy cannot be allowed to consume the whole meaning. Therefore, in suggesting that political science is oriented to the study of policy, there is no intention to

14. H. Simon, D. Smithburg, and V. Thompson, in their *Public Administration*, elevate administrative practices to a central place in political research. See also F. M. Marx, ed., *Elements of Public Administration* (New York: Prentice-Hall, 1946), ad hoc.

15. P. H. Odegard and A. E. Helms, *American Politics* (New York: Harper, 1947), 2nd ed., p. 2.

mistake its subject matter for the kind of legal construction prominent until quite recently. I am suggesting rather that political science is concerned with every way in which values are allocated for a society, whether formally enunciated in a law or lodged in the consequences of a practice.

It would be manifestly erroneous to urge, however, that political science attempts to understand the way in which society allocates all its values. Political science is concerned only with authoritative allocations or policies. This is the reason why Lasswell's intention, as we saw in the preceding section, to describe political science as the study of the distribution and composition of value patterns in society must be considered far too broad. We set this matter aside at the time, but we are now ready to return to it. We can see now that political scientists have never been concerned with so extensive a problem, nor for that matter is Lasswell himself in most of his own practical research.

If political science sought to explore the total value pattern of society it would have to embrace all social science. The reason for this is that all social mechanisms are means for allocating values. The structure and processes of society determine the social statuses that we have and the roles that we perform; these in turn enable us to acquire certain benefits or rewards not available to others. Our economic statuses and roles, for example, help to determine the economic benefits that we get in the processes of production and exchange. Similarly our class, educational, religious, and other institutions help to distribute unequally other advantages available in a society.[16] Every other set of institutions helps in one way or another to distribute the values in a society.

But none of these modes for allocating desirable or undesirable things need be authoritative. Political science can learn much from the other social sciences because they are all interested to some degree in how institutions distribute what we consider to be advantages or disadvantages. I am suggesting, however, that political research is distinctive because it has been trying to reveal the way in which values are affected by authoritative allocation. We must inquire, therefore, into the characteristics that lend the color of authority to policies. This brings us to the second of the three concepts just mentioned.

Although the literature is replete with discussions about the nature of authority,[17] the meaning of this term can be resolved quickly for our purposes. A policy is authoritative when the people to whom it is intended to apply or who are affected by it consider that they must or ought to obey it. It is obvious that this is a psychological rather than a moral explanation of the term. We can

---

16. P. Sorokin, *Social Mobility* (New York: Harper, 1927).

17. For a discriminating bibliography see Simon, Smithburg, and Thompson, *Public Administration*, pp. 571–72.

justify its use in this way because it gives to the term a meaning that enables us to determine factually whether a group of people do in practice consider a policy to be authoritative.

I do not, of course, intend to argue that political science ought to or does ignore the moral aspect of authority; a later chapter will deal with the necessary moral foundations of all political research. However, my point here is that the grounds upon which a person accepts a policy as authoritative can be distinguished from the actual acceptance of the authority of the policy. Acceptance of a policy may flow from a number of sources: moral, traditional or customary, or purely from fear of the consequences. Thus when Congress passes a law, we may consider this formal expression of policy to be authoritative because we agree with its immediate desirability or even with the moral premises out of which it stems. Normally, of course, if we accept a law that we dislike, we do so because in our hierarchy of values the maintenance of a constitutional system may take priority over disobedience to any one policy. Conceivably, however, we could reject this moral premise as the reason for agreeing to the authority of the policy; acceptance might flow simply from a desire to conform, fear of coercion, or total indifference and apathy.

For many purposes, examination of the grounds for accepting the authority of policy might be vital. For purposes of identifying the subject matter of political research, however, whatever the motivations, a policy is clearly authoritative when the feeling prevails that it must or ought to be obeyed. In the present context, therefore, authoritative will be used to mean only that policies, whether formal or effective, are accepted as binding.[18]

It is a necessary condition for the existence of a viable society that some policies appearing in a society be considered authoritative. But a moment's reflection will reveal that political science is not initially and centrally interested in all authoritative policies found in a society. For example, the members of any association, such as a trade union or a church, obviously consider the policies adopted by their organization authoritative for themselves. The constitution and by-laws of an association constitute the broad formal policy within the context of which members of the organization will accept lesser policies as authoritative. Minorities within the group, while they remain as members, will accept the decisions and practices of the group as binding, or authoritative, for the whole membership.

---

18. In one of his penetrating asides, Max Weber has expressed this idea neatly. "When we inquire as to what corresponds to the idea of the 'state' in empirical reality," he observes, "we find an infinity of diffuse and discrete human actions, both active and passive, factually and legally regulated relationships, partly unique and partly recurrent in character, all bound together by an idea, namely, the belief in the actual or normative validity of rules and of the authority-relationships of some human beings towards others." E. A. Shils and H. A. Finch, *Max Weber on the Methodology of Social Sciences* (Glencoe, IL: Free Press, 1949), p. 99.

In organizations that are less than society-wide we have, therefore, the existence of a variety of authoritative policies. And yet, in spite of the fact that for the members of the organization these policies carry the weight of authority, it is at once apparent that political science does not undertake to study these policies for their own sake. Political science is concerned rather with the relation of the authoritative policies, made in such groups as associations, to other kinds of policies, those that are considered authoritative for the whole society. In other words, political research seeks first and foremost to understand the way in which values are authoritatively allocated, not for a group within society, but for the whole society.

The societal nature of policy is therefore the third conception helpful in isolating the subject matter of political research. We must, however, clarify the meaning of this a little further. In suggesting that policy is of central interest when it relates to a whole society, I do not intend to imply that every policy, to be societal in character, must apply in its immediate consequences to each member of a society. Clearly, policy is selective in its effects, however generally it may be stated. The point is that even though a policy, such as an income-tax law or regional legislation like the TVA Act, may take away or give to only a part of the people in a society, in fact the policy is considered to be authoritative for all. To put this in its legal form, a law as executed may affect the activity of only a few persons in a society, yet in a constitutional political system it will be considered legal and binding by all. This is simply a particular way of saying that where a society exists there will always be a kind of allocation of values that will be authoritative for all or most members of a society even though the allocation affects only a few.

My point is, in summary, that the property of a social act that informs it with a political aspect is the act's relation to the authoritative allocation of values for a society. In seeking to understand all social activities influencing this kind of allocation, political science achieves its minimal homogeneity and cohesion.

The Behavioral Approach in Political Science: Epitaph for a Monument to a Successful Protest

Robert A. Dahl

Perhaps the most striking characteristic of the "behavioral approach" in political science is the ambiguity of the term itself, and of its synonym "political behavior." The behavioral approach, in fact, is rather like the Loch Ness monster: one can say with considerable confidence what it is not, but it is difficult to say what it *is*. Judging from newspaper reports that appear from time to time, particularly just before the summer tourist season, I judge that the monster of Loch Ness is not Moby Dick, nor my daughter's goldfish that disappeared down the drain some ten years ago, nor even a misplaced American eight heading for the Henley Regatta. In the same spirit, I judge that the behavioral approach is not that of the speculative philosopher, the historian, the legalist, or the moralist. What, then, is it? Indeed, does it actually exist?

I.

Although I do not profess to know of the full history of the behavioral approach, a little investigation reveals that confusing and even contradictory interpretations have marked its appearance from the beginning. The first sightings in the roily waters of political science of the phenomenon variously called political behavioral approach, or behavioral(ist) research, evidently occurred in the 1920s. The term "political behavior," it seems, was used by American political scientists from the First World War onward.[1] The honor of first adopting the term as a book title seems to belong, however, not to a political scientist but to the American journalist Frank Kent, who published a book in 1928 entitled *Political Behavior, The Heretofore Unwritten Laws,*

Reprinted in a somewhat shortened version from *American Political Science Review* 55 (1961): 763–72.
    1. David Easton, *The Political System* (1953), p. 203.

Customs, and Principles of Politics as Practised in the United States.[2] To Kent, the study of political behavior meant the cynical "realism" of the tough-minded newspaperman who reports the way things "really" happen and not the way they're supposed to happen. This meaning, I may say, is often implied even today. However, Herbert Tingsten rescued the term for political science in 1937 by publishing his path-breaking *Political Behavior: Studies in Election Statistics.* Despite the fact that Tingsten was a Swede, and his work dealt with European elections, the term became increasingly identified with American political science.

The rapid flowering of the behavioral approach in the United States no doubt depended on the existence of some key attitudes and predispositions generated in the American culture—pragmatism, factmindedness, confidence in science, and the like.[3] But there were also at least six specific, interrelated, quite powerful stimuli.

One was Charles E. Merriam. In his presidential address to the American Political Science Association in 1925, Merriam said: "Some day we may take another angle of approach *than the formal, as other sciences do,* and begin to look at *political behavior* as one of the essential objects of inquiry."[4]

During the next decade under Merriam's leadership at the University of Chicago, the Department of Political Science was the center of what would later have been called the behavioral approach. A number of the political scientists who subsequently were widely regarded as leaders in introducing that approach into American political science were faculty members or graduate students there: for example, Harold Lasswell was a faculty member and V. O. Key, Jr., David Truman, Herbert Simon, and Gabriel Almond, all graduate students in Merriam's department before the Second World War. Chicago was not the only place where the new mood of scientific empiricism was strong. At Cornell University, for example, G. E. G. Catlin was expounding similar views.[5] But the collective impact of "the Chicago school" as it was sometimes called, was greater than that of a single scholar.

A second force was the arrival in the United States in the 1930s of a considerable number of European scholars, particularly German refugees,

---

2. Kent's earlier book, *The Great Game of Politics* (1924), made no pretence of being systematic and continued to be widely read by students of American politics, but within a few years *Political Behavior* fell into an obscurity from which it has never recovered.

3. Cf. Bernard Crick, *The American Science of Politics, Its Origins and Conditions* (London, 1959).

4. "Progress in Political Research," *American Political Science Review* 20 (February 1926): 7, quoted in David B. Truman, "The Implications of Political Behavior Research," Social Science Research Council *Items* (December 1951): 37. (Emphasis added.)

5. See Catlin's *Science and Method of Politics* (1927). Another early example of the behavioral approach was Stuart Rice, *Quantitative Methods in Politics* (1928). Rice had received his Ph.D. at Columbia University.

who brought with them a sociological approach to politics that strongly reflected the specific influence of Max Weber and the general influence of European sociology. American political science had always been strongly influenced by Europeans. Not only have Americans often interpreted their own political institutions most clearly with the aid of sympathetic foreigners like de Tocqueville, Bryce, and Brogan, but American scholars have owed specific debts to European scholarship. The first American university chair in political science (actually in history and political science), established in 1858 at Columbia, was occupied by the liberal German refugee Francis Lieber. In the second half of the nineteenth century, many of the leading academic advocates of a "science of politics" sought to profit from the methods and teachings in some of the leading European universities.[6]

In the 1930s, there was once again an abrupt revival of European influences as the life of American universities was enriched by the great influx of refugee scholars.

A number of these scholars who came to occupy leading positions in departments of sociology and political science insisted on the relevance of sociological and even psychological theories for an understanding of politics. They drew attention to the importance of Marx, Durkheim, Freud, Pareto, Mosca, Weber, Michels, and others. Although some of them might later reject the behavioral approach precisely because they felt it was too narrow, men like Franz Neumann, Sigmund Neumann, Paul Lazarsfeld, Hans Speier, Hans Gerth, Reinhard Bendix, and many others exerted, both directly and indirectly, a profound influence on political research in the United States. Political sociology began to flourish. Political scientists discovered that their sociological colleagues were moving with speed and skill into areas they had long regarded as their own.

The Second World War also stimulated the development of the behavioral approach in the United States, for a great many American political scientists temporarily vacated their ivory towers and came to grips with day-to-day political and administrative realities in Washington and elsewhere: a whole generation of American political science later drew on these experiences. The confrontation of theory and reality provoked, in most of the men who performed their stint in Washington or elsewhere, a strong sense of the inadequacies of the conventional approaches of political science for describing reality, much less for predicting in any given situation what was likely to happen.

Possibly an even bigger impetus—not unrelated to the effects of the

---

6. Cf. Crick, *The American Science of Politics,* pp. 21–31. Crick notes that "The Fifth Volume of the Johns Hopkins University *Studies in Historical and Political Science* published a long study, edited by Andrew D. White, 'European Schools of History and Politics' (December 1887). It reprinted his Johns Hopkins address on 'Education in Political Science' together with reports on 'what we can learn from' each major European country." Fn. 1, p. 27.

War—was provided by the Social Science Research Council, which has had an unostentatious but cumulatively enormous impact on American social science. A leading spirit in the council for the past two decades has been a distinguished political scientist, E. Pendleton Herring. His own work before he assumed the presidency of the council in 1948 reflected a concern for realism, for breaking the bonds of research confined entirely to the library, and for individual and group influences on politics and administration. In the mid-1940s Herring was instrumental in creating an SSRC committee on political behavior. The annual report of the SSRC for 1944–45 indicated that the council had reached a

> decision to explore the feasibility of developing a new approach to *the study of political behavior.* Focused upon *the behavior of individuals* in political situations, this approach calls for examination of the political relationships of men—as citizens, administrators, and legislators—by disciplines which can throw light on the problems involved, with the object of *formulating and testing hypotheses,* concerning *uniformities of behavior* in different institutional settings. (Emphasis added.)

In 1945 the council established a Committee on Political Behavior, with Herring as the chairman. The three other members[7] were also well known political scientists with a definite concern about the state of conventional political science. In 1949, the council, together with the University of Michigan's Department of Political Science and its Institute for Social Research, held a week's conference on research on political behavior at Ann Arbor. The topics covered help to provide an implicit definition of the term: papers were presented on regional politics, the possible contributions of related social sciences (e.g., George P. Murdoch, the anthropologist, discussed the "Possibility of a General Social Science of Government"), voting behavior, political attitudes, groups, and methodological problems.[8]

Near the end of 1949, a new SSRC Committee on Political Behavior was appointed, with V. O. Key, Jr., as the chairman. In 1950, this committee succinctly defined its task: "The committee is concerned with the *development of theory* and *improvement in methods* which are needed if *social science research* on the *political process* is to be more effective."[9] This committee has been an active stimulant in the growth of the behavioral approach down to the

---

7. Herbert Emmerich, Charles S. Hyneman, and V. O. Key, Jr.

8. Alexander Heard, "Research on Political Behavior: Report of a Conference," Social Science Research Council *Items* (December 1949): 41–44.

9. Social Science Research Council *Items* (June 1950): 20. (Emphasis added.)

present time; indeed, in recent years (under the chairmanship of David Truman) the committee has also awarded research grants.

The fifth factor was the rapid growth of the "survey" method as a tool available for the study of political choices and attitudes, and specifically of the behavior of voters. Where Tingsten had necessarily relied on aggregate voting statistics, the survey method provided direct access to the characteristics and behavior of individuals: an advantage that anyone who has ever labored with aggregate data is quick to recognize. As survey methods became more and more "scientific," particularly under the auspices of the Survey Research Center of the University of Michigan and the Bureau of Applied Social Research at Columbia, political scientists found their presumed monopoly of skills in the scholarly interpretation of voting and elections rudely destroyed by sociologists and social psychologists who in a series of path-breaking studies of presidential elections began to convert the analysis of voting from impressionistic—even when it was brilliant—history or insightful journalism to a more pedestrian but occasionally more impressive and convincing empirical science. To political scientists dissatisfied with the conventional methods and manners of the discipline, the new voting studies offered encouragement. For in spite of obvious defects, the voting studies seemed to provide ground for the hope that if political scientists could only master the tools employed in the other social sciences—survey methods and statistical analysis, for example—they might be able to go beyond plausible generalities and proceed to test hypotheses about how people in fact do behave in making political choices.

A sixth factor that needs to be mentioned is the influence of those uniquely American institutions, the great philanthropic foundations—especially Carnegie, Rockefeller, and more recently Ford—which because of their enormous financial contributions to scholarly research, and the inevitable selection among competing proposals that these entail, exert a considerable effect on the scholarly community. The relationship between foundation policy and current trends in academic research is too complex for facile generalities. Perhaps the simplest accurate statement is that the relationship is to a very high degree reciprocal: the staffs of the foundations are highly sensitive to the views of distinguished scholars, on whom they rely heavily for advice, and at the same time because even foundation resources are scarce, the policies of foundation staffs and trustees must inevitably encourage or facilitate some lines of research more than others. If the foundations had been hostile to the behavioral approach, there can be no doubt that it would have had very rough sledding indeed. For characteristically, behavioral research costs a good deal more than is needed by the single scholar in the library—and sometimes, as with the studies of voting in presidential elections, behavioral research is enormously expensive.

In the period after the Second World War, however, the foundations—reflecting important trends within the social sciences themselves, stimulated by the factors I have already mentioned—tended to view interdisciplinary and behavioral studies with sympathy. The Rockefeller Foundation, for example, had helped finance the pioneering panel study by Lazarsfeld, Berelson, and Gaudet of voting in the 1940 presidential election in Erie County, Ohio, and it has also, almost singlehandedly, financed the costly election studies of the Survey Research Center at the University of Michigan. In the newest and richest foundation, Ford, the short-lived Behavioral Sciences Program probably increased the use and acceptability of the notion of behavioral sciences as something both more behavioral and more scientific than the social sciences (I confess the distinction still remains cloudy to me despite the earnest attempts of a number of behavioral scientists to set me straight). The most durable offshoot of the Behavioral Sciences Program at Ford is the Center for Advanced Study in the Behavioral Sciences at Palo Alto. Although the center has often construed its domain in most catholic fashion—the "fellows" in any given year may include mathematicians, philosophers, historians, or even a novelist—in its early years the political scientists who were fellows there tended to be discontented with traditional approaches, inclined toward a more rigorously empirical and scientific study of politics, and deeply interested in learning wherever possible from the other social sciences.

All these factors, and doubtless others, came to fruition in the decade of the 1950s. The behavioral approach grew from the deviant and unpopular views of a minor sect into a major influence. Many of the radicals of the 1930s (professionally speaking) had, within two decades, become established leaders in American political science.

Today, many American departments of political science (including my own at Yale) offer undergraduate or graduate courses in political behavior. Indeed, in at least one institution (the University of Michigan) political behavior is not only a course but a field of graduate study parallel with such conventional fields as political theory, public administration, and the like—and recently buttressed, I note enviously, with some fat fellowships.

The presidency of the American Political Science Association furnishes a convenient symbol of the change. From 1927, when Merriam was elected president, until 1950, none of the presidents was prominently identified as an advocate of the behavioral approach. The election of Peter Odegard in 1950 might be regarded as the turning point. Since that time, the presidency has been occupied by one of Merriam's most brilliant and intellectually unconventional students, Harold Lasswell, and by three of the four members of the first SSRC Committee on Political Behavior.

Thus the revolutionary sectarians have found themselves, perhaps more rapidly than they thought possible, becoming members of the establishment.

II.

I have not, however, answered the nagging question I set out to answer, though perhaps I have furnished some materials from which an answer might be derived. What *is* the behavioral approach in political science?

Historically speaking, the behavioral approach was a protest movement within political science. Through usage by partisans, partly as an epithet, terms like political behavior and the behavioral approach came to be associated with a number of political scientists, mainly Americans, who shared a strong sense of dissatisfaction with the achievements of conventional political science, particularly through historical, philosophical, and the descriptive-institutional approaches, and a belief that additional methods and approaches either existed or could be developed that would help to provide political science with empirical propositions and theories of a systematic sort, tested by closer, more direct and more rigorously controlled observations of political events.

At a minimum, then, those who were sometimes called "behaviorists" or "behavioralists" shared a mood: a mood of skepticism about the current intellectual attainments of political science, a mood of sympathy toward "scientific" modes of investigation and analysis, a mood of optimism about the possibilities of improving the study of politics.

Was—or is—the behavioral approach ever anything more than this mood? Are there perhaps definite beliefs, assumptions, methods or topics that can be identified as constituting political behavior or the behavioral approach?

There are, so far as I can tell, three different answers to this question among those who employ the term carefully. The first answer is an unequivocal yes. Political behavior is said to refer to the study of *individuals* rather than larger political units. This emphasis is clear in the 1944–45 SSRC report (which I quoted earlier) that foreshadowed the creation of the Political Behavior Committee. This was also how David Easton defined the term in his searching analysis and criticism of American political science published in 1953.[10] In this sense, Tingsten, Lasswell, and studies of voting behavior are prime examples of the behavioral approach.

The second answer is an unequivocal no. In his recent *Political Science: A Philosophical Analysis* (1960), Vernon Van Dyke remarks: "Though stipulative definitions of *political behavior* are sometimes advanced, as when a course or a book is given this title, none of them has gained general currency."[11] Probably the most eloquent and resounding "No!" was supplied

---

10. David Easton, *The Political System* (1953), pp. 201–5.

11. As we shall see, Van Dyke distinguishes the term "behavioral approach" from "political behavior."

three years ago by an editorial in *PROD,* a journal that some American political scientists—and many of its readers—probably regarded as the authentic spokesman for the newest currents among the avant-garde of political behavior. As an alumnus of both Merriam's Chicago department and the SSRC Committee on Political Behavior, the editor of *PROD,* Alfred de Grazia, could be presumed to speak with authority. He denied that the term referred to a subject matter, an interdisciplinary focus, quantification, any specific effort at new methods, behaviorist psychology, "realism" as opposed to "idealism," empiricism in contrast with deductive systems, or voting behavior—or, in fact, to anything more than political science as something that some people might like it to be. He proposed that the term be dropped.[12]

The third view is perhaps no more than an elaboration of the mood I mentioned a moment ago. In this view the behavioral approach is an attempt to improve our understanding of politics by seeking to explain the empirical aspects of political life by means of methods, theories, and criteria of proof that are acceptable according to the canons, conventions, and assumptions of modern empirical science. In this sense, "a behavioral approach," as one writer recently observed, "is distinguished predominantly by the nature of the purpose it is designed to serve. The purpose is scientific. . . ."[13]

If we consider the behavioral approach in political science as simply an attempt to make the empirical component of the discipline more scientific, as that term is generally understood in the empirical sciences, much of the history that I have referred to falls into place. In a wise, judicious, and until very recently neglected essay entitled "The Implications of Political Behavior Research," David Truman, writing in 1951, set out the fruits of a seminar on political behavior research held at the University of Chicago in the summer of 1951. I think it is not misleading to say that the views Truman set forth in 1951 have been shared in the years since then by the members of the Committee on Political Behavior. He wrote:

> Roughly defined, the term political behavior comprehends those actions and interactions of men and groups which are involved in the process of governing. . . . At the maximum this conception brings under the rubric of political behavior any human activities which can be said to be a part of governing.
>
> Properly speaking, political behavior is not a "field" of social science; it is not even a "field" of political science.

---

12. "What is Political Behavior?," *PROD,* July 1958.
13. Ibid., p. 159.

Political behavior is not and should not be a specialty, for it represents rather an orientation or a point of view which aims at *stating all the phenomena of government in terms of the observed and observable behavior of men.* To treat it as a "field" coordinate with (and presumably isolated from) public law, state and local government, international relations, and so on, would be to defeat its major aim. That aim includes an eventual reworking and extension of most of the conventional "fields" of political science. . . .

The developments underlying the current interest in political behavior imply two basic requirements for adequate research. In the first place, research must be systematic. . . . This means that research must grow out of a precise statement of hypotheses and a rigorous ordering of evidence. . . . In the second place, research in political behavior must place primary emphasis upon empirical methods. . . . Crude empiricism, unguided by adequate theory, is almost certain to be sterile. Equally fruitless is speculation which is not or cannot be put to empirical test.

The ultimate goal of the student of political behavior is the development of a science of the political process. . . .[14]

Truman called attention to the advantages of drawing on the other social sciences and cautioned against indiscriminate borrowings. He argued that the "political behavior orientation . . . necessarily aims at being quantitative wherever possible. But . . . the student of political behavior . . . deals with the political institution and he is obliged to perform his task in *quantitative terms if he can and in qualitative terms if he must.*" (Emphasis added.) He agreed that "inquiry into how men *ought* to act is not a concern of research in political behavior" but insisted on the importance of studying values as "obviously important determinants of men's behavior."

Moreover, in political behavior research, as in the natural sciences, the values of the investigator are important in the selection of the objects and lines of inquiry. . . . A major reason for any inquiry into political behavior is to discover uniformities, and through discovering them to be better able to indicate the consequences of such patterns and of public policy, existing or proposed, for the maintenance or development of a preferred system of political values.

Truman denied that "the political behavior orientation implies a rejection of historical knowledge. . . . Historical knowledge is likely to be an essential

---

14. Social Science Research Council *Items* (December 1951): 37–39. (Emphasis added.)

supplement to contemporary observation of political behavior." Finally, while suggesting that the conventional graduate training of political scientists needed to be supplemented and modified, Truman emphatically opposed the notion that the behavioral approach required "the elimination of . . . traditional training."

> Any new departure in an established discipline must build upon the accomplishments of the past. Although much of the existing literature of politics may be impressionistic, it is extensive and rich in insights. Without a command of the significant portions of that literature, behavioral research . . . is likely to be naive and unproductive. . . . Many attempts made by persons not familiar with the unsystematized facts [have been] substantively naive even when they may have been methodologically sound.

I have cited Truman's views at length for several reasons: because I wholeheartedly agree with them; because they were expressed a decade ago when the advocates of the behavioral approach were still searching for acceptance and self-definition; because they have been neglected; and because I believe that if the partisans and critics of "political behavior" and "the behavioral approach" had read them, understood them, and accepted them as a proper statement of objectives, much of the irrelevant, fruitless, and ill-informed debate over the behavioral approach over the past decade need never have occurred—or at any rate might have been conducted on a rather higher level of intellectual sophistication.

III.

Thus the "behavioral approach" might better be called the "behavioral mood" or perhaps even the "scientific outlook."

The representatives of the "scientific outlook" are, it seems to me, right in saying that it is a little early to appraise the results. We shall need another generation of work before we can put the products of this new mood and outlook in political science in perspective. Nonetheless, I believe it may be useful to make a tentative if deliberately incomplete assessment.

The oldest and best example of the modern scientific outlook at work is to be found in studies of voting behavior using survey methods. These begin with *The People's Choice*,[15] a study of the 1940 presidential election first published in 1944, and end—for the moment at least—with the magnificent

---

15. Paul F. Lazarsfeld, Bernard Berelson, and Hazel Gaudet, *The People's Choice* (New York, 1944).

study of the 1956 election entitled *The American Voter*.[16] It is no exaggeration to say that in less than two decades this series of studies has significantly altered and greatly deepened our understanding of what in some ways is the most distinctive action for a citizen of a democracy—deciding how to vote, or indeed whether to vote at all, in a competitive national election.

Although in a field as ambiguous and rich in contradictory hypotheses as political science, it is nearly always possible to regard a finding as merely confirming the obvious, in fact a number of the findings point in rather unexpected directions: e.g., that "independent" voters tend to be less interested, involved, or informed than partisan voters;[17] that socioeconomic "class" whether objectively or subjectively defined is not a factor of constant weight in American presidential elections but a variable subject to great swings; and that only a microscopic proportion of American voters can be said to bring any ideological perspectives, even loosely defined, to bear on their decisions. Where once one might have asserted these propositions or their contraries with equal plausibility, the evidence of the voting studies tends to pile up in a single direction. Moreover—and this is perhaps the most important point of all—these studies are cumulative. The early studies were highly incomplete and in many ways unsatisfactory. They were subject to a good deal of criticism, and properly so. Even the latest ones will not escape unharmed. Yet it seems to me there has been a steady and obvious improvement in quality, range, and depth.

The voting studies may have provided an indirect stimulus to the "scientific outlook" because of a psychological effect. It seems to be beyond much doubt that some political scientists, particularly younger ones, compared the yield produced by the methods used in the studies on voting with the normal yield of conventional methods and arrived at the inference—which is probably false—that the application of comparable new methods elsewhere could produce a comparable gain in results.

A closely related topic on which the scientific outlook has, in my view, produced some useful and reliable results of great importance to an understanding of politics is in the general domain of political participation.

Since I am not responsible for a complete inventory, I shall limit myself to mentioning one more subject where the behavioral mood has clearly made itself felt. This is in understanding the psychological characteristics of *homo*

---

16. Angus Campbell, Philip Converse, Donald Stokes, and Warren Miller, *The American Voter* (New York, 1960), a study extended and refined by the same authors in "Stability and Change in 1960: A Reinstating Election," *American Political Science Review* 55 (1961): 269–80.

17. A finding, incidentally, that may have to be revised in turn. A recent re-analysis of the data of the voting studies, completed after this paper was prepared, has turned up new evidence for the active, interested independent voter. William Flanigan, *Partisanship and Campaign Participation* (Ph.D. dissertation, Yale University Library, 1961).

politicus: attitudes, beliefs, predispositions, personality factors. The range of "behavioral" scholars and research in this area is very great, though the researchers and the research may not always bear the professional label "political science." A few scattered names, titles, and topics will indicate what I have in mind: Lasswell, the great American pioneer in this area; Cantril; Lane; McClosky; Adorno et al., *The Authoritarian Personality;* Almond, *The Appeals of Communism;* Stouffer, *Communism, Conformity and Civil Liberties;* and Lipset, "Working Class Authoritarianism" in *Political Man.* The fact that these scholars bear various professional labels—sociologist, psychologist, political scientist—and that it is not easy to read from the professional or departmental label of the author to the character of the work itself may be regarded by some political scientists as an appalling sign of disintegration in the distinctive properties of political science, but it is also a sign of the extent to which a concern by "behavioral scientists" with similar problems now tends to transcend (though not to eliminate entirely) differences in professional origins.

IV.

What of the yield in other matters that have always been of concern to students of political life? There are a number of important aspects of political studies where the behavioral mood has had, is having, or probably soon will have an impact, but where we must reserve judgment for the time being simply because the results are too scanty.

A good example is the analysis of political *systems.* The most distinctive products of the behavioral mood so far have dealt with *individuals*—individuals who vote, participate in politics in other ways, or express certain attitudes or beliefs. But an individual is not a political system, and analysis of individual preferences cannot fully explain collective decisions, for in addition we need to understand the mechanisms by which individual decisions are aggregated and combined into collective decisions. We cannot move from a study of the attitudes of a random sample of American citizens to a reasonably full explanation of, say, presidential nominations or the persistent problems of policy coordination in the United States.

Yet one classic concern of students of politics has been the analysis of *systems* of individuals and groups. Although the impact of the scientific outlook on the study of political systems is still unclear, there are some interesting straws in the wind. Recently a number of political scientists have followed sociologists into the study of local communities as systems of influence or decision-making.[18] Deutsch reflects the behavioral mood in his study

18. Cf. Janowitz, ed., *Community Political Systems* (1961); Edward Banfield, *Political Influence* (1961); and the English study by Birch and his colleagues at the University of Manchester, *Small Town Politics* (1959).

of international political systems.[19] A number of other studies are in process that may help us formulate some new, or if not new then more persuasive, answers to some ancient questions.[20] But until more evidence is in, anyone who does not believe he knows a priori the outcome of this present expression of the scholar's age-old quest for knowledge will perhaps be pardoned if he reserves judgment and awaits the future with skepticism—mixed, depending on his prejudices, with hope or dread.

V.

Where will the behavioral mood, considered as a movement of protest, go from here? I think it will gradually disappear. By this I mean only that it will slowly decay as a distinctive mood and outlook. For it will become, and in fact already is becoming, incorporated into the main body of the discipline. The behavioral mood will not disappear, then, because it has failed. It will disappear rather because it has succeeded. As a separate, somewhat sectarian, slightly factional outlook it will be the first victim of its own triumph.

Lest I be misunderstood in what I am about to say, let me make clear that the present and probable future benefits of the behavioral revolt to political studies seem to me to outweigh by far any disadvantages. In retrospect, the "behavioral" revolt in political science was, if anything, excessively delayed. Moreover, had that revolt not taken place, political science would have become increasingly alienated, I believe, from the other social sciences. One consequence of the behavioral protest has been to restore some unity within the social sciences by bringing political studies into closer affiliation with theories, methods, findings, and outlooks in modern psychology, sociology, anthropology, and economics.

But if the behavioral revolt in political science has helped to restore some unities, it has shattered others; and the fragments probably cannot ever again be united exactly along the old lines. There are, so to speak, five fragments in search of a unity. These are: empirical political science, standards of evaluation, history, general theory, and speculation.

The empirical political scientist is concerned with what *is*, as he says, not with what *ought* to be. Hence he finds it difficult and uncongenial to assume the historic burden of the political philosopher who attempted to determine, prescribe, elaborate, and employ ethical standards—values, to use the fashionable term—in appraising political acts and political systems. The behaviorally minded student of politics is prepared to *describe* values as empirical data; but, qua "scientist," he seeks to avoid prescription or inquiry into the

19. E.g., in his *Nationalism and Social Communication* (1953).

20. For an interesting example of an application of the behavioral mood to comparative politics, see Stein Rokkan and Henry Valen, "Parties, Elections and Political Behavior in the Northern Countries: A Review of Recent Research," *Politische Forschung* (1960).

grounds on which judgments of value can properly be made. To whom, then, are we to turn for guidance on intricate questions of political appraisal and evaluation? Today, probably no single professional group is qualified to speak with wisdom on all important political alternatives.

It may be said that this is the task of the political philosopher. But the problem of the political philosopher who wishes to engage in political evaluation in a sophisticated way is rendered ever more formidable by the products of the behavioral mood. An act of political evaluation cannot be performed in a sterile medium free from contamination by brute facts. Surely no one today, for example, can intelligently consider the relative merits of different political systems, or different arrangements within a particular political system, unless he knows what there is to be known about how these systems or arrangements work, what is required to make them work, and what effects they have on participants. No doubt the specialist who "knows the facts"—whether as physicist, physician, or political scientist—sometimes displays great naïveté on matters of policy. Still, the impatience of the empirical political scientist with the political philosopher who insists upon the importance of "values" arises in part from a feeling that the political philosopher who engages in political evaluation rarely completes all his homework. The topic of "consensus" as a condition for democracy is a case in point; when the political philosopher deals with this question, it seems to me that he typically makes a number of assumptions and assertions of an empirical sort without systematic attention to existing empirical data, or the possibility of gaining better empirical data.[21] Obviously some division of labor will always be necessary in a field as broad as the study of politics, but clearly the field needs more people who do not regard rapid shifts of mood—I mean from the behavioral to the philosophical—as a symptom of severe schizophrenia.

Second, in his concern for analyzing what *is,* the behavioral political scientist has found it difficult to make systematic use of what *has been:* i.e., with history. In a trivial sense, of course, all knowledge of fact is historical; but I am speaking here of the history of the historian. Despite disclaimers and intentions to the contrary, there seems to me little room for doubt that the actual content of almost all the studies that reflect the behavioral mood is ahistorical in character. Yet the scientific shortcomings of an ahistorical theory in political science are manifest, and political scientists with "behavioral" predispositions are among the first to admit them. As the authors of *The American Voter* remark:

---

21. In 1942, in *The New Belief in the Common Man,* C. J. Friedrich challenged the prevailing generalizations about the need for consensus (ch. 5). However, his challenge seems to have met with little response until 1960, when Prothro and Grigg reported the results of an empirical study of consensus on "democratic" propositions in Ann Arbor, Michigan, and Tallahassee, Florida. See their "Fundamental Principles of Democracy," *Journal of Politics* (May 1960): 276–94.

In somewhat severe language, theory may be characterized as a generalized statement of the inter-relationships of a set of variables. In these terms, historical description may be said to be a statement of the values assumed by these variables through time. . . .

If theory can guide historical descriptions, the historical context of most research on human behavior places clear limitations on the development of theory. In evolving and testing his theoretical hypotheses the social scientist usually must depend on what he is permitted to observe by the progress of history. . . . It is evident that *variables of great importance in human affairs may exhibit little or no change in a given historical period.* As a result, the investigator whose work falls in this period *may not see the significance of these variables* and may fail to incorporate them in his theoretical statements. And even if he does perceive their importance, the *absence of variation will prevent a proper test of hypotheses* that state the relation of these factors to other variables of his theory. (pp. 8–10, emphasis added)

There are, I think, a number of nodes around which a unity between behavioral political studies and history may be expected to grow. Because it is unreasonable to suppose that anything like the whole field of history will lend itself successfully to the behavioral approach, both historians and political scientists might profitably look for targets of opportunity on which the weapons forged by modern social science can be brought to bear. In this respect the work of the American historian, Lee Benson, seems to me particularly promising. By the application of rather elementary methods, which the historian has not been prone to employ, including very simple statistical analysis, Benson has shown how the explanations of five eminent American historians of four different presidential elections are dubious, if not, in fact, downright absurd.[22] The sociologist, S. M. Lipset, has also contributed a new interpretation of the 1860 election, based upon his analysis of Southern voting patterns in the presidential election of that year and in referenda on secession a few months later.[23] Benson has also turned his attention both to Charles A. Beard's famous interpretation—which Beard called an economic interpretation—of the creation and adoption of the American Constitution, and to the latter-day critics of Beard's somewhat loosely stated theory; he demonstrates convincingly, at least to me, some of the gains that can arise from a greater methodological sophistication on matters of causation, correla-

---

22. See his "Research Problems in American Political Historiography," in Komarovsky, ed., *Common Frontiers of the Social Sciences* (1957).

23. "The Emergence of the One-Party South—the Election of 1860," in *Political Man* (1960).

tion, and use of quantitative data than is customary among professional historians.[24]

In addition to these targets of opportunity that occur here and there in historical studies, a problem that obviously needs the joint attention of historian and "behavioral" political scientist is the matter of political change. To the extent that the political scientist is interested in gaining a better understanding of political change—as, say, in the developing countries, to cite an example of pressing importance—he will have to work with theories that can only be fully tested against historical data. Unfortunately, the atheoretical or even antitheoretical biases of many historians often make their works a storehouse of data so vast as to be almost unmanageable for the theorist. Rather than demand that every theorist should have to become his own historian, it may be more feasible to demand that more historians should become theorists, or at any rate familiar with the most relevant issues, problems, and methods of the modern social sciences.

I have already implied the third unity that needs to be established, namely a unity between empirical political studies and a concern for general theory. The scientific outlook in political science can easily produce a dangerous and dysfunctional humility: the humility of the social scientist who may be quite confident of his findings on small matters and dubious that he can have anything at all to say on larger questions. The danger, of course, is that the quest for empirical data can turn into an absorbing search for mere trivialities unless it is guided by some sense of the difference between an explanation that would not matter much even if it could be shown to be valid by the most advanced methods now available, and one that would matter a great deal if it should turn out to be a little more or a little less plausible than before, even if it still remained in some considerable doubt. So far, I think, the impact of the scientific outlook has been to stimulate caution rather than boldness in searching for broad explanatory theories. The political scientist who mixes skepticism with methodological rigor is all too painfully aware of the inadequacies of any theory that goes much beyond the immediate data at hand. Yet it seems clear that unless the study of politics generates and is guided by broad, bold, even if highly vulnerable general theories, it is headed for the ultimate disaster of triviality.

Finally, I should like to suggest that empirical political science had better find a place for speculation. It is a grave though easy error for students of politics impressed by the achievements of the natural sciences to imitate all their methods save the most critical one: the use of the imagination. Problems of method and a proper concern for what would be regarded as an acceptable test of an empirical hypothesis have quite properly moved out of the wings to

_____

24. Lee Benson, *Turner and Beard, American Historical Writing Re-Considered* (1960).

a more central position on the great stage of political science. Yet surely it is imagination that has generally marked the intelligence of the great scientist, and speculation—oftentimes foolish speculation, it turned out later—has generally preceded great advances in scientific theory. It is only fair to add, however, that the speculation of a Galileo, a Kepler, a Newton, or an Einstein, was informed and controlled by a deep understanding of the hard empirical facts as they were known at the time: Kepler's speculations always had to confront the tables of Tycho Brahe.

There is every reason to think that unities can be forged anew. After all, as the names of Socrates, Aristotle, Machiavelli, Hobbes, and Tocqueville remind us, from time to time in the past the study of politics has been altered, permanently, by a fresh infusion of the spirit of empirical inquiry—by, that is to say, the scientific outlook.

Political Science and Political Education

Norman Jacobson

Much of this essay falls within the realm of speculative thought. Since it is in the nature of speculation that one's words may appear immodest and his conclusions often eccentric, I shall state my arguments at the outset without pausing to elaborate them. The arguments themselves are quite simple. Each of them will reappear later on clothed, I hope, in more attractive dress.

Two varieties of political thought contended for the allegiance of the American people at the founding of the new nation. The two seem irreconcilable in certain crucial respects.

One was notable for its expression of friendship and brotherhood, for its insistence upon individual spontaneity and uniqueness, and for its disdain for material concerns; it was intuitive and unsystematic in temper. The other displayed a preoccupation with social order, procedural rationality, and the material bases of political association and division; it was abstract and systematic in temper.

The exponents of the latter point of view, having put their opponents to rout, assumed the responsibility for organizing the government and politics of the country. They enacted their psychological, social, economic, and political theories into fundamental law, then erected institutions designed to train generations of citizens to prefer certain goods and conduct over all others.

The basis for contemporary political analysis in America is to be found in the conjunction of prescriptive theories (the Constitution) and behavioral categories (science). The link between them is forged in the political thought of the founders.

Because this is not easily perceived, while the success of political analysis in the United States is unquestioned, many of us are tempted to believe that our scientific categories possess universal applicability, or are well on the way to achieving this status. What is often missed is the symbiosis of prescription and analysis, a cooperative venture for the production of individuals who are at once citizens and specimens. In this sense, our politics make an indispens-

Reprinted from *American Political Science Review* 57 (1963): 561–69.

able contribution to our science, while as political scientists, we ourselves are schoolmasters to a nation.

But that symbiotic system is scarcely perfect, nor will it ever become so. Political behavior is no synonym for human nature. Any theory which denies a place to uncongenial modes of thinking and feeling, despite the fact that such modes have always existed and are even now threatening to reach epidemic proportions, ignores them at its peril. To label them deviant or anomalous does not help matters. A theory can stand just so much strain, and a balanced theory demands openness to the possibility at least of complementary characteristics. The wave theory of Huygens was safely dead and buried for over a century, until resurrected as a challenge to the scientific hegemony of Newton.

Lest all of this sound far-fetched, speculation on what political analysis would look like today had the vanquished been the victors, might allay some of the skepticism. Were that the case, our present apparatus might prove adequate solely to the description of deviant behavior, what at present appears perfectly sound and functional; and I might now be advocating the relevance of the ideas of Madison and Hamilton for a balanced political theory.

One might conceivably reject all my arguments by merely asserting that the reason the victors won at all, was that their ideas were the only ones in accord with an objective political reality. But to assert that is to deny the very possibility of political change, to say nothing of education, and to withhold from the founders the credit for having brought into existence a novel system of government.

In sum, our political science has succeeded to the extent that the Constitution has performed its supreme function, the political education of the citizens. Any combination of descriptive and prescriptive theories, backed by the irresistible authority of a monolith, must appear unbeatable. More than that, the behavior it encourages must appear natural, an expression of tendencies latent in all human associations regardless of culture, institutions, or ideology. These tendencies, long since realized at home, burst for expression in other lands, particularly in the emergent nations, and theories made in America are today presented as a gift to all mankind. I predict without fear of contradiction that such theories will prove relatively successful wherever their underlying assumptions themselves become entrenched in the thoughts and ways of a people.

What I am trying to say is that the naturalness of patterns of behavior, and the apparent universality of analytic categories designed to comprehend them, stem from a gigantic self-fulfilling prophecy at work in the American polity; or, if you prefer the words of Machiavelli to those of Merton, what we have witnessed thus far is a demonstration of the dictum that only armed prophets succeed.

I.

To the Revolutionary generation in America it was axiomatic that in all times and circumstances government is a necessary evil. Society, produced by the wants of mankind, encourages felicity through uniting our affections. Government, stemming from the vices of men, is a negative force designed to restrain our excesses. Society is a blessing in every state, a loving and indulgent patron, tolerant, as nature herself, of the variety of being and experience. Government, even in its best state, is a punisher. The conclusion drawn from this by Thomas Paine and his comrades in arms was inescapable: that government is best which governs least.

But the men who drafted the Constitution proceeded on a different theory. While they agreed that government is a punisher, they were fearful that this unpleasant duty might be shirked, and they knew that in the absence of coercion the passions in men would neither relent nor be contained. This conviction dictated the outcome of their work. For sustained somberness of mood, the Constitution of the United States is extraordinary. Its authors anticipated little good, but mainly evil: war, universal corruption, public insolence and insubordination. Nor did they expect much else of themselves. In addition to formal checks upon the power of those in positions of responsibility and trust, provision is explicitly made against incursions into the public treasury and into the purses of kings and satraps. No sooner is the plan announced for the selection of representatives of the people and their organization into two Houses, than procedures are established for the punishment of members guilty of disorderly conduct and the expulsion of troublemakers. And why not? Venality and recalcitrance are as natural to men as the air they breathe.

A crescendo is reached in Article I, Section 8, the crucial enabling section of the Constitution, where the specific powers granted Congress are enumerated. As an expression of political prescience, of the sort of conduct to be expected from strangers and countrymen alike, the words of the authors leave little to the imagination. Pirates and felons are seized, counterfeiters are apprehended, bankrupts are dealt with, militiamen disciplined, captures effected on land and sea, insurrections suppressed, wars fought, invasions repelled. Threats to order were everywhere, and Section 8 takes on the aspect of a demonology of politics, foreign and domestic. Of the functions and powers set down, around two-thirds are devoted to crime and punishment, war, invasion and rebellion. The rest, save a very few, concern taxation and commerce. Beset by dangers, real and fancied, the authors of the Constitution meant their government to be frankly disciplinary and punitive. Today we call such men realists.

The special tone of the Constitution emerges even more clearly when it is compared with the mood set in the Articles of Confederation. That document attempts to come to grips with many of the same problems, yet the contrast is striking. The Articles open with warm sentiments of esteem and respect, of mutual friendship, fraternity, and independence, and close on a stirring note of dedication: each delegate agreed to "solemnly plight and engage the faith" of his constituents in the noble work ahead, a phrase reminiscent of the closing sentiments in the Declaration of Independence. One is tempted to wonder whether a Madison, a Hamilton, or a Jay could even then have listened to such lofty hopes without a smile of contempt.

The Articles had as their avowed purpose to establish conditions for mutual friendship not only among the governments, but "among the people of the different States in this Union." The Constitution set as its purposes to perfect the Union, establish Justice, insure domestic Tranquility, provide for the common Defence, promote the general Welfare, and secure unto posterity the Blessings of Liberty, in that order. The significance of the shift such as that from friendship to justice is of the greatest importance. In it may be found clues to contrasting theories of politics and of the conduct to be expected of civilized men. Sentiments of friendship are always directed toward the particular person, association, or neighborhood; sentiments of justice thrive upon the impersonal. The first class of sentiments is palpable and calls forth a response; the second is abstract and depends upon laws and procedures. The one arises from particularity or prejudice, from affection for the unique individual, the unique fraternity, the unique countryside; the other demands objectivity and is universal. It is precisely here that we can appreciate the incompatibility of the theories informing the two documents, with the resulting contrast in expression. The Articles of Confederation read like the work of a band of hopeful amateurs. But the Constitution is the product of a group of sophisticated professionals, men well versed in the day-by-day practice of a craft.

Words such as objectivity, universality, system, realism, possess a certain resonance. Do we actually mean to describe men of action rather than scholars, architects of government rather than professional political scientists? And the other set of words—subjectivity, uniqueness, inspiration, sentiment—what sense do they convey in political studies? We seem to have stumbled upon early counterparts of our present-day humanists who persist in the ways of at least one honored tradition in political theory: intuitive, idealistic, lacking the professional touch.

Choose at random any of a number of imprecise, tentative, sprawling provisions of the Articles and match them with similar provisions in the Constitution. The effect produced by this is striking, as striking perhaps as comparing a rambling passage in a contemporary writer on political morality with one in the crisp, authoritative style of an analyst of data. Where the

Constitution, with professional clarity and dispatch, prohibits any state "to engage in war, unless actually invaded, or in such imminent danger as will not admit of delay," the language of the Articles betrays a charming, though inconvenient, naïveté: "No State shall engage in any war without the consent of the United States in Congress assembled, unless such State be actually invaded by enemies, or shall have received certain advice of a resolution formed by some nation of Indians to invade such State, and the danger is so imminent as not to admit of a delay until the United States in Congress assembled can be consulted."

Where the Constitution simply provides for the Supreme Court to hear "controversies between two or more States," the Articles establish a procedure for settling such disputes that is so unwieldy as to be well nigh unworkable. There are petitions, hearings, commissioners chosen by lot, solemn oaths, judgments lodged among the acts of Congress, and so forth. It is an unbelievably complicated system, and in the description requires almost twice the number of words it took the authors of the Constitution to enumerate all the powers of Congress.

In crossing the rustic terrain of the Articles of Confederation, we are likely to trip over tents, "field-pieces," and other items of "camp-equippage," or be ordered to stand aside as militiamen, "clothed, armed, and equipped" in a "soldier-like manner," are marched to places appointed by Congress. By the time of the Constitution the litter has been swept away, and a citizen army disciplined to the standards expected of a proud nation takes the field. A few scant years had elapsed, yet we witness the passing of a world. Gone is the minuteman of government; the professional soldier builds his fortress upon the ground where once the scattered tents were pitched. Whether the obliteration of a style signifies the death of the urge it was meant to express, however, is another matter.

It is not my intent to account for this interesting change historically, but to describe the differences in analytic terms, the better to point up a contrast between revolutionary ideals and constitutional practice, and to suggest similarities to styles in scholarship. If American political science has been successful, it is to a certain extent owing to the success of the system devised by the founders to produce citizens more concerned with formal justice than with friendship, with interest than with brotherhood, and with SES than with honor. Justice, interest, and socioeconomic status are obviously amenable to quantitative treatment. Friendship, brotherhood, and honor—suffice it to say, less so. Fortunate indeed is the student of interest group politics, of cross-pressures and social stratification. What if, instead of the prudence of James Madison, the pieties of Thomas Paine had become the chief text for political education in America?

II.

It was Paine's lot in life to be the carrier of a disease which has never failed to alarm those who seek salvation in prudence, and duty in conserving the present: rulers, scribes, churchmen, property-holders, in short the managers and teachers of mankind. This disease induces in its victims a collective hallucination, the recurrent fantasy of smashing the here and now—castle, temple, academy, and countinghouse—on the path back to paradise, back to the sweet innocence of the Garden of Eden. The same madness which tempted men to strive for the impossible in all things, which set modern science on its prodigious course and freed literature and the arts, had assumed a recognizable shape in politics long before the advent of science, literature, and art as we know them, long before the Renaissance or the Enlightenment. From the old to the new Atlantis, from the playground of the gods and the Golden Age to More's Utopia, from Winthrop's city on the hill to Rousseau's rustic democracy, the political madness was the dream of America. Yet for some reason, the dream had never materialized. Now, for the first time, the prize actually lay within the grasp of men.

Thomas Paine knew why the dream had failed. It was because men had failed themselves. By a shameful want of moral courage, mankind had surrendered up its birthright: "the palaces of kings are built upon the ruins of the bowers of paradise."

In the beginning, as he pictured it, there were a handful of persons settled in some sequestered corner of the earth, separate from the rest. Dwelling in a blessed state of natural liberty, their first thought was society. The human being is unfitted for perpetual solitude and turns to his fellows for assistance and relief of his loneliness, lest in the absence of society a man perish before he dies. Society then, with its reciprocal blessings and delights, is as natural to men as personal liberty and, in its pristine state, requires neither government nor laws. But since nothing under heaven is impregnable to vice, human society suffers a fall from grace. As men begin to pursue their own advantage and grow lax in their duty and attachment to one another, the social bond is threatened with dissolution. It is selfishness which in the end makes government a necessity.

The first form of government was a free assembly of all persons held in the open air, under the leafy bower of that ubiquitous tree in the garden. Political history as we know it has actually begun, and will run its course to the despotism of the one or the tyranny of the few. For on that day, men yielded up the most precious quality of primordial society—simplicity. Governments will move from complication to complexity, then will have the audacity to claim that only government itself, and more government, is capable of delivering order out of confusion. Kingship is introduced, nobles appear on the scene, persons of wealth enter into league with them, and ordinary men awaken to find that they have been torn from nature and cut off from societal affections, that they are pawns in the games of the powerful. There is no doubt that Paine intended this as a thumbnail sketch of the rise of European civilization.

The emigrants to America from all lands fled not the embrace of a loving parent, but the cruel grip of the monster government, which had slain society, the natural guardian of men. They were bent on recreating a free society, restoring to themselves the blessings of friendship and brotherhood. "O! ye that love mankind!," Paine cried, "Ye that dare oppose not only the tyranny but the tyrant, stand forth! Every spot of the old world is overrun with oppression. Freedom hath been hunted round the globe. Asia and Africa have long expelled her. Europe regards her like a stranger, and England hath given her warning to depart. O! receive the fugitive, and prepare in time an asylum for mankind."

The hour was late, but an opportunity was present to men which had not been theirs since the days of Noah, before greed had once again polluted the earth. "We have it in our power," Paine exhorted his brothers, "to begin the world over again." With the birthday of a new world at hand, how paltry was action based on prudence or personal advantage. How vain was suspicion or distrust, when all a man had to do to grasp paradise was "to hold out to his neighbor the hearty hand of friendship, and unite in drawing a line, which, like an act of oblivion shall bury in forgetfulness every former dissension." The way to purification, the way back to the familial affections of natural society, was through collective expiation of the original sin, which was not a sin against God at all, but of brother against brother, as a punishment for which governments were imposed upon men. You may say that this is magic, pure and simple, and you would be right. But strange to tell, the magic worked, at least for the time it took to win a war against odds and to confirm the faith of mankind in the possibility of goodness. Then, like the magician himself, Paine's magic was tossed on the scrapheap of history.

It is obvious that passions such as those expressed by Paine have little to do with self-interest, property divisions, factions, and the like. He quite plainly lacked patience with such considerations, "when weighed against the business of a world." Here, we are tempted to say, he comes very close to reminding us that only the moral plight of the world was his Father's business. Paine was bitterly opposed to the contention, popular among lawyers, politicians, and merchants of his day, that a war of independence may justly be fought on grounds of commercial principle. To fight "merely to enforce the repeal of a pecuniary law, seems as unwarrantable by the divine law, and as repugnant to human feelings, as the taking up arms to enforce obedience thereto. The object, on either side, doth not justify the means; for the lives of men are too valuable to be cast away on such trifles." Besides, pecuniary concerns are a curse to freedom and an enemy to national loyalties. The man who is more troubled about his purse than about his countrymen is a slave to fear, and submits to power "with the trembling duplicity of a spaniel." Those who prepare diligently and marry well, who build their careers, settle for less than the truth in human affairs, prefer security to greatness, and counsel prudence over love, are the false prophets and betrayers of a nation.

In a brief fancy entitled "Cupid and Hymen," Paine explores the conflicting demands placed upon individuals and nations by sentiments of love on the one hand, and considerations of utility on the other. It seems that Hymen, god of marriage, had eluded his master and arranged a match on earth without prior knowledge of the god of love. The victims were to be a beautiful young maiden and a stodgy old property owner; the considerations, material comfort and security. When he learns of this, Cupid is furious with his clerk and heaps abuse upon him:

> 'Tis my province to form the union, and yours to witness it. But of late you have treacherously assumed to set up for yourself. 'Tis true you may chain couples together like criminals, but you cannot yoke them like lovers; besides, you are such a dull fellow when I am not with you, that you poison the felicities of life. . . . At best you are but a temporal and temporary god, whom Jove has appointed not to bestow, but to secure happiness, and restrain the infidelity of mankind.

To refrain from endowing the actors and their words with political meanings would be most difficult, especially since the story first appeared in the year 1775. The maiden is America, the wealthy landlord, Europe; the voice of Hymen is the voice of interest, and Cupid represents the noble ideals of love, friendship, freedom, and respect. The term "union" is too prominent to be missed. Where Hymen would contaminate the spring of nationhood at its source, Cupid means to release a powerful erotic flow in the service of community. Hymen offers a truce among thieves. Cupid holds out the promise of unity through love. Hymen is the punisher, Cupid the patron. (Lest I be accused of playing fast and loose with writings not explicitly on politics but on love and marriage, let me note that any man who insists upon interpreting even dreams *politically,* which Paine does in his poetic fantasy, "The Dream Interpreted," is probably so constituted as to have everything remind him of politics.)

In the course of this dramatic confrontation, Hymen utters an ominous threat. "You are not of such importance in the world as your vanity thinks," he says, and then announces a bold plan to join Plutus, god of riches, in an alliance against Love. The fear which haunted Paine was that love might conceivably fail in a contest against the combined strengths of wealth and governmental power. Ease, not privation, constitutes the gravest danger to collective happiness. If a combination of politicians and property owners were to convince the American people to accept ease, rather than dare happiness through love and friendship, all might be lost. The country would settle down to a long "sluggish calm" and the ideals which America had come into the world to realize, be put to rest forever.

Paine was a believer in the ancient adage that youth is the seedtime of good habits, applied equally to nations as to individuals. He was determined to instruct his young charge well, before seductive promises of private advantage, class interest, and public order could turn her head. Paine's message was at the same time savage and devout: true, it breathed intimacy, friendship, affection, and concord; but never far from the surface was a terrible anger and a wounded dignity. Paine called for revenge against the surrogates of those responsible for having seduced mankind into giving up its birthright of freedom and brotherhood in the first place. But there were other voices in the land, and they drowned out his own, in the solemn hope that none quite like it would ever be heard again.

If Paine is guilty of allowing all to Cupid and nothing to any other god, his opponents do not make this mistake. At the very outset of *The Federalist,* in the second, third, and fourth paragraphs of Number 1, we are skillfully prepared for the counsels of Hymen. The author obligingly acknowledges the moral superiority of Cupid, but is impressed with the practical difficulties in the way of his demands. Political reality will not stand for it. A polity constructed on such noble feelings as "philanthropy," "patriotism," or other sentiments "unperplexed and unbiased by considerations not connected with the public good," is "more ardently to be wished than seriously to be expected." Political truth is everywhere confronted by established institutions, "particular interests," "passions," "prejudices," "avarice, personal animosity, party opposition, and many other motives not more laudable." There are always those jealous of personal power, others of emolument. Some men, seized with "perverted ambitions," deliberately subordinate the public good to their own advantage. Yet perhaps the greatest obstacle to decency in public affairs is not the conscious evildoer, but the man of good will who, "led astray by preconceived jealousies and fears," commits "honest errors" of judgment. So long as these are the facts of political life, exhortations to friendship and brotherhood will not suffice. The only feasible response is of the sort to be found in Article I, Section 8 of the Constitution.

At the risk of boring you with still one more discussion of *Federalist* Number 10, let me look briefly at that essay, for it is there that the assumptions laid bare in the first paper are transmuted into political theory, thus establishing the affinity between political education and political science ex-

isting in America today. The mortal enemies of popular governments in all
times and in all places have been "instability, injustice, and confusion." It is
the intent of the author of Number 10 to discover whence these evils arise, and
to prescribe workable remedies against them. The causes are ultimately found
in the psychology of the individual, and the cure in a complex system of
government designed to control the results of human destructiveness.

The chief threat is the uncontrolled effects of faction, and "the latent
causes of faction are . . . sown in the nature of man." Because reason is
fallible, men will hold differing opinions. And because reason is so often
linked to self-love, men's opinions are propelled by their passions, provoking
mutual animosities, jealousies, and fears. Nor is that all. There is an innate
diversity in the faculties of men leading them to choose diverse means to
gratify diverse ends. Since the first object of government is to protect these
faculties, it follows that diversity in individual purposes, tastes, habits, and
behavior is a perennial condition of civilized existence. Furthermore, unequal
faculties give rise to external inequalities, which lead in turn to clusters of
interests, eventuating in a division into groups and parties.

Add to this division religious differences, differences of political belief,
personal attachment to leaders "ambitiously contending for preeminence and
power," and men are inflamed with a spirit of partisanship that renders them
"much more disposed to vex and oppress each other than to cooperate for their
common good. So strong is this propensity of mankind to fall into mutual
animosities, that, where no substantial occasion presents itself, the most
frivolous and fanciful distinctions have been sufficient to kindle their un-
friendly passions and excite their most violent conflicts." Paine would concur
that men tend to mistake the trivial for the profound, and to contend over it,
but he built no theories upon this observation. Instead, he dismissed the
matter with the characteristic comment that "suspicion is the companion of
mean souls, and the bane of all good society." In this sense, both Madison and
Paine could agree that interest politics is scarcely an ideal politics, based as it
is upon division and mutual hostility. Where they depart, obviously, is on the
question of whether to institutionalize it, and to instruct the citizens in its
precepts. The decision to offer this kind of instruction is as responsible for the
analytic categories of students of contemporary politics as it is for the activities of those who engage in it.

The term "interest" is used advisedly, for Madison argued that of all
possible sources of factious behavior the various and unequal division of
property is the most enduring. At the same time, the impulse to acquire
property appears wholly admirable. It is neither trivial nor unworthy of respect, as Paine had contended. Now, Madison knew as well as we do that men
have very many impulses, some just as "natural" as acquisitiveness. Either he
was unimpressed with the empirical significance of these for politics, or he

disputed the justice of their claim to public recognition—in short their desirability. While both Madison and Paine appealed to history, and although history showed the same face to both of them, a face marred by interest, avarice, and a lust for power, the values which they discovered in it are radically different. For Madison, what has been must be; for Paine what has been must be changed. In this, Madison and the political scientist are alike: fact is lawful sovereign. In this, Paine and the humanist are alike: fact is often the tyrant to be overthrown.

In Madison's final scheme, property is tied to the individual, factions to property, freedom to factions, and republican institutions to freedom. The central problem is how to permit the passionate pursuit of interest, while assuring social peace and stability. The solution is an ingenious system designed to control the deleterious effects of faction, while at the same time encouraging individual assertiveness. The public good is a resultant of material appetites, molded into rational form in the group, and propelled onto the political stage in conflict with all other group interests. This activity has since come to be known as the political process.

The Federalist, like the Constitution it advocated, is the product of professionals, and the language of Number 10 is suggestive not only of professional politics, but of professional political science. It will come as no shock that its authors should frequently sound like contemporary group theorists, for they also believed that any sensible discussion of politics must start from interest, ambition, and power, and eventuate in a search for the means of control. The dominant note is struck in the opening passage of Number 10, where an appeal is made to "the evidence of known facts," not idle conjecture, and before the essay is done we are treated to the familiar attack upon idealists, philosophers and dreamers, referred to in the text as "Theoretic politicians." The following sentence might well serve as a model for recent political science writing, and could as easily have been composed by Bentley as by Madison: "The inference to which we are brought is, that the *causes* of faction cannot be removed, and the relief is only to be sought in the means of controlling its *effects.*" Politics deals with manifest behavior, and governance has as its chief function the discovery and implementation of rational means of control. In scientific terms, all of this sounds perfectly acceptable. The study of politics is the study of assigned effects, not a metaphysical questing after causes. The authors of *The Federalist* created the apparatus for controlling these effects; professional social scientists have developed the techniques for analyzing them.

"We must," Bentley said, "deal with felt facts and with thought facts, but not with feeling as reality or thought as truth. We must find the only reality and the only truth in the proper functioning of the felt facts and the thought facts in the system to which they belong." The *only* reality and the *only* truth are to be discovered in the political *effects* of individual thoughts and feelings, as they manifest themselves functionally within a given system. Bentley, no less than Madison, finds it necessary to repudiate faculties, ideas, and ideals as *causes*, before his program for political science can be launched. Even if such "causes" do exist, as latent forces within men, until they are expressed politically they must be ignored. Following the characteristic procedure of the political realist, Bentley rescues the corpus of politics from the morass of rhetoric into which it had plunged, then moves to a description of political behavior exclusively in terms of observed effects. Society is an idea ghost, the individual an unwieldy abstraction, sentiments—where not factitious—are too slippery to serve as a hook into political reality. The hope rests with process analysis, and to demonstrate its possibilities Bentley focused his attention upon the activities of political interest groups. What he had to say is acknowledged as a major contribution to American political science.

I do not intend to suggest an actual identification of contemporary political science with the ground-breaking work of Bentley. The stress is laid exclusively upon the *intermediary* function of Bentley and some of his fellows in influencing the course of contemporary analysis. For, intentionally or not, Bentley provided the firmest link between the authors of *The Federalist* and modern students of politics. The parties meet upon the familiar ground of political pluralism. Similar styles of thinking converge on a common object, one to coerce and control, the other to describe and predict. Political education and political science reinforce one another.

Although his influence proved most decisive of all, Bentley was not alone in setting the direction for modern political science in America. His friend and collaborator, John Dewey, also played a major part in encouraging political scientists to forsake cosmic speculations for group analysis. Like Bentley and Madison, Dewey distrusted all theories tainted with idealism. "Fraternity, liberty, and equality," he wrote, are "hopeless abstractions," whose assertion leads to "mushy sentimentalism or else to extravagant and fanatical violence." In the concrete, there are only groups. Dewey meant his "doctrine of plural forms" as a literal statement of fact, and he lashed out at those who accept the political reality of anything beyond the group. For him, the state was "pure myth," and society merely "an abstraction." The import of such terms is unmistakable. Dewey wished to rid political science of the influence of the academic Tom Paines, the "Theoretic politicians" of the modern day.

Finally, I must mention Charles Beard, another who found his text in *The Federalist* papers. The search for meaning beyond individual interest and group rationality is, in Beard's words, utterly "unreal, so ill-adapted" to the facts. Whoever indulges himself in this manner is "not a man of science" at all, "or a detached scholar," but a "propagandist." "In the world of natural science," he wrote, "men do not tarry long with hypotheses that will not square with observed phenomena. Shall we in the field of political science cling to a delusion that we have to deal only with an abstract man divorced from all economic interests and group sentiments?" Beard is right. It would be a delusion to deal with political materials in that way, particularly in America where our institutions, customs, and ideals, our very Constitution and the motives which inspired it, compel us to act always upon economic interests and group sentiments. Nor is Beard himself a propagandist. His science confirms his judgment, and leads him to the inescapable conclusion that only they are propagandists who desire to alter the tendencies either of science or of society. Effective political preference, that is, a prescriptive system which can count upon the authority of institutions to enforce it, is still the surest foundation upon which to erect a science of politics.

From a scientific point of view, this makes sense. The physical scientist seeks the idea in the mind of the Creator which would allow him to comprehend all of creation. "I want to know how God created this world," Einstein was fond of saying. "I want to know his thoughts, the rest are details." But the scientist is seriously handicapped in his quest. He must impute the idea to the mute Force responsible for existence; he has to move always from data to design, backwards from fact to theory. The political scientist, on the other hand, is privileged to know the idea in advance, the thoughts in the mind of those responsible for American political existence. He already has his theory. But he also faces a difficulty, precisely opposite to that confronting the physical scientist. Everything he sees fits, and what does not fit is anomalous. Yet each advance in his science contributes not only to filling in the details of political existence, but to the fulfillment of the scheme of an all-too-human creator, fallible as the rest of us. Can this be one reason at least why the political scientist refuses to be content with interpreting the behavior of 200 million people—a stupendous achievement in itself—but reaches out to comprehend all of political existence by means of a universal science? Whatever the conclusion, one thing seems plain enough: Madison could as easily have replied to Albion Small as to Rousseau, and Bentley might have had as enjoyable a time of it demolishing Paine as he did Spencer.

III.

"He who dares to undertake the making of a people's institutions," said Rousseau, "ought to feel himself capable, so to speak, of changing human nature. . . ." Circumstances toward the end of the eighteenth century presented men of knowledge and power with a unique opportunity. They dared to make the institutions of a people and, if the authors of the American system were not sanguine about the possibility of changing human nature, they were determined to shape individual and collective behavior to desired ends. The outcome of the experiment, arranged with intelligence and care, has amply justified the faith of its designers. Whatever the verdict on human nature, there can be no doubt that the behavior of generations of Americans has responded to the genius of its Legislator. In so doing, it has also gratified the scientific needs of the observer. The founders provided more than a theory, they set the conditions for its verification. Political science has supplied the means, joining with political education to produce an impeccable tautology.

But not quite. The latent tension existing between the diffuse, protean, frequently contradictory demands of human nature, and the predictable responses required in all systems of rationalized behavior, has not been resolved once and for all. The rationality of the founders, expressed in forces and vectors, weights and balances, might have overwhelmed the impulsive arguments of Thomas Paine, but the triumph of formal rationality did not necessarily abolish the strivings for which he sought recognition.

Contrary to popular impression, in certain basic things Paine was not a rationalist but an organic thinker, profoundly conservative despite his radical tone, scarcely a modern at all. Like Rousseau, he was a magnificent contradiction, and I have obviously chosen to portray only that side of him which exemplifies the recalcitrance of the primitive towards the strident rationality of a mechanistic age. The reason I have celebrated the heroism of Paine's defense of nature against artifice, particularly in *Common Sense,* must also be obvious. His words testify to the existence of passions and hopes to which the Federalists responded with trepidation and present-day scientists respond with impatience. Paine stands to the unexpressed yearnings of men as James Madison does to the expressed rationality of their behavior. "Fraternity," Thoreau said, "is a word in everyone's heart, but on no one's lips." A polity which denies to its citizens the expression of heartfelt sentiments does not thereby expel them from the human breast.

Madison tried very hard not to be contradictory, and his efforts are justly celebrated. But there is a possibility that the materials he dealt with are contradictory and that, however suppressed or inhibited, certain powerful components of man's nature return to haunt us, whether we be rulers or scientists. Men can be pious as well as prudent, exuberant as well as staid, extravagant as well as sober, magical as well as reasonable. Just so long as these dangerous qualities are kept out of politics, they are seen as no threat to political or scientific rationality. Wherever they do irrupt into behavior, the sorts of calculations indispensable to Madison's Constitution and Bentley's science are placed in jeopardy. Those who overtly express such qualities are termed by the authorities delinquents, troublemakers, or criminals. Political scientists call them deviants, anomics, or outsiders.

Even before the experiment was very old, men of acute intelligence had perceived the precariousness of the balance between behavior and impulse in America. Simply stated, the rationalized activities of Americans, their pursuit of material comforts to the detriment of the social affections, apparently failed to gratify some crucial human needs. Tocqueville gazed with compassion upon that "strange melancholy which often haunts [Americans] in the midst of their abundance, and that disgust at life which sometimes seizes upon them in the midst of calm and easy circumstances." Could the strange melancholy have been an implicit recognition that America was not Eden, and the disgust a sign that they had failed her? For some reason, friendship, brotherhood, and community had neglected to accompany the hopes of men across the Atlantic. Emerson expressed the same thought, in much the same language. American society was "devoured by a secret melancholy which breaks through all its smiles and all its gaiety and games." As usual, it was left to Thoreau to have the last word, and that word was definitive: "The mass of men lead lives of quiet desperation." Paine's vengeance had been visited against the wrong people.

The American dream is far from dead, however, although for many it has turned into a nightmare. Men and women seek friendship in interest groups, brotherhood in political parties, a sense of purpose in the PTA, and piety in hate groups. We know that this sort of behavior is dysfunctional, that these people suffer from distorted perception, that they are the potential victims of rabble-rousers or the tools of scheming opportunists. But even though we tell them so, they persist. The spectacle a few years ago of a member of the United States Senate, repository of the federal principle designed by the founders to thwart dangerous passions and to disperse them, performing the role of a majoritarian demagogue to tyrannize over private citizens as well as the other branches of government, is a powerful case in point. Some important human needs were suffering neglect, and the senator took full advantage of the situation. Yet at the very moment when we are threatened with becoming a nation of deviant cases, and when the words long in so many hearts are at last on so many lips, we seem intent upon putting the system to work in other nations of the world.

There appears in a recent *Bulletin* of the Social Science Research Council the report of an Inter-American Conference on Research and Training in Sociology. It could just as easily have been a conference in the field of political science, for the considerations are identical. During the course of the meeting there was a growing impression that many Latin Americans "regard the work of empirical sociological research as a threat to values and social structures they consider vital to the cohesion of Latin American Society." Nevertheless, the situation is far from hopeless. The report mentions with approval the recent "receptivity in government and other circles to the possible usefulness of sociological research in guiding the direction and pace of plans for economic development," as well as the presence of "political leaders who recognize that sociological research may be able to provide rational bases for practical measures of social amelioration." Social science can be of "unparalleled aid both in *channeling social changes* and in *overcoming resistance to them,* so as to maximize the chances for peaceful growth through democratic procedures rather than through forcible and totalitarian methods."

These, to be sure, are worthy ends, and I have no quarrel with them. But I do have a question. How does it happen that a body of theories and techniques, defended at home on the grounds of strict scientific objectivity, can when taken abroad become a mechanism for channeling social changes and overcoming resistance to them, in short, a device of political education? I have tried to suggest that political science in America has been the rational outgrowth of an established political system. What we are now witnessing is the attempt to export a science in the hope that a foreign authority will provide sanctions powerful enough to turn scientific ideals into political reality. There can be no plainer evidence for the intimate relation between political science and political education.

Whether we wish it or not, as American political scientists we today wear the toga of the Legislator, to instruct half the nations of the globe. By giving them our science, we risk giving them our laws as well. In this perilous state, we could do worse than to recall the warning of Rousseau, that giving laws to men is the prerogative of a god, and bears the responsibility of a god.

Part 4
Departures/1970–1992

Introduction

Nearly a quarter-century has passed since APSA President David Easton announced that "a new revolution is under way in American political science, . . . the post-behavioral revolution." The discipline, Easton argued, needed this new revolution because "the last revolution—behavioralism" had been overtaken by social and political crises in the public world. These crises had revealed how inattentive political science had been to questions of relevance, action, and "the brute realities of politics." Easton was by no means counseling or even prophesying "an end to political science," as did other members of the discipline at the time. Rather, he hoped to clarify the normative premises and social responsibilities of political science, as well as to encourage a speculative imagination and even a few "outrageous hypotheses" about politics of the kind that Robert Lynd had called for thirty years earlier in *Knowledge for What?*[1] Whether all of this has been realized over the course of the last two decades is open to doubt. But we certainly have had no other revolution since then. We are still in a postbehavioral era.

The idea of a post*behavioral* political science reinforces the historical importance of behavioralism in shaping the discipline's twentieth-century identity. The idea of a *post*behavioral political science underscores a sense of the irretrievability of the behavioral past and a more generalized consciousness of temporality and change. It is therefore not surprising that there has been such a revival of interest in recent years in the disciplinary history of political science (as outlined in the General Introduction above). Moreover, *post*behavioralism also evokes the sense of anxiety and crisis that brought it about in the first place. For many in the discipline, there is the feeling that the last two decades have been marked by widespread "uneasiness . . . not of the body, but of the discipline's soul."[2] Others have chimed in that the discipline is adrift, disenchanted, afflicted with tragedy, or alienated from its roots.[3]

---

1. David Easton, "The New Revolution in Political Science," *American Political Science Review* 63 (1969): 1051–61; Marvin Surkin and Alan Wolfe, eds., *An End to Political Science* (New York: Basic Books, 1970); and Robert Lynd, *Knowledge for What? The Place of Social Science in American Culture* (Princeton, NJ: Princeton University Press, 1939).

2. Gabriel Almond, "Separate Tables: Schools and Sects in Political Science," *PS* 21 (1988): 838.

3. See, among others, Heinz Eulau, "Drift of a Discipline," *American Behavioral Scientist*

Amidst these unsettling diagnoses of the discipline, postbehavioral political scientists would seem to agree that the discipline was deeply altered by the political events, social movements, and cultural turmoil of the 1960s. Urban riots, student protests against the Vietnam War, and the rise of feminism, among other things, sparked a reaction that was virtually without precedent in the discipline. Never before had the profession's organizational hierarchy and the intellectual assumptions governing research been subject to so much debate and contention, nor its legitimacy and public role so questioned.

Conflict about theoretical orientations, the status of science, the meaning of professionalism, and the social composition of the discipline led to divisive debates. Sometimes the debates took organizational form, as in the challenge by the Caucus for a New Political Science to "the establishment" candidates for office at the 1969 APSA meetings, over which Easton presided. More often the debates were in print, as in the publication in 1970 of *Politics and Community: Dissenting Essays in Political Science* and the formation of a new journal of political criticism, *Politics and Society*.[4]

Yet the intense period of debate between critics and defenders of the American political order—as well as of science, objectivity, pluralism, and quantification in the discipline—was actually quite short-lived. By the mid-1970s, postbehavioral political science settled down to the less confrontational enterprise of refining research programs and developing new theories and methods. Older approaches and philosophies, once the subject of behavioral attack, were recast and reintroduced. Thus, despite all the initial ferment and the lingering anxiety, postbehavioralism has turned out to provide an intellectual ambience for a great deal of scholarly production that most agree is not governed by some overall purpose or mission. Scholars go their own ways, do their own things, or sit at their own separate tables.

In the subfield of American politics alone, the range of recent scholarly production has proved to be somewhat daunting. Behavioral political science was often attacked for its political irrelevance; in the last two decades students of public policy and political economy have created a veritable industry. Behavioralism was scorned for its scientism; today, scientific claimants exist alongside many political philosophers who question the very idea of a genuine science of politics. Behavioralism was rejected for its attachments to a liberal status quo; today, the ideological range of political science has broadened to give greater voice to conservatives, radicals, and feminists. Behavioralism

---

21 (1977): 3–10; David Ricci, *The Tragedy of Political Science* (New Haven, CT: Yale University Press, 1984); and the essays by David Easton and Raymond Seidelman below.

    4. Sanford Levinson and Philip Green, eds., *Power and Community: Dissenting Essays in Political Science* (New York: Pantheon, 1970); also see Surkin and Wolfe, eds., *An End to Political Science,* and Theodore Lowi, "The Politicization of Political Science," *American Politics Quarterly* 1 (1973).

was attacked for its ahistorical neglect of the state; today, ventures linking historical inquiry with rational-choice theory are increasingly published, as is a "new institutionalism" that echoes many of the discipline's prebehavioral concerns and preoccupations.[5]

The six essays in this section present different historical reflections on the discipline. They remember, and enter into, some of the more important recent debates in political science, including those that brought about post-behavioralism in the first place and those that intimate what departures we are presently undertaking.

In their effort to characterize the postbehavioral present, the essays by David Easton and Raymond Seidelman offer contrasting overviews of the history of political science. In his essay, originally an address to the Shanghai Academy, Easton argues that behavioralism represents the third stage in the discipline's development, having superceded the formal and traditional stages. It marked "the central transformation of political science in this century" because it supplied "theoretical coherence" to a discipline that had lacked it since its inception. Yet behavioralism was subsequently and rightly taken to task for its political quietism, its "indifference to moral judgments," and its "profound forgetfulness about the history of political systems." Post-behavioralism has absorbed these criticisms, Easton argues. It has permitted healthy dialogue between competing points of view and a "more relaxed," less positivistic view of science that promotes "no single, fixed kind of intellectual product." This genuine advantage is nonetheless counterbalanced by another: that "there are now so many approaches to political research that political science seems to have lost its purpose." It is as yet unclear, therefore, what new directions and departures the discipline will take.

Seidelman offers a more sharply critical rendition of the mood prevalent in this postbehavioral era, even as he intimates considerable praise of the prebehavioral past. He argues that the discipline ought not to be judged internally, that is, by its ideas and theories alone. Rather, its historical claims as a savior and helpmate to liberalism require an external evaluation, that is, by the discipline's public political ambitions and its attempted transformation of political conditions and events. Since the discipline traditionally sought to be a science *of* and *for* liberal politics, Seidelman argues that any meth-

---

5. Examples of new work are numerous but would certainly include, for the new institutionalism, Stephen Skowronek, *Building a New American State* (Cambridge, MA: Cambridge University Press, 1982); for public choice, Kenneth Shepsle, "Studying Institutions: Some Lessons from the Rational Choice Approach," *Journal of Theoretical Politics* 1 (1989); for political economy, Charles Lindblom, *Politics and Markets* (New York: Basic Books, 1977); and for comparative history and the state, Theda Skocpol, *States and Social Revolutions* (Cambridge, MA: Cambridge University Press, 1976), and Peter B. Evans, Dietrich Rueschemeyer, and Theda Skocpol, eds., *Bringing the State Back In* (Cambridge, MA: Cambridge University Press, 1985).

odological or theoretical program, including behavioralism and its successors, ought to be judged in these demonstrably political terms. To Seidelman, the initial postbehavioralist critique of the past did recapture the discipline's important reformist identity. But many postbehavioralists have by now largely rejected what he calls "reform political science." Only a few others bear the current burdens of its history.

In essays originally published ten years ago, Charles E. Lindblom and William H. Riker offer further contrasting views about the discipline's past and its postbehavioral condition. They also display competing theoretical and historiographical postures about what political scientists have done and ought to be doing when they judge the present debates in terms of those of the past.

In his 1981 presidential address to the APSA, Lindblom criticizes what he takes to be the insularity of contemporary political science from "radical" perspectives about the nature of political power and democracy in America. The works most intent on their scientific objectivity and sophisticated methodology, as, for example, studies of political socialization, are the "most vulnerable to the charge from radical political science that we have without evidence fallen into a complacent view of the liberal democratic process." Lindblom refuses to side with the radical critics of mainstream political science because of their "questionable methods." But he does argue that the discipline's historical identity has been undermined by the propensity of mainstream scholars to say conventional and even "silly things," and by its unwillingness to take on a greater dose of radical thought.

Riker is not interested in "criticism or philosophic speculation" but in the advance of science. Close attention to the methodological and theoretical program of rational-choice theory can make good the claims of science and also obviate the sorts of claims that Lindblom makes. In evidence, Riker offers the scientific history of Maurice Duverger's proposition that "the simple-majority single-ballot system favors the two-party system." Over the course of a century of patient research on the explanatory foundations of what has become known as "Duverger's law," political scientists displayed "increasing scientific sophistication" and have now demonstrated the scientific power of models based on individual rational choice. In Riker's view, rational-choice theory holds out the promise in this postbehavioral era of vindicating the discipline's historical aspirations to the scientific accumulation of knowledge.

Many postbehavioral critiques of mainstream political science stress the absence of systematic attention to issues of race, class, and gender in the discipline's history. Helene Silverberg's new essay chronicles and criticizes some of the ways in which feminism and gender have been incorporated into political science analysis in the last twenty-five years. A "behavioralist compromise" between feminists and political scientists brought about a substantial increase in published research on women's political behavior and on the relationship between the sexes. However, the feminist revolution must press beyond this sort of research strategy by analyzing gender, which Silverberg understands as a "category of analysis" that "provides a theoretical lens through which the inequalities of power between men and women can be seen to structure (and be structured by) the organization of political, social, and economic life." A compromise with the "new institutionalism," she argues, is the most promising way for feminist scholars in the empirical subfields of political science to progress.

Theodore J. Lowi's recent (1991) presidential reflections on the discipline's past and present complete this section as well as the volume as a whole. Lowi argues that political science's disciplinary identity was originally shaped by the fact that it emerged before the growth of a large and powerful nation state. But as the American state transformed itself into a "Leviathan," political science transformed itself into a "dependent variable" of the state it studied and still studies. To Lowi, American political scientists have therefore "become what we study." In the postbehavioral present, this has meant, among other things, that the language of economics has come to predominate in political science, just as it has in the discourse of the state. Yet Lowi sees a way out of "becoming what we study," and that is by rediscovering "the satisfaction in having made a good guess about what makes democracy work and a good stab at improving the prospect of rationality in human behavior." Here, then, is an opportunity—expressed repeatedly by political scientists during the discipline's history—for us now "to meet our own intellectual needs while serving the public interest."

Taken together, these essays by no means exhaust the current range of postbehavioral political science or the ways it remembers the history of the discipline. Yet there is sufficient range to appreciate the point behind Lowi's observation that, today, "there is not one political science but several, and each is the adaptation to what it studies." This would appear to be the state— or, rather, the states—of the discipline for some time to come.

Political Science in the United States:
Past and Present

David Easton

Political science has been defined in many ways—as the study of power, the study of the monopoly of the legitimate use of force, the study of the good life, of the state, and so on. If there is one thing that distinguishes Western political science, it is that it has not yet arrived at a consensus on how to describe its subject matter at the most inclusive level. For reasons that are elaborated at length elsewhere (Easton 1981a), I have chosen to characterize political science as the study of the way in which decisions for a society are made and considered binding most of the time by most of the people. As political scientists, we are interested in all those actions and institutions in society more or less directly related to the way in which authoritative decisions are made and put into effect, and the consequences they may have (Easton 1981b). To seek to understand political life is to address oneself to the study of the authoritative allocation of values (valued things) for a society.

In effect, this description applies to any and all political systems, whether modern or ancient, large or small, industrialized or agricultural, mass or tribal, and so on. It is probably fair to say that this way of identifying political systems seems to have won the favor of many political scientists over the last quarter of a century. Thereby we are able to distinguish our interests from those of economists, anthropologists, sociologists, and other social scientists.

With this conception of the study of politics, let us now turn to an examination of what has been happening in Western, especially United States, political science during the twentieth century. It has passed through four stages. Each of these has been distinctive. Each has been incorporated in and,

This essay first appeared in the Chinese language in *Political Science and Law* (January 1984), a journal of the Shanghai Academy of Social Sciences, and in English in *International Political Science Review* 6 (1985): 133–52. It was republished in David Easton and Corinne Schelling, eds., *Divided Knowledge* (Beverly Hills, CA: Sage, 1990), chap. 2. Reprinted by permission of Sage Publications, Inc. Copyright © 1991 by Sage Publications, Inc.

one hopes, improved upon by each succeeding stage. I shall give the following names to these stages: the formal (legal), the traditional (informal or prebehavioral), the behavioral, and the postbehavioral. I discuss each in turn.

The Formal and Traditional Stages

Toward the latter part of the nineteenth century, political science started out with the conviction that once the laws governing the distribution of power in a political system have been described, we will have obtained an accurate understanding of how political institutions operate. Students of politics assumed that there was a reasonably close fit between what constitutions and laws said about the rights and privileges people held in various political offices and the way in which they acted in those offices.

Late in the nineteenth century, Walter Bagehot in Great Britain, followed by Woodrow Wilson in the United States (where he was a student and later a professor), made a major discovery. To everyone's surprise, they found that around the formal structure of political offices and institutions there were all kinds of informal behavior and organizations in which power over decision making might lie. Bagehot, Wilson, and others discovered them in the informal committees of their respective legislatures and in the political parties. Later scholars added interest or pressure groups to a growing list of informal institutions to be taken into account.

These findings introduced a new stage in the development of political science, dividing attention away from the formal, legal structures to the informal practices surrounding them. This change, which had occurred toward the end of the nineteenth century, was in full swing by the 1920s. People who were trained in the United States from the 1920s to the 1940s were exposed largely to what has come to be called traditional political science, the name for the second distinctive phase of political research in the twentieth century. During this period, training included a great deal of attention to the operation of political parties and their effect on Congress or Parliament and to the growth, in the United States, of pressure groups and other types of groups. The latter were drawn to our attention and analyzed in depth, initially by Arthur Bentley (1908), who was ignored at the time, and later, in new ways, by Pendleton Herring (1929) and David Truman (1951).

Methodologically, this traditional period was one in which more attention was paid to mere description and the collection of information about political processes than to overarching theories about how they operated. In fact, however, a latent theory unobtrusively guided research. Even though most of the scholars of that period were not conscious of it, they really say the political process is a giant mechanism for making decisions. Decisions were, as one scholar, Merle Fainsod (1940), put it, a product of a "parallelogram of forces." This meant that when decisions were to be made, whether at the legislative or administrative levels, they were seen as being subjected to a vast array of pressures from social groups—from political parties, from other parts of the bureaucracy itself, from interest groups, from public opinion, and so on. These pressures played against each other, developing a parallelogram of forces that, through bargaining, negotiation, adaptation, compromise, and adjustment (terms commonly used to describe the process), would arrive at some equilibrium point for that time and place. This equilibrium point would yield a particular policy, or the policy could be called the point of equilibrium among the various competing forces pressing against the decision makers. If at some time one of these social forces should change, for example, because of a change in the economic structure, in the social attitudes, or in the occupants of decision-making roles, demands for modification of old policies or for the introduction of new policies might arise. Competition among the various groups for influence over the policy would then begin again, and a new point of equilibrium might be achieved (Easton 1981a). As I have indicated, for the most part, this equilibrium theory remained only latent in the literature.

The characteristic methods of research during this traditional period were no less informal than their theoretical base. Few special methods were used for the collection of data or for their analysis. Methods were not considered to be problematic, that is, as areas that required special attention or skills. Everyone was equally well equipped to collect and analyze information about politics. As a result, there were no formal or specified methods for testing the reliability of information acquired or of findings and interpretations based upon such information.

In addition, it was often difficult to distinguish whether the research worker was expressing his or her own preferences or was, in fact, describing how institutions operate and how people behave in political life. Statements relating what should be and what is were often almost inextricably intertwined. Facts and values played havoc with each other.

Finally, my own experience as a graduate student reflects the lack of theoretical coherence of traditional political science. At Harvard University, I took many different courses in political science. They covered the history of political thought, municipal or local politics, constitutional law, foreign policy, government regulation of industry, interest or pressure groups, international relations, the governments of specific foreign countries, and lawmaking in Congress. At the end of my graduate training my head was in a whirl. No one had ever tried to help me understand why my interest in politics required me to be exposed to such a wide variety of subject matters aside from the fact that, loosely, they all had to do with something called government. I gained no sense of a basis upon which I could infer that political science formed a coherent body of knowledge. There was no theoretical framework into which, for example, I could place all these courses or by which I could check their relevance.

Political theory might have been the area in which, because of its name, I might have expected to find the opportunity to address this. But theory turned out to be devoted largely to the study of the history of political thought. Such history was, of course, interesting and important in itself, but it did not fulfill what might have been one of the functions of theory in, say, economics, chemistry, or physics, namely, the conceptualization of the discipline in part or as a whole.

The traditional stage then was one in which political science discovered the rich body of informal activities out of which public policy was formed. Yet it was a period during which description was often hard to distinguish from values, when theory did not measure up to the promise implicit in its name, and when method was so taken for granted that it was nonproblematic.

The Behavioral Stage

The formal-legal and traditional periods were the first two phases of recent times. They were displaced by the so-called behavioral revolution in American political science, which rapidly spread to many other parts of the world. This third phase began after World War II although it had its roots in the earlier period. Without question, this is the central transformation that has occurred in Western political science in this century.

Despite the common root in the English terms, behaviorism and behavioralism, the two have little in common and should not be confused. Political science has never been behavioristic, even during the height of its behavioralistic phase. *Behaviorism* refers to a theory in psychology about human behavior and has its origins in the work of J. B. Watson. I know of no political scientist who subscribes to this doctrine. Indeed, I know of no political scientist, although there may be the occasional one, who accepts even the psychological theory of B. F. Skinner, the founder of the "operant conditioning" school of psychology and the modern successor to Watson.

The only real relationship between the terms behaviorism and behavioralism is that both focus on the behavior of human actors as the appropriate source of information about why things happen as they do. Both also assume that a methodology based on that of the natural sciences is appropriate for the study of human beings. Thus, aside from this acceptance of the individual as the focus of research and of scientific method, there is little resemblance between these tendencies.

Behavioralism in political science had the following major characteristics, which distinguished it from earlier stages in the study of political science (Easton 1962). Behavioralism, first, held that there are discoverable uniformities in human behavior and, second, that these can be confirmed by empirical tests. Third, behavioralism showed a desire for greater rigor in methods for the acquisition and analysis of data. Methods themselves became problematic. They could no longer be taken for granted. Courses and books on methods for acquiring and analyzing data, once nonexistent, became commonplace. Quantification, whenever possible and plausible, assumed an important place in the discipline. As a result, during the 1950s and 1960s, political science became adept at using a vast array of increasingly sophisticated and empirical and quantitative techniques—questionnaires, interviews, sampling, regression analysis, factor analysis, rational modeling, and the like.

Fourth, the behavioral movement committed itself to much greater theoretical sophistication than existed in the past. The search for systematic understanding, grounded in objective observation, led to a marked shift in the meaning of theory as a concept. Traditionally, in the distant past, theory had been philosophical in character, asking questions about the nature of the good life. In more recent times, it had become largely historical, seeking to explicate and account for the emergence of political ideas in past centuries. Behavioral theory, on the other hand, is empirically oriented. It seeks to help us explain, understand, and, if possible, predict the way people behave politically and the way political institutions operate.

A considerable amount of the energies of theoreticians in this period went into the construction of empirically oriented theory at various levels of analysis. So-called middle-range theory has sought to build theories about large segments of the discipline, as in the case of power pluralism, which offers a theory of democratic systems, game theory, or public-choice theory (Riker and Ordeshook 1973).

In part, however, theory was of the broadest character, called general theory. This type of theory sought to provide an understanding of political systems at the most inclusive level. Structural-functional theory and systems analysis (Easton 1981b) represent two major theoretical efforts of such broad scope.

Fifth, many behavioralists felt that the values of the research worker and of society could be largely excluded from the process of inquiry. Ethical evaluation and empirical explanation were viewed as involving two different kinds of statements that clarity required to be kept analytically separate and distinct. Behavioralism adopted the original positivist assumption (as developed by the Vienna Circle of positivists early in this century) that value-free or value-neutral research was possible. Although some of us, including myself (Easton 1981a, chapter 9), did not share this point of view, it is nevertheless correct to suggest that it was a dominant one during the height of the behavioral stage. As a result, among the priorities of interesting and acceptable things to do, moral inquiry receded far into the background.

Sixth, behavioralism represented a new-found emphasis on basic or pure theory as against applied research. Its assumption was that the task of the social scientist was to obtain fundamental understanding and explanation. It was felt that only after we have reliable understanding of how political institutions operate and people behave politically would it be possible to apply such knowledge, with confidence, to the solution of urgent social problems. The period of behavioralism, therefore, helped to divert the interests of scholars from social reform and encouraged them to set their sights on the needs of scientific development as a guide to research.

How can we explain the behavioral revolution of the 1950s and 1960s in the United States? It was clearly a product of a number of complex tendencies. It was part of the natural evolution of the discipline. The common sense, proverbial style of traditional political science, with its dependence on historical description and impressionistic analysis, had simply exhausted itself. A developing mass-industrialized society could not cope with its social problems with explanations of the degree of unreliability offered by traditional research. Too many difficulties in understanding political institutions and processes had been left unresolved. The epistemic successes of the natural sciences and of other social sciences, such as psychology and economics, using more rigorous methods of data collection and of analysis, left their impact on political science as well. They suggested alternatives that led political analysis away from "common" sense to "scientific" sense in which theoretical rather than social criteria defined the problems of research and technical skills took the place of mere description and common-sense methods.

In addition, however, there were social forces that encouraged a commitment to the introduction of science into the study of politics. Early in the cold war period in relations between the United States and the Soviet Union, especially during the Korean War (1950–53), Senator Joseph McCarthy inaugurated and led a reign of psychological and legal terror against liberals and others in the United States. Scholars were selected as particularly vulnerable targets for attack. McCarthyism succeeded in driving underground an interest in social reform and critical theory.

From this perspective, objective, neutral, or value-free research represented a protective posture for scholars, offering them intellectually legitimate and useful grounds for fleeing from the dangers of open political controversy. This is perhaps an instance in the evolution of knowledge in which inadvertent gains may have been won for the wrong reasons. McCarthyism, of course, had nothing to do with the emergence of behavioralism as a new approach to political research. It represented simply a historical circumstance that drove an interest in social reform underground. In doing so, it led scholars into politically less dangerous grounds of basic research, an area that, as it turned out, had major benefits to offer for the development of political science.

In addition to McCarthyism, another important social condition contributed significantly to the sustenance of behavioralism. Post–World War II prosperity, with its associated conservatism of the 1950s and the early 1960s, led to the prevalent view that ideology had indeed come to an end in the United States. Rapid economic growth offered material benefits to all segments of the population, even to the poorest. Critical social thought, including critical liberalism itself, seemed to all but disappear in the United States and, with it, all semblance of ideological conflict. Bell (1960) wrote a distinguished book entitled *The End of Ideology* that expressed this conviction.

In retrospect, it is clear that ideology had not disappeared but only seemed to have ended, because mainstream, liberal-conservative ideology was dominant and unchallenged for the moment. There were no major contenders. This situation, of course, changed during the late 1960s with the rise of the civil rights movement on behalf of blacks. But prior to this period, contending ideologies did recede or go underground. This lack of challenge to established ideologies turned the social sciences away from social problems as a source of inspiration for its research toward criteria internal to social theory, derivative from the logic of the development of social science itself. This gave social science the appearance of withdrawing from society into an ivory tower of scientific research, at least if one took the rhetoric of social research at its word.

It is clear that what from a social point of view could be interpreted as a retreat from social responsibility by social scientists, from the point of view of science could be interpreted as a breathing spell free from social involvement. This had the effect of enabling political science to address, in a relatively undisturbed atmosphere, many technical matters that have become central to its development, such as the place of theory in social research, the need for rigorous methods of research, the refinements of techniques for acquiring and analyzing data, the establishment of standards of professionalism among political scientists and social scientists in general, and so on.

In short, we can now recognize the behavioral phase as one in which the social sciences, for whatever historical reasons and fortuitous circumstances, were busy strengthening the scientific bases of their research. The cost was a significant withdrawal from an interest in social criticism and social involvement.

The Postbehavioral Stage

What I have called the postbehavioral revolution—a name now generally used for this next phase—began during the 1960s and is still with us today (Easton 1969). It represents a deep dissatisfaction with the results of behavioralism but has not led to the abandonment of scientific method in political science. It is, however, leading to a substantial modification of our understanding of the nature of science, and it is a movement that is still evolving.

Why did the postbehavioral movement arise? What were its sources? In the United States, this movement accompanied the so-called countercultural revolution, which arose in the West, and touched the East as well, during the later 1960s and early 1970s. It represented a period of worldwide social change. Much of the leadership came from large masses of students congregated in rapidly growing colleges and universities around the world. In the United States, it had its origins in the civil rights movement, especially after the 1954–1955 Supreme Court decisions against educational segregation of blacks, and was accompanied by demands for the improvement of the condition of blacks and other minorities and by widespread protests during the Johnson and Nixon administrations against the Vietnam War. It was most clearly evident in new attitudes toward forms of dress, sexual behavior, the place of women and minorities in society, poverty, respect for the physical environment (pollution, atomic waste, the dangers of nuclear energy), and social inequality. The postbehavioral movement, in its broadest meaning, represented the awakening of the modern world to the dangers of rapid and unregulated industrialization, ethnic and sexual discrimination, worldwide poverty, and nuclear war.

This is not the place to describe this movement in detail. All we need to do is to draw attention to the impact that the countercultural revolution of the 1960s and 1970s had on the social sciences in general and on political science in particular. For social scientists, it raised the question as to why we were unable to foresee the kinds of problems, just mentioned, that became salient in this period. In addition, even if the social sciences had foreseen some of these problems, how did it happen that they did nothing about them? It appeared that the social sciences had simply withdrawn into an ivory tower. Questions such as these led to large-scale debates on the nature of our discipline and what it ought to be.

From these debates several things are now clear. The original commitment to science during the behavioral period, that is, during the 1950s and 1960s, has been seriously questioned. Some of the criticisms of scientific method reflect well-known arguments inherited largely from the nineteenth century: Human behavior is composed of too many complex variables and therefore we are not likely to be able to discover any lawlike regularities; unlike atoms, human beings are not determined. They have free will, and therefore their actions can never be predicted even on a probable basis. Even if the methods of the natural sciences have manifested great epistemic success, this is because they deal with inanimate matter. Atoms, however, do not have feelings or intentions that, by their very nature, are unpredictable or inaccessible to observation or prediction.

Other criticisms of social science were directed to its positivistic claims that behavioral research was value free. As I mentioned earlier, some social scientists had proclaimed the "end of ideology." With the countercultural movement came the argument that all social research is, on the contrary, really shot through with ideology. The point was advanced that the claim that social science was valuationally neutral was possible only because social science had assumed the ideological coloring of the status quo (bourgeois liberalism) and the existing power structure. Its ideological premises were at one with those of the establishment and disappeared into the received views of the day. This claim to false objectivity was seen as serving the interests of the establishment. It seemed to justify or excuse the withdrawal of social scientists from involvement in social issues, to divert social inquiry from urgent social problems, and thereby to allow the status quo to go unchallenged.

This attack on the ideologic presuppositions of scientific method in the study of society broadened into a wholesale challenge of the epistemological and ontological bases of social research. In a widely read book, *The Structure of Scientific Revolutions* by T. Kuhn (1962), the view was advanced that all science, natural as well as social, is essentially an irrational process. In this book, scientific change is no longer seen as the product of a gradual accumulation of knowledge and understanding; change now represents only the shift of scientists from acceptance of an existing paradigm or set of ideological and other presuppositions to a new one, for a variety of explainable reasons. The history of science, from this point of view, appears as a random shift from one set of premises (paradigms) governing research to another.

Despite the initial impact of this book, it is now realized that this criticism, in denying the possibility of any objective and cumulative knowledge, went far beyond the realm of necessity and plausibility (Suppe 1977). The criticism did however draw attention to the need to reconsider how we do manage to acquire a valid understanding about the real world despite the fact that research may be saturated with evaluative presuppositions.

I have touched only briefly on the fierce attacks that have been launched against scientific method since the 1970s. They have, however, led to serious reassessments of the original commitment to the positivistic conception of scientific method that was prevalent during the behavioral period of the 1950s and 1960s. We can see the results of this reassessment in the current approaches to political inquiry, which are far more diverse than during the behavioral period. The earlier impressionistic methods have even regained some plausibility, as has the method of interpretive understanding (*verstehen*) put forward at the turn of this century by Max Weber. We have also witnessed the reemergence of proponents of Marxism as an alternative way to develop a social science (Ollman and Vernoff 1982; Poulantzas 1973).

Indeed, there are now so many approaches to political research that political science seems to have lost its purpose. During the 1950s and 1960s, in the behavioral phase, there was a messianic spirit and collective effort in the promotion and development of the methods of scientific inquiry even while there continued to be opposition to it. Today there is no longer a single, dominant point of view or one that unmistakably catches the imagination, especially of younger members of the profession. Nor is there even a single defensive adversary. The discipline is fragmented in its methodological conceptions, even though it is probably fair to say that scientific inquiry still represents the mainstream. However, it is not, as we shall see in a moment, only science in the old positivistic sense. Instead we are adding a new and more relaxed understanding of the nature of science itself. In addition to losing its sense of a dynamic purpose concentrated on the pursuit of scientific validity, political science seems to have lost its core. There was once agreement that political science was a study of values or of the good life. Also, if it will not seem self-serving on my part to say so, there was a dominant point of view. If there was any single comprehensive description of the subject matter of political science it was to be found in the notion that it studied the authoritative allocation of values for a society. This was a conception that I had put forward in 1953 in my book, *The Political System* (Easton 1981a), and it found widespread acceptance.

Today, however, students are no longer certain what politics is all about. They may be even less concerned than they were in the past. Political science as a study of the state, a conception that, after World War II, had been driven out by the idea of the political system, has now been revived. It has accompanied the reemergence, in U.S. political science at least, of Marxist and quasi-Marxist points of view (Easton 1981c) and in them, of course, the state is a central concept.

What is being offered today to draw the discipline together, to give it a sense of common purpose, and to provide alternative methods, if any, for inquiry? Here is where the real difficulty arises. As the 1990s begin, political science is still trying to develop a new sense of identity and a new drive or sense of purpose. We are clearly in a transition phase, and it is difficult to predict just where we will end up. We look fragmented and display a great variety of objectives for the very reason that theories, methods, and perspectives are still being questioned, that is, they are in the process of change.

We can get some flavor of the reconstruction taking place by recounting the different interests and approaches of U.S. political science, at least at the present time. Theoretical Marxism, after lying dormant in U.S. social science since the 1940s (even though very much alive in Europe), was reintroduced during the 1970s. However, no single orthodoxy in the Marxist methods or theories has been adopted. The fragmentation of European Marxism is reflected in its American renaissance. We find all schools of Marxism represented—critical theory, humanist, cultural, structural, as well as ortho-dox. All have had some impact on U.S. political science, although structural Marxism, as developed by Althusser and Poulantzas, has probably been the most influential.

What is clear, however, is that in being absorbed into U.S. social re-search, the various schools of Marxism have been attenuated; most inquiry is only quasi-Marxist in character. Even in that form, however, the revival of Marxist thinking has brought to political science a renewed awareness of the importance of history and of the significance of the economy, social classes, and ideology, as well as the total social context (the social formation, as Althusser would phrase it). As of the moment, with the disintegration of the socialist-bloc countries, the emergence of *perestroika* in the USSR, and the outbreak of democratic ideologies in Eastern Europe, it is not yet clear what effect these events will have on the plausibility of Marxist theories for future social inquiry.

The mainstream of U.S. political science has, however, moved off in a variety of other directions. The interests of the behavioral period in voting, judicial, legislative, administrative, and executive behavior as well as in interest groups, parties, developing areas, and the like have continued. But during the postbehavioral period new topics of political research have arisen to satisfy the desire to understand the new concerns typical of this period—environmental pollution, ethnic, racial, social and sexual equality, and nu-clear war, for example.

In the search for answers to urgent social issues such as these, political science in this period has joined all other social sciences in making an extraor-dinary commitment of its resources to the application of knowledge. We witness this in the rapid and widespread growth of the so-called policy-analysis movement. Literally hundreds of institutes have arisen not only for the understanding of the way in which policies are formed and implemented, but for the formulation of policy alternatives to help solve the urgent social problems facing all societies at the present time. These institutes ring the changes on all questions of policy creation and execution: What are the policies in various areas? How are they formed? What alternatives are ne-glected or rejected and why? What are their consequences, direct or indirect? To what extent do they fulfill their ostensible objectives (contributing to the emergence of a vast subfield of policy evaluation)? How does a given set of present policies influence subsequent policies (the feedback process)? Be-cause the effects of policies are felt not only in the political sector but also in most other areas of study, policy institutes typically have been built around interdisciplinary curricula (Fleishman 1990, chapter 9). In this way policy research has reawakened the hope of an earlier day for integrating the social sciences, at least in the application of its knowledge.

Another shift in interest that is part and parcel of this new policy orientation is reflected in the rebirth of the field of political economy. In the nineteenth century, as modern political science was evolving, economics and politics had already shown a close and natural affinity, as revealed in the work of John Stuart Mill, which he explicitly called political economy, and of Karl Marx. The revival of this link, beginning in the 1970s, is in part attributable, of course, to the revival of Marxist thought. But it has also blossomed independently through efforts to show the numerous relationships between the state of the economy on the one hand and political events and institutions on the other (Frolich and Oppenheimer 1982; Monroe 1983).

As I have just noted, political economy is a return to a traditional combination of interests common in the nineteenth century. But perhaps the most dramatic shift in perspectives has occurred recently in a different area, in what I shall call cognitive political science. The emergence of this approach reflects a movement away from the attempt to understand political phenomena as exclusively a product of nonrational processes, that is, as a product of social forces that influence decisions and actions of political actors and institutions.

The starting assumption of cognitive political science is that there is a strong rational component to political behavior. This can mean one of two things: that human beings do act rationally or that we can better understand their behavior if we adopt rationality as an assumption.

Whereas the outcome of empirical scientific research consists of generalizations about behavior that are grounded in observations, the products of the cognitive approach are models about how human beings would or should act under varying circumstances if they were to act rationally. The product of inquiry takes the form of rational-choice models, game theories, or other kinds of so-called rational-actor models (Downs 1957; Kramer and Hertzberg 1975; Riker and Ordeshook 1973; Taylor 1975). For some political scientists, these models only tell us how persons might behave if they acted rationally. They are of value insofar as we can compare actual behavior with the model in order to try to account for the deviance from the model. For others, however, these models represent the way in which people actually do behave. The assumption of rationality becomes a reality (Riker and Ordeshook 1973). For still others, however, rational models represent ways in which people should behave if they are to conform to rational norms, and such norms are assumed to be desirable in themselves. Rational models may, therefore, depict formal calculi of rational behavior, actual strategies of choice, or preferred strategies, if one values rational behavior.

Not only empirically oriented research but political philosophy also has been a major beneficiary of the rational approach. Rational modeling has breathed new life into political philosophy. During the behavioral period, moral research had all but died out for reasons already mentioned. Values were sometimes thought to be mere expressions of preferences, as in economics to this day. In the current postbehavioral period, renewed efforts are under way to demonstrate that there is a rational basis for moral argument and judgment. Most of the work in this area has been inspired by John Rawl's *A Theory of Justice* (1971), itself influenced by economic modeling and game theory. In this book, the author attempts to develop valid and demonstrable criteria of justice derivable from the assumption of rational action. Using a similar convention about rational behavior, others have turned to the task of developing moral theories about equality, freedom, international justice, legitimacy, and the like (Beitz 1979; Elster 1986; Fishkin 1982; Lehrer and Wagner 1981).

Political philosophy is not alone in this new approach. It was preceded by and has in turn reinforced the application of the rational-actor approach in the areas of voting behavior and public choice, and as a technique has spread to other fields of political inquiry. In its essence, it reflects the theoretical approach of contemporary economics and in fact even borrows economic theories for application to political situations (Downs 1957; Kramer and Hertzberg 1975).

This rationalistic approach has not been without its critics, and their voices have been growing in number and intensity. In part they have challenged the rationality assumption on the grounds that actors do in fact behave nonrationally and irrationally and that prediction of the behavior of individuals or of aggregates unnecessarily handicaps itself by failing to take such facts into account (Eckstein 1988; Elster 1989; Jarvie 1984; Mansbridge 1990; Quattrone and Tversky 1988). In part, however, the rational model has been accused of being overly reductionist in assuming that individual attributes, such as rationality, can explain all behavior. Such a model fails to take into account systematically the institutional and structural context that may determine, or, at the very least limit, actors, severally or as aggregates (Easton 1990; March and Olsen 1989). By the beginning of the 1990s, however, it would appear that these increasing reservations about the applicability of the rationality model have not prevented it from carving out a sizable and, from all appearances, an enduring niche for itself in the discipline.

In substantive areas such as those just mentioned—policy analysis, political economy, and what I have called cognitive political inquiry (rational modeling and the new political philosophy)—there has been little difficulty in going beyond the range of interests characteristic of the behavioral period and in adding to the latter's methodological perspectives. However, in the matter of actual methods of empirical research and in the fundamental premise that human behavior is subject to scientific inquiry, much less success has been met in finding an alternative, despite the current pervasive criticism of scientific method.

Few people believe any longer in the value neutrality of science. That scientific concepts are value-laden can no longer be denied. But that this does not invalidate the search for objective knowledge and understanding is equally undeniable. How both these statements can be true is still the subject of much debate (Lakatos and Musgrave 1970; Suppe 1977).

What, however, do the critics of scientific method offer as an alternative to the methods of science? This is where the real difficulty for the critics arises. The only formal alternative, that is, the only alternative that involves something that looks like a method that can be articulated, formalized, and communicated to succeeding generations is Weberian interpretive (*verstehen*) or empathetic understanding. This method has been and continues to be discussed, and in recent years the interest in the writings of Max Weber has increased enormously. As yet, however, no one has been able to formalize, systemize, or standardize the so-called interpretive method in a way that makes it readily communicable to those who would seek to learn it. Despite this irreducible inexpressibility, strangely enough, many radical critics of conventional social science have adopted this method, implicitly or otherwise. This is especially strange as its inventor, Max Weber, has been called "the Karl Marx of the bourgeoisie."

The Present and the Future

The many, often conflicting tendencies in postbehavioral political science in the West make it difficult to draw general conclusions about the state of the discipline. Because political science is still in the process of change, as the 1990s begin we cannot speak of a single, dominant tendency or direction. If there is one, however, we can probably find it in the fact that most leading members of the discipline continue to accept the appropriateness for social inquiry of the scientific methodology found to be so successful in the natural sciences.

It would be misleading, however, to assume that our understanding of scientific method today is the same as it was during the behavioral period. Our conception of science has not stood still; it is itself undergoing change.

We no longer cast ourselves in the image of the positivist ideal of science. An incipient transformation is under way that may well displace that image with a new one. If so, this is probably the most dramatic thing that is happening in the social sciences, though most social scientists may not yet be aware of it.

Positivism as represented in the thinking of the Vienna Circle during the 1920s was largely subsumed, if not consciously articulated, as behavioralism took shape, especially during the 1950s and 1960s. In this image, the ideal product of scientific inquiry would be a body of knowledge, based on axioms, with statements of relationships or generalizations that could be ultimately formalized, especially through the use of mathematics, and that would be well grounded in objective observations.

This model is still entertained by many social scientists, especially those who happen to be in areas where it can be either achieved or approximated, as, for example, in the areas of public choice and rational modeling. There, formal mathematization of propositions works well if only because it is intrinsic to the method of analysis in those areas. There are vast fields in political science, however, indeed most of political science to this point, that have not yielded this kind of intellectual product. Yet these areas of political science are clearly subject to rigorous inquiry through the use of the normal rules of logic, through careful acquisition of data consistent with the canons of science, and through equally sophisticated analysis of these data. The outcomes, though, do not measure up to the positivistic ideal of an axiomatized and mathematized set of propositions. Does this mean that they are not acceptable as scientific conclusions?

During the positivistic behavioral phase of political science, the answer might have been affirmative. Today, under the more relaxed understanding of science that is growing within philosophy of science, a different answer can be offered, one that accepts nonaxiomatized and nonmathematical statements as an integral part of scientific knowledge, even in its ideal form.

Philosophy of science is that special discipline in the West that is concerned with understanding the nature of science—how it acquires knowledge (epistemology) and the nature of the world we wish to know and understand (ontology). The findings of philosophy of science itself, no less than the findings of any other discipline, are subject to change and, we hope, improvement. Like other fields of inquiry it grows and changes. Although at one time philosophers of science, under the sway of early positivism, did indeed conceive of the appropriate outcomes of scientific inquiry in the manner of the positivists of the Vienna Circle, today, most recent findings are moving in a far less monolithically mathematical direction. No longer do all philosophers of science see science as restricted to a single kind of formalized product in the image of classical positivism. In a more skeptical mood, philosophers of science are now beginning to recognize that if we are able to understand science, we ought not to accept some abstract analysis of the nature of science as an adequate description of the way science operates to acquire valid knowledge. Rather, we are better advised to look at what scientists actually do.

When we do look at the history of scientific practices we find that a larger variety of research products are accepted as useful and necessary than we would have guessed if we had confined ourselves to the positivistic interpretation. Philosophy of science is now discovering that there are many varieties of outcomes with which scientists seem to be satisfied. These outcomes seem to answer the kinds of problems that are being asked in a particular area of science even if the outcomes do not look like the formal or mathematical models of early positivism. For example, systems of classification, taxonomies, conceptual frameworks, and qualitative generalizations about evolutionary processes that do not permit prediction need have little to do with formal models or mathematized propositions. Yet in the various sciences in which they are found, such as botany and biology, they are just as acceptable as final products (Hanson 1969; Shapere 1974; Suppe 1977; Toulmin 1972).

If this is happening in the natural sciences where the success of their methods cannot be denied, then it ought not to be any less true in the social sciences. In this view, then, systematic classifications of political phenomena, for example, or conceptual frameworks, as developed in my own thinking in systems analysis, would be just as normal a product of scientific inquiry as any generalization about politics or any mathematical model. The only question one must ask is whether, at the time, the intellectual product satisfies the needs of a would-be scientific discipline, such as political science, in terms of rigorous and testable understanding. That is to say, if the knowledge we acquire seems to help us in attaining satisfactory explanation or adequate understanding of an empirically grounded sort, then that is the most that we can ask of the methods of science. The history of inquiry in the natural sciences now seems to reveal that, despite what classical positivism would have us believe, there is no single fixed kind of intellectual product that can be designated as appropriate and necessary to achieve understanding of any given phenomena.

As the 1990s begin, the postbehavioral stage that we have just discussed is still evolving. It will be some time before a definitive statement can be made about how it finally differs from behavioralism and about the new direction in which it may be leading political science. One thing is clear, however. It had its birth in efforts to cope with some of the unresolved problems generated by behavioralism: the indifference to moral judgments; the excessive commitment to formal mathematized statements flowing from the use of scientific method; the focus on theoretical criteria to the neglect of social issues; the preoccupation with social forces as determinants of behavior, overlooking, in the process, important cognitive (rational) elements; and a profound forgetfulness about the history of political systems that helps to shape their present.

In trying to cope with these problems bequeathed by behavioralism, however, we can assume that postbehavioralism is busily generating its own difficulties. Some of these are already obvious; others undoubtedly will emerge as new contemporary explanations exhaust their own potential. For example, in emphasizing the need to apply whatever knowledge we have to the solution of urgent social issues, we have already run into major difficulties in trying to reintegrate the various highly specialized disciplines. Descartes taught us that understanding requires decomposition and analysis of a subject matter. Application of knowledge to the solution of social problems, however, requires the reassembly of the specialized knowledge of the various social sciences. We are still at a loss about how to do this. Application of knowledge has also diverted scarce resources from the continued search for fundamental knowledge so that we are already being called upon to reassess the appropriate division between applied and so-called pure research. Computer technology will clearly change the character of major aspects of research in all the social sciences, including political science, in ways that we can only guess at the present time. And finally, the growing international character of research raises fundamental issues about the universality of concepts in the social sciences as contrasted with the culturally conditioned nature of most thinking about social problems. Can we develop a genuinely transnational social science when different national cultures approach problems of understanding social phenomena in such transparently different ways, often with such different concepts?

To enter into a discussion of the impact of issues such as these on political science would, however, take us too far afield from our present purpose, an analysis of the four basic stages—formal-legal, traditional, behavioral, and postbehavioral—through which political science in the United States has passed in the twentieth century. These issues may, however, foreshadow a fifth stage that we have not yet begun to enter.

REFERENCES

Beitz, C. R. 1979. *Political Theory and International Relations.* Princeton, NJ: Princeton University Press.

Bell, D. 1960. *The End of Ideology: On the Exhaustion of Political Ideas in the Fifties.* Glencoe, IL: Free Press.

Bentley, A. 1949. *The Process of Government.* Cambridge, MA: Harvard University Press. (Originally published in 1908.)

Downs, A. 1957. *An Economic Theory of Democracy.* New York: Harper.

Easton, D. 1962. "The Current Meaning of 'Behavioralism' in Political Science." Monograph. *Annals of the American Academy of Political and Social Science,* 1–25.

Easton, D. 1969. "The New Revolution in Political Science." *American Political Science Review* 60: 1051–61.

Easton, D. 1981a. *The Political System.* New York: Knopf. (Originally published in 1953.)

Easton, D. 1981b. *A Framework for Political Analysis.* Chicago: University of Chicago Press. (Originally published in 1965.)

Easton, D. 1981c. "The Political System Besieged by the State." *Political Theory* 9: 303–25.

Easton, D. 1990. *The Analysis of Political Structure*. New York: Routledge.

Eckstein, H. 1988. "A Culturalist Theory of Political Change." *American Political Science Review* 82: 789–804.

Elster, J. 1989. *Solomonic Judgments: Studies in the Limitation of Rationality*. New York: Cambridge University Press.

Elster, J., ed. 1986. *Rational Choice*. New York: New York University Press.

Fainsod, M. 1940. "Some Reflections on the Nature of the Regulatory Process." In *Public Policy*. Cambridge, MA: Harvard University Press.

Fishkin, J. S. 1982. *The Limits of Obligation*. New Haven: Yale University Press.

Fleishman, Joel L. 1990. "A New Framework for Integrating Policy Analysis and Public Management." In *Divided Knowledge*, ed. David Easton and Corinne Schelling. Beverly Hills, CA: Sage.

Frolich, N., and Oppenheimer, J. A. 1982. *Modern Political Economy*. Englewood Cliffs, NJ: Prentice-Hall.

Hanson, N. R. 1969. *Perception and Discovery*. San Francisco: Freeman Cooper.

Herring, P. 1929. *Group Representation before Congress*. Baltimore, MD: Johns Hopkins University Press.

Jarvie, I. C. 1984. *Rationality and Relativism*. London: Routledge and Kegan Paul.

Kramer, G. H., and Hertzberg, J. 1975. "Formal Theory." In *Handbook of Political Science*, ed. F. I. Greenstein and N. W. Polsby, vol. 3, chap. 7. Reading, MA: Addison-Wesley.

Kuhn, T. 1962. *The Structure of Scientific Revolutions*. Chicago: University of Chicago Press.

Lakatos, I., and Musgrave, A. 1970. *Criticism and the Growth of Knowledge*. Cambridge: Cambridge University Press.

Lehrer, K., and Wagner, C. 1981. *Rational Consensus in Science and Society*. Dordrecht, Holland: Reidel.

Mansbridge, J. J., ed. 1990. *Beyond Self-Interest*. Chicago: University of Chicago Press.

March, J. G., and Olsen, J. P. 1989. *Rediscovering Institutions: The Organizational Basis of Politics*. New York: The Free Press.

Monroe, K. 1983. *Presidential Popularity and the Economy*. New York: Praeger.

Ollman, B., and Vernoff, E. 1982. *The Left Academy: Marxist Scholarship on American Campuses*. New York: McGraw-Hill.

Poulantzas, N. 1973. *Political Power and Social Classes*. London: New Left Books: Sheed and Ward.

Quattrone, G. A., and Tversky, A. 1988. "Contrasting Rational and Psychological Analysis of Political Choice." *American Political Science Review* 82: 719–36.

Rawls, J. 1971. *A Theory of Justice*. Cambridge, MA: Harvard University Press.

Riker, W. H., and Ordeshook, P. C. 1973. *An Introduction to Positive Theory*. Englewood Cliffs, NJ: Prentice-Hall.

Shapere, D. 1974. "Discovery, Rationality and Progress in Science." In *PSA 1972: Proceedings of 1972 Biennial Meetings of Philosophy of Science Association*, ed. K. Schaffner and P. Cohen, pp. 407–19. Dordrecht, Holland: Reidel.

Suppe, F. 1977. *The Structure of Scientific Theories*. Urbana: University of Illinois Press.

Taylor, M. 1975. "The Theory of Collective Choice." In *Handbook of Political Science,* ed. F. I. Greenstein and N. W. Polsby, vol. 3, pp. 413–18. Reading, MA: Addison-Wesley.

Toulmin, S. 1972. *Human Understanding.* Princeton, NJ: Princeton University Press.

Truman, D. 1951. *The Governmental Process.* New York: Knopf.

Political Scientists, Disenchanted Realists, and Disappearing Democrats

Raymond Seidelman

For the greater part of its history, American political science has been tied to its political sibling, American reform liberalism. This tether has provided the discipline with a strong while often troublesome identity. At the same time, the discipline's efficacy has sometimes suffered the consequences of liberalism's fate in the polity at large.

The story I want to tell here is about the relatively recent demise of that relationship in the postbehavioral era, one prompted by the decline of liberal politics since the late 1960s and exacerbated by the conservative political climate of the Reagan/Bush years of the 1980s. My remarks will be confined to the discipline's core, the study of American politics, and it will strongly reenforce the view that political science has, at last, departed from its past into a multiplicity of directions. Mine is a self-consciously critical perspective on our discipline today, as it is designed to highlight the features of our present postbehavioral condition that supply both continuities and breaks with the political science past.

In what follows, I will briefly trace the origins and recent history of political science as a science *of* and *for* American reform politics. By the late 1960s, that sort of science was in trouble, for it had largely failed to account for the conflicts then occurring in the polity. What remained of it took a threefold course in the last two decades. First, a reform science of politics lived on as a species of organizational revolt, better known as the Caucus for a New Political Science. Second, reform political science moved beyond considerations of power and participation in American politics through the growth of the subfield of academic political theory. And third, reform political science has moved beyond its own liberalism by employing tried-and-true

Previously unpublished essay. This work was first delivered as a lecture at the University of Tulsa's "Symposium on the History of the Social Sciences" in October, 1987. Thanks to Eldon Eisenach and Michael Mosher of the University of Tulsa and James Farr of the University of Minnesota for helping it to become something more.

approaches to contradict the very hopes and identities of its academic forebears.

Political Science and Political Identity

Until the middle of this century, organized political science grew with the
premise and expectation that it would position itself above the arcane provincialism of the two dominant American political traditions. Like other Progressives whose company they kept, political scientists first opposed what might
be called the "institutionalist" tradition. From the Federalists onwards, this
"first" tradition featured fear of majoritarian government and created a political order where power was balanced against power, ambition against ambition, interest against interest, and center against periphery. Without human
agency, constitutional structure imposed an impersonal, mechanical harmony.
For political scientists at the turn of the century, the result was a polity sorely
in need of institutional modernization and reconstruction. Not only were the
knowledgeable and the altruistic probably excluded from political power, but
legitimacy and authority were denied to a potentially benign and positive
state. In the proper context, a strong state, backed by responsible democratic
majorities, could be formed so that the excesses of a tumultuous modernity
could be tamed and shaped.

Arrayed not only against the institutionalist tradition, political scientists
also lamented the preeminence of its opposite, the "radical democratic,"
"second" political tradition. From Paine to the Populists, radical democrats
inveighed against strong and centralized state power as a threat to majoritarian
democracy and local community. Radical democrats appealed for a local,
popularly controlled, nonbureaucratic order within a personal, egalitarian,
and virtuous political culture. For political scientists, radical democrats
thereby immersed themselves in a fruitless struggle to stop the locomotive of
modern history. As America now spanned a continent, radical democrats
persisted in trying to reconstruct face to face communities in hopeless circumstances (Wiebe 1967).

In rejecting these two traditions, political scientists sought to create a
reformist, statist, and democratic "third tradition," resting heavily on the
increased authority of political and social sciences themselves. Through their
studies and public activities, political science founders and most of the
discipline's prominent leaders sought to close the gap between the uncontrolled pace of change and the persistence of two political traditions rooted in
the concerns of the eighteenth century. Firm admirers of political power
exercised by expert public bureaucracies and confident about the potential
common sense of properly educated public opinion, political scientists began
with the notion that scientific language was not just an academic discourse but

a political one. Walter Lippmann (1961) perhaps best captured this complementarity of science and politics when he said: "Science . . . is the un-
frightened, masterful and humble approach to reality—the needs of our nature
and the possibilities of the world. The scientific spirit is the discipline of
democracy, the escape from drift, the outlook of free men. Its direction is to
distinguish fact from fancy, its enthusiasm is for the possible, its promise is
the shaping of fact to a chastened and honest dream." If nothing else, here is a
distinctively American definition of the scientific ideal. While critical of
institutionalism and radical democracy, leading political scientists of the early
generations based their claims on the expectation that "scientifically
grounded" liberal politics could find deep roots in the American terrain, even
among contemporary elites and publics who thought and acted otherwise.
Perhaps that is why the definitions of science offered by scholars like Lester
Ward, Arthur Bentley, Woodrow Wilson, Frank Goodnow, or Charles Merriam sound remarkably vague by contemporary standards. The use of the
word "science" was not much more or less than the assertion that human
institutions, and especially American ones, were not unchangeable. Neither
the mechanics of institutionalists nor the fears of radical democrats were
really necessary. Skeptical about all divinely ordained ethics and static
doctrines of authority, political scientists were sure that American state power
could be constructed on the basis of democratic processes and informed
leaders and citizens.

With a number of exceptions, this was nonetheless the dominant view of
leading political scientists between 1885 and 1940. Lester Ward, Woodrow
Wilson, Charles Beard, and Arthur Bentley were certainly of this view, and
so, too, were Charles Merriam and Harold Lasswell in the 1920s and 1930s.
These are disciplinary leaders who created political meaning and a national
context for the scholarly enterprise of political science. Whatever their
differences, their idea of political science depended for its authority on the
vindication of reform claims and expectations in the American polity. Political
science would enter democratic politics not just as an academic field but as a
part of an entirely new tradition of political thinking and of counsel to the
democratic state.

That peculiar kind of partisanship even influenced the professionalization
that attended the rise of political science. Under Charles Merriam's leadership
at the University of Chicago, political science professionalization achieved an
inherently political dynamic. In Merriam's own words (1939), "the new scientific orientation, the new drive to remake the world in creative fashion, may
rest upon the assumption of faith in the common possibilities of common
humanity, . . . great human values so precious to the spirit of man are recognized and placed in a more realistic setting than ever before."

With the identity of an earlier political science, bound as Merriam's to the development of new political sensibilities in the polity itself, it is worth asking how well these expectations were met. Generally, the publics designated by reform political scientists failed to live up to their billing. As time progressed, each political science generation began to limit the range of their reform expectations for the state and democratic publics alike. Reliance on ever narrower circles of political leaders and publics grew to the point where the once broad audience of reform political science dwindled. In our own postbehavioral existence, it could be said that the audience has been reduced to colleagues and students.

Take, for instance, the proposal of Lester Frank Ward in the 1890s for a "populist sociocracy," a bureaucracy of common origins but of scientific sophistication and learning. Ward's positive science of society was self-consciously designed to provide intellectual foundations for the quite broad labor and agrarian radicalism of the 1880s and 1890s. "No one," Ward (1893) argued, "is more anxious to throttle the money power than I am." His bitter criticisms of social Darwinism and competitive capitalism were coupled with calls for a "dynamic and applied sociology and political science" leading to "controlled evolution." The horrors of American industrialization, thought Ward, had spawned a "great movement in history," naturally characterized by "strong emotion" and not always by reason. But the movement's proper object was to "checkmate the principle of competition as it manifests itself in society."

Contrast the breadth and nature of Ward's intended audience with that of Harold Lasswell, who argued forty years later that "the discovery of truth is an object of specialized research, it is no monopoly of people as people, and of the ruler as ruler" (Lasswell 1930). Or compare Arthur Bentley's call for a "middle-class counterrevolution" against the powers of trusts and corporations, an appeal directly linked to his call to study processes of government, to David Truman's 1968 warning that "if the preoccupations that in large part define a discipline are being set by the problems of public policy, then in some measure they are being set by the problems that confront the discipline as an intellectual enterprise" (Truman 1968).

The growing cleavage between professional work and political reform was accompanied by the sense that hopes for the third tradition came not from democratic publics but elites who could serve as reform vanguards in the public's absence. In his classic study of Congress, Woodrow Wilson was bold and prescient enough to urge that Congress be reformed from the outside, through the growth of "a responsible two party system" and new forms of organized popular influence over elites (Wilson 1885). Yet by Lasswell's time, political and social scientists themselves were designated as "democratic guardians," not the people acting in their collective capacity (Lasswell 1941). The classic work of pluralist political science, penned by Robert Dahl, described a chaotic policy universe infused with direction and purpose not by pluralist groups but by New Haven's chief executive, the talented Mayor Lee (Dahl 1961).

My point is that the democratic reform tradition in political science, once so broad in its expectations about the relationship between good political science and the emergence of liberal publics, gradually began to have few constituencies outside itself. This was hardly intended and was often the fruit of firsthand experience or glum research findings disconfirming once optimistic outlooks. Designated reform publics have simply refused to heed the appeals of political scientists, contradicting the "realistic" scientific expectations of their would-be guides out of the institutionalist and radical democratic dilemma.

At one level, reform political science has always possessed a kind of fated Enlightenment optimism about the receptivity of publics and elites alike to the "realistic" findings and suggestions of reform political science. Yet underneath the optimism there is a long history of disenchantment, as realistic science meets incorrigible realities. A favorite of early reform political scientists, for example, was the desire to separate politics from administration so that each could act in their proper spheres. But politics and administration, though formally separated, have had the uncanny tendency to intertwine once again. Pluralist theory promised democracy and stability, until it was discovered in the 1960s that many groups disputed the rules and the limited version of democracy pluralists described and prescribed. For seventy years, scholarship was devoted to the idea of "responsible parties," until it has finally been admitted that this is probably the feature of American political parties that one could least expect. And there are numerous studies in the reformist vein that end with calls for a "strong presidency," until the president turns out to be Johnson, Nixon, or Ollie North's boss. All of the above proposals only make scientific sense insofar as one accepts the notion that political science's primary identity must be vindicated by changing realities to match research agendas, not the other way around.

The Eclipse of Reform Science

It should be clear by now that I am arguing that the connections political science has tried to forge with reform liberalism in the polity have explained, legitimated, and provided its central identity for much of its history. Yet these connections have been far from fruitful. The reasons why are numerous, and they are perhaps instructive as well for those who try to continue this tradition in the contemporary, postbehavioral discipline.

The first reason is that the languages of political science in American politics haven't, couldn't, and probably shouldn't achieve anything like the authority other scientific languages have compiled in the transformation of nature or the organization and distribution of commodities in the corporate economy. Early political scientists liked to borrow from what they thought were the modernist methods and outlooks of the natural sciences when they thought about American politics. Still others, such as Merriam and Lasswell, liked to be thought of as political doctors attending to a weak but potentially curable patient.

Yet the subjects and objects of political science research could and would not be manipulated as easily as the Colorado River or numbers in a computer model. Unlike matter in a petri dish, Franklin Roosevelt used Charles Merriam's services as a technical adviser without subjecting himself to Merriam's doctoring. Similarly, Lester Ward's sincere efforts to shape the populist movement and channel its antiscientific enthusiasm into sociocracy seriously mistook the nature of the movement. Populists just weren't interested in sociocracy. It may be that American politics and political language are just too protean to be reduced to scientific discourse and action.

Second, their proclamations about "realism" aside, reform political scientists often wound up as political neophytes who simply misunderstood the histories and needs of the very publics that they tried to influence. For example, if there was more space, we could compose a list of the reasons why political scientists thought that the rise of the American state and the private corporation was entirely compatible with liberal democracy. We could also compose another list of the procedural reforms that were supposed to produce democratic accountability in the new hierarchies. Then we could assemble a bibliography of more recent political science studies that show why, despite the reforms, political accountability remained elusive and popular support for strong bureaucracies remained quite marginal. Even in the face of study after study that showed how American bureaucracies were captured by the very clienteles they were supposed to regulate, the utopia of the responsible and accountable bureaucracy lived on.

Third, reform political science was stymied by one of its own creations—the growth of the profession itself. The early leaders and founders of the discipline had fewer problems doing research, writing books, and gaining access to public life than their successors (Crick 1959; Somit and Tanenhaus 1967). But by hitching their star to disciplinary growth and specialization, to sophisticated methods and technologies to study political life, and by succeeding in their efforts to expand the new discipline into new graduate curricula, reform political scientists began to encounter a tougher time implanting their vision on an increasingly complex discipline. If there is anything that approximates a historical "law" in the discipline's history, it is the causal relationship between the discipline's leaders' perceptions that political science was not getting its message across and the call for the increased professionalization of the discipline itself in order to solve the problem. Even as the political claims were not realized, the professionalization once proposed as an antidote itself became a symptom.

Behavioral Interlude and Postbehavioral Impasse

To many who made the second behavioral revolution and who wrote about it, the kind of political science that emerged in the 1950s and 1960s was the crowning achievement of the discipline's history (Somit and Tanenhaus 1967). Yet from another perspective, behavioralism represents something of a distinct break from the discipline's reform political identity. Somewhere in the 1950s, reform political science became an undercurrent and behavioralism the mainstream. Several phenomena explain this development.

John Gunnell has written of the postwar behavioral revolution as a defensive response to the onslaught on reform political science launched from the Right by Leo Strauss and his followers and from the Left by the Frankfurt school (see Gunnell's essay in this volume). While reform political science and political theory had been seen as two sides of the same liberal coin throughout much of the discipline's pre–World War II history, the attack by the émigrés on liberalism hit directly at the old philosophical core of third-tradition political science. While reform political scientists had seen their liberalism in obvious and self-evident opposition to totalitarianism, their new detractors saw political science with its relativism and scientism as complicit in its rise.

The behavioral mood may be assessed as an effort to outtheorize the new challenges, but it came at great cost to reform political science. In works such as those of Heinz Eulau and David Easton, the philosophical defense of political science shifted away from a defense of the reform vocation into a defense of science, pure and simple. Critical analyses of the polity's ills gave way to methodologically sophisticated efforts to define democracy as if it was already completed in the American polity (Easton 1953; Eulau 1963).

Behavioralism might also be seen as a recognition that reform liberalism was just not all that strong in the polity itself. The qualities of quietism, complacency, and scientism later pinned on behavioral political science by its critics also reflected the disappearance of reform constituencies in the Eisenhower years. Cold War anticommunism, the fear and loathing of mass society, the critique of ideology, and the rise of pluralist theory were as much a part of the general political discourse of the 1950s as they were themes of political science itself (Connolly 1969; Green and Levinson 1970).

Finally, there is the phenomenon of yet more increased professionalization. Each succeeding generation of political scientists had criticized the preceding one for simplistic methods and premature and excessive political advocacy. Merriam had done this in *New Aspects of Politics* (1925). By the time David Easton wrote *The Political System* (1953), the scientization of political science had reached the point where it denied rather than reasserted the reform political science tradition. Behavioral scientists of the 1950s and 1960s might have been the first generation of social scientists to consider democratic publics and American institutions as mere objects of inquiry rather than as subjects of political change (Easton 1953; Poschman 1982).

Postbehavioralism and the Reform Tradition Today: The Case of the Disappearing Democracy

What, then, of the legacy of the behavioral movement in the last twenty years or so, particularly its connections with politics? Like past turnarounds in the history of political science, the postbehavioral period also began with time-honored *mea culpa* about its excessive distance from the polity and reform. Some of the reformers were those who had themselves led the behavioral revolution, such as David Easton and his 1969 appeal for a "new revolution in political science." Now, as before, the discipline sought to draw itself more closely to politics, to become more truly professional, and to revive the reform tradition by modernizing it in the light of new political conditions and the fact of disciplinary growth. And, in repetition of the past, the impetus to return to founding principles came from outside the discipline, from the very visible reality of a polity and state whose nature and trajectory could not be understood or predicted by behavioral methods or pluralist theory. Imagistically, when Dahl's *Who Governs?* and Richard Neustadt's *Presidential Power* encountered the Black Panthers and Richard Nixon's Watergate Plumbers, something in behavioral political science had to give.

Yet unlike previous refoundations in political science, the initial phase of postbehavioral ferment did not and has not achieved its political, professional, or reformist goals. In the aftermath of the sixties, there has been no Woodrow Wilson, no Progressive movement, no Charles Merriam, and no New Deal, nor even V. O. Key and rational voters, to carry the torch forward and to unify the discipline behind a common scientific and political reform agenda. Parts of political science have undeniable relevance to existential politics. Rational-choice theory and public policy are notable in this regard, but, generally speaking, these subfields cannot really be considered part of the reform political science legacy. The former seems closely tied to the rise of economic discourse in the age of Reagan, and the latter's ambitions are much more limited to the kind of technical claims that reform political scientists always tried to encapsulate within a larger political vision. Overall, the proliferation of subfields and their attendant and sometimes impenetrable languages are notable consequences of refoundation. Another is the rise of academic subcultures that, while not behavioralist, eschew public discourse nonetheless.

The Caucus for a New Political Science

What, then, became of the reform tradition in political science? One way of charting an answer to this question is to look at what became of the most outspoken organizational form of that tradition, the Caucus for a New Political Science.

Formed at the 1967 APSA meetings, the caucus's bylaws were quite forthright in their call for "a new concern in the Association for our great social crisis." The caucus would try to "stimulate research in areas of political science that are of crucial importance and have thus far been ignored" (Lowi 1973).

From its inception, the CNPS made considerable headway within the profession. After 1969, the APSA's procedures were democratized to a degree, and some elections to APSA leadership positions were contested. Annual panels devoted to critical research were established, as was a new journal, *Politics and Society,* and, much later, *New Political Science.*

Within these terms, the caucus has been a limited success. But its achievements only highlight the inherent problems in postbehavioral reform political science. Somewhere along the line, inclusion of new research and people in the APSA's convention agenda displaced or even replaced reform of the discipline's *public* role; reform politics became *disciplinary* reform politics, and the passion and power plays of real politics raged within the confines of the discipline as if the profession was the polity itself. Debate about the Vietnam War, race, class and gender inequality, and other matters were converted into debates about methods of study, promotions, hirings, and firings. In the words of one well-known caucus member, the "Caucus for a New Political Science was converted into the Caucus for a New Political Science Association" (Lowi 1973).

In the caucus, the nexus of critical political science with the prescribed rules of university success and disciplinary professionalism was never questioned. The whole panoply of ranks, Ph.D.'s, specialized research, journal articles, and arcane vocabulary was accepted. What was demanded—and largely achieved—was acceptance *into* the profession, not a rethinking of the conditions under which intellectual life was defined and sustained. Thus, absent from the caucus's efforts was the essential component of past efforts at political science refoundation. Nowhere was a reform public addressed; seldom, if at all, were bridges built between intellectual inquiry and ongoing movement politics. Instead, the caucus eschewed such connections between a "new" political science and reform movements in the polity. The "reform public" became other colleagues in the profession, and critiques became an effort to educate and mobilize other professionals.

As Alan Wolfe noted at the time (1971), those "who formed the Caucus cut themselves adrift from the dynamics of political change in America and thereby lost touch with reality." In postbehavioral political science, reform liberalism became a rather odd species of internal dissent, dedicated to self-reflection about theories and methods generated within its own ranks. In a way, such consequences are only the logical culmination of past tendencies to equate improvement of the profession with more professionalization—in Yogi Berra's terms, déjà vu all over again. Nor were political scientists alone in their penchant to equate organizational revolt with new public postures. Russell Jacoby (1987) has argued recently that public intellectuals concerned with the enrichment of the democratic debate are in very short supply across the political spectrum, and most notably on the Left.

In an earlier time, German Social Democrats and Italian Communists used to refer to the "long march through institutions" as a way of describing their political strategy. In postbehavioral political science, this strategy has been implemented in the form of the caucus. Unfortunately for the dissenters, the institutions have emerged victorious.

A Liberalism beyond Politics

Besides the caucus, much of contemporary political theory inherited the impulses and identity of reform political science. Although political theorists have waged the most concerted attack on the positivist philosophy of science in behavioral political science, the political theory subfield was undeniably born within the political science discipline. The material and bureaucratic conditions under which political theory is today produced and taught is thus closely allied with the fate of political science and its existence in universities and colleges (Gunnell 1983).

Just as much, if not more, than Ward, Wilson, Beard, and Merriam, political theorists today address what are taken to be public concerns. Like these political science predecessors, political theorists of the reform variety take seriously the revival of an active citizenry. Many write books and articles that are designed, somehow, to catalyze citizens to thought, action, and reconstitution of the terms of American public life. These are of course noble goals, befitting the historical traditions of the discipline and of American public intellectuals. Yet perhaps political theory bears more of the burdens of its disciplinary origins and development than its critique of behavioral political science might otherwise suggest.

Consider as an example of this dilemma Benjamin Barber's *Strong Democracy: Participatory Politics for a New Age* (1984). Barber's work merits consideration because it is one of the most publicized recent efforts of a political theorist to regenerate public discourse. The book is about liberalism (what he calls "thin democracy") and his alternative, "strong democracy." Thin democracy, Barber argues, does not capture the protean quality of human needs, particularly the need for communal involvement in public life. This is a time-honored critique of liberalism that may indeed require constant revival in the present American context. Since the publication of this book, Barber has become something of a public intellectual himself and certainly cannot be charged with shutting himself up in the academy.

Yet while Barber's book begins with much talk about the alienation of people from public life and the crisis of politics in the West, there is hardly a word in the entire treatise about any historical or contemporary practice, event, or behavior. There is virtually no discussion of how thin democracy as a kind of power relationship grew, what power relations it sustains, and how it effects contemporary practices. Liberalism and capitalism, strong and thin democracy, appear not as existential realities embodied in institutions, personal lives, social and political movements, or power relationships within which many are born and live. The emergence and existence of thin democracy is not really discussed; its advocates appear to be nothing more than poor political theorists with nothing to lose but their chains of weak arguments. The converse, strong democracy, assumes a curiously abstract nature as a disembodied ideal or value to which everyone should aspire. In passages like the following, Barber (1984) reveals that not much has changed about the *expectations* of reform political science:

> How then can we expect either the self-interested or the apathetic to identify with a program of participation and civic renewal in which their most immediate interests would be ignored . . . ? Through persuasion, through the self-education yielded by democratic participation itself, and through the logic of political priority which demonstrates that even in a privatistic politics dominated by economic interests, it is only the autonomy of politics and rights of citizens that give modern men and women the real power to shape their lives. (p. 265)

There is a peculiar kind of abstraction here that would appear to typify the dilemma of postbehavioral democratic political theory. Many would hope, with Barber, that the problem of self-interest in American politics could be solved in the way he prescribes. Yet it might be doubted that the kind of organized self-interest that gave us supply-side economics, Iran-Contra, and the Savings and Loan imbroglio could be wished away by such arguments. While a passage such as the one above might be convincing within the context of academic political theory, it neglects the fact that academic political theory simply does not possess the authority or the audience to justify such hopes and expectations. Like reform political scientists before him, Barber brings to his work forthright political intentions and objects. Yet partly because of the failures of reform political scientists that have been described, Barber's work assumes the intellectual authority that is in fact absent from our current politics and lacking for the reform wing of our discipline. The dilemma is only reenforced by Barber's naïveté about the complex of powerful institutions, ideas, and people that uphold "thin democracy." In the end, discussion of strong democracy appears merely as just another academic debate. Yet by the very nature and intention of Barber's argument, it cannot be.

A Politics beyond Liberalism: The Critical Pessimism of Walter Dean Burnham

There is yet a third course that reform political science has taken in the postbehavioral era, and it is best represented by the intellectual adventure of Walter Dean Burnham. Here is a scholar whose career begins with the most time-honored preoccupations of reform political science, including the belief that political science could and should help to keep alive the potential for democratic change through voting and elections. Yet such concerns lead to the kind of despair that would have surely disappointed his forebears.

In his now classic *Critical Elections and the Mainsprings of American Politics* (1970), Burnham argued that the American party system generally refracted and even repressed fundamental social conflicts and divisions in most elections. Yet occasionally and under unusual conditions, "critical" elections occurred that restored a rather tenuous balance between voting and the exercise of political power. Their periodic occurrence, as in 1896 and 1932, indicated that there were important if spasmodic episodes of democracy and that they could occur again.

Without critical elections, democratic politics itself was deemed all but impossible, as political and economic elites became ever more insulated from elections as checks on their power. The key, Burnham argued, was strong political parties. Without them, critical elections were impossible, and the civic consciousness and dispositions that were the fabric of democratic culture would erode. In its place a party of nonvoters grew, and with it a citizenry without the possibility of politics and vulnerable to the hegemony of ever more monolithic cultural, economic, and political institutions.

Its tone critical but ultimately hopeful, its methods rigorous and its prose readable, its conclusions tentative but strong enough to provoke debate with a varied lot of defenders of the U.S. party system, *Critical Elections* was in many ways the epitome of a reform political science study. Yet, reflective of the fate of this brand of postbehavioral political science, by the 1980s faith in the future had expired.

In the aftermath of the 1980 and 1984 elections, Burnham began to argue that the political system was now incapable of undergoing a critical "realignment," with all its attendant democratic possibilities. American electoral politics was, in fact, dealigning, with even sharper declines in voter turnout and accompanying decay in partisan ties and linkages amongst the mass electorate. In conjunction with defeat in Vietnam, economic decline, and cultural and social turmoil, partisan dealignment had catalyzed the formation of a sharp ideological Right intent on a "one-sided declaration of class war on most of the American people." Reform political science's traditional hopes are shattered with Burnham's (1982) simple statement that "you cannot get there from here in American politics if the direction is leftward, since the basis for a collective energizing left consciousness and will does not exist in this country. But you can if you are headed to the right."

What is one to make of all this? All of the former reform actors seem to be on Burnham's stage—the electorate, the political parties, the political actors bent on change—but they are no longer performing the old roles written for them by reform political science. Insofar as postbehavioral reformers share the traditional concerns and questions of political science, they can no longer sustain its politics. Democratic mass publics have become the atomized nonvoters of Burnham's imploding electoral universe. The positive democratic state has become the right-wing Leviathan, and American "uniqueness," once the distinctive characteristic that made American liberalism possible, is now notable for its inability to resolve social tensions democratically.

The significant point is this: the very prominent work of Walter Dean Burnham suggests that reform political science, once the core identity of the discipline, is now very near at an end.

Conclusions

Academic disciplines, like any other institutions, may thrive long after their founding identities have been forgotten, discarded, transcended, or simply altered. If this argument has any validity, postbehavioral political science may be experiencing just such a fate. In its weakened and fragmented contemporary form, the residues of reform political science seem either irrelevant, quaint, despairing, or hopelessly out of touch with broader intellectual developments in American letters and the political climate in American society.

Meanwhile, the major trends in postbehavioral political science have developed in other and varying directions. Rational-choice theory, the new institutionalism, and other schools of thought contend or sometimes just grow without contention. Given what I have argued about reform political science, all this may not be so tragic. If the core identity of political science at its origins led to disenchantment, utopianism, or poor science, lamentations about its passing may be more crocodile tears.

Yet, founding identities are surpassed and displaced at considerable cost. The case of reform political science is no exception. Just like the political liberalism to which it was so attached, reform political science had its nobler themes and moments. Among them was its penchant for criticism, its search for political clarity, and its ambition to have a transformative public role. At the very least, reform political science took the time to justify its own historical project. Can the same be said of the postbehavioral present?

REFERENCES

Barber, Benjamin. 1984. *Strong Democracy: Participatory Politics for a New Age.* Berkeley: University of California Press.

Burnham, Walter Dean. 1970. *Critical Elections and the Mainsprings of American Politics.* New York: W. W. Norton and Co.

———. 1982. "The Eclipse of the Democratic Party." *Democracy* 2:7–17.

Connolly, William E., ed. 1969. *The Bias of Pluralism.* New York: Atherton Press.

Crick, Bernard. 1959. *The American Science of Politics: Its Origins and Conditions.* Berkeley: University of California Press.

Dahl, Robert A. 1961. *Who Governs?* New Haven, CT: Yale University Press.

Easton, David. 1953. *The Political System: An Inquiry into the State of Political Science.* Chicago: University of Chicago Press.

———. 1969. "The New Revolution in Political Science." *American Political Science Review* 63:1051–61.

Eulau, Heinz. 1963. *The Behavioral Persuasion in Political Science.* New York: Random House.

Furner, Mary O. 1975. *Advocacy and Objectivity.* Lexington: University of Kentucky Press.

Green, Philip, and Sanford Levinson, eds. 1970. *Power and Community: Dissenting Essays in Political Science.* New York: Pantheon.

Gunnell, John G. 1983. "Political Theory: The Evolution of a Subfield," in *Political Science: The State of the Discipline,* ed. Ada Finifter. Washington, DC: American Political Science Association.

———. 1988. "American Political Science, Liberalism and the Invention of Political Theory." *American Political Science Review* 82:71–87.

Haskell, Thomas L. 1977. *The Emergence of Professional Social Science.* Urbana: University of Illinois Press.

Huntington, Samuel P. 1981. *American Politics: The Promise of Disharmony.* Cambridge, MA: Harvard University Press.

Jacoby, Russell. 1987. *The Last Intellectuals: American Culture in the Age of Academe.* New York: Basic Books.

Lasswell, Harold D. 1941. *Democracy through Public Opinion.* New York: Bantam Publishing.

———. 1930. *Psychopathology and Politics.* New York: Viking Press.

Lippmann, Walter. 1961. *Drift and Mastery: An Attempt to Diagnose the Current Unrest.* Englewood Cliffs, NJ: Prentice Hall.

Lowi, Theodore J. 1973. "The Politicization of Political Science." *American Politics Quarterly* 1:43–71.

Merriam, Charles E. 1925. *New Aspects of Politics*. Chicago: University of Chicago Press. (An excerpt is reprinted in this volume.)

———. 1939. *Prologue to Politics*. Chicago: University of Chicago Press.

Neustadt, Richard E. 1976. *Presidential Power*. New York: John Wiley.

Poschman, Gene. 1982. "Emerging American Social Science and Political Relevance: Extractions from a Less than Classic American Literature." Paper delivered at the 1982 American Political Science Association convention, Denver, CO.

Ricci, David M. 1984. *The Tragedy of Political Science: Politics, Scholarship and Democracy*. New Haven, CT: Yale University Press.

Seidelman, Raymond, with the assistance of Edward J. Harpham. 1985. *Disenchanted Realists; Political Science and the American Crisis, 1884–1984*. Albany: State University of New York Press.

Somit, Albert, and Joseph Tanenhaus. 1967. *The Development of Political Science: From Burgess to Behavioralism*. Boston: Allyn and Bacon.

Truman, David B. 1968. "The Social Sciences: Maturity, Relevance and the Problem of Training." In *Political Science and Public Policy,* ed. Austin Ranney. Chicago: University of Chicago Press.

Ward, Lester Frank. 1893. *Psychic Factors in Civilization*. Boston: Ginn and Co.

White, Morton. 1972. *Science and Sentiment in American Thought*. New York: Oxford University Press.

Wiebe, Robert H. 1967. *The Search for Order*. New York: Hill and Wang.

Wilson, Woodrow. 1885. *Congressional Government: A Study in American Politics*. Boston: Houghton Mifflin.

Wolfe, Alan. 1971. "Unthinking about the Thinkable: Reflections on the Failure of the Caucus for a New Political Science." *Politics and Society* 1:398–406.

Another State of Mind

Charles E. Lindblom

About liberal democracy, V. O. Key, Jr., wrote: "Political parties are basic institutions for the translation of mass preferences into public policy" (1967, p. 432). He did not write that they obstruct the translation of mass preferences into public policy. Although his formulation may be the correct one, it is not justified by any evidence and argument.

Karl Deutsch wrote that "politics has the function of coordinating the learning processes of the whole society" (1980, p. 19). He did not say "indoctrinating"—his was the kinder word "learning." Nor did he write "obstruct" or "distort" the learning processes; his word was "coordinate." How does he know his words are more accurate than these alternatives? Again, his statement is introduced as a preface to subsequent analysis, all of which simply assumes it to be true.

David Easton and Robert Hess (1962, p. 233) wrote—and Richard E. Dawson and Kenneth Prewitt (1969, p. 45n) wrote that they agree—that a political community is "a group of persons who seek to solve their problems in common through a shared political structure." They did not write that the phenomenon they sought to describe was that of prevailing over adversaries— their phrase was the more benign "solve their problems *in common*." Again, how do they know that their formulation is more accurate than the alternatives they did not choose? They do not say.

Let me interrupt this illustrative procession of witnesses, though I shall resume it shortly with younger authors. My concern is that when we, political scientists, make gratuitous claims like these, we leave mainstream American political science vulnerable—vulnerable to the charge from radical political science that we have without evidence fallen into a complacent view of the liberal democratic political process, government, and state and that we do not even bother to debate it.[1] It is, I think, largely an American problem. Euro-

Presidential Address, American Political Science Association, 1981. Reprinted in a somewhat shortened version from *American Political Science Review* 76 (1982): 9–21.

1. These vulnerable views can be and are sometimes attacked from within a broad mainline tradition, going back to Madison in the *Federalist Papers* and even earlier. My primary interest is

pean political theory has in recent years been greatly reconstructed by the incorporation of much radical thought. If these European developments can be taken as leading, American thought is a decade or two behind.

Two Views of Liberal Democracy

To see whether there is any merit to so bruising a charge, let me first lay out—very briefly because it is familiar—the simplest elements of the democratic political system and state as they have often appeared since World War II in respectable circles in much of theoretically oriented American political science.[2] I shall also lay out a simple synthetic dissenting view that captures much of the radical concept of the democratic state. They will be two views of what democracy is, not what it ought to be. After laying them out, I propose to appraise basic elements of the conventional view that I have chosen to discuss.

A Conventional Intellectual Tradition in American Political Science. According to views common in theoretical circles of the profession in which broad generalization is attempted—and for which I shall offer further documentation—the political system called democratic in the West is best understood as a distinctive kind of mutual-benefit society. However imperfect, it provides some degree of social order, as well as widespread benefits beyond that. In Deutsch's term, it "coordinates the learning processes." In Easton and Hess's, it attacks "problems in common." In Key's, it "translates mass preferences into public policy."

Conflict abounds, however, in this view of the democratic state, running in all directions. The state is therefore also seen as a conflict-resolving system—a theme so common as hardly to require documentation. The theme can be traced back to Hobbes and earlier; and among contemporary voices that sound it is Dahl's in the opening pages of his *Democracy in the United States* (1972). It also opens the analysis of politics in Prewitt and Verba's *Introduction to American Government* (1977).

---

in their vulnerability from any source of attack. I give special attention, however, to the radical attack for several reasons: the magnitude of the assault, the sharpness of issues posed, and a concern that radical thought is likely to be undervalued as a corrective to the problem.

2. There are, of course, other mainstream traditions. I am trying to capture an intellectual tradition in mainstream theory construction, one of recent unchallenged prominence in American political science. I think it has already lost much of its earlier vitality, for two different reasons. On the one hand, its persuasiveness has already declined among some political scientists. On the other hand, it is less vital because it is taken for granted in many circles. It remains strong, as I see it, sometimes all the stronger for being taken for granted, for therefore remaining only implicit, and for directing research attention down some avenues rather than others without explanation or justification.

The concept of the state or government as a common-benefit organization has to be reconciled with the concept of the state as conflict resolver. The reconciliation is easy. Everyone is seen as wanting a core of much the same fundamental services or benefits: law and order, national defense, and a prosperous economy, among others. Ordinarily, only secondary conflict develops within such an agreed fundamental set of desires. Class conflict is only one important conflict among many.

The specialized political machineries of these systems (elections and legislative representation, for example) are seen as necessary instruments for holding government or the state responsible to society as a whole by placing important powers in the hands of all—with some approximation to equality in the distribution of these powers. It is believed that some consequential approach to equality, even if distant, is achieved and justifies interpretation of the system as benefiting, however unequally, almost everyone.

In this conventional intellectual tradition, the disproportionate political influence or power of elites is recognized. But their disproportion does not deny any of the above characteristics of democracy; all that is required is that elites be held accountable. Some political scientists, David Truman (1959) among them, go further to make elites the guardians of democracy, on the grounds that they are more committed to it than are nonelites.

Pluralism is not a necessary feature of this picture. It is at most secondary and is absent from some versions.

A Synthesis of Dissent. An alternative view captures the most basic features of dissenting Marxist and other radical thought on liberal or bourgeois democracy. A transitional form, liberal democracy can be understood only in light of where it came from. If we cut into the historical process at a stage at which humankind has already developed a complex social structure marked by substantial specialization of function, we see that some subsets of the population at that time rule others and enjoy various advantages denied to other subsets. Once such a degree of complexity is realized, a high degree of political inequality and resultant conflict thereafter become universal historical phenomena—in all places and at all times, though less in some circumstances than in others.

There is some cohesion or cooperation, much though not all of it unintended and without self-awareness, among the advantaged on one hand and the disadvantaged on the other. Most radicals would say that this is the distribution of property rights that has for the last few centuries marked off the two loose, somewhat cohesive, aggregates. That the disadvantaged and the advantaged each cohere loosely is critical to the model, and the usual word for each of the aggregates is class. Within, between, and jointly among the advantaged and disadvantaged aggregates are conflicting subgroups. But the most critical conflict is between the two aggregates, even if it is suppressed and consequently not recognizable as a conflict by such mainstream political scientists as I am summarizing.

The liberal democratic political systems of the world have to be understood as the present institutionalized form of that struggle. Democratic institutions represent the present alignment, strengths, and formal authority of advantaged and disadvantaged groups. Democracy did not come about through any agreement between advantaged and disadvantaged groups that henceforth the political system should be operated for the benefit of all. These systems represent social machinery for converting the age-old struggle into a more peaceful one than it would otherwise often be, but not for terminating the struggle.

For the advantaged groups in these systems, the principal effort is to keep such advantages as they have, even if it has become impolite for them to say so. For the disadvantaged groups, the principal effort is to reduce the degree of inequality, or exploitation, or dominance—the dissenters do not all use the same terms. A principal weapon of the advantaged groups, which have always been more educated and have had instruments of communication available to them (ranging from the Church in times past to the mass media today), is indoctrination of the disadvantaged groups to induce them to believe in the rightness of their disadvantaged position and of the difficulty, in any case, of doing anything about it. Hence, the principal purpose of most members of the disadvantaged groups is no more than to protect such gains as are already won and to pursue others only timidly and fitfully.

It is then argued that the political systems of the West are, as a consequence, not mainly mutual-benefit or common-purpose systems. Both sides share an interest in some common purposes, such as in some degree of social order and organized economic production. But many interests are shared only in the sense that two nations at war have shared interests in methods of communication between them and in the exchange of prisoners. Their common interests are usually best understood as serving more fundamental conflicting interests. Some of the common interests of the advantaged and disadvantaged are best understood as no more than common interests in keeping the struggle from escalating.

Finally, specific mechanisms of government like mass elections and broad legislative representation are concessions (wrung from a bourgeoisie that earlier won these gains for itself) that have grown out of historical struggle. For the disadvantaged, the gains are significant. They are, however, so far from perfect instruments of popular control and political equality that they leave many opportunities for the advantaged to continue their predominance of control and other advantages. If, in the eyes of the disadvantaged, the purpose of these mechanisms is or ought to be the establishment of popular control and political equality, in the eyes of the advantaged the point of establishing them was to make no more than necessary concessions, sometimes of more apparent than genuine significance.

The relation between polity and economy is a key issue in the dissenters' model. Orthodox Marxism often tended toward a conspiratorial model of dominance by property, yet those at the frontiers of current Marxist thought have moved far from such a position. They are now exploring more carefully qualified and specific hypotheses. I attribute to contemporary radical thought a concept of the state as much more autonomous than that in traditional Marxism.

In some formulations, the state achieves autonomy because of the existence of competing capitalist fractions, to no single one of which the state is subordinate. In other formulations, the state to a degree responds to demands from the working class and is therefore not wholly subordinate to property. Or the state has to provide welfare benefits to all classes because they each provide an input necessary to the productive system. In still another formulation, the state responds to all interests within a set of constraints that protect the survival of capitalism. Some Marxists have also introduced explicit elements of pluralism into their analyses.

The dissenting view draws no great number of adherents in the American political science profession. But many of us are aware that some of our students, including many of the brightest, are exploring it independent of our tutelage. They claim to be finding intellectual nourishment in such sources as Habermas (1976), Poulantzas (1973), Miliband (1969), Offe (1976), O'Connor (1973), Lukes (1974), Mandel (1974), and Gough (1975), among others who are being widely cited in a new literature on the state. The hold of the conventional theory on political science is indicated by a striking fact that, although scholars like those just named write about politics, they come to it from sociology, philosophy, economics, and history, as well as disproportionately from European intellectual traditions to which American political science is cool. Very few come from American political science—and of this particular list, none. Radicals do not see political science as a well-designed discipline; its very definition is an obstruction, they will say, to necessary research. Our discipline itself is a formidable difficulty in the way of some of our younger colleagues.

The Nondissenting Dissenter. In their choice between these two pictures of democratic politics, a wider array of political scientists than first appears holds to the conventional one. So persuasive is the conventional picture that even some forms of dissent among political scientists do not break with it. Lowi's polemic (to use his own term) against interest-group liberalism in *The*

End of Liberalism (1979) makes no sense if the radical picture of the political system is correct. Only on the assumption that the political system might be and should be evaluated as a mutual-benefit organization, a problem-solving mechanism for the good of all, can he be indignant that it has drifted off course.

Dye and Zeigler set out to attack pluralist interpretations of democratic systems. Yet they propose an alternative in which the political system is still a mutual-benefit association whose elites "may be very 'public-regarding' and deeply concerned with the welfare of the masses" (Dye and Zeigler 1970, pp. 1–2).

Similarly, Dolbeare and Edelman, who desire in their textbook to give full hearing both to the conventional and what they call the challengers' models of the American political system, categorically declare by way of introduction that people "erect governments to maintain order, further mutual goals, and promote general well-being" (Dolbeare and Edelman 1981, p. 7).

I am suggesting that scholars of a wide range of ages, temperaments, and schools of thought are largely committed to the conventional view and give little sustained analytical attention to the radical model. My list of samples above is illustrative of the variety.

An Incomplete Breakaway. In recent decades, some significant attempts have been made by members of the conventional school to break out of its confines with frames of reference or theories that would then permit an eyes-open choice among existing or yet-to-be-developed theories. A monumental attempt of this kind—on a functional framework—has been that of Almond and Powell (1966) on foundations they attribute, in part, to Easton. Their analysis of the political process is worked out with such extraordinary care that it can accommodate both the dominant and the radical pictures.

For their discussions of democratic politics, however, they choose, without any explicit defense of their choice, the conventional view. For example, although interest aggregation might, according to their framework, largely neglect the interests of the disadvantaged, they appear to take it for granted that in democratic politics it does not. Having developed a framework that will work for either the conventional or radical view of democracy, they work it for the conventional one.

In addition, their framework seems to have been designed with an eye on variables that best fit the conventional view. For one thing, the framework is structural-functional with debt to Parsons; it therefore habitually identifies functions served for the whole society rather than some functions for the advantaged and others for the disadvantaged. Although fundamental and continuing struggle between the two groups is neither denied in the framework nor impossible to place in it, it is difficult to fit the struggle in. To fit it would require that a strained interpretation be given to such societywide functional categories as interest articulation and interest aggregation. It is possible to consider the advantaged group's interest in exploiting the disadvantaged as just another interest to be articulated and aggregated, but one cannot help wondering about the usefulness of these terms—articulation and aggregation—for describing such a situation. To make the point vividly by analogy, though with some exaggeration: if a racketeer shakes down a tradesman for monthly protection payments, we could say that in so doing he is both articulating his own interests and aggregating his and the tradesman's. But the concepts would seem strained.

Do We Know That the Dominant Model Is Superior?

At this point, the questions are: How solid, verified, or even thoughtful is the conventional tradition? Why do we think our picture is more useful for political science than the radical picture? Let us examine some of the differences between the two. I propose to do so without any appeals to the vocabulary of radical thought and without any radical methodological stances; nor shall I ascend to the philosophy of science.

Common Purposes Versus Struggle. Is it known—is it settled—that the primary motivation among leaders and ordinary citizens is the pursuit of those benefits they share in common? Clearly not. Empirical evidence does not establish even a thin case that, on this point, the conventional view is correct.

What do we actually observe when we observe political life? We observe millions of ordinary people pursuing a variety of objectives. Even to an experienced observer, it is not at all clear that certain objectives common to all occupy much of their energies. On the other hand, neither is it obvious that the various partisans cohere either deliberately, tacitly, or unintentionally into two loose coalitions, the advantaged and the disadvantaged, each pursuing distinctive conflicting objectives. In short, we actually observe forms of behavior that the dominant view wants to construe one way and the radical the other. A principal task of a scientific political science might be to research the issue. Conventional political science has no grounds for simply holding to its present view to the neglect of the radical one.

There seems to be a way to escape making such a concession to the radical model. We can argue as many do—Dolbeare and Edelman (1981) most explicitly among those cited above—that a political system, government, or state is necessary for law and order. We simply cannot imagine doing without it—all people need it whether they know it or not. Hence, it makes a certain kind of sense to say that fundamentally the state's purpose is (for the benefit of all) law and order and other necessary benefits. In an earlier analogy, however, we noted that to carry on international warfare seems to require that some system of communications between the warring nations be kept open and that they thus can be seen as joining in pursuit of that common purpose. But it would confuse our understanding of war if we called it a common-purpose activity. We would do better to see it as a struggle moderated by some common concerns. Similarly, perhaps, the democratic state is an institutionalized form of a struggle to which such necessary common purposes as observers see are secondary. Until that possibility is more carefully examined, the conventional view is not persuasive.

More important, by what logic does a purpose rather than any other important variable dictate how we should build analytic models? As a guide to what goes into models or theories, there is no logical imperative that requires that an essential social purpose must be made the centerpiece.

Perhaps we are still missing something. Perhaps the emphasis in the conventional view on certain common purposes rather than on struggle between advantaged and disadvantaged is not meant to assert or imply any *fact*, historical or contemporary. Perhaps it is only intended to lay out a fruitful strategy, thus to imply a judgment about method—that we shall get more results if we study the state in the light of certain necessary functions than if we study it as though it were an institutionalized form of a long-standing struggle. If this is so, perhaps all variants of the conventional view represent a commitment to structural-functionalism, though only a few are explicitly so labeled.

I do not want to undertake at this point a survey of the pros and cons of structural-functional analysis. But if structural-functionalism is a requirement of good social science—which is not obvious at all—note that the radical model is often put in structural-functional terms. Some advocates of the radical model subscribe to such propositions as that the state's function is to preserve the advantages of the advantaged. I take it that they mean that the state is a structure serving such a function for the ruling class, whether members of the ruling class know it or not. Similarly, many Marxist statements about the working class attribute functions to it. We do not often recognize structural-functionalism in radical thought because the functions postulated are not for the whole society but instead for either the advantaged or the disadvantaged or for an abstraction like "the development of the productive forces."

Have we any reason to assume that the nation-state society is the correct social group for which functions and structures are to be analyzed? Or that the functions explored should be stabilizing functions? Do we have any reason to say we know that structural-functional analysis is inappropriate when used to analyze the functions performed for subgroups or for social change rather than for stability? Must structural analysis be limited to its particular formulation in conventional theory?

Thus we come to the end of our first line of inquiry into analyzing the state or government as a kind of mutual-benefit organization versus analyzing it as an institutional form of struggle between advantaged and disadvantaged. If neither position is wholly satisfactory, as I believe to be the case, we have nevertheless found no solid ground for choosing the first approach over the second. The radical model begins with what may be a historical fact, a struggle, while conventional theory begins with allegations about necessity without connecting that necessity to facts about participants' behavior. There is, consequently, a slightly stronger a priori or question-begging tone to conventional than to radical thought. But our purpose is not to evaluate the relative merits of the two models but only to try to understand the grounds on which the advocates of the dominant model might be justified in holding confidently to it. So far, we have found no grounds.

Diversified Conflict: Second Line of Defense. Perhaps I am giving too much attention to the "common benefits" theme in conventional theory. A mainstream political scientist might want to play it down, arguing instead that the critical point of difference between the two views is that one asserts diversified conflict in all directions, the other asserts a more fundamental conflict between advantaged and disadvantaged, each as loosely cohesive groups.

As a defense for conventional theory, the tactic will not quite do. For one thing, as my quotations have shown, the assertion of common benefits and of their central importance to the understanding of democratic politics is hardly an only secondary feature of conventional theory.

Second, the conventional emphasis on diversified conflict to the near exclusion of attention to conflict between advantaged and disadvantaged is, I shall argue below, an intellectual habit of focusing on manifest conflict rather than an emphasis warranted by empirical comparison of the two patterns of conflict which are not equally manifest.

I do not have to show that the radical view of the pattern of conflict is correct, mainstream view wrong. All I must do is show that the mainstream view is unsubstantiated and that there is an issue between the two views that has not been carefully investigated. On whether the conflict is dichotomous or not, consider the distribution of wealth. It is not conclusive evidence that the advantaged cohere in the perpetuation of their advantages, but it is a phenomenon of such striking character as to make such an hypothesis worthy of investigation. So also are patterns in the perpetuation of educational inequality that persist despite public education and state universities. So also is the frequency with which government subsidies turn out to be for the benefit of the well-off rather than for the disadvantaged for whom they are ostensibly designed. So also are differences in teachers' treatment of children of different socioeconomic class. All of these examples, and many more easily listed, should stir our curiosity about the radical model of conflict. Proving nothing but suggesting much to which much mainstream political science has been indifferent, they undercut confidence in the conventional picture of diversified conflict.

The ordinary or daily business of politics, it might be replied, is resolution of conflicts of a highly diversified sort. What we can observe on the political agenda is diversified conflict. That, consequently, is what democratic politics is all about. What we can see is what is really happening. What we cannot see, or cannot see very clearly, we must not only doubt, but we must also entertain a strong presumption against its existence. In one formulation in the mainstream literature that caught my eye, it is said that, so long as men have liberty to express their views, conflicts will exist—as though conflict does not exist unless made so conspicuously manifest. Indeed, I think one of the misunderstandings separating mainstream and radical political science is that the one often identifies conflict with such expressions of it as liberty permits while the other is sensitive to repressed conflict.

Let me further examine this "politics is what we see" argument in defense of the conventional view of diversified conflict—in three steps.

The first possible point of vulnerability in the argument is the counter argument that what we do not see can be seen if we look harder. Radical political science often argues hypotheses about those parts of the social world, such as indoctrination, most difficult to see. It also warns us against imputing to the unseen the same characteristics as mark the seen. Some mainstream political scientists consequently allege that radicals hold a conspiracy theory of political life. Some radicals do, but that is not characteristic of radical political science. The unseen that interests them is no more conspiratorial than, and is in many ways comparable to, Smith's hidden hand, though a less benign hidden hand—perhaps a hidden fist. Their hypotheses, like earlier hypotheses about the once unseen backside of the moon, are not to be discredited solely because of formidable difficulties in proof so long as they are willing, as at least some are, to specify what phenomena they would seek to observe if they actually became observable.

The second point of vulnerability in the "politics is what we see" defense of conventional theory is the possibility that, as good scientists, we have to explain both what exists and what does not exist. Radicals believe so—that nonoccurrences require explanation. Sherlock Holmes had to explain why the dog did not bark. If people do not have liberty to express their conflicts, we must often explain why. John Gaventa, our Woodrow Wilson prizewinner for this year, says he had to turn traditional political science around—to ask why rebellion in Appalachia does not occur (1980, p. vi). That is no less a scientific question than why rebellions occur when they do. That many conflicts between advantaged and disadvantaged, which radicals think are fundamental, *do not appear* on the political agenda is a good scientific hypothesis. And if they exist and do not so appear, why they do not is a good scientific question.

The third point of vulnerability of the "politics is what we see" defense of conventional theory is that all the statement means is that "we"—we political scientists—do *not* see and that it is for other kinds of social scientists to observe. Sometimes I hear the opinion that although some of the phenomena in the radical model may exist (indoctrination of the disadvantaged by the advantaged, for example), they are not part of the political process. They are prepolitical, or at least nonpolitical; and they deserve investigation not by our discipline but by sociologists, social psychologists, and anthropologists. For, again, politics is what goes on in the political process, not what does not go on in it.

Such an argument is not a good reason for rejecting the radical model. It is only an argument about disciplinary lines, and it throws some light on why radicals usually find the lines that define political science unacceptable.

I would conclude that for these three reasons the "politics is what we see" defense of conventional theory is extremely weak and the radical criticism of that defense is highly plausible.

I grant, however, that radical political scientists have been short on empirical research into the unseen. That fact cannot be used to deny the inadequacies of the conventional thought; it points, however, to a potential available to radical thought to verify its model.

Scientific Neutrality: Third Line of Defense. A third line of defense for conventional theory is that its propositions are more neutral—they commit you to less—than those of the radical model. To assert, even with historical evidence, a fundamental struggle in politics between advantaged and disadvantaged seems to assert a highly questionable proposition. To study the political system as a system into which we are all drawn because of a common concern for law and order seems safer scientifically.

It is not a very good argument. Even if the state does provide law and order and certain other shared benefits, one takes a position—with no satisfactory evidence—if one asserts that participants are drawn into politics and motivated by those functions of the state. There is nothing neutral at all about such a position. It may seem to be a colorless, nonprovocative kind of position to hold; but it is nevertheless an exposed, unproved position, no less so than the belief in struggle between advantaged and disadvantaged.

I shall go further in showing that conventional theory is far from neutral, whatever "neutral" might be defined to be. It departs from neutrality in the specific sense that it claims that democratic politics are at root benign. It grants, of course, that democratic governments make mistakes, are sometimes harsh, and occasionally sink into violence or repression. But its fundamental characterization of these systems is as benign.

V. O. Key, Jr., for example, takes a benign view: "legitimization of the view that the preferences of the governed shall be accorded weight by governors constitutes the moral basis of popular government, an ethical imperative that in mature democracies is converted into consistent habits and patterns of action among those in places of authority and leadership" (1967, p. 412). The quoted sentence characterizes democracy as so benign that it sounds like the statement of an ideal, but he writes it as a statement of fact.

The benign view is missing from the radical model, in which politics is a struggle between adversaries. In some older and contemporary Marxist versions of the radical model, the state is malevolent rather than benign; but usually the model depicts the political process as a mixture of benignity and malevolence unless, more neutrally, it is simply described by reference to historical causation. We cannot categorically say that the radical view is superior, but we clearly have no grounds for declaring the dominant benign view to be the more neutral. Hence, the third line of defense of the dominant model will not hold.

The Wrong Questions: Fourth Line of Defense. A fourth line of defense is this: perhaps the trouble with the radical model is that people who use it ask the wrong questions. I suggest that the very questions that radicals have long raised about democratic politics are being raised belatedly by mainstream political scientists in acknowledgment of their importance. Among others, they are questions about political indoctrination, about rising expectations and other sources of new popular demands on government, about corporatism, and about increasingly tense conflict between popular demands and the needs of business (a conflict highlighted in the Reagan administration's declared position that the economy cannot prosper without a reduction in popular demands for regulation and entitlements). These questions include, consequently, new interests in the politics of inflation growing out of possible connections between inflation and magnitude of demands made on government.[3]

These questions connect with even larger questions about the viability and efficacy of democracy, questions that radical thought has long approached with a useful skepticism that is free of certain defects of mainstream thought.[4]

For attacking these questions, it is not at all obvious that conventional theory is superior to the theory of struggle between advantaged and disadvan-

---

3. Some examples of the radical literature on these issues are to be found in Lindberg et al. (1975), Crouch (1979), and O'Connor (1973).

4. The tendency of radicals to turn every apparent strength in democratic politics into a weakness has not gone any further than the mainstream tendency to convert every apparent defect into a strength. Berelson made apathy a strength; Truman made elite privilege a bulwark of democracy, and some of you have read Lindblom on the blessings of fragmentation.

taged. The literature on these questions is clearly greatly enriched by the radical contribution, the best of which is of a quality that warrants the attention of all mainstream political scientists (despite their habit of regarding contributions from that quarter as falling outside the essential literature of the profession). The fourth line of defense, in short, is no defense at all.

A Brief Case Study

I now propose a case study: the literature on political socialization. In it, we can find concrete examples of the weaknesses of conventional theory to solidify the foregoing analysis.

To begin with, in their view of the democratic political process as benign, many conventional scholars see political socialization as a life-long process, even if especially critical in childhood, in which citizens "mature." Socialization helps the citizen to "comprehend" and to "evaluate." It gives him "cognitive growth" and "increasing grasp" (Dawson and Prewitt 1969, pp. 16–17 and 56). Such a view slights the possibility that socialization is intellectually confining, is sometimes crippling, may reduce understanding, and may obstruct the development of skill in evaluation. But which of these it does, or in what mixture, is as important a question for political science as can be imagined. To begin analysis of socialization, as some studies do, with exclusive reference to its benign effects and never to turn to its more questionable effects is, by any scholarly standard, dubious if not unacceptable.

An analytic problem arises because "learning," like "socialization," can refer to developmental or other processes through which persons improve their grasp of reality, improve the accuracy of their perceptions, and develop skills in perception, analysis, and evaluation. Or it can refer to the effect of influences on the mind that reduce these very competences, as when a person learns that he is destined to fail in anything he attempts or learns from an abusive parent to trust no one. These two kinds or effects of learning—one benign, the other not—are simply not separated in much mainstream political science. And thus both terms "socialization" and "learning"—against which radical thought would pose such a term as "indoctrination"—though pretending to scientific neutrality, take a position: specifically, that learning and socialization are to be viewed as bringing people into society rather than as obstructing their social capacities.

That this process, which might variably be called socialization, learning, or indoctrination, goes by the benign name of socialization in the literature of political science illustrates the disposition of the dominant model to find benefits for all in political processes, thus benefits for the abstraction called "society." That disposition confuses the study of socialization in other ways too. Easton and Dennis are an example. They are much too careful to fall into the trap of associating socialization with maintenance of the status quo; it may also be an agent of change, they say. Notwithstanding, they finally work toward what they consider to be the theoretical significance of socialization, which is its effects on system persistence. They conceive of these effects as the capacity of sets of behavior that allow institutions of value to persist even when their specific forms change (Easton and Dennis 1969, pp. 36–38 and 47–48). System persistence is, again, a benefit for society, a benefit for all. It renders Easton and Dennis unable to examine the extent to which the process they study, whether called socialization or indoctrination, is an instrument through which the advantaged, with their advantages in the control of communications, teach the disadvantaged to accept their disadvantages. Again, I do not have to argue that the latter interpretation of the process would be the correct one, only that users of the dominant model formulate their inquiries so that they do not investigate it as a possibility.

Easton and Dennis subsequently take note of the possibilities that the process they call socialization teaches citizens to curb their demands. The process of constraining demands is a process which on some counts seems to make a democracy more viable, yet on other counts argues that democracy is much less democratic than we have supposed. In such a benign view of demand constraint as Easton and Dennis's, this great issue is missed.

Greenstein's views on socialization avoid many of the traps into which the dominant model seems to have lured political scientists, but consider the following benign picture: "The long-run effect of media attention is probably to build up, gradually and inadvertently, an awareness of basic elements in the political system" (Greenstein 1968). Suppose that I reverse the meaning of the sentence, rewriting it to read that the effects are to reduce awareness of the most basic elements. How could he claim that his sentence is any better than mine?

In the same article, Greenstein moves from "socialization" to "learning," and then without explanation to the term "education." He might have moved, but did not, toward the term "indoctrination" instead of "education." With that word "education" he chooses, perhaps with little self-awareness, to put the best possible interpretation on a two-faced process. We must turn to the radical model if we are to see the other side.

To the dominant model may perhaps also be attributed a gap in socialization studies. Users of the model are familiar with widely circulating propositions that democracy is impossible without some degree of agreement on fundamentals, at least on rules of the game and among elites. Believing that such agreement is functional for society, they have invested little effort in explaining how it comes about. They can of course point to the socialization mechanisms—family, school, peer groups, the media—which pass the agreed beliefs of one generation on to the next. That approach leaves wholly unexplained the agreement that is already formed when transmitted. How does it come about that certain transmitted beliefs and values are agreed rather than diverse? That we do not understand.

We fall into a bad habit of simply taking for granted that people in any society will think alike, as though agreement were a natural phenomenon that requires no explanation. Even natural phenomena require explanation. Moreover, on some beliefs and values, people differ greatly; only on some do they cluster. Agreement on political fundamentals cries for an explanation. Why, how, through which mechanisms do people come to think alike about political fundamentals?

While conventional theorists are on the whole satisfied merely to note that agreement of certain kinds is necessary and therefore to turn off the search for how it is in fact accomplished, radical theorists have at least some hypotheses to offer. The hypotheses derive from the first feature of their model that we identified above—that political democracy is a transitional phase in a long-standing struggle between advantaged and disadvantaged. The democratic political system has a history; it cannot be understood without reference to its historical origins. If we then look for an explanation of political agreement, we shall find it not in studies of contemporary socialization, though they may give us new chapters for an old story, but in a history in which, as Marx said, the ruling ideas have been the ideas of the ruling class. We shall find it in tendencies toward agreement that were set in motion many centuries ago through such instruments of indoctrination of the disadvantaged by the advantaged as the shaman and later the priest of the Middle Ages. The mechanisms include, through processes of cultural diffusion not well researched, the permeation in more recent history of entire societies with such doctrines as were codified by John Locke and Adam Smith.

Attempting to understand this history, Gramsci (1968) offers propositions, which we may regard as hypotheses well worth study, on cultural hegemony and on the role of intellectuals. In recent years, Habermas and Marcuse have grappled, though not lucidly, with some hypotheses based on Weber on how technology and markets bring about a pervasive purposiveness in human relations that induces acquiescent likemindedness.

We do not know whether the radical hypotheses are true, but they are meaty. They are also sophisticated in their understanding that in opinion formation, just as Adam Smith asserted for the market, much is accomplished through social life without organized intent—often with no intent at all to produce the results actually effected. The hypotheses are an advance over no hypothesis at all from mainstream study of socialization.

Conclusion

Neither in our four lines of defense nor in our brief case study of the socialization literature have we found any grounds for confidence in the conventional theory on democratic politics. I have not, however, argued the superiority of radical over conventional theory. The conclusion is not that the radical is superior but only that mainstream political science ought to bring it in from the cold. The conventional theory creaks and on the evidence here leads political scientists to say silly things.

We cannot, in a final desperate move, reject the radical model because radicals practice questionable methods. My argument has been that, on its own terms, conventional theory is seriously defective and that, presented in mainstream language and concept and without acceptance of any but the most familiar methodology, the radical model is not obviously inferior.

Radical political scientists, however, annoy many of us with their excursions into phenomenology, hermeneutics, interpretive theory, and critical theory. Yet, so many in the mainstream join in certain of these excursions that we can no longer afford to deprecate them. The radicals' use of these new methods as well as the older habits of Marxist method does, I grant, create a chasm between radical and most mainstream thought. And many mainstream scholars, myself included, have made little attempt to cross it. We are also rebuffed by what we are fairly confident are serious shortcomings in much radical writing. It is sometimes insular and arrogant, sometimes humorlessly incapable of self-criticism. Its terms sometimes defy association with any observable real-world process. It begs questions. And its authors, themselves feeling rebuffed, sometimes make no attempt to communicate beyond a privileged radical circle with its private language—thus also excusing themselves from demands for evidence. But the clichés of some radical thought are no more relevant to my argument than the fatuities of some mainstream thought. My argument has not been that radical thought is a model for all of us. It has been instead, to say it once more, that conventional theory is embarrassingly defective. It greatly needs to call more heavily on radical thought.

REFERENCES

Almond, Gabriel A., and C. Bingham Powell, Jr. 1966. *Comparative Politics.* Boston: Little, Brown.
Cohen, Ronald, and Elman R. Service, eds. 1978. *Origins of the State.* Philadelphia: Institute for the Study of Human Issues.
Crouch, Colin. 1979. "The State, Capital, and Liberal Democracy." In *State and Economy in Contemporary Capitalism,* ed. Colin Crouch. London: Croom Helm.
Dahl, R. A. 1972. *Democracy in the United States.* Chicago: Rand McNally.
Dawson, Richard E., and Kenneth Prewitt. 1969. *Political Socialization.* Boston: Little, Brown.
Deutsch, Karl. 1980. *Politics and Government.* Boston: Houghton Mifflin.
Dolbeare, Kenneth M., and Murray J. Edelman. 1981. *American Politics.* 3d ed., rev. Lexington, MA: D. C. Heath.

Dye, Thomas R., and L. Harmon Zeigler. 1970. *The Irony of Democracy.* Belmont, CA: Wadsworth.

Easton, David, and Jack Dennis. 1969. *Children in the Political System.* New York: McGraw-Hill.

Easton, David, and Robert Hess. 1962. "The Child's Political World." *Midwest Journal of Political Science* 6: 229–46.

Gaventa, John. 1980. *Power and Powerlessness.* Urbana: University of Illinois Press.

Gough, Ian. 1975. "State Expenditure in Advanced Capitalism." *New Left Review* 92: 53–92.

Gramsci, Antonio. 1968. *The Modern Prince and Other Writings.* Translated by Louis Marks. New York: International Publishers.

Greenstein, Fred I. 1968. "Socialization: Political Socialization." Part 3 in *International Encyclopedia of the Social Sciences,* ed. David L. Sills, vol. 14, pp. 551–55. New York: The Macmillan Company and The Free Press.

Habermas, Jurgen. 1976. *Legitimation Crisis.* London: Heinemann.

Key, V. O., Jr. 1967. *Public Opinion and American Democracy.* New York: Knopf.

Lindberg, Leon, et al., eds. 1975. *Stress and Contradiction in Modern Capitalism: Public Policy and the Theory of the State.* Lexington, MA: Lexington Books.

Lowi, Theodore J. 1979. *The End of Liberalism,* 2d ed. New York: W. W. Norton.

Lukes, S. 1974. *Power: A Radical View.* London: Macmillan.

Mandel, Ernest. 1974. *Late Capitalism.* London: New Left Books.

Miliband, Ralph. 1969. *The State in Capitalist Society.* New York: Basic Books.

Mouzelis, Nicos. 1980. "Reductionism in Marxist Theory." *Telos* 45: 173–85.

O'Connor, James. 1973. *The Fiscal Crisis of the State.* New York: St. Martin's Press.

Offe, C. 1976. "Political Authority and Class Structure." In *Critical Sociology,* ed. P. Conneton. Harmondsworth, Middlesex, England: Penguin.

Polsby, Nelson W. 1980. *Community Power and Social Theory.* New Haven, CT: Yale University Press.

Poulantzas, Nicos. 1973. *Political Power and Social Classes.* London: New Left Books.

Prewitt, Kenneth, and Sidney Verba. 1977. *Introduction to American Government.* New York: Harper and Row.

Truman, David. 1959. "The American System in Crisis." *Political Science Quarterly* 74: 481–97.

Weissberg, R. 1974. *Political Learning, Political Choice and Democratic Citizenship.* Englewood Cliffs, NJ: Prentice-Hall.

The Two-Party System and Duverger's Law: An Essay on the History of Political Science

William H. Riker

One defining characteristic of science as distinct from belles lettres, criticism, and philosophic speculation is the accumulation of knowledge in the form of more or less verifiable propositions about the natural world. In the conventional view of science, propositions are verified deductively when they are inferred indisputably from an axiom system and verified empirically when they have survived repeated attempts at falsification (Popper 1963). In practice, however, scientific propositions are typically neither so theoretically indisputable nor so empirically unfalsifiable as the conventional view suggests. Rather, most reported tests of propositions involve either discrediting a theory or successful falsification. The triumphant scientist then replaces the proposition he or she has falsified with a revised one, which passes the test that the initial proposition failed. When I speak of a more or less verified proposition, therefore, I mean the one that is the current end point of a series of revisions and that is, at least provisionally, accepted by the relevant portion of the scientific community (Riker 1977). By the phrase "accumulation of knowledge" we mean not only that the corpus of propositions is growing but also that each one of the series of revisions is more general or more precise than its predecessor.

In this view, every branch of science has a history which is a chronicle of the marginal revisions of propositions leading up to the currently accepted ones. This is what Thomas Kuhn (1970) calls "normal science." Political science, which is my concern in this essay, has, however, often been said to have no history, which is of course merely a way of saying that it contains no accumulation of knowledge and that it is therefore not a branch of science. Many political scientists have been persuaded to believe this assertion, so that in despair they are inclined to abandon the search for scientific generaliza-

Reprinted in a somewhat shortened version from *American Political Science Review* 76 (1982): 753–66.

tions. (This despair is, I believe, the root of the movement toward phenomenology and hermeneutics and other efforts to turn political science into a belles-lettristic study.)

The rationale for the assertion that political science lacks a history is that political institutions, the main topic of generalizations in the field, are themselves so evanescent that the subject and predicate classes of scientific propositions change more swiftly than the propositions can be perfected. It is indeed true that in comparison with the physical and biological sciences, which deal with the unchanging properties of matter, and even in comparison with psychological sciences, which deal with the relatively more plastic properties of the human psyche, the habits and institutions studied in the social sciences are swiftly changing. But generalizations are neither so hard to come by nor so hard to perfect as this criticism implies. Many of the propositions of social science involve an interplay between permanent psychological characteristics of humans and institutional structures. This feature implies some degree of permanence for the subject and predicate classes of generalizations in social science. For example, the law of demand in economics—that, with appropriate qualifications, demand curves do not slope upward—is mainly psychological in character and is indeed a better formulated and more thoroughly verified law of behavior than any to be found in the science of psychology itself. Even when the psychological component is smaller and the institutional component is larger than in the law of demand, as is typical in political science, lasting generalization is still possible because many institutions (e.g., voting and decisions by forming coalitions) are, when abstractly described, at least as old as written history.

It should be the case, therefore, that political science, like any other science, has a history, even if it has not heretofore been chronicled. My intention in this essay is to demonstrate that a history does exist, and my vehicle is a particular series of reformulations called Duverger's law. I am not undertaking this demonstration out of chauvinism, merely to claim for students of politics the name and privilege of scientists, but rather to show that the accumulation of knowledge is possible even when dealing with such fragile and transitory phenomena as political institutions (Riker 1977). This is also why I deal with Duverger's law, a not very well accepted proposition dealing with institutions of only the last two hundred years. If it is demonstrated that knowledge has accumulated, even in this not yet satisfactorily formulated "law" about an ephemeral institution, then I will have demonstrated at least the possibility of the accumulation of knowledge about politics.

I.

Duverger's law proposes that "the simple-majority single-ballot system favors the two-party system." Duverger described this sentence by saying: "Of all the hypotheses . . . in this book, this approaches most nearly perhaps to a true sociological law" (Duverger 1963, p. 217). Related to this sentence is another, which Duverger did not elevate to the status of law: "the simple-majority system with second ballot and proportional representation favors multi-partyism" (Duverger 1963, p. 239). I will refer to the first proposition as the law and to the second proposition as the hypothesis. These propositions distinguish among three kinds of electoral systems, which, although far from a complete list of the systems in current use, are the only ones used widely enough to admit the observation of their relationship with the number of political parties:

(1) *Plurality voting*—rather misleadingly called the simple-majority, single-ballot system by Duverger—in which the unique winner is the candidate with the most votes. With two or fewer candidates, the winner has a simple majority of the votes cast; with three or more candidates, the winner may have only a plurality.

(2) *Run off majority voting* among three or more candidates with two ballots, in which at the first ballot the winners are the two candidates with the largest and second largest number of votes, and, at the second ballot between exactly these two, the winner is the candidate with a simple majority. Coupled with the two-ballot system are various alternative vote methods in which counting, rather than voting, occurs twice, using the same definition of winning as in the two-ballot system.

(3) *Proportional representation,* in which the winners are those candidates who obtain some quota of votes, usually $v/(s + 1)$ or $(v/(s + 1)) + 1$, where v is the number of votes cast and s is the number of winners to be selected. Since $s > 1$, some winners must have less than a plurality.

Although it is easy to clarify Duverger's terminology, it is not at all easy to straighten out the ambiguity in his statement of the relationship between electoral systems and the number of parties. Is plurality voting a necessary condition of the two-party system? or a sufficient condition? or both? or neither? The claim that the relation is "a sociological law" suggests causality or a necessary and sufficient condition, whereas the use of "favors" suggests the relationship is at best probabilistic, not deterministic. I suspect the formulation was deliberately ambiguous because the author was not himself entirely certain of what he wanted to claim. Just what the claim *ought* to be is not immediately obvious, so I will settle the question as I survey the present state of knowledge about Duverger's law.

II.

Duverger's sentences appeared in print in 1951, but as is usually the case with scientific laws, similar propositions had already been widely discussed and reformulated with some increasing degree of sophistication.[1] Indeed, related propositions appeared in popular discussion almost as soon as methods other than plurality voting were proposed or adopted for legislative elections in which large numbers of people were expected to vote. Such electorates were constituted in America in the eighteenth century and in Western Europe in the late nineteenth century. Once these large electorates existed, there also existed a motive for politicians to attempt to devise appropriate methods to manipulate outcomes in elections, and hence methods other than plurality voting were discussed and adopted. Naturally proponents and opponents of alternative methods also thought deeply about the consequences of alternative methods and thus began to discuss propositions related to Duverger's law.

These propositions were to be expected, and it is quite likely that there is indeed some demonstrable relation between electoral forms and the structure of the party system. Whatever their other ideological or programmatic functions, political parties serve to organize elections. (For a recent elaboration, see Katz 1980.) Politicians and candidates with some common interests—perhaps only a common desire to win or perhaps also a common ideology or a common identification with a group—appeal to voters under a common banner, and thereby generate political parties. Since one motive for the common appeal is the desire to win, it is not surprising that the constitutional definitions of winning have an effect on the parties thereby generated. If winning is defined as the most votes, that is, as a plurality, then one might reasonably expect a two-party system owing to the necessity under this definition of maximizing votes. Since the best way, in the long run, to get the most votes is to get more than half, each of two parties might be expected to structure a coalition in the hope, *before the election*, of getting a majority. Alternatively, if winning is defined as more than half the votes at a runoff election, candidates do not necessarily have to maximize votes at the initial election—the second most votes initially may be enough to win in the end. And if winning is defined as the achievement of some number of votes less than half (as is necessarily the case under proportional representation), then the necessity of maximizing disappears entirely. In short, when the definition of winning forces candidates to maximize votes in order to win (as in plurality systems), they have strong motives to create a two-party system; but when the definition of winning does not require them to maximize votes (as in runoff and proportional systems), then this motive for two parties is absent.

The twin conditions of a large electorate and proposals for methods other than plurality voting were met in Europe in the latter half of the nineteenth

---

1. It is customary to call the law by Duverger's name, not because he had much to do with developing it but rather because he was the first to dare to claim it was a law. The memorial honors, therefore, a trait of character as much as a scientific breakthrough.

century, but general public discussion on the subject did not appear until the 1850s. In 1859, Thomas Hare in *The Election of Representatives* set forth an elaborate method of proportional representation, the single transferable vote, and in 1861, John Stuart Mill popularized it in *Considerations on Representative Government,* which contained a philosophical justification of Hare's method. Mill believed Parliament should contain "not just the two great parties alone," but representatives of "every minority . . . consisting of a sufficiently large number," which number he defined precisely as the number of voters divided by the number of seats (Mill 1910, p. 263). He expected the proposed system would produce Tory free traders and Tory corn law supporters without upsetting the two-party system.

Quite recently Duff Spafford sent me what he and I believe is the earliest known explicit statement of the law. Henry Droop, an English barrister, advocate of proportional representation and inventor of the Droop quota, wrote in 1869 about plurality voting:

> Each elector has practically only a choice between two candidates or sets of candidates. As success depends upon obtaining a majority of the aggregate votes of all the electors, an election is usually reduced to a contest between the two most popular candidates or sets of candidates. Even if other candidates go to the poll, the electors usually find out that their votes will be thrown away, unless given in favour of one or other of the parties between whom the election really lies.

By 1881 he was prepared to argue "these phenomena [i.e., two-party systems] I cannot explain by any theory of a natural division between opposing tendencies of thought, and the only explanation which seems to me to account for them is that the two opposing parties into which we find politicians divided in each of these countries [United Kingdom, United States, etc.] *have been formed and are kept together by majority voting*" [emphasis added; Droop means, of course, plurality voting].

This is the earliest explicit statement of Duverger's law that I have seen. By 1901 it was a commonplace.

III.

In the previous section I reported a gradual development culminating in a clear and unambiguous statement of both Duverger's propositions twenty years after Hare and seventy years before Duverger. In the succeeding half-century, scholarly support became quite general, so that it was indeed reasonable for Duverger to call one of them a law. The general theme of this development is that of an initial skepticism followed by increasing acquiescence.

A. Lawrence Lowell, whose books on comparative politics dominated the field at the turn of the century, thought that the two-party system was essential for effective parliamentary government. He attributed this system in Great Britain to the historical experience of the English people, but he also thought that the absence of it in France was owing to the majority system and the second ballot (Lowell 1896). Thus, in effect, he accepted Duverger's hypothesis but not Duverger's law. Other prominent scholars of that period were less clear. Ostrogorski, for example, was so eager to do away with political parties by his own pet reforms that he never quite diagnosed the causes of structural features of parties (Ostrogorski 1908, vol. 2, p. 705). Practical publicists, excited by the controversy over proportional representation, which was considered or adopted in most European countries between 1900 and 1925, tended to favor proportional representation if they belonged to parties without a majority and to oppose it if they belonged to parties with the majority or close to it. Implicitly, therefore, they behaved as if they agreed with Duverger's law. One author who explicitly stated this belief was J. Ramsay MacDonald, later a Labour prime minister, who wrote frequently against proportional representation and clearly explained the forces involved in Duverger's law (MacDonald 1909, p. 137). On the other hand, most minority publicists were not so frank; when they favored proportional representation, they typically denied Duverger's hypothesis (on the effect of proportional representation) and pointed out that countries without proportional representation often did not have two-party systems. Conversely, those opposed to proportional representation were not quite sure.

Two strands of intellectual development removed the doubts. One was the spread of dissatisfaction in the 1930s with proportional representation; the other was an increased scholarly examination of the origins of the two-party system that characterized the successful American polity. Since the dissatisfaction with proportional representation relates to Duverger's hypothesis (that proportional representation caused multiple parties, the lesser of Duverger's two propositions), I will skip over most of that debate, which was especially aimed at identifying the reasons for the initial successes of the German National Socialist Party. An excellent example of the effect of that experience is observable in the two editions of a Fabian Society tract by Herman Finer, a prominent student of comparative politics. In the initial edition (1924), he criticized proportional representation in much the same way as had MacDonald fifteen years earlier, that is, as a system that confused responsibility. In the second edition (1935), however, he added a postscript in which he blamed proportional representation in Italy and Germany for increasing the number of political parties. Then he attributed the weakness of executives and the instability of governments to the multiplicity of parties, and he explained the rise of Mussolini and Hitler as a reaction: "people become so distracted by fumbling governments, that they will acquiesce in any sort of dictatorship" (Finer 1935, p. 16). Hermens's *Democracy or Anarchy: A Study of Proportional Representation* (1941) constitutes the most elaborate indictment of this electoral system for its encouragement of National Socialism, and although not published until 1941, its evidence had been widely circulated for several years before that. Finer and Hermens were frequently quoted, and the collection of evidence on this subject by Hermens and others (e.g., Mellen 1943) had, I believe, a significant persuasive effect in support of Duverger's hypothesis.

The scholarly study of the two-party system tended to increase the evidence for and scholarly certainty about Duverger's law. Arthur Holcombe, a prominent American political scientist in the first half of the century, affirmed Duverger's law as early as 1910 (Holcombe 1910). Although in a popular textbook published as late as 1919 W. B. Munro attributed the two-party system to the "practical capacity of the Anglo-Saxon race" (Munro 1919, p. 329), and although authors of other popular textbooks of the next decade, e.g., Charles Merriam, E. M. Sait, and Frederic Ogg, avoided the subject entirely, by 1933 the notion was well established that plurality voting for executives generated the American two-party system. This example of presidential and gubernatorial elections proved extraordinarily convincing, and within a decade the more general form of Duverger's law was enshrined in popular American textbooks. Thus Carl Friedrich observed that the "single member district with plurality elections . . . forces the electorate to make up its mind between two clear-cut alternatives" (Friedrich 1937, p. 290), and E. E. Schattschneider wrote that the "single-member-district-system-plus-plurality-elections . . . discriminates *moderately* [emphasis in original] against the second party, but against the third, fourth, and fifth parties the force of this tendency is multiplied to the point of extinguishing their chances of winning seats altogether," a force that thereby guarantees exactly two parties (Schattschneider 1942, p. 75). V. O. Key, Jr. (1949) even applied the idea of the law to the superficially one-party system of the states of the old Confederacy, observing that where primary elections in the one main party were conducted with the plurality rule, there was bifactionalism, and where conducted with the runoff majority rule, there was multifactionalism.

Scholarly acceptance of both Duverger's law and Duverger's hypothesis was therefore quite general by the time he formulated them. Duverger's own contribution was twofold: First, he distinguished sharply between the law and the hypothesis, which previously had often been mistakenly interpreted as duals of each other. (Since plurality and proportional systems are only two out of many, the absence of one does imply the presence of the other.) Second, he collected and systematically arranged a large amount of historical evidence in support of both sentences so that their full significance was apparent.

IV.

Of course, acceptance and utterance do not make statements true. The history of these sentences in the next thirty years consists mainly in collecting evidence for and against their truth and revising their formulation and adjusting the rational-choice model within which they fit. Since it is just exactly this activity that constitutes the daily life of science, the fact of a substantial amount of testing out and reformulating of Duverger's hypothesis and law is evidence of the accumulation of knowledge I am trying to describe.

I start with Duverger's hypothesis (that proportional representation and majority systems favor multiparty systems). Clearly Duverger himself was uneasy about the hypothesis, did not call it a law, and asserted it only as a probabilistic association, not a deterministic one.

The rational-choice theory, standing implicitly behind the hypothesis, is that proportional representation and the second-ballot runoff both offer politicians an incentive for the formation of new parties and do not give them any disincentive. The incentive is that, given particular configurations of potential coalitions, these systems sometimes permit new parties (and heretofore-excluded politicians) to get a bit of political influence with relatively few votes. That is, in these systems a new party does not have to get the most votes to win, merely some indefinite number less than the most. Under proportional representation, the candidate or list with the second most votes can always win seats and sometimes so can candidates with the third or fourth most votes. Indeed, the purpose of the system is to encourage this result. In the runoff majority system a candidate who initially has the second most votes can ultimately win, provided the supporters of eliminated candidates vote for her or him at the second ballot. Hence, if a group of politicians can see a chance to come in second or third, it is often worthwhile to form a new party. In the plurality system, on the other hand, this positive incentive is turned into a disincentive because it is rare for the prospective builders of a new party to see a chance to come in first past the post. This system, then, constitutes a real disincentive because the leaders of the new party are likely to be regarded as politically irrelevant. This disincentive is absent from proportional representation and runoff systems, however, because even leaders of failed parties are welcome in expanded coalitions of continuing parties. Neither feature of this incentive system is strong enough to permit one to say for certain that these electoral systems favor multiple parties. The incentive is weak because it operates only when people want to form new parties for other reasons. However, there are surely many configurations of potential coalitions, configurations lasting through many elections, that do not render it likely that new parties will come in second (probably the case in Austria) or even third (probably the case in Ireland). Similarly the absence of a disincentive for new parties within the system of proportional representation itself is not very important. Although the existence of proportional representation prohibits the direct use of the disincentive inherent in plurality voting, there are other kinds of efficacious disincentives that can be combined with proportional representation, as has been done in Germany and perhaps Austria. So the incentive is not sufficient and the disincentive is not necessary. Hence the hypothesis cannot be deterministically valid, although doubtless there is a fairly strong probabilistic association between proportional representation or runoff elections on one hand and the multiparty system on the other.

V.

We can therefore abandon Duverger's hypothesis in its deterministic form (although it is still useful for practical life) and proceed to the more interesting question of Duverger's law, relating plurality elections and two-party systems. The difficulties with the law are less formidable. There are indeed counterexamples, but not, I believe, definitive ones, so that the law may possibly survive with appropriate revisions. If we can also fit it to an adequate theory, it may even be persuasive.

The two most pressing counterexamples to Duverger's law are in Canada and India, where despite plurality elections there are distinctly more than two parties. In Rae's study of 121 elections in 20 countries, 30 elections were conducted under plurality rules and seven of these—all in Canada—resulted in more than 10 percent of the votes for a third party. Rae attributed the Canadian deviation to the fact that, geographically, local parties survive as the main parties in some provinces while they are third parties nationally. Doubtless this situation derives from the extreme decentralization of Canadian government, wherein the chance of provincial control is of itself enough to motivate political action.

On the basis of the Canadian exception, Rae reformulated Duverger's law from "the simple-majority, single-ballot system favors the two-party system" to "plurality formulae are always associated with two-party competition except where strong local minority parties exist" (Rae 1971, p. 95).

The Indian counterexample is more difficult to deal with. India began plurality elections about the same time Duverger formulated his law, and only once has something approaching a two-party election been held.

On another occasion (Riker 1976), I have offered the explanation that because Congress, the largest party in India, includes the median of the voters arranged on an ideological spectrum, Congress has most of the time been the second choice of many voters on both its right and its left. Hence, the party has probably been a Condorcet winner most of the time, although it has never obtained an absolute majority.[2] Congress has been clearly defeated only when the opposition has been so consumed with intense popular hatred of Mrs. Gandhi or with intense elite lust for ministerial office that politicians and voters alike could put aside their ideological tastes and act as if they ordered their preferences with Congress at the bottom of the list. When they have done so, they have defeated Congress in both state and national elections. Then, typically, coalitions of each end against the middle (like Janata in 1977–79) have dissolved and Congress has won again, presumably as the Condorcet choice. With these thoughts in mind, I constructed a model in which, with rational participants who wished to maximize political satisfaction, i.e., for office and ideological tastes, a multiparty equilibrium was consistent with plurality elections. The essence of this model was that some party in the multiparty system was regularly a Condorcet winner. Utilizing this feature, it is possible to revise Duverger's law further, incorporating Rae's revision, to account for both of the apparent exceptions, Canada and India.

In my revision the law reads:

> Plurality election rules bring about and maintain two-party competition except in countries where (1) third parties nationally are continually one of two parties locally, and (2) one party among several is almost always the Condorcet winner in elections.

Note that this formulation is deterministic—an attempt to avoid the ambiguity of Duverger and Rae. The law asserts that, with the exceptions noted, the plurality rule is a sufficient condition for a two-party system. It is not, however, an assertion of a causal relation, inasmuch as the plurality rule clearly is not a necessary condition (vide, Austria).

VI.

The revised law is entirely consistent with our knowledge of the empirical world, accounting both for the long history of two-party competition in Anglo-American countries with plurality voting and for the apparent exceptions like Social Credit in Canada, the Irish in Britain in the nineteenth century, the multiparty grouping around Congress in India, and the few third parties in the United States that have survived more than one election. But the law itself is entirely empirical, the record of observations. It explains nothing and tells us nothing about why it works. It is the task of science to explain the law by incorporating it as a necessary inference inside a theory. Thus it is appropriate to look at the theory that subsumes the law.

Duverger offered two theoretical explanations for why the plurality rule

---

2. A Condorcet winner is a candidate who can beat any other in a pairwise contest.

destroys third parties: (1) a "mechanical effect" of underrepresenting losing parties; and (2) a "psychological factor" in that voters do not want to waste their votes on losers. Both these reasons derive (implicitly) from a view of both politicians and voters as rational actors, i.e., expected utility maximizers. The mechanical effect gives politicians an incentive to abandon parties that win even less than they might be expected to; the psychological factor gives voters, observing wasted votes and even votes that, being wasted, indirectly contribute to the victory of least-liked parties, an incentive to vote for their second choices. If both these propositions are correct, they can be combined, as they were by Duverger, into a theoretical explanation of the operation of the law.

The existence of the mechanical effect was disputed by Grumm on the basis of a modest bit of evidence (Grumm 1958). But Rae showed definitively by an empirical comparison that plurality rules gave a greater relative advantage to large parties over small ones than did proportional representation rules (Rae 1971, pp. 88–92). Sprague (1980) carried Rae's analysis quite a bit further by calculating precisely how much plurality systems are biased against third parties.

The main dispute is about the validity of the psychological factor, which Downs bluntly described thus:

> A rational voter first decides what party he believes will benefit him most; then he tries to estimate whether this party has any chance of winning. He does this because his vote should be expended as part of a selection process, not as an expression of preference. Hence even if he prefers party A, he is "wasting" his vote on A if it has no chance of winning, because very few other voters prefer it to B or C. The relevant choice in this case is between B and C. Since a vote for A is not useful in the actual process of selection, casting it is irrational. (Downs 1957, p. 48)

What Downs describes has come to be called "sophisticated" voting, by which is meant that the voter takes account of anticipated votes by others and then votes so as to bring about the best realizable outcome for himself, regardless of whether or not his vote is sincere, i.e., for his preferred alternative.

In the election of single executives, if sophisticated voting occurs, it always works against third parties. (Indeed, early statements of Duverger's law in the United States, e.g., by MacMahon [1933], emphasized the special importance of the elected executive in bringing the psychological factor into play.) In the election of members of a legislature, however, which of the several parties is weakened by sophisticated voting depends on conditions in the constituency. If the third party nationally is the weakest locally, then sophisticated voting by its supporters weakens it. However, if the third party nationally is one of the two larger parties locally, then sophisticated voting by supporters of the weakest party (i.e., one of the two larger parties nationally) strengthens the third party. This latter effect is probably what has kept alive the Liberal party in Britain and some Canadian third parties. Because third parties remain third parties, however, the main force of sophisticated voting must work against third parties.

Given the significance of sophisticated voting in the explanation of why Duverger's law works, one very important question is: Does sophisticated voting occur? That is, are ordinary voters clever and bold enough to vote against their true tastes?

Shively (1970) made the first attempt to discover sophisticated voting. He interpreted Duverger's law (rather too broadly, I think) as the sentence: "Where the likelihood that a party can win . . . is low, voters are less likely to continue voting for it, or . . . to begin voting for it." For a test, he created an index of the likelihood of winning and regressed the change of a party's proportion of the vote in two consecutive elections on this index. He expected a positive association, i.e., low likelihood linked with decline in share of votes, but he got a negative one. This result led him to further statistical manipulation and a reinterpretation which he believed supported the law, though only weakly. Hence he concluded that the psychological factor had "a trivial impact on election outcomes."

Given the empirical strength of Duverger's law at the institutional level, these results from electoral data were, to say the least, perplexing. Since Shively's form of the hypothesis and his method were far too gross to study the truly relevant behavior, however, other scientists have looked more precisely at voters' desertion from third parties. These investigators have found a relatively large amount of sophisticated voting in Britain, Canada, Germany, and the United States, as described in Spafford (1972); Lemieux (1977); Cain (1978); Fisher (1974); Black (1978, 1980); and Bensel and Sanders (1979).

VII.

The evidence renders it undeniable that a large amount of sophisticated voting occurs—mostly to the disadvantage of the third parties nationally—so that the force of Duverger's psychological factor must be considerable. It seems initially appropriate and attractive, therefore, to construct a theory to explain Duverger's law out of the theory of rational choice. Nevertheless, we cannot do so blithely. In the first place, not everyone votes sophisticatedly, although the evidence collected here suggests that most people who "should" do so by reason of the expected utility calculus probably do so in fact. It is difficult, however, to build a theory on behavior that is not certainly universal, and even if it is universal, there remains a serious and unresolved paradox in the argument, which is that the expected utility calculus of voting may itself be irrational.

In Downs's statement of the theory, which I cited previously, the rational voter should expend his vote "as part of the selection process," not as "an expression of preference." Yet this statement may be indefensible because, as Downs himself pointed out (1957, pp. 36–50, 260–76) and as Ordeshook and I have elaborated (Riker and Ordeshook 1968), it may be impossible for an individual to influence the selection process. One interpretation of influence is the chance to make a tie or to break a tie that occurs in the absence of the individual's vote. This chance is, of course, extremely tiny in most elections in the modern state. Under this definition, it is objectively the case that one cannot expect to contribute much to the decision process. If so, the rational action may be simply to express a preference.

Ferejohn and Fiorina (1974, 1975) have suggested that individuals do not calculate their chance of influence but merely their satisfaction, minimizing thereby the maximum regret they would feel if an undesired candidate won. The debate over the relative merits of minimax regret and expected utility is extensive (Beck 1975; Mayer and Good 1975). Although the bulk of the evidence about the way people behave now seems to favor expected utility (Black 1978; Cain 1978; Aldrich 1976), still the fact that the minimax regret interpretation can be put forward plausibly suggests that some people may be interested merely in utility, not expected utility.

The direction one must go, I believe, is to turn attention away from the expected utility calculus of the individual voter and to the expected utility calculus of the politician and other more substantial participants in the system. The groups and individuals who buy access and the politicians who buy a future have substantial interests, and it is their actions to maximize expected utility that have the effect of maintaining the two-party system under plurality voting.

One especially interesting feature of politics under plurality rules is that minor parties regularly appear. The reason, I believe, is that quite reasonably not all voters vote sophisticatedly. Instead they are willing to support a program that appeals to their ideological taste. Potential politicians are in turn often willing to experiment with and invest in new programs and platforms to form a possible winning venture. Since some of these win locally, they can remain in the system for a long time. In the United States there is the additional attraction to politicians in that we have a two-ballot majority system (rather than a plurality system) at the electoral college level, which encourages third parties because their leaders may convince themselves that they have a chance to throw the election into the House of Representatives (Bensel and Sanders 1979). Coupling the interest of potential leaders with the sincere behavior of many voters, one understands why there is an almost constant supply of third parties.

The interesting question about such parties is not why they begin but why they fail. I believe the answer is that donors and leaders disappear. A donor buys future influence and access, and many donors are willing to buy from any party that has a chance to win. (In the United States, at least, many donors give to *both* parties.) But as rational purchasers they are not likely to donate to a party with a tiny chance of winning, and in a plurality system, most third parties have only that chance, because plurality rules give large parties a large relative advantage over small parties (Rae 1971, pp. 88–92; Sprague 1980). Similarly a potential leader buys a career, and as a rational purchaser he has no interest in a party that may lose throughout his lifetime. So the answer to the question of failure is that third parties are rejected in the rational calculus of expected utility especially by leaders, though also in the calculus by many simple voters. Any adequate theory to subsume Duverger's law must, I believe, begin there, which is a task for scholars in the next decade.

VIII.

I began this survey of the history of Duverger's law to demonstrate that a history existed. I think it is clear that in a forty-year period in which writers struggled to enunciate it, through another half-century, when it was clarified until Duverger asserted it as a law, and in the succeeding thirty years, it has been examined with increasing scientific sophistication:

- empirically: Counterexamples have been analyzed and the law revised to subsume them.
- theoretically: A theory of the behavioral forces involved has been enunciated and revised. From the first enunciation by Droop, the law has been implicitly embedded in a rational-choice theory about the behavior of politicians and voters. This theory has been rendered more and more explicit, especially in the last two decades, so that recent empirical work consciously invokes the rational-choice model.
- and as a source of hypotheses: Propositions inferred from it have been tested as, for example, the inquiry about sophisticated voting was undertaken because, if the law is valid and if the theory is appropriate, something like sophisticated voting must occur.

Of course, there is much yet to be done. If the theory is revised along the lines I have suggested, conditions to cover the counterexamples will doubtless be clarified and simplified. And there are more polities to examine. Recently Nigeria has adopted plurality voting, and its future experience with or without a two-party system will be another test of the law.

Although we are only part way along in this history, it still seems to me that the law is much more defensible than when Droop uttered it a century ago. Many—perhaps most—political scientists who specialize in the study of political parties now accept the law (e.g., Katz 1980, who, however, thought it applied particularly at the local level). Still, not all political scientists are convinced it is valid, and that is exactly as it should be, for skepticism about supposed truths is the heart of science. Still nearly everyone would agree, I believe, that there has been some accumulation of knowledge, and that is what I set out to demonstrate.

REFERENCES

Aldrich, J. H. 1976. "Some Problems in Testing Two Rational Models of Participation." *American Journal of Political Science* 20: 713–33.

Beck, N. 1975. "The Paradox of Minimax Regret." *American Political Science Review* 69: 918.

Bensel, R. F., and Sanders, E. 1979. "The Effect of Electoral Rules on Voting Behavior: The Electoral College and Shift Voting." *Public Choice* 34: 69–85.

Black, J. H. 1978. "The Multicandidate Calculus of Voting: Application to Canadian Federal Elections." *American Journal of Political Science* 22: 609–38.

Black, J. H. 1980. "The Probability-Choice Perspective in Voter Decision Making Models." *Public Choice* 35: 565–74.

Cain, B. E. 1978. "Strategic Voting in Britain." *American Journal of Political Science* 22: 639–55.

Canon, B. C. 1978. "Factionalism in the South: A Test of Theory and a Revisitation of V. O. Key." *American Journal of Political Science* 22: 833–48.

Carstairs, A. M. 1980. *A Short History of Electoral Systems in Western Europe.* London: George Allen and Unwin.

Downs, A. 1957. *An Economic Theory of Democracy.* New York: Harper & Bros.

Droop, H. R. 1871. "On the Political and Social Effects of Different Methods of Electing Representatives." London Juridical Society *Papers* 3: 469–507.

Droop, H. R. 1881. "On Methods of Electing Representatives." *Journal of the Statistical Society* 44: 2.

Duverger, M. 1963. *Political Parties: Their Organization and Activity in the Modern State.* North, B. and North, R., tr. New York: Wiley, Science Ed.

Ferejohn, J. A., and Fiorina, M. P. 1974. "The Paradox of Not Voting: A Decision Theoretic Analysis." *American Political Science Review* 68: 525–36.

———. 1975. "Closeness Counts Only in Horseshoes and Dancing." *American Political Science Review* 69: 920–25.

Finer, H. 1924. Rev. 1935. *The Case against Proportional Representation, Fabian Tract No. 211.* London: Fabian Society.

Fisher, S. L. 1974. "A Test of Anthony Downs' Wasted Vote Thesis: West German Evidence." Unpublished paper prepared for the Public Choice Society, New Haven, CT.

Friedrich, C. J. 1937. *Constitutional Government and Politics: Nature and Development.* New York: Harper & Bros.

Grumm, J. 1958. "Theories of Electoral Systems." *Midwest Journal of Political Science* 2: 357–76.

Hare, T. 1859. *The Election of Representatives, Parliamentary and Municipal.* London: Longmans Green.

Hermens, F. 1941. *Democracy or Anarchy: A Study of Proportional Representation.* Notre Dame, IN: Review of Politics.

Holcombe, A. 1910. "Direct Primaries and the Second Ballot." *American Political Science Review* 5: 535–52.

Katz, R. S. 1980. *A Theory of Parties and Electoral Systems.* Baltimore: Johns Hopkins University Press.

Key, V. O., Jr. 1949. *Southern Politics.* New York: Alfred A. Knopf.

Kuhn, T. S. 1970. *The Structure of Scientific Revolutions.* 2d ed. Chicago: University of Chicago Press.

Lemieux, P. 1977. *The Liberal Party and British Political Change: 1955–1974.* Ph.D. dissertation, Massachusetts Institute of Technology.

Lowell, A. L. 1896. *Government and Politics of Continental Europe.* 2 vols. Boston: Houghton Mifflin.

MacDonald, J. R. 1909. *Socialism and Government.* London: Independent Labour Party.

MacMahon, A. W. 1933. "Political Parties, United States." In *Encyclopedia of the Social Sciences,* ed. A. Johnson, 6: 596–601. New York: Macmillan.

Mayer, L., and Good, I. J. 1975. "Is Minimax Regret Applicable to Voting Decision?" *American Political Science Review* 69: 916–17.

Mellen, S. L. W. 1943. "The German People and the Post-war World." *American Political Science Review* 37: 607–25.

Mill, J. S. 1861. *Considerations on Representative Government.* In *Utilitarianism, Liberty, and Representative Government,* ed. A. D. Lindsay. London: J. M. Dent (Everyman Ed. 1910).

Munro, W. B. 1919. *The Government of the United States.* New York: Macmillan.

Nanson, E. J. 1882. *Transactions.* Melbourne: Proceedings of Royal Society of Victoria, 19: 197–240.

O'Leary, C. 1961. *The Irish Republic and Its Experiment with Proportional Representation.* Notre Dame, IN: University of Notre Dame Press.

———. 1979. *Irish Elections 1918–77: Parties, Voters and Proportional Representation.* New York: St. Martin's Press.

Ostrogorski, M. 1908. *Democracy and the Organization of Political Parties.* 2 vols. New York: Macmillan.

Popper, K. 1963. *Conjectures and Refutations: The Growth of Scientific Knowledge.* London: Routledge and Paul.

Rae, D. W. 1971. *The Political Consequences of Electoral Laws.* Rev. ed. New Haven, CT: Yale University Press.

Riker, W. H. 1976. "The Number of Political Parties: A Reexamination of Duverger's Law." *Comparative Politics* 9: 93–106.

———. 1977. "The Future of a Science of Politics." *American Behavioral Scientist* 21: 11–38.

Riker, W. H., and Ordeshook, P. C. 1968. "A Theory of the Calculus of Voting." *American Political Science Review* 62: 25–42.

Schattschneider, E. E. 1942. *Party Government.* New York: Farrar and Rinehart.

Shively, W. P. 1970. "The Elusive Psychological Factor: A Test for the Impact of Electoral Systems on Voters' Behavior." *Comparative Politics* 3: 115–25.

Spafford, D. 1972. "Electoral Systems and Voters' Behavior: Comment and a Further Test." *Comparative Politics* 5: 129–34.

Sprague, J. 1980. *On Duverger's Sociological Law: The Connection between Electoral Laws and Party Systems.* Political Science Paper No. 48. Photocopy. St. Louis: Washington University.

Weiner, M. 1957. *Party Politics in India: The Development of a Multiparty System.* Princeton, NJ: Princeton University Press.

Gender Studies and Political Science: The History of the "Behavioralist Compromise"

Helene Silverberg

The Root is Man.
　　　　　—Heinz Eulau, *The Behavioral Persuasion in Politics*

Some twenty years have passed since feminist scholars first began to challenge the content, substance, and research agendas of the academic disciplines. These methodological challenges, brought to the university by a new generation of scholars influenced by the political turbulence of the 1960s, have generated some of the most exciting research of the past decades. The persistence, strength, and steady growth of this new scholarship has now established the study of women as a legitimate focus of academic research. Today, almost half of all universities have a women's studies program, the women's studies community has its own organizations and journals, and almost all disciplines (including the "hard" sciences) have produced a substantial body of literature on women (Boxer 1982; Chamberlain 1988). However, a glance across the disciplines suggests the radically uneven response to the challenges posed by feminist scholars.

Despite a substantial increase in published research on women and politics, the feminist revolution has barely begun in the empirical subfields of political science. Feminist political scientists have pursued extensive and valuable work on subjects ranging from the origins of women's movements to the underrepresentation of women in legislative bodies. But compared to theoretical developments in the humanities, the large quantity of feminist work in political science has had remarkably little impact on the discipline as a whole. Within the last ten years (1980–90), the *American Political Science Review* (*APSR*) has published only two articles and three research notes on women,[1] while the *Publications of the Modern Language Association*

Previously unpublished essay.

1. These two articles were Eileen McDonaugh and H. Douglas Price, "Woman Suffrage in the Progressive Era: Patterns of Opposition and Support in Referenda Voting, 1910–1918," *APSR* 79(2): 415–35; Nancy Hirschmann, "Freedom, Recognition, and Obligation: A Feminist Ap-

(*PMLA*) and the *American Historical Review* (*AHR*) published dozens during the same period. Nor has feminist political science work been especially well received in the interdisciplinary women's studies community. Work by political scientists is strikingly underrepresented in journals such as *Signs* and *Feminist Studies*. Moreover, the amount of published material on women by feminist political scientists has been declining for at least the past five years.

The single most important contribution of contemporary feminist scholarship has been the recent emergence of gender as a category of analysis. It is the third phase of a three-stage process of theoretical development. In the first stage, feminist scholars simply appended women to established agendas of research. In the second stage, the social relations between the sexes became itself a new *topic* of research. This work focuses on the unequal power in the relations between men and women and examines historically specific patterns of struggle and compromise between them.[2] The structure of this analytical approach is similar to research on class relations that explores patterns of interaction between workers and management.

During the third and current stage, feminist scholars have employed gender as a new *category of analysis*. Used in this way, gender provides the theoretical lens through which the inequalities of power between men and women can be seen to structure (and are structured by) the organization of political, social, and economic life (Scott 1986). An example from the new feminist scholarship on the welfare state is perhaps most illustrative. Classic theories of the origin and development of the welfare state have commonly used class as their primary category of analysis. This scholarship has assumed that the welfare state emerged out of the contested intersection of capitalism, citizenship, and democracy (Briggs 1961; Marshall 1963; Titmuss 1958). As historian Linda Gordon has noted, however, this view of the evolution of the welfare state is implicitly based upon male workers' confrontation with late nineteenth-century capitalism and the state. It neither describes women's relationship to capitalism and the state during industrialization, takes account of their participation in the establishment of social welfare policy, nor explains the sexually differentiated programmatic structure of welfare states. Feminist scholarship employing gender as a category of analysis can do so (Gordon 1990).

proach to Political Theory," *APSR* 83(4): 1227–44. The three research notes were Jerry Perkins and Diane Fowlkes, "Opinion Representation versus Social Representation; Or, Why Women Can't Run as Women and Win," *APSR* 74(1): 92–103; Virginia Sapiro, "When Are Interests Interesting: The Problem of Political Representation of Women," *APSR* 75(3): 701–16; Timothy Bledsoe and Mary Herring, "Victims of Circumstances: Women in Pursuit of Public Office," *APSR* 84(1): 213–24.

2. Christine Stansell, a prominent feminist historian, defines a gender system as "all of those arrangements of work, sexuality, parental responsibility, psychological life, assigned social traits and internalized emotions through which the sexes defined themselves respectively as men and women." *City of Women* (Urbana: University of Illinois Press, 1987), p. xii.

This essay argues that feminist political scientists have failed to make the methodological transition from a focus on women (stage one) to the use of gender as a category of analysis (stage three) because of the confluence of three specific developments in the 1970s: (1) the dominance of the behavioralist paradigm in political science; (2) the professional imperatives experienced by feminist scholars entering political science at that time;[3] and (3) the emergence of the feminist movement. During the 1970s, the efflorescence of political activity by women provided the terrain on which this first generation of feminist scholars was able to reconcile the competing claims of feminism and political science. The resulting "behavioralist compromise" enabled feminist political scientists to pursue research on women (stage one), but it simultaneously raised methodological obstacles to the emergence of gender as a category of analysis in political science (stage three). An alliance with the increasingly prominent historically oriented and interpretive "new institutionalism" can, I argue, provide the necessary methodological underpinnings for the emergence of gender as a category of analysis in political science.

Behavioralism and the Origins of Research on Women and Politics

Like other scholarly fields, political science research on women has moved in a cyclical fashion over the decades since the discipline was founded in the United States. During the early twentieth century, when the first wave of the feminist movement forced open higher education to women, a handful of women entered the newly established political science graduate programs at the University of Chicago, Johns Hopkins, and Columbia. These women initiated the first systematic research on women and politics as part of their social reform activities during the Progressive era (Breckinridge 1933; Fitzpatrick 1990). Research on women rapidly dwindled in the 1920s with the withdrawal of women from academic careers and political life, and virtually disappeared in the 1930s and 1940s. The most important exceptions during these years were the publication of Charles Merriam and Harold F. Gosnell's *Non-Voting: Causes and Methods of Control* (1924), which examined women's voting behavior four years after their enfranchisement, and Sophonisba Breckinridge's *Women in the Twentieth Century: A Study of Their Political, Social, and Economic Activities* (1933), written for Herbert Hoover's President's Research Committee on Social Trends.[4] With these ex-

---

3. It is important to note that not all women political scientists were, or are, feminists and, second, that not all feminist political scientists were inclined to do their research on women. In this essay I am specifically referring to feminist women political scientists who sought to do research on women.

4. Breckinridge obtained a Ph.D. in political science at the University of Chicago in 1901 and a J.D. from the University of Chicago's law school in 1904. On Breckinridge, see Edith

ceptions,[5] however, the almost exclusively male discipline of the interwar period engaged in an atheoretical "hyperfactualism" (Easton 1971) that did not even examine the fact of women's participation in politics.[6]

The ascendance of behavioralism in the 1950s revived scholarship on women and politics, though it did not, of course, set out to do this. As postwar political scientists increasingly turned their attention to the investigation of individual and group political behavior, they invariably stumbled upon women's extensive postwar civic activities. However, the two research traditions established during these years, the survey research studies of mass political behavior and the "community power" studies, led political scientists down well-defined methodological paths. This had distinct theoretical implications for the study of women's political activity. In *Who Governs?* (1960), Dahl sought to challenge stratification theory, in which a socioeconomic elite was said to dominate political life. His categories of analysis therefore embraced hierarchies of power within the political arena. As a result, Dahl failed to attribute any theoretical significance to women's prominent role in education politics in New Haven through the local Parent-Teacher Association (1960, pp. 156–58). For Dahl, the Parent-Teacher Association was just another example of the relationship between leaders and constituents in local politics.[7] Polsby (1963) and Wolfinger (1974) similarly failed to attribute any theoretical significance to the patterns of women's political participation they described.

By contrast, survey researchers' methodology and research questions compelled them to focus theoretical attention on women. In *The People's Choice* (1948), where women make their first appearance in postwar American political science, Lazarsfeld, Berelson, and Gaudet distinguished carefully between the sexes in their examination of the role of the family in the development of individual political attitudes (Lazarsfeld, Berelson, and Gaudet 1948, pp. 140–42). Berelson and Lazarsfeld's next study, *Voting*

Abbott, "Sophonisba Breckinridge over the Years," *Social Service Review* 22(4): 417–23. On the President's Research Committee on Social Trends, see Barry Karl, "Presidential Planning and Social Science Research: Mr. Hoover's Experts," *Perspectives in American History* 3 (1969): 347–409.

5. There were two other notable exceptions, but they were not written by American political scientists. They were Herbert Tingsten, *Political Behavior: Studies in Election Statistics* (London: P. S. King and Sons, 1937) and Maurice Duverger, *The Political Role of Women* (Paris: UNESCO, 1955).

6. The *American Political Science Review* published only two articles on women during the interwar period, both by women: Alzada Comstock, "Women Members of European Parliaments," *APSR* 20 (1926): 379–83; Marguerite Fisher and Betty Whitehead, "Women's Participation in National Party Nominating Conventions, 1892–1941," *APSR* 38 (October 1944): 395–403.

7. This point is firmly underscored by Dahl's use of gender-neutral language; members of the PTA are most frequently referred to as "people" or "parents."

(1954), extended this investigation of the differences between the sexes from the family into the political arena. In one of the most important theoretical innovations of this literature, *Voting* systematically examined women's behavior in a variety of political roles (e.g., as voters, party activists, and union members). By the time Campbell, Converse, Miller, and Stokes published *The American Voter* in 1960, sex was a well-established independent variable in survey research. Between 1948 and 1972, survey research produced the first large body of systematic research on women's political behavior since the Progressive era.

This large and highly influential body of work created what I have called the "behavioralist approach" to research on women and politics. Two aspects of this approach are especially noteworthy. First, survey researchers defined women's political behavior in precisely the same terms as they did men's. They examined women's voting turnout rate, their attendance at political meetings, and their financial contributions to political campaigns. But this definition of political behavior, though ostensibly gender-neutral, was clearly based on the norm of male political behavior in the 1940s and 1950s. It excluded, for example, women's extensive political activity through civic organizations, such as the League of Women Voters or the Parent-Teacher Association. As a result, survey researchers came to view women's political behavior as inadequate and inferior to men's. Some drew a less flattering picture of "femina politica" than others. Lane (1959, pp. 209–16) concluded that women were moralistic, intolerant, uninformed, and personality- rather than issue-oriented in comparison to men. Campbell, Converse, Miller, and Stokes (1960, pp. 483–93) took a more sympathetic view of women's low levels of political activity, suggesting that women were unfortunate victims of lagging sex-role change.

Second, survey researchers universally agreed that sex roles were responsible for sex differences in political behavior. According to this view, female socialization fostered an interest in private and family matters, whereas male socialization fostered an interest in public, political matters. Although sex roles were not considered to be biologically mandated, survey researchers of this period believed they embodied a division of labor that was both natural and appropriate. Greater political activity by women, it was argued, would jeopardize the stability of the family and therefore of the United States. "Apolitical Woman"—with the possible exception of regular trips to the polling booth on election day—was, in fact, the bulwark of postwar American democracy.[8] The discipline's claims to scientific objectivity notwithstanding, however, such

---

8. See, for example, Lane's comment on the consequences of increased political activity for women: "Would it be wise to reinforce the feminist movement, emphasizing politics on the women's page along with the garden club and bridge club news . . . ? No doubt something along

value-laden views of women's "proper place" could not flourish for long in the rapidly changing profession of the 1970s.

In the late 1960s, women began to reenter political science graduate programs in large numbers. As had happened at the turn of the century, the resurgence of the feminist movement and the growth of higher education enabled many young women to undertake advanced training in political science. Many of them were already swept up in feminist activities and others were drawn into women's liberation during their graduate school years. But although their arrival reversed the decline of the number of women granted Ph.D.'s in political science that had begun in the 1920s, this did not immediately alter the social structure of the profession. Women were still largely excluded from the most prestigious graduate schools, many received only an M.A., others taught only part time, and most were concentrated in small liberal arts colleges (especially the women's colleges), state universities, or two-year institutions where their energies were necessarily directed toward teaching rather than scholarship (Schuck 1969, 1970; Chamberlain 1988). In the face of rising expectations and blocked opportunities, these women formed part of a growing constituency available for mobilization against the established structure of the postwar profession.

In the late 1960s, a group of these women joined a number of their male colleagues in a short-lived insurgency within the American Political Science Association. The Caucus for a New Political Science, the first organized expression of discontent in the profession, made several efforts to attract women to its ranks.[9] But neither the male-dominated caucus nor the slow-moving APSA Committee on the Status of Women, appointed by APSA President David Easton in March 1969, were able to contain women's discontent. At the APSA annual meeting in August 1969, a small group of women founded the Women's Caucus for Political Science (WCPS). Like the Caucus for a New Political Science, the women's caucus hoped to promote both intellectual and organizational change.[10]

---

these lines could be done, but it is too seldom remembered by the American society that working girls and career women, and women who insistently serve the community in volunteer capacities, and women with extracurricular interests of an absorbing kind are often borrowing their time and attention and capacity for relaxed play and love from their children to whom it rightfully belongs. As Kardiner points out, the rise of juvenile delinquency (and, he says, homosexuality) is partly to be attributed to the feminist movement and what it did to the American mother." *Political Life*, p. 355.

9. The caucus's efforts to attract women included the creation of its own Commission on the Status of Women in the Profession, chaired by Alan Wolfe, and a campaign to have the American Political Science Association establish a similar commission. See "Supplement to Professional Notes," *PS* 1 (Fall 1968): 17–18. On the rise and fall of the caucus see Lowi (1972) and Wolfe (1970).

10. On the origins and early aspirations of the Women's Caucus, see its statement in *PS* 2 (Fall 1969): 678.

The intellectual and political diversity of the women's caucus, however, worked to displace emerging theoretical debates with professional concerns. The WCPS drew its leadership from among graduate students, adjunct faculty, and part-time lecturers scattered across the subfields in the discipline. In its earliest years, the women's caucus also attracted radical and socialist feminists with ties to women's liberation as well as feminists more sympathetic to the style and goals of liberal feminism.[11] Since women's caucus members were linked only by their sex and their common opposition to sex discrimination in political science, the WCPS focused its attention on professional concerns. It participated in APSA elections, developed new grievance procedures, drew up sexual harassment guidelines, attacked antinepotism laws, and generally helped to lower the barriers to women's advancement in the profession.[12] But its failure to serve as a forum for scholarly debate and methodological revision left it permanently on the sidelines of new feminist intellectual developments already under way in the discipline.

In 1974, a handful of feminist political scientists began to provide the first structural critiques of behavioralist political science from a feminist perspective. Bourque and Grossholtz (1974) and Elshtain (1974) challenged the idea of value-free research by attacking the sexist interpretations of women's political behavior in some of behavioralism's most influential texts. More important, these essays also exposed the male political norm that lay behind the discipline's purportedly gender-neutral categories of analysis. Political science's definition of "the political," which focused primarily on governmental institutions, formal political processes, and public policy, was especially rejected. These feminist scholars embraced the early feminist movement's central precept and challenged the discipline to expand its definition of "the political" to include "the personal." The actual content of this departure was left quite vague, but the implied research agenda pointed toward an examination of the sexual division of labor in the family, reproduction, and sexuality. It was, seemingly, a rejection of political science.

Simultaneously, a second and much larger group of women began to lay the terms of a compromise between feminism and political science. These women explicitly embraced behavioralist assumptions and methods and sought to turn them to new, feminist ends. In 1974, the first survey research studies focused solely on women voters and political elites were published (Jacquette 1974; Kirkpatrick 1974), and several more followed over the next decade (Diamond 1977; Kelly and Boutilier 1978; Sapiro 1983). In focusing

---

11. Ibid; also Kay Klotzberger, "Political Action by Academic Women," in Alice Rossi and Anne Calderwood, eds., *Academic Women on the Move* (New York: Russell Sage, 1973). Klotzberger was a founder of the WCPS and first chair of the WCPS as well as a member of the APSA Committee on the Status of Women.

12. The activities of the WCPS can be traced in *PS*. See also the article by Klotzberger (n. 11).

specifically on women's behavior, these feminist political scientists partially departed from the research tradition established by their male predecessors. But their methodological continuity with postwar behavioralists was most striking.

Changes in the discipline in the 1970s strengthened the hand of feminists seeking a compromise[13] with political science. Male sociologists and political scientists, such as Gamson (1975), Oberschall (1973), Lowi (1971), and Lipsky (1968), had already begun to expand political science's scholarly domain beyond the narrow limits of early behavioralism. The new definition of political behavior included the new forms of political activity characteristic of the 1960s and 1970s, such as social movements and interest groups. The expansion of the discipline's jurisdiction in this way enabled feminist political scientists to append women to mainstream research agendas without having to challenge the larger questions, categories, and models of the discipline. In 1975, the APSA gave its imprimatur to this approach by awarding the first prize for the Best Work on Women in Politics to a book that used women as a case study, employing social movement theory. Jo Freeman's *The Politics of Women's Liberation: A Case Study of an Emerging Social Movement and Its Relation to the Policy Process* consummated what I have called the "behavior alist compromise." With a few exceptions, most feminist research in the empirical subfields of political science has followed this methodological format.

During the 1980s, feminist political scientists embraced the linguistic shift from the word "sex" to the word "gender." Klein's book, titled *Gender Politics* (1984), announced the prominence of the new language in the discipline. But the shift to the new term obscured the continuity of the old methodological approach. Feminist political scientists' definition of gender simply reiterated the logic of political socialization and the assumptions of behavioralism. In a usage characteristic of feminist political scientists in the 1980s, Sapiro (1983, p. 36) explained gender as "the sociocultural manifestations of being a man or woman, . . . [the] learned significance of one's sex." Defined this way, gender remained simply an alternative term for sex roles. It did not include the key concepts of either stage-two or stage-three feminist scholarship: It did not, for example, take account of the role of power in the relations between the sexes, nor did it employ gender as a theoretical lens on political life. Thus Klein, Sapiro, and other prominent feminist political scientists in the early 1980s remained firmly within the terms of the behavioralist compromise.

---

13. I here use the term "compromise" in the way that political scientists have traditionally employed such terms as "class compromise" or "postwar settlement." That is, I do not in any way mean to imply self-consciously intentional acts of "compromise" on the part of feminist scholars. To the contrary, the term is meant to suggest the outcome of a historically situated, institutionally structured conflict in which both sides search for an accommodation.

It is important to note that feminist scholarly work in political theory has followed a different path over the last two decades. The postwar split between empirical political science and political theory (Gunnell 1988) provided feminist political theorists with a freedom to explore new questions and approaches denied their empirical colleagues. Within the first generation of feminist political theorists, divergent political commitments fostered two methodological trajectories. Radical and socialist feminists, who were especially attracted to the subfield in the mid-1970s, began immediately to apply their analytical tools to explaining the nature and origins of women's subordination in contemporary society. They produced several anthologies that sought to integrate Marxism and feminism into a theory explaining women's oppression under "capitalist patriarchy" (Eisenstein 1979; Sargent 1981; Hartsock 1983). At the same time, Susan Moller Okin (1979) and Jean Elshtain (1981) led scholarly efforts by liberal feminists to explore the hidden gender assumptions of the political philosophy canon. In both cases, this work involved more than simply adding women to the established research agenda in political theory. Feminist theorists focused almost immediately on the social relations between the sexes (stage two).

In contrast to developments in empirical political science, shifts in political theory in the early 1980s enabled feminist theorists to embrace gender as a category of analysis in their work. The intellectual heirs of earlier feminist scholars concerned with contemporary problems extended gender analysis to current debates about sex, abortion, and the new reproductive technologies. Feminist theorists also increasingly used gender as their analytical framework for exploring issues not obviously related to women, such as justice, rights, contract, and citizenship (Dietz 1987; Okin 1989; Pateman 1988; Sunstein 1990). As in other areas of the discipline, however, there has been insufficient dialogue between feminist political theorists and feminist empirical political scientists. As a result, the emergence of gender as a category of analysis (stage three) in the subfield of political theory has had little influence over the course of feminist empirical work, at least to date.

The frustration of feminist scholarship in political science appears especially prominent when compared to developments in the humanities. The absence of a single dominant paradigm in these disciplines in the 1970s facilitated the transition from sex to gender as a new category of analysis. As early as 1975, historian Natalie Davis encouraged her colleagues to study "the significance of the sexes" (stage two) rather than focus narrowly and separately on women (stage one) (1975, p. 90). Little more than a decade later, the publication of Joan Scott's important *AHR* essay, "Gender: A Useful Category of Historical Analysis" (1986), confirmed a trend already under way in the humanities. By the mid-1980s, political science was clearly lagging behind several other disciplines.

Sex and Gender in Political Science

Why were feminist political scientists unable to make the methodological transition in the 1980s to gender as a category of analysis? The answer lies in the specific historical conditions of the 1970s. The emergence of the feminist movement during that decade enabled feminist political scientists to use behavioralism to reconcile the competing claims of feminism and political science—but primarily on political science's terms. Once in place, however, the terms of the behavioralist compromise actually prevented the emergence of gender as a category of analysis in the discipline. Gender analysis would have to wait until the historical underpinnings of the behavioralist compromise began to erode in the mid-1980s.

Postwar behavioralists incorporated women into their research by introducing sex as an independent variable into the lexicon of political science. This approach to research on women was directly derived from the basic methodological assumptions of their paradigm. Behavioralists insisted that interests and preferences determining political behavior were exogenous to the political system. They simply extended this general principle to the differences in political behavior their studies revealed (or, more precisely, constructed) between men and women. As Campbell, Converse, Miller, and Stokes (1960, pp. 484–85) argued:

> The basic differences that mark the political participation of men and women we take to lie in vestigial sex roles. . . . A sex role for political behavior includes, then, that portion of expectations about behavior proper for a male or female that involves political responses. A century ago political sex roles were clear-cut. A man was supposed to be the political agent for the family unit. A woman not only had no need to concern herself with politics; to one degree or another, political activity was unseemly for her. . . . Yet social roles are deeply ingrained in day-to-day assumptions about behavior in any culture, and these assumptions are not rapidly uprooted. Decades after the first successes of the suffragettes many wives wish to refer our interviewers to their husbands as being the person in the family who pays attention to politics. Or the woman may say in so many words: "I don't know anything about politics—I thought that business was for men, anyway."

Campbell, Converse, Miller, and Stokes merely assumed a causal relationship between sex roles and political behavior; *The American Voter* provided no direct evidence for this linkage. The emergence of "political socialization" as a subspecialty in American politics in the early 1960s provided the key, purportedly "scientific" evidence of causality between sex role socialization and political behavior.[14] Thus a fully formulated and widely accepted approach to research on women was available when the first generation of feminists entered the discipline in the late 1960s.

Behavioralism proved to be highly receptive to their efforts to reconcile their feminist and professional commitments. These women could not simply embrace the behavioralist tradition as formulated by their male predecessors, since the pre-1970 scholarship clearly subordinated women's political behavior to larger, ostensibly gender-neutral questions about "How the Voter Makes up His Mind in a Presidential Campaign," "Opinion Formation in a Presidential Campaign," or "Why People Get Involved in Politics."[15] Determined to bring women's political behavior out from under the shadows of postwar behavioralism, this first generation of feminist political scientists turned the behavioralist approach on its side: they applied behavioralist assumptions and research tools specifically to women's burgeoning political activity in the 1970s.

The resurgence of the feminist movement in the public debates of the 1970s was thus the key historical condition that made possible what I have called the behavioralist compromise. Women's extensive political activity in the 1950s through voluntary, nonpartisan, civic associations, such as the Parent-Teacher Association and the League of Women Voters, had fallen outside the channels of politics for which the categories of behavioralism had been constructed. Thus the politically active women of the 1950s and 1960s had been judged less political than men by the political scientists of those years. But during the late 1960s, women's political behavior began spilling out of the domain of voluntary association into political channels, which behavioralist categories could register as political activity. The founding of the National Organization for Women in 1966 and the Women's Strike for Equality in 1970, the creation of the National Women's Political Caucus in 1971, the election of several new women to Congress in 1972, and the initiation of organized lobbying for new public policies for women indicated the growing convergence of the bases and forms of men's and women's political behavior. Women could therefore simply be added to established research agendas on social movements, interest groups, electoral politics, congressional politics, political elites, and so on. Not surprisingly, the first published research of this first generation included studies of women party activists, women voters, and women state legislators (Kirkpatrick 1974; Jacquette 1974; Diamond 1977). The feminist movement outside the academy thus made it possible for femi-

---

14. For a brief early history of this subspecialty, see Fred Greenstein, *Children and Politics* (New Haven: Yale University Press, rev. ed., 1979), pp. 5–15.

15. These are the subtitles of Lazarsfeld, Berelson, and Gaudet, *The People's Choice* (1948); Berelson, Lazarsfeld, and McPhee, *Voting* (1954); and Lane, *Political Life* (1959), respectively.

nist political scientists to accept (indeed, enthusiastically embrace) the terms of behavioralism and to carve out a new field of scholarly expertise called "women and politics."

Once in place, the behavioralist compromise was sustained by the particular distribution of its benefits. It enabled feminist political scientists to reconcile their feminism with the imperatives of professional advancement. The new field of women and politics permitted feminists to claim a special place for themselves in political science departments. The behavioralist compromise was also good for the feminist movement. Few feminist organizations and nonuniversity research centers were financially able to develop the in-house technical expertise necessary to pursue their electoral, legal, and policy activities. The behavioralist compromise enabled them to rely on feminist political scientists to supply the needed data on women's political behavior. Feminist political scientists were, of course, happy to oblige.

But the behavioralist compromise benefitted political science as a discipline most of all. It increased political science's legitimacy by implicitly confirming the claim that its methods, assumptions, and categories were neutral, universal, and objective, permitting all groups to be studied equally. In exchange, the discipline acknowledged women as a valid research subject, precisely because feminist researchers accepted and used the methods and techniques of behavioralist political science in their work. In 1983, the APSA published a five-volume series of review essays, sample syllabi, and suggested readings to assist faculty in integrating women into the political science teaching curriculum (APSA 1983).

Finally, the behavioralist compromise flourished between the mid-1970s and mid-1980s because it had uncontested explanatory power for the specific research questions feminist political scientists asked during these years. The emergence in the public world of feminist interest groups, feminist electoral activities, feminist legal battles, and feminist lobbying for new public policies for women excited feminist political scientists and demanded scholarly attention. But the particular methodological orientation of the feminist research agenda of the past two decades cannot be viewed as a simple and straightforward response to the efflorescence of women's political activity in the 1970s and 1980s. It was also a function of the behavioralist training feminist political scientists had themselves received. Feminist scholars who adopted the behavioralist paradigm found, not surprisingly, that the questions they were able to ask were particularly well answered in behavioralist terms. But this did not mean that they were the best or the sole research questions feminist political scientists could ask.

Feminist political scientists paid a high price for the emergence of the behavioralist compromise. The behavioralist compromise had restricted the development of feminist scholarship in three significant ways. First, it had severely limited the dialogue between political scientists and scholars in other disciplines interested in gender studies. Though feminist political scientists had produced an enormous body of research on women and politics, this work was methodologically incompatible with the standards of women's studies research. It was therefore of limited interest to other feminist scholars, most of whom were now attuned to work employing gender as a category of analysis. At the same time, feminist political scientists did not generally benefit from the rich interdisciplinary debates in women's studies. As women's studies research became increasingly sophisticated and more deeply committed to gender as a category of analysis, the theoretical gap between political scientists and other feminist scholars grew increasingly large.

Second, the behavioralist compromise had also limited feminist political scientists' dialogue with other political scientists. Feminist scholars were hard-pressed to demonstrate their contribution to political science's body of theoretical knowledge. The behavioralist compromise had provided feminist scholars with a new area of expertise, but few made any claims to a distinct body of theory. Nor were feminist scholars able to apply the methods of the behavioralist compromise in a way that substantially challenged existing empirical political science theories. From Freeman's *Politics of Women's Liberation* in 1975 to the most recent studies by Klein (1984), Sapiro (1983), Katzenstein and Mueller (1987), the empirical feminist scholarly tradition in the discipline was more likely to apply, than revise, theories current in the discipline.

Finally, the behavioralist compromise limited feminist political scientists' dialogue with each other as scholars. As a research approach, it proved unable to unify feminist political scientists into an influential intellectual force in the discipline. By its very logic, which subordinated the study of women to the conceptual terms of behavioralism, the behavioralist compromise scattered feminist scholars across the subfields of political science. It also enjoined them to address their work to these subfields, rather than toward any common feminist theoretical concerns. The expansion of work on women therefore led to a large but fragmented literature on women and politics, which reproduced itself as new graduate students interested in pursuing research on women were themselves dispersed across the discipline's subfields.[16]

Some of these concerns were raised in a steady stream of review essays and articles in the late 1970s (Boals 1975; Jacquette 1976; Carroll 1979). There was unanimous agreement on the importance of the new data collected,

---

16. For the past several years, the fall issue of *PS* has listed political science dissertations in preparation. A quick glance reveals that projects on women are scattered across the subfields and seem to have more in common with other projects in their subfield than with each other.

but many feminist political scientists expressed concern about the weak the-oretical contribution this work was making to the discipline. As the conditions underpinning the behavioralist compromise eroded in the mid-1980s, how-ever, the way has been opened for feminists in the discipline to forge a new compromise with political science.

Toward Gender as a Category of Analysis in Political Science

In the early 1980s, political science entered a period of methodological flux. As the behavioralist paradigm's influence finally waned, the conditions that had sustained the academic settlement between feminists and political science for almost two decades also began to erode. The time is now ripe for feminist political scientists to renegotiate the terms of understanding between femi-nism and the discipline. Although a number of alternative paradigms are now available, an alliance with the historically oriented, interpretive "new institu-tionalism" would, I believe, provide the firmest methodological footing for the emergence of gender as a category of analysis in political science. This would, in turn, help revitalize feminist scholarship in the discipline.

In the early 1980s, the three pillars supporting the behavioralist com-promise began to crumble. First, what remained of the behavioralist paradigm came under renewed fire from two distinct intellectual approaches in the discipline that both claimed the name of the "new institutionalism." New institutionalist critiques of behavioralism differed from those associated with the Caucus for a New Political Science and were far more successful in undermining behavioralism's power, because they focused on its meth-odological assumptions rather than its alleged irrelevance. Scholars working in both the formal or rational-choice new institutionalist tradition, as well as those working in the historical and interpretive new institutionalist tradition, attacked behavioralism for its failure to consider the institutional constraints on individual choice and collective decision making (McCubbins and Sullivan 1987; Riker 1983; Skowronek 1982; Weir, Orloff, and Skocpol 1988). Al-though there continues to be debate over whether the new institutionalism constitutes the paradigm shift some of its advocates have claimed (Almond 1988), March and Olsen's pioneering essay in the *American Political Science Review* announced the emergence of a new scholarly impulse—if not a full-fledged new paradigm—in the discipline (March and Olsen 1984).

By the early 1980s, the second and third pillars supporting the behavior-alist compromise also began to crumble. Feminists entering political science in the early 1980s were far less inclined than their predecessors to commit themselves to research on women in politics. Like many of the men in their cohort, this second generation of feminist political scientists was attracted to the new and unusually exciting developments occurring around the world. By contrast, the feminist movement in the United States, particularly after 1982, grew increasingly moribund. Not only did this deter new feminist political scientists from pursuing feminist scholarship, it also significantly reduced the range of topics that could be assimilated to the behavioralist compromise. Although the defeat of the Equal Rights Amendment and the emergence of a "gender gap" in voting patterns in the early 1980s generated a spurt of research on these topics (Klein 1984; Mueller 1988; Mansbridge 1986; Hoff-Wilson 1986), the decline of feminist activity in the public arena significantly reduced the feminist agenda in political science. By comparison to the 1970s, however, feminist political scientists published only a limited number of books and articles in the 1980s.

The current weakness of the behavioralist compromise, and the present methodological flux in the discipline more generally, provides feminist political scientists with an unusual opportunity to rethink the future direction of feminist scholarship in the discipline. In my opinion, an alliance with the historically oriented, interpretive new institutionalism would provide the best possibility for the revitalization of feminist scholarship in political science. Specifically, the underlying methodological assumptions of this approach are uniquely compatible with the "social constructionist" impulse at the heart of women's studies. Unlike behavioralism or rational choice, the historically oriented, interpretive new institutionalism assumes that preferences are endogenous to (that is, constructed in) politics. Accordingly, politics could be understood not simply as the "authoritative allocation of values" (Easton 1971) or the process through which "who gets what, when, how" (Lasswell 1936). Politics could also be viewed as a primary mechanism through which definitions of womanhood and manhood are defined, sexuality is conceptualized, and reproductive activity delineated.

Gender as a category of analysis has the potential to open each of the three dialogues that the behavioralist compromise foreclosed in the 1970s. First, feminist political scientists would be able to participate more fully in the interdisciplinary debates of women's studies. The mechanisms through which gender is constructed would no longer seem to lay outside the political arena as they had under the terms of the behavioralist compromise. Thus feminist political scientists would be able to enrich women's studies' understanding of the origin and dynamics of gender systems by modifying the society-oriented perspective it inherited from social history.

Second, gender as a category of analysis would open an equally rich, and long-needed, dialogue between feminist political scientists and others in the discipline. As a new theoretical lens through which subjects of long-standing interest to political scientists could be examined, gender as a category of analysis could help place the social relations between the sexes at the center of the discipline's research agenda. Recent work by Skocpol and Ritter (1991), Nelson (1990), and Sapiro (1986), for example, has clearly demonstrated the constitutive role of gender relations and ideologies in the administrative distinctions between the contributory social insurance approach of workmen's compensation (intended primarily for men) and the means-tested approach to Aid to Families with Dependent Children (AFDC), intended primarily for women. Clearly, many additional areas of interest to political scientists invite a gender analysis.[17]

Finally, gender as a category of analysis would help foster a more fruitful conversation among feminist political scientists. Under the terms of the behavioralist compromise, feminist scholars' dispersion across the subfields fragmented feminist scholarship both substantively and theoretically. By contrast, gender as a category of analysis could unite feminist political scientists by providing common methodological ground for scholars with different substantive interests. Just as the methodology of rational choice has enabled political scientists working in different subfields to pursue a common theoretical agenda and, perhaps more importantly, to establish a recognized and influential intellectual community in the discipline, gender as a category of analysis would foster closer intellectual cooperation among feminist scholars.

Conclusion

From the outset, the goal of feminist scholarship has been to change existing structures of knowledge, not simply to add women to established research agendas. This goal has been easier to realize in the humanities than in the social sciences. In political science, the convergence of the behavioral revolution in postwar political science, the professional and political concerns of feminist political scientists in the 1970s, and the emergence of the feminist movement provided the conditions for a rather uneasy settlement between feminism and political science for more than two decades. But short-term legitimacy for feminist scholarship was clearly gained at the expense of long-term theoretical significance. Gaining legitimacy for research on women is inherently linked to a methodological challenge this work did not, and could not, raise.

Feminist scholarship in political science does not require abandoning fundamental presuppositions of political science, such as positivism, hypothesis-testing, and the requirement of falsifiability, as some feminist

---

17. For purposes of my argument, feminist scholars do not necessarily need to subscribe (implicitly or explicitly) to the new institutionalism. My point is simply that the growing prominence of the new institutionalism has created a much more sympathetic intellectual environment for scholarly work employing gender as a category of analysis.

critics of social science have suggested. Rather, broader use of gender as a category of analysis in political science would open the way for a compromise between feminism and political science on terms that would enrich both feminist scholarship and political science.

REFERENCES

Almond, Gabriel. 1988. "The Return to the State." *American Political Science Review* 82(3): 853–74.
American Political Science Association. 1983. *Citizenship and Change: Women and American Politics.* 5 vols. Washington, DC: American Political Science Association.
Berelson, Bernard, Paul Lazarsfeld, and William McPhee. 1954. *Voting.* Chicago: University of Chicago Press.
Boals, Kay. 1975. "Review Essay: Political Science." *Signs* 1(1): 161–74.
Bourque, Susan, and Jean Grossholtz. 1974. "Politics as Unnatural Practice: Political Science Looks at Women's Participation." *Politics and Society* 4(2): 225–66.
Boxer, Marilyn. 1982. "For and About Women: The Theory and Practice of Women's Studies in the United States." *Signs* 7(3): 661–95.
Breckinridge, Sophonisba. 1933. *Women in the Twentieth Century: A Study of Their Political, Social, and Economic Activities.* New York: McGraw Hill.
Briggs, Asa. 1961. "The Welfare State in Historical Perspective." *Archives Europeannes de Sociologie* 2(2): 221–58.
Campbell, Angus, Philip E. Converse, Warren E. Miller, and Donald E. Stokes. 1960. *The American Voter.* New York: John Wiley and Sons.
Carroll, Berenice. 1979. "Review Essay: Political Science, Part I: American Politics and Political Behavior." *Signs* 5(2): 289–306.
Chamberlain, Mariam K., ed. 1988. *Women in Academe: Progress and Prospects.* New York: Russell Sage.
Dahl, Robert A. 1960. *Who Governs?* New Haven: Yale University Press.
Davis, Natalie Zemon. 1975. "Women's History in Transition: The European Case." *Feminist Studies* 3(3/4): 83–103.
Diamond, Irene. 1977. *Sex Roles in the State House.* New Haven: Yale University Press.
Dietz, Mary G. 1987. "Context Is All: Feminism and Theories of Citizenship." *Daedalus* 116(4): 1–24.
Easton, David. 1971. *The Political System.* 2d ed. New York: Knopf.
Eisenstein, Zillah, ed. 1979. *Capitalist Patriarchy and the Case for Socialist Feminism.* New York: Monthly Review Press.
Elshtain, Jean. 1974. "Moral Woman and Immoral Man." *Politics and Society* 4(4): 453–73.
———. 1981. *Public Man, Private Woman: Women in Social and Political Thought.* Princeton: Princeton University Press.

Fitzpatrick, Ellen. 1990. *Endless Crusade*. New York: Oxford University Press.
Frankovic, Kathleen. 1977. "Sex and Voting in the United States House of Representatives, 1961–1975." *American Politics Quarterly* 5(1977): 315–30.
Freeman, Jo. 1975. *The Politics of Women's Liberation*. New York: David McKay.
Gamson, William. 1975. *The Strategy of Social Protest*. Homewood, IL: Dorsey.
Githens, Marianne, and Jewell Prestage, eds. 1977. *A Portrait of Marginality*. New York: David McKay.
Gordon, Linda. 1990. "The New Feminist Scholarship on the Welfare State." In *Women, the State, and Welfare*, ed. Linda Gordon, pp. 9–35. Madison: University of Wisconsin Press.
Gunnell, John G. 1988. "American Political Science, Liberalism, and the Invention of Political Theory." *American Political Science Review* 82(1): 71–87.
Hartsock, Nancy. 1983. *Money, Sex, and Power: Toward a Feminist Historical Materialism*. New York: Longman.
Hoff-Wilson, Joan. 1986. *Rights of Passage*. Bloomington: Indiana University Press.
Jacquette, Jane, ed. 1974. *Women in Politics*. New York: John Wiley.
———. 1976. "Review Essay: Political Science." *Signs* 2(1): 147–64.
Katzenstein, Mary, and Carol Mueller, eds. 1987. *The Women's Movements of the United States and Western Europe*. Philadelphia: Temple University Press.
Kelly, Rita Mae, and Mary Boutilier. 1978. *The Making of Political Women*. Chicago: Nelson-Hall.
Kirkpatrick, Jeane. 1974. *Political Woman*. New York: Basic Books.
Klein, Ethel. 1984. *Gender Politics*. Cambridge, MA: Harvard University Press.
Klotzberger, Kay. 1973. "Political Action by Academic Women." In *Academic Women on the Move*, ed. Alice Rossi and Ann Calderwood, pp. 359–91. New York: Russell Sage.
Lane, Robert. 1959. *Political Life*. Glencoe, IL: Free Press.
Lasswell, Harold D. 1936. *Politics: Who Gets What, When, How*. New York: McGraw-Hill.
Lazarsfeld, Paul, Bernard Berelson, and Hazel Gaudet. 1948. *The People's Choice*. New York: Columbia University Press.
Lipsky, Michael. 1968. "Protest as a Political Resource." *American Political Science Review* 42(4): 1144–58.
Lowi, Theodore J. 1971. *The Politics of Disorder*. New York: Basic Books.
———. 1972. "The Politics of Higher Education: The Case of Political Science." In *The Post-Behavioral Era: Perspectives on Political Science*, ed. George Graham and George Carey. New York: David McKay.
McCubbins, Mathew, and Terry Sullivan, eds. 1987. *Congress: Structure and Policy*. New York: Cambridge University Press.
Mansbridge, Jane. 1986. *Why We Lost the ERA*. Chicago: University of Chicago Press.
March, James G., and Johan Olsen. 1984. "The New Institutionalism: Organizational Factors in Political Life." *American Political Science Review* 78(3): 734–49.
Marshall, T. H. 1963. *Class, Citizenship, and Social Development*. Garden City, NY: Doubleday.
Merriam, Charles E., and Harold Gosnell. 1924. *Non-Voting: Causes and Methods of Control*. Chicago: University of Chicago Press.

Mueller, Carol, ed. 1988. *The Politics of the Gender Gap.* Beverly Hills, CA: Sage Publications.

Muncy, Robin. 1990. *Creating a Female Dominion.* New York: Oxford University Press.

Nelson, Barbara. 1990. "The Origins of the Two-Channel Welfare State: Workmen's Compensation and Mothers' Aid." In *Women, Welfare, and the State,* ed. Linda Gordon, pp. 123–51. Madison: University of Wisconsin Press.

Oberschall, Anthony. 1973. *Social Conflict and Social Movements.* Englewood Cliffs, NJ: Prentice-Hall.

Okin, Susan Moller. 1979. *Women in Western Political Thought.* Princeton, NJ: Princeton University Press.

———. 1989. *Justice, Gender, and the Family.* New York: Basic Books.

Pateman, Carole. 1988. *The Sexual Contract.* Stanford: Stanford University Press.

Polsby, Nelson W. 1963. *Community Power and Political Theory.* New Haven, CT: Yale University Press.

Riker, William H. 1983. "Political Theory and the Art of Heresthetics." In *Political Science: The State of the Discipline,* ed. Ada Finifter. Washington, DC: American Political Science Association.

Sapiro, Virginia. 1983. *The Political Integration of Women.* Urbana: University of Illinois Press.

———. 1986. "The Gender Basis of American Social Policy." *Political Science Quarterly* 101(2): 221–38.

Sargent, Lydia, ed. 1981. *Women and Revolution: A Discussion of the Unhappy Marriage of Marxism and Feminism.* Boston: South End Press.

Schuck, Victoria. 1969. "Women in Political Science: Some Preliminary Observations." *PS* 2(4): 642–53.

———. 1970. "Femina Studens Rei Publicae: Notes on Her Professional Achievement." *PS* 3(4): 622–28.

Scott, Joan. 1986. "Gender: A Useful Category of Historical Analysis." *American Historical Review* 91(5): 1053–75.

Skocpol, Theda, and Gretchen Ritter. 1991. "Gender and the Origins of Social Policy in the United States." *Studies in American Political Development* 5(1): 36–93.

Skowronek, Stephen. 1982. *Building a New American State.* New York: Cambridge University Press.

Sunstein, Cass, ed. 1990. *Feminism and Political Theory.* Chicago: University of Chicago Press.

Titmuss, Richard. 1958. *Essays on "The Welfare State".* London: Allen and Unwin.

Ware, Susan. 1981. *Beyond Suffrage.* Cambridge, MA: Harvard University Press.

Weir, Margaret, Ann Orloff, and Theda Skocpol, eds. 1988. *The Politics of Social Policy in the United States.* Princeton, NJ: Princeton University Press.

Wolfe, Alan. 1970. "Unthinking about the Thinkable: Reflections on the Failure of the Caucus for a New Political Science." *Politics and Society* 1(3): 393–406.

Wolfinger, Raymond. 1974. *The Politics of Progress.* Englewood Cliffs, NJ: Prentice-Hall.

The State in Political Science: How We Become What We Study

Theodore J. Lowi

This presidential pilgrimage is over, and I can report that the American Political Science Association is alive and well. But a pilgrimage is not a journey into happiness. A pilgrimage is a search, and no pilgrimage is fulfilled until the pilgrim returns and shares the pains of discovery.

From out of their early pilgrimage, the Quakers cried: "Speak truth to power." From out of my pilgrimage I responded, "Who's listening?" And "What truths do we have to impart?" On my pilgrimage I listened in on the conversation between political science and power, and it is my duty to report that the terms of discourse have been set by power. We are not the teachers we have thought ourselves to be.

The insights of my pilgrimage began with my awakening to the following facts: First, that American political science is itself a political phenomenon and, as such, is a product of the American state. Second, that there is not one science of politics but several, and each is the outcome of a particular adaptation to what it studies. And third, that even assuming we are all sincerely searching for the truth (and it is more interesting to assume that), there are reasons other than the search for truth why we do the kinds of political science we do, and there are reasons other than the search for truth why particular subdisciplines become hegemonic. In sum, every regime tends to produce a politics consonant with itself; therefore every regime tends to produce a political science consonant with itself. Consonance between the state and political science is a problem worthy of the attention of every political scientist.

To explore the relation between the state and political science, I have chosen case studies of the three hegemonic subdisciplines of our time—public opinion, public policy, and public choice—preceded by an overview of the

Presidential Address, American Political Science Association, 1991. Reprinted from *American Political Science Review* 86 (1992): 1–7.

transformation from the old to the new state, and the old political science to the new. I will conclude with a brief evaluation of the consequences for political science of being a "dependent variable."

There is no need to document for political scientists the contention that the American state until the 1930s was virtually an oxymoron. The level of national government activity was almost as low in 1932 as it had been in 1832. However, although a number of large social movements had failed to expand the national government after the Civil War, they had succeeded in nationalizing the focus of American politics. The Civil War and industrialization had contributed to this by making us one nation in fact. The *Wabash* case (1886) had contributed to this with the doctrine that the state governments were constitutionally incompetent to confront the nationalizing economy. The media had contributed to this by finding their new independence in a transference of their dependence from the highly localized political parties to the corporations seeking mass sales through advertising.

Political science as a profession was a product of this nationalization of political focus. Intellectual historians such as Somit and Tanenhaus (1967) and Seidelman and Harpham (1985) report that the APSA was part of the progressive reform movement, and Somit and Tanenhaus report that only 20 percent of the first decade's membership were "professors and teachers" (p. 55). From out of the beginnings in the 1890s, where the writing was "legalistic, formalistic, conceptually barren and largely devoid of what would today be called empirical data" (ibid., p. 69), the founders of the association were committed to political realism, which meant facts, the here and now, and the exposure of the gap between the formal institutions and the realities. James Bryce, in his address as the fourth association president in 1909, urged political scientists to "keep close to the facts. Never lose yourself in abstractions. . . . The Fact is the first thing. Make sure of it. Get it perfectly clear. Polish it till it shines and sparkles like a gem" (quoted in Somit and Tanenhaus 1967, p. 70). The title of Woodrow Wilson's presidential address to the seventh annual meeting of APSA was "The Law and the Facts" (1911), and early in his speech he said, "I take the science of politics to be the accurate and detailed observation of [the] processes by which the lessons of experience are brought into the field of consciousness, transmuted into active purposes, put under the scrutiny of discussion, sifted, and at last given determinate form in law" (p. 2). But these were not facts for themselves alone. Some early political scientists were active reformers, others were radical muckrakers, and a few may have been completely aloof. But facts were to be put in the service of assessment: Did a given political institution meet its purpose? According to Wilson (1911), political scientists should serve as a kind of "self-constituted commission . . . to discover, amidst our present economic chaos, a common interest, so that we might legislate for the whole country instead of this, that, or the other interest, one by one" (pp. 6–7).

There is no evidence to suggest that the founding generation was trying to form an intelligentsia—defined as an organization of intellectuals in opposition to the state. There was, in fact, no state to organize against. If anything, there was a memory trace of the two states that conducted the most devastating total war in history up to 1865. But both states were dismantled quickly after the Civil War and were folded back into the "stateless polity" of the restored Union (Bensel 1990). One could say, however, that the early APSA was a kind of *counter*intelligentsia formed in defense of a state that did not yet exist. The political science of the entire first generation of the APSA was formed around politics—the observable, the immediate, and the near-run purpose to be served. But politics was not only a phenomenon, it was a problem. For example, to Goodnow, the purpose of political science was to show "particularly from a consideration of political conditions as they now exist in the U.S., that the formal governmental system as set forth in the law is not always the same as the actual system" (quoted in Ross 1991, p. 274). And for most of them, there was a handy solution to the problem of politics, and that solution was government—properly characterized as the "building of a new American state" (Skowronek 1982). This goal of a new American state can in turn be characterized as a stateless government, or an enlightened administration. Woodrow Wilson, while still an obscure professor of political science at Johns Hopkins, sounded the call for the study of administration in 1887. This should be understood, however, within the context of his still larger declaration that the era of constitution-making was closed "so far as the establishment of essential principles is concerned" (quoted in Ross 1991, p. 275). Administration could be a solution to politics because, in Wilson's words, we could have the Prussian state breathe free American air (Wilson 1887). As Seidelman puts it (1985, p. 44), "the study of politics for Wilson thus had to evolve into a study of America's cultural uniqueness and European administration." Wilson was confirming the inarticulated major premise of political science, that the American system was permanent and that the science of politics involved the study and assessment of political things within a permanent, and unique, context. We were one republic, then and forever. Political scientists could remain a counterintelligentsia not because all members shared the Lockean liberal consensus, but because they were scientists in the state-building business—even while, as with Bentley, they were attacking the very concept of the state as "soul stuff" (Seidelman and Harpham 1985, pp. 70–71). For the same reason, political science was atheoretical. Works produced by the founding generation stand up well even by today's standards of science and are superior to most of ours in the quality of the knowledge they brought to bear and in their use of the English language. But the work remained essentially empirical and became almost technocratic in its participation in the reform movement, primarily because it had no concept of an alternative regime in America.

It should have been unmistakably clear to any political scientist of 1887 or later that the American system after the Civil War was a new regime, deserving a new enumeration. Why not the Second Republic? The answer is that that would have suggested an impermanence to the American regime— the possibility of a third and a fourth republic. My wife sometimes introduces me to her friends as her first husband. That is a sobering sobriquet. Political science was atheoretical because it had no concept of a Second Republic or of any other alternative regime. Eventually, political scientists would virtually rewrite democratic theory to accommodate political parties and would rewrite republican theory to accommodate the devolution of constitutional powers from Congress to the presidency; but this was not a self-conscious act of political theory; this was part of the study of what Goodnow called the "political conditions as they now exist." In the stateless polity of the founding epoch, the science of politics was the study of politics and of political institutions within a timeless as well as a uniquely American framework.

In my opinion, the golden age of American political science came toward the end of this founding epoch, which corresponds, of course, with the end of the stateless polity. Works of political science of the 1930s and 1940s were magnificent in their ability to describe a complex political whole; they were thorough, honest and imaginative in their use of statistics to describe a dynamic reality; they were powerful and cogent in pointing out flaws and departures from American ideals. But this was the sentimental part of my journey. To yearn for those particular studies of elections, case studies of interest groups and policy making, histories of party systems, and representation in Congress is to yearn also for the luxury of the First Republic, now that we are irreversibly in the second and possess at least the bare beginnings of an awareness of the possibility of regime change in America.

Surely by now there has been, in fact, a change of regime, and I call it the Second Republic for lack of an established enumeration. It is not the French state or the Prussian state. But at least we can say that the American state is no longer an oxymoron. Here, all too briefly, are its relevant high spots: First, it is a positive state, not a reactive state, and from the start it was centered on the executive branch. Second, constitutional limits on the powers of the national government over the economy, and constitutional limits on the distribution of power among the branches within the national government were very quickly laid to rest. Third, many aspects of politics that had traditionally been private—such as registration, ballots, election administration, nomination, job patronage, polling, and campaign finance—have been governmentalized. That is, modern government has assumed responsibility for its own politics. Fourth, political parties, like nuclear families, have declined for lack of enough to do. Fifth, bureaucracy, independent of party and Congress, expanded in size and scale, approaching autonomy as a social force. And sixth, but intimately connected with five, government has become intensely committed to science. This was no accident, and it is no mere policy. Science is an inherent part of the new, bureaucratized American state, in at least two dimensions: First, it involves a commitment to building science as an institution; that is, a commitment to government *for* science. Second, it involves a commitment to government *by* science; that is to say, it involves scientific decision making. This has been properly characterized as technocratization, which I take to mean "to predict in order to control" (cf. Mills 1959, p. 113). But another and, to me, more interesting but less appreciated part of this aspect of the expansion of science is that *economics has replaced law as the language of the state.*

As Tocqueville said of the First Republic, so we may say of the second, that "a new science of politics is needed for a new world" (quoted in Wood 1969, opening epigraph). But life is not quite so simple. If modern states are differentiated, there are almost certain to be several sciences of politics rather than just one. We tend to call these subdisciplines, but despite continuities and overlaps, they are quite distinct. Each can be understood as a product of the phenomena it studies, but I am concerned here not to explain or to place them all but only to understand the hegemonics of disciplines—why the three approaches in particular became hot topics and when.

The first case is public opinion. Some call it behavioral science. I think I am more accurate calling it the subdiscipline of public opinion. Observers from an alien intellectual planet would find it most peculiar that the study of individual opinions and attitudes could be called behavioral—until they deconstructed the discourse between the new bureaucratized state and the new political science. Here is my deconstruction:

1. If science is to be public, it must be neutral.
2. It must also be rational and therefore concern itself with rational phenomena—i.e., orderly, repeatable, predictable phenomena. This is precisely what makes science and bureaucracy so compatible. Here is Karl Mannheim, over twenty years before the behavioral revolution: "Bureaucratic thought is permeated by measurement, formalization, and systematization on the basis of fixed axioms . . . [such that] only those forms of knowledge were legitimate which touched and appealed to what is common to all human beings" (1936, pp. 118 and 167).
3. Science also has to be microscopic, down to the irreducibly smallest unit. *It is no paradox that as our state grew larger, the units of analysis in our social science became smaller.* This is a profoundly important aspect of rationality: out of small units, large numbers grow, and large numbers behave according to the regularities of math-

ematical probability. In this context it is easy to understand why
Arthur Bentley's appeal "to fashion a tool," with the group as the
smallest unit of analysis, was first uttered in 1907 and not really
heard, or responded to, until over forty years later.
4. Science, like administration, has to follow a prescribed method. As
Robert Wiebe put it, "bureaucratic thought . . . made 'science' practically synonymous with 'scientific method.' Science had become a
procedure . . . rather than a body of results" (1967, p. 147).
5. And finally, the language itself has to be microscopic—that is, science has to be translated into the language of variables.

The phenomena and methodology of public opinion obviously meet all
the requirements of a science that would be consonant with bureaucratic
thinking. And now consider the units of analysis within the sample surveys
that give public opinion its link to political behavior—voting and participation. These display an even stronger consonance with the state, in that these
are approved political behavior, i.e., political behavior sponsored by the state
and needed by regimes and elites to maintain their legitimacy.

Some see behavioral science as a large step toward hard science, and
through that, an advancement toward greater enlightenment about society and
politics. I don't disagree. But my political analysis tells me also that the
hegemony of the subdiscipline of behavioral science or public opinion was to
a large extent a product of its compatibility with bureaucratic thoughtways
rather than the result of successful discourse within political science.

It is important to emphasize, however, the hegemony of the subdiscipline
of public opinion is a case of natural selection, not one of political maneuver-
ing or intellectual opportunism. Anyone personally acquainted with the
people who made the behavioral revolution in political science would agree
that if political skill were required to succeed, there would be no survey
research centers, probably no behavioral science at all. It is their very lack of
attention to playing the political game that makes the success of their field so
interesting. The explanation is to be found not in politics in the vulgar sense
but politics in the higher sense—the politics of state-building.

The Second Republic that had put a new emphasis on science also determined what that science would be. The capacity to engage in public opinion
research in political science had been in existence since at least the late
nineteenth century. Statistics, which takes its name from state and statist,
reached maturity still earlier in the nineteenth century and grew in importance
as states democratized and individuals began to count for something. Sampling was also well advanced and widely practiced, especially in the agricultural sciences (Porter 1986, pp. 23–25). Even opinion-polling in political
campaigns was actually tried at least as early as 1892, albeit over the objec-

tions of many defenders of the sanctity of elections (Jensen 1969, pp. 228–29). And it was picked up by advertising companies and newspapers soon after. Yet, public opinion did not become the hegemonic subdiscipline of political science until the Second Republic.

Case two. Public policy as a subdiscipline of political science has an even longer genealogy than public opinion, although it was more than a decade later to emerge as a hegemonic subdiscipline. The study of public policy begins, of course, with the study of legislation, whose history is usually traced out from divine law through common law to something called positive law, to indicate the demystification of law and the deliberateness of modern laws. There is then one later stage called public policy, indicating the intervention of administration between legislature and citizen. Public policy is a term of art reflecting the interpenetration of liberal government and society, suggesting greater flexibility and reciprocity than such unilateralist synonyms as law, statute, ordinance, edict, etc. Public policy began to gain some currency in public administration in the 1930s, and public administration had been one of the hegemonic subdisciplines in the political science of the stateless polity I refer to as the First Republic. The decline and transfiguration of public administration gives us the key to public policy. Traditional public administration was almost driven out of the APSA by the work of a single, diabolical mind, that of Herbert Simon. Simon transformed the field by lowering the discourse. He reduced the bureaucratic phenomenon to the smallest possible unit, the decision, and he introduced rationality to tie decisions to a system—not to any system but to an economic system. His Ph.D. was in political science; his Nobel award was in economics.

Now, Simon didn't accomplish this all by himself. His intellectual tour de force was made possible by actual changes in the administrative institutions of the Second Republic. Administrative authority in the First Republic partook of a fairly well established tradition of separating public from private life by a variety of legal rules and procedures that comprise what Joseph Vining calls the "masterful myth of the 'rule of law.'" In the Second Republic, these rules and myths broke down—not spontaneously but in face of the rise of economic thinking in the corporate world as well as in government (Vining 1978, p. 27).

It is in this context that modern public policy became a hegemonic subdiscipline in political science, overshadowing behavioralism itself. The study of public policy in the political science of the First Republic drew upon public law and institutional economics. Some of that old-fashioned public policy study exists today. However, the modern approach is more appropriately called public policy analysis, which draws upon macroeconomic methods and economic systems thinking. The best way to demonstrate the size and character of this new subdiscipline of political science is to point to the presence of the policy analysis courses within political science departments and the explosive growth of the separate policy analysis programs and the economics requirements in the schools of public affairs and public policy and in the law schools. All the students in those places are learning the new language of the state.

Case three. It does no disservice to the subdiscipline of public choice to tie it to another of Karl Mannheim's 1929 observations, that in the political science of a bureaucratic state, "an economic man, a political man, etc., irrespective of time and race, could be constructed on the basis of a few axiomatic characteristics" (1936, pp. 167–68). Mannheim continues: "Only what could be known by the application of these axioms was considered as knowable. Everything else was due to the perverse 'manifoldness of the real,' concerning which 'pure' theory need not worry itself" (p. 168). Compare this to Kenneth Arrow's assertion made in a boastful spirit nearly forty years later that any assumption other than the rational actor leads to mysticism and irrationality (Goldfield and Gilbert 1990, pp. 14–15).

This gives us a start toward a political explanation for why public choice has become probably the hottest thing going in political science today.

Totally aside from whatever merits it may have as a method and however true its truths may be, public choice is hegemonic today for political reasons, or to be more dignified about it, for reasons of state. Let me dramatize this in quite tangible rational-actor terms: most of the luminaries in this subfield of political science came from, serve in, or are substantially associated with the same "freshwater" universities that kept burning the flame of laissez-faire ideology. Chicago, Rochester, Washington University of St. Louis (and we should not overlook the St. Louis Federal Reserve staff) (Johnson 1991). Here again we are confronting not political opportunism but institutional consonance, a symbiotic relationship between state and political science.

The affinity between modern bureaucratic government and economics, already strong, was further strengthened by the revival of the political popularity of laissez-faire ideology within the Republican party. For most of this century, laissez-faire liberalism (erroneously called conservative) had been the Republican party's center of gravity, but after the Depression it had had little effect on voters and even less on intellectuals in the social sciences. Few intellectuals figured in national Republican party circles. "Conservative intellectual" was just another oxymoron. Today, of course, Republican administrations are overflowing with intellectuals, as are affiliated think tanks and the op-ed pages of the major newspapers. I see no signs yet of a Republican takeover of the APSA, but I do see one beneficiary of the Republican party era in political science, and that beneficiary is public choice. People of merit inhabit this subfield, but its hegemony has little to do with their merit. Their success as a group was entirely fortuitous.

We political scientists enjoy the primitive wisdom of Mr. Dooley; and Mr. Dooley's best-known scientific proposition probably was that "no matter whether th' constitution follows th' flag or not, th' supreme court follows th' iliction returns." A more dignified Dooley would say, "The APSA follows Leviathan."

I conclude with what are to me the three principal consequences of following Leviathan too closely. First, we have as a consequence failed to catch and evaluate the significance of the coming of economics as the language of the state. Second, we have failed to appreciate how this language made us a dismal science like economics. Third, having been so close to Leviathan, we failed to catch, characterize, and evaluate the great ideological sea changes accompanying the changes of regime.

First, then, why economics? Of what use is economic analysis to politics? Since economics was always a deeply flawed predictive science, why was it so attractive to policy makers and bureaucrats in the new state, and why to political science? My evaluation was inspired in part by an observation made thirty years ago by the distinguished economic philosopher Joan Robinson: "Economics . . . has always been partly a vehicle for the ruling ideology of each period as well as partly a method of scientific investigation" (1962, p. 1). And my answer is that *economic analysis is politically useful because it closes off debate,* especially in a highly public representative assembly such as Congress. The rise of economics as the language of the state parallels the decline of Congress as a creative legislature. (A more extensive argument on this point can be found in Lowi [1991].) Policy-making powers are delegated less to the agency and more to the decision-making formulas residing in the agency. The use of economic analysis to close off debate was strengthened as Republicans discovered that economic analysis could be used as effectively for them as for the Democrats—merely by manipulating the cost rather than the benefits side of the cost/benefit analysis. I recommend John Schwarz's evaluation of Murray Weidenbaum's outrageous manipulation of the "costs of regulation," which supported the Reagan administration's commitment to deregulation (1988, pp. 90–99). But I must confess that both the Democratic and the Republican politicians were smarter than the political scientists because they took the stuff as weaponry, while we took it as science. We swallowed economics before subjecting it to a political analysis.

We should have seen that economics rarely even pretends to speak truth to power. If substantive truths were claimed, there would be room for argument. But economics, particularly as a policy science, stresses method above all. And the key to the method is the vocabulary of economics, which is the *index.* An index is not a truth but an agreement or a convention among its users about what will be the next best thing to truth. M_1, the Dow, the CPI, unemployment, GNP. This is the new representative government: an index representing a truth. Indexes have analytic power because they fit into defined systems; and, of course, systems are also not truths but are only useful fictions. This, by the way, is not an attack on indexes *or* systems. It is just a political evaluation of indexes and systems.

Now to the second of my consequences, that the modern bureaucratic state has made political science just another dismal science. By dismal I don't mean merely the making of gloomy forecasts in the Malthusian tradition. By dismal today I mean the absence of passion.

During my pilgrimage, the most frequent complaints I heard were against the *APSR*. I join in at least one of these, and I don't limit it just to the *APSR*: too few of the articles seek to transcend their analysis to join a more inclusive level of discourse; and there is consequently little substantive controversy. The response is that a scientific journal must be dedicated to replication and disproof. But actually, very few pieces independently replicate anything, and even so, replication alone is dismal stuff. Political science is a harder science than the so-called hard sciences because we confront an *un*-natural universe that requires judgment and evaluation. Without this there can be no love of subject, only vocational commitment to method and process. The modern state has made us a dismal science, and we have made it worse by the scientific practice of removing ourselves two or three levels away from sensory experience. Political scientists always quantified, whatever and whenever they could. And most tried to be rigorous. But they stayed close to sensory experience. Even with our original mechanical helper, the counter-sorter device, it was possible to maintain a sensory relation to the data. What a pleasure it was to watch the cards seek their slots. And what a pity today that the empiricists have only their printout.

Finally, I turn to our failure to catch and evaluate adequately the ideological sea changes accompanying the changes of regime. Time permits only the barest inventory of missed opportunities, but I think they will speak for themselves.

The perspective of nearly fifty years makes it easy to see what we did not catch about the New Deal as a regime change. Although political scientists caught the new liberalism in the air, they failed to evaluate whether all the elements of this ideology were consistent with liberalism or with constitutionalism. They failed, for example, to capture and evaluate the significance of "administrative law." They noticed but merely celebrated the delegation of power from Congress to the executive branch. At the time it meant only the fulfillment of the New Deal program. Even as time passed, our tendency was to render each change consistent with our existing model of the political system. There was virtually no serious political science inquiry into whether the changes in constitutional doctrine, governmental structure, and policy commitments constituted a regime change. Some Republicans suggested

America had become a socialist regime, but political science did not respond to this challenging formulation. It should be a matter of ultimate interest as well as enjoyment to fight intensely over the identification of criteria for determining when a political change is sufficient to constitute a regime change. The New Deal helped give us a new political science but did not provide sufficient inclination to evaluate what was new.

We are at this moment in the presence of another failure, to catch the nature and significance of the ideological shift accompanying the current Republican era. The inability of the Reagan administration to terminate any important New Deal programs should have led at least to a reflection on the nature of the New Deal as a regime change. Even a post hoc evaluation would be useful. Meanwhile, the Republican era has brought with it some profound ideological changes that political science is failing to capture, even though our own public opinion polls are sensing them. Political science has failed to catch and evaluate the two separate components of the Republican coalition— the old, laissez-faire liberalism and the genuine native conservatism. Political science has stood by and permitted Republican candidates and staff intellectuals to treat the traditional laissez-faire core of the Republican party as conservative and then to compound the felony by stigmatizing liberalism as an alien belief system akin to socialism. This profound misuse of rich terminology is literally poisoning political discourse in the United States, and political science has to take a lot of the blame for this. We also did not catch the rise of the genuine conservatism; although our polls were picking up significant reactionary movements, we continued to treat the Falwell phenomenon and such predecessors as the Christian Anticommunist Crusade as aberrant. And we have witnessed passively the joining of laissez-faire liberalism with genuine right-wing conservatism as though they are consistent in their opposition to big government. Laissez-faire liberal Republicans, supported by their economists, embrace an ideal of radical individualism and view all government as a threat to freedom. In contrast, genuine conservatives are not individualists but statists. The state they want is tight and restrictive police control by state and local governments, but they are statists nevertheless. Genuine conservatives were never really at home with purely market relations, and they have never espoused the ideal, much less the methodology, of rational individualism. (Many conservative Catholic lay intellectuals have tried in vain to establish a comfortable concordance with free-market liberalism.) Conservative intellectuals are now writing the poetry of executive power and are the authors of most of the writing that bashes Congress and the politics of representative government. Just as political scientists did not catch the ideological significance of the propresidential power writings of the New Deal supporters in the 1950s and early 1960s, we are now not catching the significance of the fact that most of the current propresidential power writing is by the far right.

The far-right intellectuals are also writing a significant proportion of the new work on the founding—the purpose of which is not only to contribute to historical scholarship but to reconstitute the constitution in such a way as to place the presidency above the law and affirmative action beneath it.

No effort has been made to camouflage my antagonism to Republican-era ideology. But my own personal position is irrelevant. Political scientists of left, right, and center are at unity in their failure to maintain a clear and critical consciousness of political consciousness. Causal and formal analyses of the relations among clusters of variables just won't suffice. Nor will meticulous analysis of original intent. It is time we became intellectuals.

At the end of my pilgrimage, I have come to the conclusion that among the sins of omission of modern political science, the greatest of all has been the omission of passion. There are no qualifications for membership in the APSA, but if I had the power to establish such standards they would be something like this: one must love politics, one must love a good constitution, one must take joy in exploring the relation between the two, and one must be prepared to lose some domestic and even some foreign policy battles to keep alive a positive relation between the two. I do not speak for the passion of ideology, though I don't count it out. I speak for the pleasure of finding a pattern, the inspiration of a well-rounded argument, the satisfaction in having made a good guess about what makes democracy work, and a good stab at improving the prospect of rationality in human behavior.

Regime changes throughout the world since 1989 ought to give us a clearer perspective on some new sciences of politics. Although only a few of the world's regime changes will be liberal democracies, they are stimulating tremendous demand for transferrable insights about the workings of liberal democratic institutions, especially American. May this demand draw American political scientists out of the shadow of American Leviathan upward and outward, toward a level of discourse worthy of the problem. This is not an opportunity to play philosopher king. It is an opportunity to meet our own intellectual needs while serving the public interest. And we need not worry how to speak truth to power. It is enough to speak truth to ourselves.

REFERENCES

Bensel, Richard F. 1990. *Yankee Leviathan—The Origins of Central State Authority in America, 1859–1877.* New York: Cambridge University Press.
Goldfield, Michael, and Alan Gilbert. 1990. "The Limits of Rational Choice Theory." Paper presented at the annual meeting of the American Political Science Association, San Francisco.
Jensen, Richard. 1969. "American Election Analysis." In *Politics and the Social Sciences,* ed. S. M. Lipset. New York: Oxford University Press.

Johnson, Peter. 1991. "Unpopular Measures: Translating Monetarism into Monetary Policy in the Federal Republic of Germany and the United States, 1970–1985." Ph.D. diss., Cornell University.

Lowi, Theodore J. 1991. "Knowledge, Power, and the Congress." In *Knowledge, Power, and the Congress,* ed. William H. Robinson and H. Wellborn Clay. Washington, DC: Congressional Quarterly Inc.

Mannheim, Karl. 1936. (German edition, 1929.) *Ideology and Utopia.* New York: Harcourt Brace Jovanovich.

Mills, C. Wright. 1959. *The Sociological Imagination.* New York: Oxford University Press.

Porter, Theodore M. 1986. *The Rise of Statistical Thinking, 1820–1900.* Princeton, NJ: Princeton University Press.

Robinson, Joan. 1962. *Economic Philosophy.* New York: Doubleday Anchor Books.

Ross, Dorothy. 1991. *The Origins of American Social Science.* New York: Cambridge University Press.

Schwarz, John E. 1988. *America's Hidden Success.* New York: W. W. Norton.

Seidelman, Raymond, with the assistance of Edward J. Harpham. 1985. *Disenchanted Realists: Political Science and the American Crisis, 1884–1984.* Albany: SUNY Press.

Skowronek, Stephen. 1982. *Building a New American State: The Expansion of National Administrative Capacities, 1877–1920.* New York: Cambridge University Press.

Somit, Albert, and Joseph Tanenhaus. 1967. *The Development of Political Science: From Burgess to Behavioralism.* Boston: Allyn and Bacon.

Vining, Joseph. 1978. *Legal Identity: The Coming of Age of Public Law.* New Haven, CT: Yale University Press.

Wabash, St. Louis, and Pacific Railway v. Illinois. 1886. 118 U.S. 557.

Wiebe, Robert. 1967. *The Search for Order, 1877–1920.* New York: Hill and Wang.

Wilson, Woodrow. 1887. "The Study of Administration." *Political Science Quarterly* 2: 202–17.

Wilson, Woodrow. 1911. "The Law and the Facts." *American Political Science Review* 5: 1–11.

Wood, Gordon S. 1969. *The Creation of the American Republic, 1776–1787.* New York: Norton Library.

Contributors

Terence Ball is professor of political science at the University of Minnesota. He is the author of *Transforming Political Discourse* (1988) and editor or coeditor of *Idioms of Inquiry* (1987), *Conceptual Change and the Constitution* (1988), and *Political Innovation and Conceptual Change* (1989). He has also written numerous essays on the philosophy of the social sciences and the history of political thought.

Charles A. Beard (1874–1948) has a long list of accomplishments: historian and political scientist, professor of public law at Columbia (1907–17), president of both the American Political Science Association and the American Historical Association, social and political reformer and critic, and consultant to state and city governments. Along with other Progressive intellectuals, Beard propounded a "new history," dwelling on the whole context of human activity as essential to the understanding and transformation of political institutions. The appearance of his *Economic Interpretation of the Constitution* (1913) and subsequent related books revolutionized the study of the Constitution. In the 1920s and 1930s, Beard became a vocal critic of what he saw as the excessive objectivity and empiricism of political science, and became active in antifascist and antiwar political causes. Works from this period include *The Rise of American Civilization* (1927, with Mary Beard) and *The Open Door at Home* (1934, with G. E. Smith).

John W. Burgess (1844–1931) founded the extremely influential School of Political Science at Columbia in 1880, four years after assuming a professorship in the university's law school. Raised in Tennessee in a pro-Union family, he served in the federal army before studying at Amherst and then at Berlin under Mommsen, Treitschke, Droysen, and von Gneist. These German and nationalist influences left their mark on Burgess who, at Columbia from 1879 to 1912, theorized about the state, national sovereignty, racialism, constitutional law, and historical methodology. Besides his most important work, *Political Science and Comparative Constitutional Law* (1890), Burgess was the author of many historical and political works on the Civil War, reconstruction, World War I, presidential administrations, and German-American relations.

Robert A. Dahl is professor emeritus at Yale University, where he has taught in the Department of Political Science for most of his professional career. Dahl is known for his theoretical work and case studies in the pluralist theory of politics. In *A Preface to Democratic Theory* (1956) Dahl attempted to compare the Madisonian theory of factions with the actual practice of American interest groups. His most well-known and still controversial work is *Who Governs? Democracy and Power in an American*

City (1961), which tests elite and pluralist theories of democracy through an examination of the politics of New Haven, Connecticut. Dahl also pioneered postwar studies of public policy and administration with his *Politics, Economics and Welfare* (1953, with Charles Lindblom). His recent works on democratic theory include *Democracy and Its Critics* (1990). He served as APSA president in 1967.

David Easton is a distinguished professor at the University of California, Irvine, and taught for most of his career at the University of Chicago. He served as president of the American Political Science Association in 1969. Easton is a major figure in the development of behavioral political science after World War II. In *The Political System* (1953), he launched criticisms of political science in the 1930s for its lack of sophistication and backwardness in developing scientific theories of politics. A pioneer in the introduction of systems analysis into the study of the political process (see *A Systems Analysis of Political Life* [1965]), Easton applied it in the late 1960s to the study of the political socialization of children. His recent works include *The Analysis of Political Structure* (1990) and editorial contribution to *The Development of Political Science: A Comparative Survey* (1991, with Luigi Graziano and John G. Gunnell).

James Farr, one of the coeditors of this volume, is professor of political science at the University of Minnesota. Coeditor of *After Marx* (1984) and *Political Innovation and Conceptual Change* (1989), he has published several essays on the history and philosophy of political inquiry, especially concerning the problem of interpretation.

John G. Gunnell is professor of political science at the State University of New York at Albany. Gunnell has written about the philosophy of the social sciences and the origins and history of political theory in the United States. His principal published works include *Philosophy, Science, and Political Inquiry* (1975), *Political Theory: Tradition and Interpretation* (1979), and *Between Philosophy and Politics: The Alienation of Political Theory* (1986).

Norman Jacobson taught political theory at the University of California, Berkeley, until his retirement. One of the most influential teachers of political theory in recent times, Jacobson has authored *Pride and Solace: The Functions and Limits of Political Theory* (1978) and many articles on American political thought.

Harold D. Lasswell (1902–78) received his Ph.D. from the University of Chicago, with Merriam as his principal adviser, taught at Chicago (1924–38), later at Yale (1945–75), and served as APSA president in 1956. Lasswell was the author and coauthor of over forty books and is responsible for, among other things, the introduction of psychology, quantitative and qualitative content analysis, and communications theory into the discipline of political science, the collection of comprehensive data on world social and political trends, the study of propaganda, political elites, and technocracy, and the development of the idea of the policy sciences. His principal works include *Psychopathology and Politics* (1930), *Politics: Who Gets What, When, How* (1936), *Power and Society* (1963, with Abraham Kaplan), and *World Politics and Personal Insecurity* (1935).

Francis Lieber (1800–72) emigrated from Germany in 1827 and taught at South Carolina College from 1838 until 1856. He accepted Columbia's professorship in history and political science in 1857, the first such chair in the United States, and was later a founding member of the American Social Science Association. First editor of the *Encyclopaedia Americana* (1829–45), Lieber was the author of *Legal and Political Hermeneutics* (1837–39), *Manual of Political Ethics* (1838), *Civil Liberty and Self-Government* (1853), and several other works, including some of the *Instructions* that codified the rules of war for the Union Army during the Civil War. In these works, Lieber articulated theories of the state, nationalism, political economy, education, penology, international law, and constitutional interpretation that were influential during the greater part of the nineteenth century.

Charles Lindblom is professor of political science at Yale University and served as APSA president in 1981. Lindblom began his career with a critique of "rational" models of public administration and policy-making decisional processes, stressing the role of short-term political and other factors. He collaborated with Robert Dahl on *Politics, Economics and Welfare*, a major pluralist account of American policy making. In the 1970s and 1980s, Lindblom examined the tension between democracy and capitalism in *Politics and Markets* (1978) and *Democracy and the Market System* (1988).

Benjamin E. Lippincott (1902–88) was a democratic theorist and student of American politics particularly interested in distributive justice, social responsibility, and government control of the economy. He received his Ph.D. from the London School of Economics in 1930, having studied under Harold Laski. His academic career was spent entirely at the University of Minnesota, where he authored, among other books, *On the Economic Theory of Socialism* (1938), *Victorian Critics of Democracy* (1938), and *Democracy's Dilemmas* (1965). After retirement, he endowed the Benjamin Evans Lippincott Award in Political Theory that the APSA awards annually.

Theodore J. Lowi is John L. Senior professor of American Institutions at Cornell University. A major critic of "interest group liberalism" and the liberal state, Lowi is also noted for his innovations in the theory of public policy and the study of presidential power and its excesses in the contemporary American political order. His major publications include *Private Life and Public Order* (1968), a significant critique of the influence of technocracy on politics, two editions of *The End of Liberalism* (1969 and 1978), and *The Personal President: Power Invested, Promise Unfulfilled* (1985). Lowi served as APSA president in 1991.

Charles E. Merriam (1874–1953) transformed the University of Chicago's political science department into the chief center for graduate training in the "new" political science, helped generate contacts between philanthropists and the social sciences, served on numerous advisory committees during the Roosevelt and Hoover administrations, and was president of the APSA in 1924. A student of William Dunning and John Burgess at Columbia University, Merriam expanded his original interests in liberal political theory to encompass advocacy of a new "science of democratic possibilities," which would point toward an increase in government authority and popular political support for increased governmental functions. His principal works include *A History of American Political Theories* (1903), *Non-Voting: Causes and Methods of Control* (1924, with Harold Gosnell), *New Aspects of Politics* (1925), and numerous reports on civic education, administrative management, and economic planning.

David M. Ricci teaches political science at the Hebrew University of Jerusalem and has written extensively about disciplinary debates in American political science. His published books include *Community Power and Democratic Theory* (1971) and *The Tragedy of Political Science: Politics, Scholarship and Democracy* (1984).

William H. Riker, professor of political science at the University of Rochester, served as APSA president in 1983. Riker introduced and elaborated social and rational choice models in political science, and has been a strong proponent of scientific analyses in the discipline. His major works include *An Introduction to Positive Political Theory* (1973, with Peter Ordeshook) and *Liberalism against Populism: A Confrontation between the Theory of Democracy and the Theory of Social Choice* (1982).

Dorothy Ross is Arthur O. Lovejoy professor of history at Johns Hopkins University. She is the author of *G. Stanley Hall: The Psychologist as Prophet* (1972) and *The Origins of American Social Science* (1991), as well as many influential articles on American intellectual history and on the disciplinary development of the modern social sciences in the United States.

Raymond Seidelman is an associate professor of political science at Sarah Lawrence College. His *Disenchanted Realists: Political Science and the American Crisis, 1884– 1984* (1985, with the assistance of Edward Harpham) traces the history of political science and its relationship to liberal reform politics in the United States. Seidelman is presently at work on a textbook in American politics and a book on the social and cultural causes of American nonvoting. He is a coeditor of this volume.

Helene Silverberg is assistant professor of politics at Princeton University. She writes in the fields of American politics and women and politics. In addition to her contribution in this volume, she has authored "Feminism and Political Science" in *Western Political Quarterly* (1990).

Leonard D. White (1891–1958) was one of the most important scholars of the "public administration movement" in the 1920s, 1930s, and 1940s. He taught at the University of Chicago and served on the Committee on Administrative Management in the Roosevelt administration. His major works include *Introduction to the Study of Public Administration* (1926) and *The City Manager* (1927). He served as APSA president in 1944.

W. W. Willoughby (1867–1945) was among the more important founders of the American Political Science Association, serving as its secretary-treasurer from 1903 to 1914, as president in 1913, and as long-time editor of the *American Political Science Review.* Willoughby's teaching career was spent entirely at Johns Hopkins, one of the premier institutions of graduate training in the social sciences in the United States. His most influential works were in the areas of public law, political theory, and international relations. His principal theoretical interests in the nature and ethical basis of state authority were developed in *The Nature of the State* (1896), *Social Justice* (1900), and *The Constitutional Law of the United States* (1910).

Woodrow Wilson (1856–1924) was one of the major proponents of a "new" science of politics as a professor at Princeton and as that university's president, before becoming governor of New Jersey (1902–10) and then president of the United States (1913–21). An admirer of English constitutionalism and German theories of the state, Wilson argued in *Congressional Government* (1885), *The State: Elements of Historical and Practical Politics* (1889), and elsewhere that the parliamentary and bureaucratic institutions of the modern state represented a high point in human evolution. He focused on how administrative and institutional change could be brought about by blending scientific expertise with the liberal democratic heritage embedded in American political institutions and customs.

Bibliography

The list below, though far from exhaustive, is designed to aid the reader interested in further research in American political science history. This bibliography includes works in the following five areas:

I. General book-length commentaries and histories about political and social science in America written *before* 1945, including those works written in a particular period, or by or about a particularly important figure. Also included are major works that influenced the writing of political science history.
II. General book-length commentaries and histories about political and social science in America written *after* 1945, including those works written about a particular period or figure in political science's past.
III. Selected articles that are commentaries and/or histories of political and social science in America, written *before* 1945.
IV. Selected articles that are commentaries and/or histories of political and social science, written *after* 1945.
V. Disciplinary classics—book-length works that provide important historiographical positions and claims in the context of writing about another topic, or works that have particularly influenced those who have written about the history of political science.

I. Commentaries and Histories before 1945

Beard, Charles A. *A Charter for the Social Sciences*. New York: Charles Scribner's Sons, 1932.
———. *The Nature of the Social Sciences*. New York: Charles Scribner's Sons, 1934.
Bryce, James. *The American Commonwealth*. New York: Macmillan and Co., 1888.
Burgess, John W. *Political Science and Comparative Constitutional Law*. Boston: Ginn and Co., 1891.
Catlin, George E. G. *The Science and Methods of Politics*. New York: Alfred A. Knopf, 1927.
Fess, Simeon D. *The History of Political Theory and Party Organization in the U.S.* Dansville, NY: World's Events Publishing, 1907.
Gettell, Raymond G. *Introduction to Political Science*. Boston: Ginn, 1922.
Lynd, Robert S. *Knowledge for What? The Place of Social Science in American Culture*. Princeton, NJ: Princeton University Press, 1939.
Haddow, Anna W. *Political Science in American Colleges and Universities, 1636–1900*. New York: Appleton, 1939.

Jacobson, Gertrude Ann, and Miriam Lipman. *Political Science*. New York: Barnes and Noble, 1937.

Merriam, Charles E. *American Political Theories*. New York: Macmillan & Co., 1903 and 1920.

———. *History of the Theory of Sovereignty since Rousseau*. New York: Columbia University Press, 1900.

———. *New Aspects of Politics*. Chicago: University of Chicago Press, 1925.

Murray, Robert H. *The History of Political Science from Plato to the Present*. New York: Appleton, 1925.

Ogg, Frederic A., and P. Orman Ray. *Introduction to American Government*. New York: Century, 1922.

Pollock, Frederick. *An Introduction to the History of the Science of Politics*. London, 1890.

Sabine, George. *History of Political Theory*. New York: Holt, 1937.

Seeley, John R. *Introduction to Political Science*. London, 1896.

Ward, Lester Frank. *Dynamic Sociology or Applied Social Science*. New York: Appleton, 1883.

White, Leonard D., ed. *The Future of Government in the United States: Essays in Honor of Charles E. Merriam*. Chicago: University of Chicago Press, 1942.

Wilson, Woodrow. *The State: Elements of Historical and Practical Politics*. Boston: D.C. Heath, 1889.

Woolsey, Theodore Dwight. *Political Science, or the State Theoretically and Practically Considered*. New York: Scribner, Armstrong and Co., 1877.

II. Commentaries and Histories after 1945

Almond, Gabriel A. *A Discipline Divided*. Beverly Hills, CA: Sage Publications, 1990.

American Political Science Association. *Goals for Political Science*. New York: William Sloane, 1951.

Anckar, Dag, and Erkki Berndtson, eds. *Political Science between the Past and the Future*. Helsinki: Finnish Political Science Association, 1988.

Andreski, Stanislav. *Social Sciences as Sorcery*. New York: St. Martin's Press, 1972.

Baer, Michael A., Malcolm E. Jewell, and Lee Seligman, eds. *Political Science: Oral Histories of a Discipline*. Lexington: University Press of Kentucky, 1991.

Ball, Terence, ed. *Idioms of Inquiry: Critique and Renewal in Political Science*. Albany: State University of New York Press, 1987.

Ball, Terence, James Farr, and Russell L. Hanson, eds. *Political Innovation and Conceptual Change*. New York: Cambridge University Press, 1989.

Barrow, Clyde W. *Universities and the Capitalist State*. Madison: University of Wisconsin Press, 1990.

Bernstein, Richard J. *The Restructuring of Social and Political Theory*. Philadelphia: University of Pennsylvania Press, 1978.

Bledstein, Burton J. *The Culture of Professionalism*. New York: Norton and Co., 1976.

Borning, Bernard C. *The Political and Social Thought of Charles A. Beard*. Seattle: University of Washington Press, 1962.

Brecht, Arnold. *Political Theory: The Foundation of Twentieth Century Political Thought*. Princeton: Princeton University Press, 1959.

Brown, Bernard E. *American Conservatives: The Political Thought of Francis Lieber and John W. Burgess*. New York: Columbia University Press, 1951.

Brown, JoAnne, and David van Keuren, eds. *The Estate of Social Knowledge*. Baltimore: Johns Hopkins University Press, 1991.

Charlesworth, James C., ed. *The Limits of Behavioralism in Political Science*. Philadelphia: American Academy of Political Science, 1962.

————. *Contemporary Political Analysis*. New York: Free Press, 1967.

Collini, Stefan, Donald Winch, and John Burrow. *That Noble Science of Politics: A Study in Nineteenth Century Intellectual History*. Cambridge: Cambridge University Press, 1983.

Connolly, William E., ed. *The Bias of Pluralism*. New York: Atherton Press, 1969.

Crick, Bernard. *The American Science of Politics: Its Origins and Conditions*. Berkeley: University of California Press, 1959.

Crotty, William J., ed., *Political Science: Looking to the Future*. Evanston, IL: Northwestern University Press, 1991.

Degler, Carl N. *In Search of Human Nature: The Decline and Revival of Darwinism in American Social Thought*. New York: Oxford University Press, 1991.

Dryzek, John S. *Discursive Democracy: Politics, Policy and Science*. Cambridge: Cambridge University Press, 1990.

Easton, David. *The Political System: An Inquiry into the State of Political Science*. New York: Knopf, 1953.

Easton, David, John Gunnell, and Luigi Graziano, eds. *The Development of Political Science: A Comparative Survey*. New York: Routledge, 1991.

Eulau, Heinz. *The Behavioral Persuasion in Politics*. New York: Random House, 1963.

Eulau, Heinz, ed. *Crossroads of Social Science: The ICPSR 25th Anniversary Volume*. New York: Agathon, 1989.

Eulau, Heinz, and James G. March. *Political Report of the Behavioral and Social Science Survey Committee*. Englewood Cliffs, NJ: Prentice Hall, 1969.

Eulau, Heinz, and James G. March, eds. *Political Science*. Englewood Cliffs, NJ: Prentice Hall, 1969.

Falco, Maria J. *Truth and Meaning in Political Science*. Columbus: Merriam Co., 1973.

Finifter, Ada W., ed. *Political Science: The State of the Discipline*. Washington, DC: American Political Science Association, 1983.

Fowler, Robert Booth. *Believing Skeptics: American Political Intellectuals, 1945–1964*. Westport, CT: Greenwood Press, 1978.

Freidel, Frank. *Francis Lieber: Nineteenth Century Liberal*. Baton Rouge: Louisiana State University Press, 1947.

Furner, Mary O. *Advocacy and Objectivity: A Crisis in the Professionalization of American Social Science, 1865–1905*. Lexington: University Press of Kentucky, 1975.

Gordon, Scott. *The History and Philosophy of Social Science*. London: Routledge, 1991.

Graham, George J., and George W. Carey, eds., *The Post-Behavioral Era*. New York: McKay, 1972.

Green, Philip, and Sanford Levinson, eds. *Power and Community: Dissenting Essays in Political Science*. New York: Pantheon, 1969.

Greenstein, Fred I., and Nelson W. Polsby, eds. *Handbook of Political Science*. Reading, MA: Addison-Wesley, 1975.

Gunnell, John G. *Political Theory: Tradition and Interpretation*. Cambridge: Winthrop, 1979.

———. *Between Philosophy and Politics: The Alienation of Political Theory*. Amherst: University of Massachusetts Press, 1986.

Gutmann, Amy. *Democratic Education*. Princeton, NJ: Princeton University Press, 1987.

Gutting, Gary, ed. *Paradigms and Revolutions: Applications and Appraisals of Thomas Kuhn's Philosophy of Science*. Notre Dame, IN: University of Notre Dame Press, 1980.

———. *Michel Foucault's Archaeology of Scientific Reason*. Cambridge: Cambridge University Press, 1990.

Haskell, Thomas L. *The Emergence of Professional Social Science: The American Social Science Association and the Nineteenth Century Crisis of Authority*. Urbana: University of Illinois Press, 1977.

Hays, Samuel P. *Conservation and the Gospel of Efficiency*. New York: Atheneum, 1964.

Herbst, Jürgen. *The German Historical School in American Scholarship*. Ithaca, NY: Cornell University Press, 1965.

Hollinger, David. *In the American Province*. Bloomington: Indiana University Press, 1985.

Hoxie, Gordon. *The Faculty of Political Science at Columbia University*. New York: Columbia University Press, 1955.

Hyneman, Charles S. *The Study of Politics: The Present State of American Political Science*. Urbana: University of Illinois Press, 1959.

Irish, Marian D. *Political Science: Advance of the Discipline*. Englewood Cliffs, NJ: Prentice Hall, 1968.

Isaak, Alan C. *Scope and Methods of Political Science: An Introduction to the Methodology of Political Inquiry*. Homewood, IL: Dorsey Press, 1969.

Jacoby, Russell. *The Last Intellectuals*. New York: Basic Books, 1987.

Janos, Andrew C. *Politics and Paradigms: Changing Theories of Change in the Social Sciences*. Stanford, CA: Stanford University Press, 1986.

Kariel, Henry S. *The Decline of American Pluralism*. Stanford, CA: Stanford University Press, 1962.

Karl, Barry D. *Charles E. Merriam and the Study of Politics*. Chicago: University of Chicago Press, 1974.

Kress, Paul F. *Social Science and the Idea of Process: The Ambiguous Legacy of Arthur Bentley*. Urbana: University of Illinois Press, 1973.

Kuhn, Thomas. *The Structure of Scientific Revolutions*, 2d ed. Chicago: University of Chicago Press, 1970.

Lakatos, Imre. *The Methodology of Scientific Research Programmes*. Cambridge: Cambridge University Press, 1978.

Landau, Martin. *Political Theory and Political Science.* New York: Macmillan, 1972.

Larson, Magali Sarfatti. *The Rise of Professionalism: A Sociological Analysis.* Berkeley: University of California Press, 1977.

Leonard, Stephen T. *Critical Theory in Political Practice.* Princeton, NJ: Princeton University Press, 1990.

Lipset, Seymour Martin, ed. *Politics and the Social Sciences.* New York: Oxford University Press, 1969.

———. *The First New Nation.* New York: Norton, 1973.

Lynn, Naomi B., and Aaron B. Wildavsky, eds. *Public Administration: The State of the Discipline.* New York: Agathon, 1989.

McCoy, Charles, and John Playford, eds. *Apolitical Politics: A Critique of Behavioralism.* New York: Crowell, 1967.

MacKenzie, W. J. M. *The Study of Political Science Today.* London: Macmillan, 1970.

MacRae, Duncan. *The Social Function of Social Science.* New Haven, CT: Yale University Press, 1976.

Manicas, Peter. *A History and Philosophy of the Social Sciences.* New York: Basil Blackwell, 1987.

Marcell, David W. *Progress and Pragmatism.* Westport, CT: Greenwood Press, 1974.

Natchez, Peter B. *Images of Voting: Visions of Democracy.* New York: Basic Books, 1985.

Nelson, John S., ed. *What Should Political Theory Be Now?* Albany: State University of New York Press, 1983.

Neustadt, Richard E., and Ernest R. May. *Thinking in Time: The Uses of History for Decision Makers.* New York: Free Press, 1986.

Oleson, Alexandra, and John Voss, eds. *The Organization of Knowledge in Modern America, 1860–1920.* Baltimore: Johns Hopkins University Press, 1979.

Pocock, J. G. A. *Politics, Language, and Time.* London: Methuen, 1972.

Pool, Ithiel de Sola, ed. *Contemporary Political Science—Toward Empirical Theory.* New York: McGraw-Hill, 1967.

Popper, Karl. *Objective Knowledge.* Oxford: Oxford University Press, 1972.

Proctor, Robert N. *Value-Free Science? Purity and Power in Modern Knowledge.* Cambridge: Harvard University Press, 1991.

Purcell, Edward A. *The Crisis of Democratic Theory.* Lexington: University Press of Kentucky, 1973.

Ranney, Austin, ed. *Essays on the Scientific Study of Politics.* Urbana: University of Illinois Press, 1962.

Ricci, David M. *The Tragedy of Political Science: Politics, Scholarship and Democracy.* New Haven, CT: Yale University Press, 1984.

Riker, William H. *Liberalism against Populism: A Confrontation between the Theory of Democracy and the Theory of Social Choice.* San Francisco: Freeman, 1982.

Rodgers, Daniel T. *Contested Truths: Keywords in American Politics since Independence.* New York: Basic Books, 1987.

Rorty, Richard, J. B. Schneewind, and Quentin Skinner, eds. *Philosophy in History.* Cambridge: Cambridge University Press, 1984.

Ross, Dorothy. *The Origins of American Social Science.* Cambridge: Cambridge University Press, 1991.

Runciman, W. G. *Social Science and Political Theory.* Cambridge: Cambridge University Press, 1963.

Ryan, Alan. *Philosophy of the Social Sciences.* New York: Pantheon, 1970.

Sartori, Giovanni, ed. *Social Science Concepts.* Beverly Hills, CA: Sage, 1984.

Seidelman, Raymond, with the assistance of Edward J. Harpham. *Disenchanted Realists: Political Science and the American Crisis, 1884–1984.* Albany: State University of New York Press, 1985.

Smith, Wilson. *Professors and Public Ethics: Studies in Northern Moral Philosophers before the Civil War.* Ithaca, NY: Cornell University Press, 1956.

Somit, Albert, and Joseph Tanenhaus. *The Development of American Political Science: From Burgess to Behavioralism.* Boston: Allyn and Bacon, 1967.

Sorauf, Frank J. *Perspectives on Political Science.* Columbus, OH: Merrill Books, 1966.

Spragens, Thomas A., Jr. *The Dilemma of Contemporary Political Theory: Toward a Post Behavioral Theory of Politics.* New York: Duneller, 1973.

Storing, Herbert J., ed. *Essays on the Scientific Study of Politics.* New York: Holt, Rinehart, 1962.

Surkin, Marvin, and Alan Wolfe, eds. *An End to Political Science?* New York: Basic Books, 1970.

Tully, James, ed. *Meaning and Context: Quentin Skinner and His Critics.* Princeton, NJ: Princeton University Press, 1988.

UNESCO. *Contemporary Political Science: A Survey of Methods.* Liège, Belgium: G. Thone, 1950.

Van Dyke, Vernon. *Political Science: A Philosophical Analysis.* Stanford, CA: Stanford University Press, 1960.

Veysey, Laurence R. *The Emergence of the American University.* Chicago: University of Chicago Press, 1965.

Voegelin, Eric. *The New Science of Politics.* Chicago: University of Chicago Press, 1952.

Wagner, Peter, Björn Wittrock, and Richard Whitley, eds. *Discourses on Society: The Shaping of the Social Science Disciplines.* Boston: Kluwer Academic Publishers, 1991.

Waldo, Dwight. *The Administrative State: A Study of the Political Theory of Public Administration.* New York: Ronald Press Company, 1948.

———. *Political Science in the United States.* Paris: UNESCO, 1956.

Ward, James F. *Language, Form and Inquiry: Arthur F. Bentley's Philosophy of Social Science.* Amherst: University of Massachusetts Press, 1984.

Weisberg, Herbert F., ed. *Political Science: The Science of Politics.* New York: Agathon, 1986.

White, Morton. *Science and Sentiment in American Thought.* New York: Oxford University Press, 1972.

Wiebe, Robert H. *The Search for Order.* New York: Hill and Wang, 1967.

Wood, Gordon S. *The Creation of the American Republic.* Chapel Hill: University of North Carolina Press, 1969.

III. Articles Written before 1945

Beard, Charles A. "Conditions Favorable to Creative Work in Political Science." *American Political Science Review* 24 (1930).

———. "Limitations to the Application of Social Science Implied in Recent Social Trends." *Social Forces* 11 (May 1933).

———. "Time, Technology and the Creative Spirit in Political Science." *American Political Science Review* 21 (February 1927).

———. "Training in Efficient Public Service." *Annals of the American Academy of Political and Social Science* 64 (March 1916).

Bryce, James. "The Relation of Political Science to History and to Practice." *American Political Science Review* 5 (1909).

Corwin, Edward S. "Democratic Dogma and the Future of Political Science." *American Political Science Review* 23 (August 1929).

Dewey, A. Gordon. "On Methods in the Study of Politics." *Political Science Quarterly* 38 (1923).

———. "On Methods in the Study of Politics, II." *Political Science Quarterly* 39 (1924).

Dewey, John. "Social Science and Social Control." *New Republic* 67 (July 1931).

Ford, Henry Jones. "The Scientific Study of Politics." *American Political Science Review* 11 (1917).

———. "Present Tendencies in American Politics." *American Political Science Review* 14 (1920).

Lasswell, Harold D. "Why Be Quantitative?" In *The Language of Politics*. New York: G. W. Stewart, 1949.

Merriam, Charles E. "The Education of Charles Merriam." In *The Future of Government in the United States,* ed. Leonard D. White. Chicago: University of Chicago Press, 1942.

———. "Presidential Address to the APSA." *American Political Science Review* 20 (1926).

Munro, William Bennett. "Physics and Politics: An Old Analogy Revised." *American Political Science Review* 22 (1928).

Odegard, Peter H. "Political Scientists and the Democratic Service State." *Journal of Politics* 2 (1940).

Parsons, Talcott. "Max Weber and the Contemporary Political Crisis." *Review of Politics* 4 (1942).

Shephard, Walter J. "Democracy in Transition." *American Political Science Review* 29 (1935).

White, Andrew Dickson. "Education in Political Science." In *Studies in Historical and Political Science*. Baltimore: Johns Hopkins University Press, 1879.

White, William Foote. "Instruction and Research: A Challenge to Political Science." *American Political Science Review* 37 (1943).

Wilson, Woodrow. "The Law and the Facts." *American Political Science Review* 5 (1911).

Worthington, T. K. "Recent Impressions of the Ecole Libre." In *Studies in Historical and Political Science*. Baltimore: Johns Hopkins University Press, 1879.

Wright, Benjamin F. "The Tendency Away from Political Democracy in the United States." *Southwest Social Science Quarterly* (June 1926).

IV. Articles Written after 1945

Agassi, Joseph. "Towards an Historiography of Science." *History and Theory* 2 (1963).

Almond, Gabriel A. "Separate Tables: Schools and Sects in Political Science." *PS* (1988).

Almond, Gabriel A., and Stephen Genco. "Clouds, Clocks and the Study of Politics." *World Politics* 29 (1979).

Anckar, Dag, and Erkki Berndtson. "The Evolution of Political Science: Selected Case Studies." *International Political Science Review* 8 (1987).

Appleby, Paul H. "Political Science: The Next Twenty Five Years." *American Political Science Review* 44 (1950).

Ball, Terence. "Power, Causation and Explanation." *Polity* 8 (1975).

———. "Models of Power: Past and Present." *Journal of the History of the Behavioral Sciences* 11 (1975).

———. "From Paradigms to Research Programs: Toward a Post-Kuhnian Political Science." *American Journal of Political Science* 20 (1976).

Barrow, Clyde W. "Charles A. Beard's Social Democracy: A Critique of the Populist-Progressive Style in American Political Thought." *Polity* 21 (1988).

Barry, Brian M. "The Strange Death of Political Theory." *Government and Opposition* 15 (1980).

Baum, William C. "American Political Science before the Mirror: What Our Journals Reveal about the Profession." *Journal of Politics* 38 (1976).

Beardsley, Philip L. "Political Science: The Case of the Missing Paradigm." *Political Theory* 2 (1974).

———. "A Critique of Post-Behavioralism." *Political Theory* 5 (1977).

Bluhm, William T. "Metaphysics, Ethics and Political Science." *Review of Politics* 31 (1969).

Bourque, Susan C., and Jean Grossholtz. "Politics as an Unnatural Practice: Political Science Looks at Female Participation." *Politics and Society* 4 (1974).

Caucus for a New Political Science. "Proposed Directions." Report of the Committee on Structure, 1975.

Cobban, Alfred. "The Decline of Political Theory." *Political Science Quarterly* 68 (1953).

de Jouvenal, Bertrand. "On the Nature of Political Science." *American Political Science Review* 55 (1961).

Deutsch, Karl W. "The Development of Communication Theory in Political Science." *History of Political Economy* 7 (1975).

Dryzek, John S. "The Progress of Political Science." *Journal of Politics* 48 (1986).

———. "Discursive Designs: Critical Theory and Political Institutions." *American Journal of Political Science* 31 (1987).

Dryzek, John S., and Stephen T. Leonard. "History and Discipline in Political Science." *American Political Science Review* 82 (1988).

Easton, David. "Harold D. Lasswell: Policy Scientist for a Democratic Society." *Journal of Politics* 12 (1950).

———. "The Current Meaning of Behavioralism." In *Contemporary Political Analysis,* ed. James C. Charlesworth. New York: Free Press, 1967.

———. "The New Revolution in Political Science." *American Political Science Review* 63 (1969).

Eulau, Heinz. "The Maddening Methods of Harold Lasswell." *Journal of Politics* 30 (1968).

Farr, James. "The History of Political Science." *American Journal of Political Science* 82 (1988).

———. "Political Science and the Enlightenment of Enthusiasm." *American Political Science Review* 82 (1988).

———. "Francis Lieber and the Interpretation of American Political Science." *Journal of Politics* 52 (1990).

Farr, James, Raymond Seidelman, John G. Gunnell, Stephen T. Leonard, and John S. Dryzek. "Can Political Science History Be Neutral?" *American Political Science Review* 84 (1990).

Friedrich, Carl J. "Political Science in the United States in Wartime." *American Political Science Review* 41 (1947).

Garson, G. David. "On the Origins of Interest-Group Theory: A Critique of a Process." *American Political Science Review* 68 (1974).

Gunnell, John G. "Political Science and the Theory of Action." *Political Theory* 7 (1979).

———. "Political Theory: The Evolution of a Subfield." In *Political Science: The State of the Discipline,* ed. Ada W. Finifter. Washington, DC: APSA, 1983.

Hanson, Donald W. "The Education of Citizens: Reflections on the State of Political Science." *Polity* 11 (1979).

Heard, Alexander. "Southern Political Science: Some Notes on Progress and Need." *Journal of Politics* 25 (1963).

Huntington, Samuel P. "Paradigms of American Politics: Beyond the One, the Two and the Many." *Political Science Quarterly* 89 (1974).

Kariel, Henry S. "Political Science in the United States: Reflections on One of Its Trends." *Political Studies* 4 (1956).

———. "Disarming Political Science." *Polity* 5 (1972).

Kavanaugh, Dennis. "An American Science of British Politics." *Political Studies* 22 (1974).

Kirn, Michael. "Behavioralism, Post-Behavioralism and the Philosophy of Science: Two Houses, One Plague." *Review of Politics* 39 (1977).

Krouse, Richard. "Polyarchy and Participation: The Changing Democratic Theory of Robert Dahl." *Polity* 14 (1982).

Landau, Martin. "The Myth of Hyperfactualism in Political Science." *Political Science Quarterly* 83 (1968).

Leiserson, Avery. "Charles Merriam, Max Weber and the Search for Synthesis in Political Science." *American Political Science Review* 69 (1975).

Lipsitz, Lewis. "Vulture, Mantis, and Seal: Proposals for Political Scientists." *Polity* 3 (1970).

Lowi, Theodore J. "The Politicization of Political Science." *American Politics Quarterly* 1 (1973).

McClosky, Robert G., and Austin Ranney. "Political Science: The State of the Profession." *Political Science Quarterly* 80 (1965).

Melanson, Philip H. "The Political Science Profession, Political Knowledge and Public Policy." *Politics and Society* 2 (1972).

———. "Bringing the Sociology of Knowledge to Bear on Political Science." *Polity* 7 (1975).

Moon, J. Donald. "The Logic of Political Inquiry: A Synthesis of Opposed Perspectives." In *Handbook of Political Science,* ed. Fred I. Greenstein and Nelson W. Polsby. Reading, MA: Addison Wesley, 1975.

Morgenthau, Hans J. "Reflections on the State of Political Science." *Review of Politics* 17 (1955).

Nettl, Peter. "The Concept of System in Political Science." *Political Studies* 14 (1966).

Oberschall, Anthony. "Paul Lazarsfeld and the History of Empirical Social Research." *Journal of the History of the Behavioral Sciences* 14 (1978).

Ollman, Bertell. "Marxism and Political Science: Prolegomenon to a Debate on Marx's Method." *Politics and Society* 3 (1974).

Petras, James F. "Ideology in United States Political Scientists." *Science and Society* 29 (1965).

Pfotenhauer, David. "Conceptions of Political Science in West Germany and the United States, 1960–1969." *Journal of Politics* 34 (1972).

Reid, Herbert G., and Ernest Yanarella. "Political Science and the Post-Modern Critique of Scientism and Domination." *Review of Politics* 37 (1975).

———. "Contemporary American Political Science and the Crisis of Industrial Society." *Midwest Journal of Political Science* 16 (1972).

Roettger, Walter B. "Strata and Stability: Reputation of American Political Scientists." *PS* 11 (1978).

Rosen, Paul L. "Science, Power and the Degradation of American Political Science." *Polity* 9 (1977).

Ross, Dorothy. "Socialism and American Liberalism: Academic Social Thought in the 1880s." In *Perspectives in American History,* no. 12. Cambridge: Harvard University Press, 1978.

Sartori, Giovanni. "Philosophy, Theory and Science of Politics." *Political Theory* 2 (1974).

Schaar, John H., and Sheldon Wolin. "Essays on the Scientific Study of Politics: A Critique." *American Political Science Review* 57 (1963).

Schwartz, David. "Toward a More Relevant and Rigorous Political Science." *Journal of Politics* 36 (1974).

Seidman, Steven, Robert Alun Jones, R. Stephen Warner, and Stephen Turner. "The Historicist Controversy: Understanding the Sociological Past." *Sociological Theory* 3 (1985).

Skinner, Quentin. "Meaning and Understanding in the History of Ideas." *History and Theory* 8 (1969).

Spence, Larry D. "Political Theory as a Vacation." *Polity* 12 (1980).

Stanyer, Jeffrey. "Irresistible Forces: The Pressures for a Science of Politics." *Political Studies* 24 (1976).

Steintrager, James. "Prediction and Control vs. the Narcissus Trance of Political Science." *Polity* 3 (1970).

Stocking, George W. "On the Limits of 'Presentism' and 'Historicism' in the Historiography of the Behavioral Sciences." *Journal of the History of the Behavioral Sciences* 1 (1965).

Susser, Bernard. "The Behavioral Ideology: A Review and a Retrospective." *Political Studies* 22 (1974).

Truman, David B. "Disillusion and Regeneration: The Quest for a Discipline." *American Political Science Review* 59 (1965).

Weinstein, Michael A. "The Inclusive Polity: New Directions in Political Theory." *Polity* 5 (1973).

Wolfe, Alan. "Unthinking about the Thinkable: Reflections on the Failure of the Caucus for a New Political Science." *Politics and Society* 1 (1971).

Wolfe, Alan, and Marvin Surkin. "Political Dimensions of American Political Science." *Acta Politica* (1967).

Wolin, Sheldon. "Paradigms and Political Theories." In *Politics and Experience,* ed. P. King. Cambridge: Cambridge University Press, 1968.

———. "Political Theory as a Vocation." *American Political Science Review* 63 (1969).

V. Disciplinary Classics with Historiographical Commentary

Bachrach, Peter, and Morton S. Baratz. *The Theory of Democratic Elitism.* Boston: Bobbs-Merrill, 1967.

Beard, Charles A. *An Economic Interpretation of the Constitution of the United States.* New York: Macmillan and Co., 1913.

Beard, Charles A., and Frederic A. Ogg. *National Governments and World War.* New York: Century, 1923.

Bentley, Arthur F. *The Process of Government.* Evanston, IL: Principia Press, 1908.

Berelson, Bernard, Paul Lazarsfeld, and William N. McPhee. *Voting.* Chicago: University of Chicago Press, 1954.

Brecht, Arnold. *Political Theory: The Foundations of Twentieth Century Political Thought.* Princeton, NJ: Princeton University Press, 1959.

Burgess, John W. *Political Science and Comparative Constitutional Law.* Boston: Ginn and Co., 1891.

Burnham, Walter Dean. *Critical Elections and the Mainsprings of American Politics.* New York: Norton and Co., 1970.

Campbell, Angus, Phillip E. Converse, Warren E. Miller, and Donald E. Stokes. *The American Voter.* New York: Wiley and Sons, 1960.

Croly, Herbert S. *The Promise of American Life.* New York: Bobbs-Merrill, 1965.

Dahl, Robert A. *A Preface to Democratic Theory.* Chicago: University of Chicago Press, 1956.

Easton, David. *The Political System*. New York: Alfred A. Knopf, 1953.

Eliot, William Y. *The Pragmatic Revolt in Politics*. New York: Macmillan and Co., 1928.

Evans, Peter, Dietrich Rueschemeyer, and Theda Skocpol, eds., *Bringing the State Back In*. Cambridge: Cambridge University Press, 1985.

Follett, Mary Parker. *The New State*. New York: Longman's and Green, 1918.

Ford, Henry Jones. *The Natural History of the State*. Princeton, NJ: Princeton University Press, 1915.

Goodnow, Frank J. *Municipal Problems*. New York: Macmillan, 1897.

Key, V. O., Jr. *Public Opinion and American Democracy*. New York: Alfred A. Knopf, 1961.

Lasswell, Harold D. *Politics: Who Gets What, When, How*. New York: McGraw-Hill, 1936.

———. *Democracy through Public Opinion*. New York: Bantam Publishing, 1941.

———. *Psychopathology and Politics*. New York: Viking Press, 1930.

———. *An Analysis of Political Behavior*. New York: Oxford University Press, 1947.

Lieber, Francis. *Manual of Political Ethics*. 2 vols. Philadelphia: J. B. Lippincott, 1838.

———. *Legal and Political Hermeneutics*. New York: Little and Brown, 1837 and 1839.

———. *Civil Liberty and Self-Government*. Philadelphia: J. B. Lippincott, 1853.

Lippmann, Walter. *Drift and Mastery*. Englewood Cliffs, NJ: Prentice-Hall, 1961.

Lowell, A. Lawrence. *Public Opinion and Popular Government*. New York: Longmans Green, 1913.

Lowi, Theodore J. *The End of Liberalism*. New York: Norton and Co., 1969.

McConnell, Grant. *Private Power and American Democracy*. New York: Alfred Knopf, 1967.

MacIver, Robert M. *The Web of Government*. Boston: Atheneum Press, 1942.

Merriam, Charles E. *American Political Ideas, 1867–1917*. New York: Macmillan and Co., 1903 and 1920.

———. *New Aspects of Politics*. Chicago: University of Chicago Press, 1924.

———. *Civic Education in the United States*. New York: Charles Scribner's Sons, 1939.

Munro, William Bennett. *The Invisible Government*. New York: MacMillan and Co., 1928.

Polsby, Nelson W. *Community Power and Democratic Theory*. New Haven, CT: Yale University Press, 1963.

Sabine, George A. *History of Political Theory*. New York: Holt, 1937.

Schattschneider, E. E. *The Semi-Sovereign People*. New York: Holt, Rinehart and Co., 1960.

Skowronek, Stephen. *Building a New American State*. New York: Cambridge University Press, 1982.

Truman, David B. *The Governmental Process*. New York: Alfred A. Knopf, 1971.

Voegelin, Eric. *The New Science of Politics*. Chicago: University of Chicago Press, 1952.

Wallas, Graham. *Human Nature in Politics*. London: Constable, 1908.

Willoughby, W. W. *The Nature of the State*. New York: MacMillan and Co., 1896.
―――. *Social Justice*. New York: MacMillan, 1900.
Wilson, Woodrow. *Congressional Government: A Study in American Politics*. Boston: Houghton Mifflin, 1885.
―――. *The State: Elements of Historical and Practical Politics*. Boston: D. C. Heath, 1889.
Wolin, Sheldon S. *Politics and Vision*. Boston: Little, Brown and Co., 1960.
Wright, Quincy. *Public Opinion and World Politics*. Chicago: University of Chicago Press, 1933.

Index

Absolutism, and study of history, 23

Adams, Herbert Baxter, 89, 142

Adams, John: and the "divine" science of politics, 15–16, 66; and economic factors in political study, 148

Adorno, Theodor, and the *Authoritarian Personality,* 218

Agassiz, Louis, 85

Almond, Gabriel, 332; and post-behavioralism, 285; and science theory debate, 187

Alpert, Harry, 208

Althusser, Louis, 301

American Association for the Advancement of Science, 82, 84

American Economics Association, 60–62, 85

American "exceptionalism": and bias of political science, 153–54; in Cold War political science, 218–19; in early political science, 19

American Historical Association, 60–62, 83

American Philological Society, 83

American Political Science Association, 15; as a "counterintelligentsia," 385; and feminism, 368–69; nonpartisanship of, 62; origins, 10, 60–62; post-behavioralism and, 319–20; relation to social sciences, 62; and study of the state, 64. *See also* Professionalization; Science of politics

American Political Science Review, 363; complaints about, 392; and historiography of political science, 9

American Revolution, and the rhetoric of science, 67. *See also* Constitution, American; Hamilton, Alexander; Madison, James

American Social Science Association, 15; birth and decline, 84–86; reform of, 17

American Voter, The, 259; and research on sexual differences in voting, 367

Anderson, William, 189

Anthropology: early development of, 86–87; relevance to political science development, 132

Anticommunism, and postwar political science, 218. *See also* Cold War

Antifederalists, and the idea of the state, 68–69

Arendt, Hannah, and critique of liberalism and the science of politics, 182, 189

Aristotle, 26, 31, 57; and economic factors in political study, 148

Articles of Confederation, political theory of, 270–71

Authoritarianism, response of political scientists to, 174–76

Authority, political, defined, 245–46

Bagehot, Walter, 292

Baldwin, Simeon, 61

Ball, Terence, 8, 204
Barber, Benjamin, and contemporary political theory, 320–22
Beard, Charles A., 8, 9; definition of politics, 114; and democratic state building, 108; economic interpretation of history of, 144; as pioneer in method, 147; and Progressivism, 109; and revolt against formalism, 107; and science and democracy, 177
Behavioralism: and American culture, 250; the Chicago School and, 250; defined, 255–56; development after World War II, 202–3; distinguished from past political science, 294–97; European influences on American version of, 251; the "first" revolution of, 108; history of in political science, 249–53; and historical study, 262–63; and liberalism, 187; as a mood, 256; and political philosophy, 180–81, 262; and reform political science, 317; and research about women, 366–68; as a revolt against political theory, 180–81; and Robert Dahl, 205. See also History of political science; Postbehavioralism; Science of politics
Behavioralist compromise, and feminism, 373–76
Behavioral revolution, 3; contrasted to traditional political science, 296; the first, 110; the second, 10. See also Behavioralism
Bell, Daniel, 297
Benson, Lee, 263
Bentham, Jeremy, 73
Bentley, Arthur, 292; as founder of modern political science, 278; and interest group theory, 278; and reform political science, 314; and political theory in the United States, 206; and revolt against formalism, 107; and science of the state, 78
Berelson, Bernard, 366
Bernard, Luther Lee, 100

Bias in political science: and middle class professors, 154–55; neglect of economic interests, 148–49; and the New Deal, 110; and political philosophy, 116; in postwar years, 218. See also Postbehavioralism
Bluntschli, Johann K., 40
Boas, Franz, 89
Bodin, Jean, 68
Bourque, Susan, 369
Brecht, Arnold, and critique of positivism, 187–88
Breckinridge, Sophonisba, 365
Brinton, Daniel, 86
Brown, Clarence (Congressman), 214
Bryce, James: and Modern Democracies, 135; originality in political science history, 149; political science of facts and, 384
Burgess, John W., 3, 8, 15–16, 18, 63, 89; and the American state, 75–77; and professionalization, 92; science of the state of, 64; and university reform, 97
Burke, Edmund, 29
Burnham, Walter Dean, and reform political science, 322–23

Calhoun, John C., 29, 69, 71
Calvin, John, 68
Campbell, Angus, 367, 372
Catlin, George E., 176
Caucus for a New Political Science, 311, 319–20; and feminism, 368–69
Causation, political, for Beard, 126
Center for Advanced Study in the Behavioral Sciences, 201
"Chicago School," the: and development of behavioralism, 250. See also Lasswell, Harold; Merriam, Charles
Chipman, Nathaniel, 69
Cicero, 15, 25
Citizenship: and the role of political science, 26–27; and "specialists on intelligence," 159–60. See also Democracy

Civic education: and American nationhood, 22–23; to Francis Lieber, 72. *See also* Democracy

Classes, social, origins of in liberal democracy, 330–31

Classical republicanism, and political science, 15

Cold War: and behavioralism, 296; effects on political science, 204; and government funding of social science, 212–14. *See also* Behavioralism

Columbia College, School of Political Science, 15, 18, 142

Consensus, as retarding political inquiry, 154

Conservatism: political science's incomprehension of, 393–94; and a science of the state, 77–78

Constitution, American: relationship to modern political science, 270–71; view of human nature in, 269. *See also* Adams, John; Hamilton, Alexander; Madison, James; Paine, Thomas

Converse, Phillip, 367, 372

Corwin, Edward S., 166

Crick, Bernard, 3–4

Criminology, and relevance to political science, 134

Curtis, George W., 84

Dahl, Robert, 8, 9, 205; and reform political science, 314–15; view of the state of, 328; and women in politics, 366

Darwinism, influence on social science, 115

De Mably, Gabriel Bonnet, 69

Democracy: conflict over meaning of, in political science, 328–31; elite theory of, 219; and findings of political science, 167–69; for nineteenth-century political scientists, 18; and political science, mid-century, 227; and political science between the wars, 108–9; and state-building in the United States, 108

Demosthenes, 29

Dennis, Jack, and political socialization, 339–40

De Tocqueville, Alexis, 63, 70, 387; and political science for a new world, 16

Deutsch, Karl, 327–28

Dicey, Albert Venn, and political psychology, 143

Dolbeare, Kenneth, 332–33

Downs, Anthony, 355, 357

Droop, Henry (English barrister), 349

Duverger, Maurice, 288, 346–47, 354–55

Duverger's Law: and development of a science of politics, 346–61; history of, 347–48

Dunbar, Charles, 86

Dunning, William, and a political science of the state, 64

Dye, Thomas, 332

Easton, David, 8, 9, 327–28; and funding of social science, 218; and political socialization, 339–40; *The Political System* and, 192–93, 205; and postbehavioralism, 285–88; and prebehavioral political science, 3–4; relationship to political theory, 183; and the "revolution" of 1969, 318; science and democracy and, 189; and the science of the state, 78. *See also* Behavioralism; Postbehavioralism; Systems theory

Economic approaches, influence in political science, 147–59

Economic interpretation of history, 130–31

Economics: Austrian school of, 130; early development of, 86; relationship to political science, 59–60, 130; and the state in America, 387; superiority to political science, 387–89

Edelman, Murray, 332, 333

Elshtain, Jean Bethke, 369, 371

Ely, Richard, 17, 89; and university origins, 97

Emmeny, Brooks, 147
Empiricism: as defect of political science, 150–53; and bias of political science, 152–53. *See also* Behavioralism; Bias in political science
Encyclopedia Americana, 71
Ethnology, relevance for political science, 133
Expertise. *See* Democracy; Public Administration; Science of Public Administration; State

Fainsod, Merle, 292
Fairlie, J. A., 62
Farr, James, 8, 18
Fascism, political science's response to, 175–76. *See also* Authoritarianism; Totalitarianism
Federalist, as source of modern political science, 276
Federalists, idea of the state, 68–69. *See also* Hamilton, Alexander; Liberalism; Madison, James
Feminism, 288–89; and behavioralist methods in political science, 369–70; political science treatment of, 371; in political theory, 371; in post-behavioral political science, 363–78; research agenda of, 374
Ferejohn, John, 357
Finer, Herman, 350
Fiorina, Morris, 357
Ford, Henry Jones, and defects of American Constitution, 120
Ford Foundation, 217
Formalism, defects of, 121–22
Foundations. *See* Philanthropy
Freeman, Jo, 370
Freud, Sigmund, 167
Friedrich, Carl, 177, 351

Gamson, William, 370
Gaudet, Hazel, 366
Gaus, John M., 213
Gaventa, John, 336

Gender: emergence as category in analysis, 372–78; in political science research, 364; and the state, 364. *See also* Feminism; Women
Germany, emigrés from, influence on American political science, 182, 189–90
Giddings, Franklin, 89
Gilman, Daniel Coit, 85
Goodnow, Frank J., 18, 61; and defects of American Constitution, 120; *Politics and Administration,* 172; as a state builder, 385
Gordon, Linda, 364
Gosnell, Harold, and political irrationality, 168
Government: changing forms of, 123; peculiar American qualities of, 120. *See also* Democracy; Public Administration; State
Gramsci, Antonio, 341
Greenstein, Fred I., 340
Griffith, Ernest, 185
Grossholtz, Jean, 369
Grotius, 15
Groups: political rationality of, 169–71; critique of theory of, 278–79. *See also* Behavioralism; Bentley, Arthur; Pluralism
Gunnell, John G., 6, 8; and behavioralism's origins, 317; and science and theory debate, 111

Habermas, Jürgen, 341
Haddow, Anna, 3
Hall, G. Stanley, 89
Hallowell, John: attacks on liberalism, 186; *The Main Currents of Modern Political Thought,* 190–91; and science theory debate, 184
Hamilton, Alexander, 15, 67, 228; and economic factors in political study, 148
Harpham, Edward J., 4
Hegel, G. W. F., 3

Hermeneutics: contemporary, 342, 346; and Francis Lieber, 71

Hermens, F., 351

Herring, E. Pendleton, 14, 292; and interest-group research, 170–71; and political science objectivity, 216

Hess, Robert, 327–28

Historians, and national freedom in the United States, 23–24

Historical comparative method, 18; in Beard, 115; merits and defects of, 149–50; for Merriam, 134

Historical method, in political science, 131, 134

Historiography of political science: and American exceptionalism, 9; and American politics subfield, 9; criteria for periodization used by, 10; general themes in, 7; methodological approaches in, 8; plurality within, 8; rationale for resurgence of, 4–8; theoretical traditions within, 8; types of, 207. *See also* Behavioralism; Democracy; History of political science; Liberalism; Postbehavioralism; Professionalization; State

History, discipline of, relationship to political science, 59–60

History, economic interpretation of, 14

History of political science: advances and difficulties of, 138–39; before the mid-twentieth century, 3; early developments in, 86–87; identity debates after World War II, 204; institutional changes after World War II, 201; intellectual change after World War II, 201–2; in the late nineteenth century, 75; at mid-century, 223–28; in the nineteenth century, 232–33; periods in, 137–38, 165, 224, 291–307; postwar political contexts and, 208–21; as a profession, 74–78; professionalization in, 8; and the state, 64, 65–79, 385–87; state of the discipline, 1

Hobbes, Thomas, 68, 71; and liberty, 31

Hoffmann, Frank S., 78

Holcombe, Arthur H., 147, 351

Huberich, C. H., 62

Human nature, and political science, 268–70

Humboldt, Alexander von, 71

Hume, David, 15, 69, 71

Individualism, and Socialism, 30–31

Inequality, conceived in radical and conventional political science, 335–36

Institute for Social Research, influence of American political science, 183–94, 201

Interest politics, origins in Madison's thought, 276–77

Irish, Marian, 217

Irrationality, in politics, 167–69

Jacobson, Norman, 8, 205–6

Jacoby, Russell, 320

James, William, 86

Janos, Andrew C., 4–5

Jefferson, Thomas, 71

Johns Hopkins University, 18; School of History and Political Science, 142

Journalism, relationship to social science, 162–63

Judson, H. P., 62

Kelsen, Hans, 188, 191

Kent, Frank, and political parties, 170, 250

Key, V. O., 327–28; benign view of state, 338; and Duverger's Law, 351

Klein, Ethel, 370

Kuhn, Thomas, 5, 299

Laissez-faire: defects of, 122; irrelevance to new industrial order, 124

Lane, Robert, 367

Lasswell, Harold, 8–9; and concept of power, 240–43; and the garrison state, 64; and philosophy of social science, 192; and political irrationality, 168–69; and reform political science, 314; and relationship to liberal democracy, 110–11

Lazarsfeld, Paul, 366

Lerner, Max, 147

Liberal democracy, theory of, 329–30. *See also* Democracy

Liberalism: and contemporary political theory, 321–22; political science's misunderstanding of, 392–93; in political science between the wars, 108–9; and scientific politics, 311–15; theory's critique of, 182–95; as a tradition in political science, 165–78

Liberty: in America, 31; and national development, 26–27

Lieber, Francis, 8, 15–17, 56, 66; concepts of the state in the United States and Europe, 70–75; defects of formalism of, 149; as founder of political science, 141

Lindblom, Charles E., 8–9; and postbehavioralism, 288

Lippincott, Benjamin Evans, 8; and "bias" in political science, 110; on defects of American political theory, 183; on state of political theory, 190

Lippmann, Walter: importance to public administration, 143; and psychology, 137; and public opinion, 170–72

Lipset, Seymour Martin, 219

Lipsky, Michael, 370

Locke, John: contrasted to contemporary political scientists, 115; and economic factors in political study, 148

Loewenstein, Karl, and scientific method, 176

Louis the Fourteenth, 23

Lowell, A. Lawrence: and Duverger's Law, 350; and public opinion research, 167

Lowi, Theodore J., 8–9; and critique of

behavioralism, 370; his liberalism, 332; and postbehavioralism, 289

Lynd, Robert S., influence on postbehavioralism, 285

Machiavelli, Niccolo, 29, 68; and origins of state concept, 236

MacIver, Robert, 235

Macy, Jesse, 62

Madison, James, 15, 71, 205, 223; compared to Paine, 277; and economic factors in political study, 148; as first U.S. political scientist, 277; political theory of, 277; and the science of government, 67

Magruder, John (U.S. General), 212

Maine, Henry Sumner, 118

Mannheim, Karl, 387; and bureaucratic thought, 390

March, James G., 376

Marcuse, Herbert, 193, 341

Markby, Sir William, 117

Marx, Karl, 63; and economic factors in political study, 148; on the modern state, 70

Marxism: and critique of liberal democratic theory, 329–30; political scientists respond to, 175; and postbehavioralism in political science, 299–301

Merriam, Charles, 3–4, 8–9; and behavioralism, 109–10, 250; on political irrationality, 167–68; and research on women, 365; on science and democracy, 178; and a science of reform politics, 313–14; and scientism, 100; view of political theory, 181

Methods: development of social surveys, 135; in early social science, 98–103; importance of quantitative, 139

Michels, Robert, 169–70

Middletown, and systematic study, 163

Mill, John Stuart, 136–37, 349

Miller, Donald, 367, 372

Mills, C. Wright, critique of postwar social science, 216
Mitchell, Wesley C., 100
Modern Language Association, 83
Montesquieu, Charles Secondat de, 15, 41, 69, 71
Moralism, contrasted to social science, 163–64
Moses, Bernard, 62
Munro, William G., 176, 351
Murray, Robert H., 3

Napoleon Bonaparte, 38
National Conference for Charities and Corrections, 85
National Conferences on the Science of Politics, 166, 173
National Opinion Research Center, 201
National Science Foundation, 211, 215
National university, and citizenship, 22
Nelson, Barbara, 378
Newcomb, Simon, 86
New Deal: effects on later political science, 208; postbehavioral misconceptions about, 392–93
New institutionalism, and feminism in political science, 376–78
New York Bureau of Municipal Research, 136, 143
Niebuhr, Barthold G., 71
Nourse, E. G., 213

Oberschall, Anthony, 370
Objectivity: in early social science, 102–3; in postbehavioral political science, 337–38; and social sciences during the Cold War, 214
Odegard, Peter H., 147
Ogburn, William F., 100, 213–14
Okin, Susan Moller, 371
Olsen, Johan, 376
Oppenheim, Felix, 191

Paine, Thomas, 205; contrasted to modern political scientists, 280; view of society and government, 272–80

Park, Robert, 100, 102
Parties, political: and Duverger's Law, 350–58; political science embrace and criticism of, 170; in U.S. democracy, 120–21
Peirce, Benjamin, 85
Peoples' Choice, The, 258; and research about women, 366
Philanthropy: and the behavioral movement, 253–54; influence on social sciences, 216–19; role in postwar political science, 215
Philosophy of science: and postbehavioral political science, 305–6
Pittsburgh Survey, 136
Plato, 71; and economic factors in political studies, 148
Pluralism: as agenda for political research, 202, 205, 292–93, 295
Pocock, J. G. A., 5
Political, the: defined, 231
Political behavior: defined, 205; study of, 210; as a subfield, 254. *See also* Behavioralism
Political economy: as a new science, 24–26; and postbehavioralism, 302; similarity of methods to political science, 145
Political education, and political science, 205–6, 268, 281–82
Political ethics, in the modern versus classical polity, 28
Political science, discipline of: conventionalism of, 333; defined, 244–47; distinguished from other fields, 245–46; identity of, 226; modern variety compared to Founders, 277; new complexity of, 125; relation to economics, 59–60, 130; relation to history, 59–60; relation to other social sciences, 230–33; role in democratic politics, 126–27; state of, 145–46; weakness of intellectual foundations of, 227. *See also* Professionalization; Science of politics

Political Science in America: Oral Histories of a Discipline, 4
Political Science Quarterly, 18
Political socialization: sex differences in, 367; weakness of conventional political science in study of, 339–41
Political system, and behavioralism, 260–61. *See also* Easton, David
Political theory: as an academic field of political science, 180–81; in the college curriculum, 27–28; as commentary on state of political science, 179–95; and feminism, 371; as a great tradition, 182; hostility of conventional political science to, 150–52; inadequacies of, 294; irrelevance of to public discourse, 321–22; origins in the United States, 179–95; and political science, 116; and postbehavioralism, 302–3; and reform political science, 320–23; relevance to political science, 133; as a subfield, 179–95
Political thought, history of, 129
Politics and administration. *See* Public Administration
Politics and Community: Dissenting Essays in Political Science, 286
Politics and Society, 286
Pollock, Frederick, 3
Positivism, postbehavioral critique of, 304–5
Postbehavioralism: and American politics, 298; contrasted to behavioralism, 298–304; and conventional political science, 332–33; definitions of, 11, 285; origins of, 298–304; and positivism, 304–5
Poulantzas, Nicos, 301
Power: as concept in political science research, 239–43; defects as analytical tool, 243; and Harold Lasswell, 241–43
Powell, G. Bingham, 332
Powell, John Wesley, 84

Presidency: political science and the, 393
Prewitt, Kenneth, 328
Private property: and democratic politics, 115–16
Process, as a method of study, 135. *See also* Bentley, Arthur
Professionalism: and democracy, 173; and end of reform political science, 314–19; middle-class bias of political science, 156–57; role in science theory debate, 195
Professionalization: competing ideas about, 94–98; of early social sciences, 88–98; and feminism, 374; German model of, 96; and growth of American state, 74–78; and industrialization, 93–94; and moral uncertainty, 93–94; and political science influence, 226; and reform political science, 316–17; and scholarly research, 96–97; in sociology, 94; sociology of, 94; and state theories, 74–78; and teaching, 95–96
Progressivism: impact on political science, 10, 165–66, 312–13; and science of the state, 78
Proportional representation, 350–51
Psychology: development of, 86–87; and early behaviorism, 99; influence on political science, 133, 167; scientism of, 108
Psychopathology and Politics, 108
Public administration: and democracy, 44, 121; and nineteenth-century political science, 17. *See also* Science of public administration
Public opinion, as a subfield of political science, 389–92
Public policy, 208; revival in postbehavioralism, 389–92; as a subfield, 389–90; tool of political research, 244–45
Publics. *See* Democracy
Pufendorf, Samuel, 71

Putnam, Frederic Ward, 86
Putnam, Herbert, 62

Radical political science: characteristics, 336–37; lessons from, 341–42. *See also* Marxism; Postbehavioralism
Rae, Douglas, 353–55
Ramsay, David, 67
Rational choice: and the American bureaucratic state, 390–91; and Duverger's Law, 352–53; and postbehavioralism, 302–3; and rise of Republican Party, 390
Rationalism, criticized in political science, 280
Reform, political: and beginnings of social science, 89–91; in early American psychology, 92; in New Deal political science, 109; and political science, 225, 323
Reinsch, Paul S., 61
Relativism: and German emigré scholars, 194; and origins of political theory, 186–87
Revolt against formalism, 107–8. *See also* Formalism
Ricci, David, 8; and liberalism in political science, 111; as skeptical historian, 4–5
Riker, William H., 8, 9; and postbehavioralism, 288
Ritter, Gretchen, 378
Robinson, James H., 144
Robinson, Joan, 391
Rockefeller Foundation, 254
Rodgers, Daniel, 76
Ross, Dorothy, 4, 8, 18; and American exceptionalism, 6
Ross, E. A., 89
Rousseau, Jean-Jacques, 118
Rowe, L. S., 62

Sabine, George, 182
St. Simon, Claude Henri de, 29
Sanborn, Frank B., 84

Sapiro, Virginia, 370, 378
Savigny, Friedrich Karl von, 71
Schattschneider, E. E., 351
Schleiermacher, Friedrich E. G., 71
Schaper, W. A., 62
Schwarz, John, 391
Science: and behavioralism, 259; defining methods of, 345; as language of political reform, 312–13; as public discourse, 387–88; and reform political science, 313–14
Science of politics: and American republicanism, 66–70; definitions of, 32, 60, 117; development of, 345–46; difficulties of, 139–41; and regime changes, 394; as a science of the state, 64–79, 387; in the United States, 141–46. *See also* Behavioralism; Political science, discipline of; Professionalization; Science of public administration
Science of public administration: and American democracy, 39–40, 42; and comparative historical method, 45–47; and constitutional law, 41; and democratic state, 44–45; distinguished from politics, 40–41; eclipse of as subfield in political science, 393; in England, 38; in France, 38; history of, 34–44; and modern state, 34–44; necessity for in modern conditions, 35–36; periodization of history of, 37; and political science, 34–44; in Prussia, 38–39; and public opinion, 42–43; in the United States, 38–39. *See also* Public administration; State
Scientism: and the comparative-historical method, 98; and decline of values, 102; critiques of, 299–300; and Darwinians, 98–99; and decline of religion in the United States, 101; in early psychology, 99; in early social science, 98–104; and liberalism, 176; limitations imposed by, 337; and natural sciences, 98; and political

Scientism (*continued*)
quietism, 101; and postbehavioralism, 304; in postwar political science, 210–14; as self-fulfilling prophecy, 279; and World War I, 103
Scott, Joan, 371
Scottish Enlightenment, 66
Schuman, Frederick, 147
Second Republic of the United States, 386–87
Seeley, John R., 3, 59
Seidelman, Raymond, 8, 385; as skeptical historian, 4–5; and postbehavioralist critique, 287
Seneca, 32
Sex. *See* Gender
Shaw, Albert, 62
Shively, W. P., 356
Silverberg, Helene, 8, 288
Simon, Herbert: concept of political science, 191–92; and public policy subfield, 389
Skinner, B. F., 294
Skinner, Quentin, 5
Skocpol, Theda, 378
Skowronek, Stephen, 385
Small, Albion, 89; and authority of social science over religion, 93; and moral connotations of science, 102; and revolt against formalism, 144
Smith, J. Allen, 147
Social psychology, 133
Somit, Albert, 2, 384
Social Science Research Council, 81–82, 252
Social sciences: American origins in Protestantism, 84–88; definitions of, 87; development as a science, 346; distinguished from natural sciences, 101; as empirical investigation, 90–91; and historical consciousness, 90; history, Civil War to 1820, 81–104; postwar support by government, 211–12; as solution to social and political problems, 91
Society, concept of, 269–70

Sociology: development of, 86, 144; influence on development of behavioralism, 251; relation to political science, 132–33
Specialists: "on intelligence," 160–61; role in a democracy, 159
Specialization, causes of, 232–33
Staatswissenschaft, 65–66
State: in America, 36–38, 56–58, 64–79; and American democracy, 44–45; and behavioralism, 108; as a common benefit organization, 328–29; competing ideas of origin of, 118–19; as concept for scientific research, 237–38; definitions of, 49, 117; and democracy, 53–58; development of, 114–15, 384; disappearance in social science, 218–19; distinguished from government, 54–56; distinguished from politics, 235–39; economics as language of, 390–91; effects on political science, 383–94; functions of, 123–24; historical ideas about the, 50–53; and history of political science, 384–86; influence from Europe on American version, 65–79; as a "limiting concept," 234; as a middle-class product in America, 154; its modern form, 35–36; as myth, 237; in nineteenth-century political science, 16–17, 70, 75–78; as opposed to the political system, 233–36; origins of, 27–28, 118–19, 235; political science conceptions of, 56–58, 108; in postbehavioral political science, 300; and public administration, 35; and radical thought, 329–31; in reform political science, 316; and social classes, 119; sovereignty of, 51–54; in Western Europe, 55–56
Stocking, George, 82
Stokes, Donald, 367, 372
Story, Joseph, 71, 73
Stouffer, Samuel, 218; and *The American Soldier,* 209
Strauss, Leo: and the crisis of liberal

democracy, 203; and critique of liberalism and political science, 182, 189, 193

Structural-functionalism: in postbehavioral political science, 334–35

Sumner, William Graham, 86

Survey Research Center (University of Michigan), 201

Surveys: development of in the United States, 136; importance of, 135; role in political science, 253

Systems theory, 230; defined, 229; development of, 205

Tanenhaus, Joseph, 2

Thucydides, 26

Tingsten, Herbert, 250

Totalitarianism, and origins of political theory, 193

Truman, David B., 292; definitions of political behavior in, 256–58; democratic elitism of, 329; and reform political science, 314

Tulane University, 61

United States Census Bureau, 142

United States Government, as funder of social sciences, 211–16

Universities, and rise of the middle class, 97

Utopias, and communism, 29

Values, and behavioralism. *See also* Behavioralism; Political Theory; Scientism

Veblen, Thorstein, and scientism, 99–100

Verba, Sidney, 328

Vietnam War, political scientists' disputes about, 220. *See also* Cold War

Vining, Joseph, 389

Voegelin, Eric, and the critique of liberalism, 185–86

Walker, Francis A., 86

Wallas, Graham: and development of political psychology, 136–37; and political irrationality, 167

Ward, Lester Frank, 84; and a science of reform politics, 314

Watson, John B., 99, 294

Weber, Max, in postbehavioralism, 299

Webster, Daniel, 29

White, Andrew Dickson, 62, 86

White, Leonard D., 8; on the postwar discipline, 204–5

Whyte, William Foote, 183

Willoughby, W. W., 3, 8–9, 16, 61, 64; and failure of liberal democracy, 174

Wilson, Francis G., and origins of political theory as a subfield, 184–85

Wilson, Woodrow, 3, 8–9, 16–17, 292; and APSA origins, 61; and *Congressional Government,* 120; historical-comparative method of, 18, 149; and reform political science, 314; and revolt against formalism, 107; and role of administrators in a democracy, 172; and the state, 64, 75, 384–85

Wolfe, Alan, 319

Wolin, Sheldon, 190

Women: in postbehavioral political science, 368–72; research about in political science, 365. *See also* Feminism; Gender

Women's Caucus for Political Science, 368–69

Women's Studies, 363

Woolsey, Theodore Dwight, 16, 56, 64, 75–76; and defects of formalism, 149

World War II, effects on political science, 10, 208, 210, 251

Wright, Benjamin, 185

Wright, Carroll D., 84, 94

Zeigler, L. Harmon, 332